LORRAINE HANSBERRY

LORRAINE HANSBERRY

The Life Behind
A Raisin in the Sun

Charles J. Shields

HENRY HOLT AND COMPANY   **H**   NEW YORK

Henry Holt and Company
Publishers since 1866
120 Broadway
New York, NY 10271
www.henryholt.com

Distributed in Canada by Raincoast Book Distribution Limited

Library of Congress Cataloging-in-Publication Data is available.

ISBN: 9781250205537

Our books may be purchased in bulk for promotional, educational, or business use. Please contact your local bookseller or the Macmillan Corporate and Premium Sales Department at (800) 221-7945, extension 5442, or by email at MacmillanSpecialMarkets@macmillan.com.

First Edition 2022

Designed by Meryl Sussman Levavi

Printed in the United States of America

10 9 8 7 6 5 4 3 2 1

To Guadalupe

> *A wife of noble character who can find?*
> *She is worth far more than rubies.*

—Proverbs 31:10

Contents

Chronology

1819 William "Bill" Hansberry, great-grandfather, born at the Salubria plantation in Culpepper County, Virginia.

1895 Carl Augustus Hansberry, father, born in Gloster, Mississippi.

1898 Nannie Louise Perry, mother, born in Columbia, Tennessee.

1914–18 Carl Augustus Hansberry and future wife, Nannie Louise Perry, arrive
in Chicago as part of the Great Migration from the South.

1919 Carl Augustus Hansberry and Nannie Louise Perry wed in Chicago.

1930 Lorraine Hansberry born in Chicago; her parents and three siblings—
Carl Jr. (1920), Perry (1921), and Mamie (1923)—reside in Bronzeville, on
Chicago's South Side.

1937 The Hansberrys move to all-white Woodlawn, where they are met with
violence and hostility; the unrest leads to a civil rights lawsuit filed by
Carl Augustus Hansberry.

1940 U.S. Supreme Court rules in favor of Hansberry.

1946 Carl Augustus Hansberry dies in Mexico.

1948 Lorraine Hansberry enrolls at the University of Wisconsin–Madison, as
a pre-journalism major; comes to the attention of the FBI for associating
with Communists.

1950 Drops out of the University of Wisconsin, studies briefly at Roosevelt
College, and moves to New York City.

1951 Begins writing for Paul Robeson's *Freedom* newspaper in Harlem; also
begins writing for several Marxist-socialist newspapers under pen names.

1951 Engaged to Roosevelt "Rosie" Jackson, a Harlem street speaker and
member of the Labor Youth League.

1952   Secretly attends the Montevideo Inter-American Congress for Peace, in Uruguay, in place of Paul Robeson, who has been forbidden by the U.S. State Department from traveling abroad. Teaches black literature at the Marxist Jefferson School of Social Science.

1953   Marries Robert (Bob) Nemiroff; moves into his apartment on Bleecker Street in Greenwich Village.

1953–54 On staff during summers at Camp Unity, in upstate New York, a Communist-affiliated family camp.

1954   Studies colonialism and Pan-Africanism under W. E. B. Du Bois; also becomes a regular speaker at rallies for social causes.

1956   Nemiroff cowrites a hit song, "Cindy, Oh Cindy." The money allows Lorraine to quit working part-time jobs in Greenwich Village and write full-time.

1957   She completes the play *A Raisin in the Sun*.

1959   *A Raisin in the Sun* opens in New Haven in January; continues to Philadelphia; and reaches Broadway in February. Hansberry becomes the first black playwright to win a Drama Critics' Circle Award. Columbia Pictures purchases film rights and asks her to write the screenplay. Hansberry is part of a circle of lesbian friends. She moves to 112 Waverly Place in Greenwich Village, where she meets and falls in love with Dorothy Secules. Hansberry and Nemiroff continue to collaborate on Lorraine's plays.

1960–64 Hansberry, now a leading black intellectual, is regularly invited to participate in public events and on television and radio.

1964   Nemiroff quietly obtains a divorce in Mexico. Hansberry's health is very poor after several operations for an ulcerated stomach and pancreatic cancer. She enters the hospital "critically ill" in October.

1964–65 Hansberry's second Broadway play, *The Sign in Sidney Brustein's Window*, after a troubled opening, continues to run with donations and fundraising until the day of Lorraine's death.

1965   Hansberry dies of pancreatic cancer in New York City on January 12.

Introduction

This book is about Lorraine Hansberry, an American playwright whose play *A Raisin in the Sun* competes with Arthur Miller's *Death of a Salesman* for the honor of the most popular work of mid-twentieth-century American theater. No other play from that era is more widely anthologized, read, or performed than Hansberry's most famous work, written when she was just twenty-nine.

Until the curtain rose on *A Raisin in the Sun* in 1959, "Never before, in the entire history of the American theater, had so much of the truth of black people's lives been seen on the stage," James Baldwin wrote. During the decade that followed, more than six hundred black theater companies opened their doors, providing venues for works by Amiri Baraka, Ed Bullins, Alice Childress, Ntozake Shange, and August Wilson—the high-water mark of twentieth-century African American drama. Had Hansberry not died at thirty-four in 1965, today she would have been an elder spokesperson in the LGBTQ and Black Lives Matter movements. Her ability to articulate and dramatize human rights would have brought her to the forefront of current thought and literature.

This biography is an attempt to situate Lorraine Hansberry with her contemporaries—midcentury American writers, artists, and activists. My approach to writing a life is to focus on what sets a person apart from others, who influenced them, and which events became turning points in their lives. Fortunately, Hansberry had a gift, or maybe an instinct, for engaging with the leading black American playwrights, novelists, activists,

and cultural leaders of her day. The richness of her private correspondence, her notes to herself, and drafts of unpublished works—curated for
twenty-five years by her former husband, Robert Nemiroff—open a window onto how Hansberry saw the world. To show her development as an
artist, I rely on her friendships, romances, ambition, and emotional struggles. She cultivated multidimensionality in her personal and professional
life, which led to new directions in her work and love affairs.

A side of her that will be new to readers is her complicated loyalty to her
family. She was raised upper-middle class, and despite being an anticapi-
talist, she enjoyed the cultural and material advantages of an upbringing
among the black elite. She stood by her family as they fought to maintain
a lifestyle that was built on a family dynasty of black free enterprise on
Chicago's South Side.

Also presented here for the first time is a domestic portrait of Hansberry and Nemiroff, and of their creative partnership. The Nemiroffs of
Greenwich Village is an unusual story.

A Note about Usage: Lorraine Hansberry was "not interested in capitalizing the first letters of the expression 'black race,'" she said in 1959,
"any more than I could imagine that anyone should wish to suddenly start
writing 'White Race.'" The reason was "American Negroes take the view
that we are a specific and not a generality." I accede to her preference and
lowercase *black* and *white* throughout the book and rely on *Negro* now and
then. "'Negro' is quite as accurate, quite as old and quite as definite as any
name of any great group of people," wrote W. E. B. Du Bois.

LORRAINE HANSBERRY

PART I

Chicago

1

Infant of the Spring

I went to Chicago as a migrant from Mississippi. And there in that great iron city, that impersonal, mechanical city, amid the steam, the smoke, the snowy winds, the blistering sun; there in that self-conscious city, that city so deadly dramatic and stimulating, we caught whispers of meanings that life could have . . .

—Richard Wright, *Black Metropolis*, Introduction

It was a warm evening for early February in Philadelphia in 1959, and the excited crowd waiting in the alley beside the Walnut Street Theatre was large. At last, the stage door opened, and an elegantly dressed young woman stepped out to a round of applause and cries of "Bravo!"

Laughing, Lorraine Hansberry turned to James Baldwin and asked him for a pen—a playwright without a pen! "It only happens once!" she said happily. He dipped into his suit jacket to find one, delighted by her "marvelous laugh," because it was loud and rowdy, in contrast to her refined voice and sophisticated dress. "I loved her," he said; "she was my sister and my comrade." She handed him her pocketbook while she reached out to the eager hands waving programs of *A Raisin in the Sun* for her autograph.

Baldwin was delighted with the play, impressed with the black ensemble, and surprised that half of the audience was black. But he understood why. It was because "black people recognized that house and all the people in it"—that house in Chicago's South Side ghetto, where the

Younger family lives in a tenement too small for their dreams.[1] In the final scene, the mother, Lena Younger, takes a last look around at the shabby rooms she's lived in for years, holding in her hand a single potted flower from the kitchen windowsill. And then she leaves and closes the door behind her, to begin a better life. The Youngers wanted out of the ghetto like millions of other black Americans. The audience got to their feet, cheered, and shouted for the author. Some stayed in their seats and cried. A woman who'd never been to a play before had bought a ticket because, she told an usher, "The word's going around my neighborhood that there's something here that has to do with me."[2] Lorraine Hansberry was a witness to the truth, and the people crowding around her now assuredly understood this and wanted to tell her—this young woman not yet thirty who knew what was in their hearts.

On the sidewalk in front of the theater, people were lingering, discussing the play. A man coming out wove between them and then continued on his way down the street. During the performance, he'd been sitting quietly listening and taking notes. He was thinking about what he'd seen, what it meant, and what he would say in his report about *A Raisin in the Sun* and its playwright for the New York office of the FBI.

The day Lorraine Hansberry was born, May 19, 1930, started out chilly, with the sun poking through shimmering rain. "I was, being May-born," she wrote, "literally an 'infant of the spring.'"[3] She was delivered at Provident Hospital, on the corner of Thirty-Sixth and Dearborn on Chicago's South Side. Provident was one of the few hospitals in the city where black physicians, refused visiting privileges at white-controlled hospitals, could attend to Negro women.[4] Lorraine's brothers and sister—Carl Jr., nearly ten; Perry, almost nine; and Mamie, almost seven—had been born at Fort Dearborn Hospital and Training School for Colored Nurses. The year Carl was born, 1920, a bomb set by racists exploded in the hallway of the nurses' residence, injuring three.

On her birth certificate, Lorraine's first name is misspelled "Loraine" and her middle name, "Vivian," is omitted. Her gender is noted, but there's no space for her race or color.[5] Her father, Carl Augustus Hansberry, and her mother, Nannie Louise Hansberry, are identified as "Negro." But someone has drawn a line through "Negro" and written "B" after her father's name, and "Bl," for "Black," after her mother's. Probably her father made the correction; he would have had the authority to do so.

The Hansberrys had accrued quite a bit of influence by the time Lorraine was born. Her father was a real estate speculator, but he preferred to be identified on the form as a "U.S. Deputy Marshal." It was a political patronage job, one of many handed out by Lorraine's mother, a Republican Ward committeewoman, a powerful position for a woman in those days. Carl found that having the silver star badge agreed with him. Leaving the Chicago Federal Building one morning, for instance, he flashed it at a mounted white police officer who was writing him a ticket for double-parking. He demanded the cop get down from his horse and apologize for interfering with official business, which he did.

Some scholars conclude that the lines drawn through "Negro" represent "a testament to the Afrocentric ideology that the elder Hansberrys bequeathed to their children."[6] But that's a revisionist wish to meet a particular agenda. The reason her father didn't approve of the word *Negro* was because the Hansberrys were upper-middle class. A speech delivered at Wilberforce University in 1938 by a member of the Boule, an elite group of black physicians, attorneys, and educators, was quite clear about the difference between *Negro* and *black*. "The word *Negro*," said the speaker, "carries with it a stigma that can never gather valuable meaning to those who live under the American flag. The terms *Negro life*, *Negro religion*, *Negro education*, *Negro society*, carry with them the inferiority-laden slave tradition. Our survival impinges definitely upon our whole-hearted adoption of the American way of life in all its aspects."[7]

Lorraine said her father was a "real 'American' type American"—a believer in progress and living the modern way.[8]

How the Hansberrys made their money is a tale of the American Dream come true—materially, anyway.

Her father, Carl, arrived in Chicago in 1916 aboard an Illinois Central train that had come up from the Mississippi Delta, completing its 750-mile run by rolling to a stop inside the largest train shed in the world, under a canopy of coal-smoked glass and arches of blackened steel. ("A first-generation Northerner" was how Lorraine liked to think of herself.[9]) From the platform, passengers walked through the city's Central Station, a nine-story Romanesque building built to serve the millions of visitors who had come to Chicago to see the 1893 Columbian Exposition. The first thing travelers leaving the station saw was enormous Grant Park, a half mile long. To the right was gray-green Lake Michigan stretching east as far as the eye could see, to where the horizon met the sky, as if Chicago were a seaport instead of an inland city of two and a half million. On the left rose a beetling wall of hotels and office buildings running the length of Michigan Avenue—the edge of downtown proper. To a newcomer, particularly one from the rural South, Chicago could be intimidating.

But Hansberry was ready for what the city could offer. At twenty-one, he was a stout young man whose build suggested physical strength. He was formal, given to a sober lifestyle, and possessed of an exceptional education for the times. His father was Elden Hayes Hansberry, a professor of ancient history at Alcorn Agricultural and Mechanical College, near the Delta town of Lorman, in Amite County, Mississippi. Professor Hansberry had died at thirty-four in 1896, leaving Carl, then just a year old, and his two-year-old brother, William Leo, with their mother, the former Harriet Pauline Bailey.[10] Harriet saw to it that her sons attended Alcorn College preparatory school. They also read deeply from their late father's personal library of classical literature and history. Carl completed his freshman and sophomore years at Alcorn College. Leo enrolled at Atlanta University and studied ancient African history under W. E. B. Du Bois, the father of sociology in the United States and a preeminent historian of black history and culture. With Du Bois's encouragement, Leo transferred to Harvard his junior year.

But Carl's interest was in America's future, not the African past. The Hansberrys had been Republicans for three generations, a political ideology rooted in nineteenth-century middle-class mores of respectability, the Protestant work ethic, self-help, and personal responsibility. Republicanism, in broad strokes, was both the political expression of Booker T. Washington's doctrine of self-improvement through enterprise and capitalism, as outlined in his hugely popular 1901 autobiography, *Up from Slavery*, and a real-world application of W. E. B. Du Bois's "Talented Tenth" leading the rest of the race.[11] Carl had come to Chicago, the fastest-growing city in the world, to make his own economic decisions, to take hold of his own destiny, just as millions had done after emancipation, when the yoke of slavery was shrugged off. In a great northern metropolis such as Chicago, his ambition would be unencumbered by Mississippi's tangle of poll taxes, literacy tests, voter suppression, violence, and fraud designed to keep a black man down. "Hasten on my dark brother, Duck the Jim Crow law," urged a 1915 poem in the *Chicago Defender*, "No Crackers North to slap your mother, or knock you on the jaw. / No Cracker there to seduce your sister, nor to hang you to a limb."

For new arrivals to Chicago needing a helping hand, like Hansberry, the South Side Wabash Avenue YMCA, the Olivet Baptist Church, and the Pilgrim Baptist Church offered social services. A nickel ride on a southbound streetcar took him past blocks of sooty gray warehouses and long, dark alleys at the end of which could be seen the tracks of the elevated train. Gradually, block by block, the buildings became "more darkly alive," wrote Langston Hughes. "Negroes leaned from windows with heads uncombed, or sat fanning themselves in doorways with legs apart, talking in kimonos and lounging in overalls, and more and more they became a part of the passing panorama."[12] This was where Lorraine's sensibilities as a playwright would develop, she said, in "that crucible, the Chicago South Side."[13]

At the end of the nineteenth century, earlier immigrants such as the ethnic Irish began to leave that part of the city as Negroes moved in. It was not a matter of class. At first, the old and new residents were on a par economically. The difference was racial—social order based on skin color.[14] During the Great Migration of World War I, blacks coming up from the South were crushed into the only housing available to them, inside the South Side Black Belt, as white Chicagoans called it. When Hansberry arrived, more than one hundred thousand people, 80 percent of them black, were residing in an area suitable for half that number, corralled into a narrow strip thirty blocks long and only a mile wide. The boundaries were Twenty-Second Street on the north, Fifty-First Street on the south, Cottage Grove Avenue on the east, and the Rock Island Railroad on the west. The residents, in a defiant spirit, voted to name their community "Bronzeville."

Shut out as they were from other neighborhoods, the residents of

Bronzeville were all kinds of people—hotel bellhops, Pullman porters, street sweepers, bankers, postal workers, cooks, slaughterhouse "cattle splitters"—jammed into the Black Belt but hoping for a better life. Every weekday morning at dawn, flocks of domestic housekeepers, practical nurses, and waitresses left for work in white neighborhoods, as if they were going up to the big house on a plantation.[15]

Being "othered" in this way played a part in creating race pride—not universally embraced by everyone, of course, but nevertheless widespread. As a playwright, Lorraine Hansberry used this strength in her work. "It's not any more difficult for me to know the people that I wrote about than it is for me to know members of my family because there is that kind of intimacy. This is one of the things that the American experience has meant to Negroes: we are one people."[16] And pressure from the black establishment in Bronzeville enforced social standards. Longtime residents felt entitled to scrutinize and correct the appearance, dress, and behavior of newcomers, to make sure they were keeping the faith and upholding conventions. Not long after Lorraine's father arrived, the *Chicago Defender* began publishing weekly "guidelines for migrant behavior," including rules about acceptable language, clothing, and personal bearing in public, such as "Don't talk so loud, we're not all deaf," and "Don't wear handkerchiefs on your head."[17]

Carl Hansberry's first priority was finding a place to live. He rented a room in a tenement at 5008 South Wabash in Bronzeville. Next, he needed a job. Purity Grocery Company on West Randolph Street hired him to unload deliveries and stock the shelves. After work, he walked fifteen blocks east in the direction of the lake, to Chicago Technical College, on South Michigan Avenue, to attend evening and weekend classes in business. His brother, Leo, had enlisted in 1917, the first year of the United States' entry into World War I, and was saving money as an army clerk to pay for Harvard. The brothers agreed that Carl would identify himself as their mother's sole supporting son, and thereby claim an exemption from the draft.[18]

And so, with his weekday routine in place—work, school, study—Lorraine's father became just another straphanger on the Halsted streetcar, swaying in the aisle, rattling into downtown, the stops clanged off by the conductor as in a never-ending prize fight. Returning to his room in Bronzeville after dinner, Carl had a few hours left to hit the books before turning off the light.

Things seemed to be going in the right direction. One evening at a meeting of the Colored Commercial Club of Chicago, he met a new member who had just arrived from Alabama, Randall Washington Hunter. Hunter was starting a private bank and proposed that Hansberry come in with him as the cashier. Because Carl was just completing a correspondence course for a certificate in accounting, the offer couldn't have come at a better time.

The R.W. Hunter and Company Bank opened in August 1918 at Forty-Eighth and South State Streets, in the heart of Bronzeville. Its mission was a noble one: "We want colored men and women to do business with one another the same as other races in this country."[19] At the ceremonial ribbon cutting, celebrated with refreshments and speeches by "prominent leaders of the race," Hunter praised Hansberry for his hard work and his ability to recruit fresh talent.[20] One of Carl's hires was a young woman for the position of teller: twenty-two-year-old Nannie Louise Perry.[21] She was petite, with light brown skin, straight black hair, and high cheekbones. Her face had wide, smooth features, giving an impression of serenity. It was said by her family that her maternal grandfather was a member of the Cherokee tribe. Like Carl, she hadn't been in Chicago very long, less than a year, making them a pair who were just beginning their adventure in the North.

Nannie had been born in 1896, the youngest of seven children of the Reverend and Mrs. Perry of the African Methodist Episcopal Church of Columbia, Tennessee.[22] Her parents raised her to be genteel and pious, but a striver, too. These qualities might seem to be slightly opposed: living a conservative, well-tempered life involving church events, calling on friends, and attending improving lectures, while at the same time expressing a frank desire to rise in the material world. But those like the Perrys entering the middle class during Reconstruction, before it ended in the mid-1870s, believed that with continued self-help, education, and respectability, economic independence would come, as predicted by Booker T. Washington. The Perry children were expected to dress tastefully, exhibit appreciation for the finer things, take part in improving activities, and

demonstrate a moderate temperament befitting a young lady or gentleman. Prudishness was commendable—it signified that one was civilized
in mind and body. When she was nineteen, Nannie Perry traveled by train
on perhaps her first independent trip, to visit relatives in Knob Creek,
Kentucky. But she went in the role of chaperone to her niece.[23] Propriety
was everything—a value she had been taught to hold dear.

Lorraine's parents were married on June 1, 1919. They found accommodation at 4316 Forty-Third Street, the only residence on the block that
would accept Negroes. Other residences were mainly boardinghouses for
single men where mealtime was a feast of accents. "You vas shust der same
like me ven you game to Chicago ten year ago," a German was overheard
scolding a fellow countryman indignantly. For their portion of the house
rent, the Hansberrys were entitled to a bedroom, kitchen privileges, and
a bathroom shared with seven other adults and their children. Lorraine's
mother was expecting her first child. Everyone in the house had one thing
in common: None was a native Chicagoan. They had all come up from the
South to make a fresh start. "Practically everybody you meets here is from
Mississippi," says a character in Lorraine's unpublished novel "All the Dark
and Beautiful Warriors." "And if they ain't they mama and papas is. This
here town ain't nothing but Mississippi done come North."[24]

Six weeks after the Hansberrys married, their future changed suddenly.
A stone-throwing fight between whites and blacks at the Twenty-Ninth
Street Beach escalated into the worst race riot in the city's history. Whites
boarded cars and began speeding into Bronzeville, firing into homes.
Some charged on foot down Thirty-Fifth Street, beating up people as
they went. Watching them approach, a Bronzeville resident looking out
his front window readied his gun. "Here they come," he said to his family.[25] The following day, Monday, thousands of black men gathered in the
center of Bronzeville. The ones in military uniform, veterans of the black
370th Infantry, attached to the Eighth Regiment Armory in Bronzeville,
organized into squads and set up communication outposts linked by telephone, constituting one of the first, and probably the largest, instances of
armed self-defense by Negroes to date in American history. On the fifth
day, a thunderstorm sent people back inside their homes, and the fighting

ended. Thirty-eight people (twenty-three black and fifteen white) were killed. More than 350 people were injured.[26]

Other riots during the "Red Summer" of 1919 erupted in Texas, Arkansas, South Carolina, Tennessee, Oklahoma, Nebraska, and Washington, DC. In Elaine, Arkansas, Nannie Hansberry's brother-in-law L. H. Johnston, a physician, and his three brothers (one of them a wounded veteran) were forced off a train and accused by a white posse of being insurrectionists. The brothers fought back and were shot to death. The Elaine Massacre took the lives of between one and two hundred black Americans.[27] Lorraine later heard the story about the Johnston brothers when she was a child, from her babysitter, Dr. Johnston's niece. Reflecting on the history of her people as an adult, she wrote to a young, white southerner, "I think, then, that Negroes must concern themselves with every single means of struggle: legal, illegal, passive, active, violent and non-violent . . . They must harass, debate, petition, boycott, sing hymns, pray on steps— and shoot from their windows when the racists come cruising through their communities. The acceptance of our condition is the only form of extremism which discredits us before our children."[28]

In the cleanup after Red Summer, along with the broken glass scattered on Bronzeville's sidewalks, R.W. Hunter and Company Bank was swept away; and with it, Carl Hansberry's position as cashier. Bank records for the private company aren't available, but why it went bankrupt in the fall of 1919 may have been a result of overzealousness. Black-run banks, in their eagerness to help the community, tended to overlook the credit histories of borrowers who were poor risks.[29] In December, Hansberry and R. W. Hunter appeared as defendants in bankruptcy court at the Chicago Federal Building. The *Chicago Tribune* ridiculed the pair of young black men who had the temerity to think they could run a bank.[30]

The Hansberrys' first child, Carl Augustus Hansberry Jr., was born on February 19, 1920. Fortunately, Carl Sr. was working at a new and sounder financial institution by then: the Douglass National Bank, named for Frederick Douglass, at Thirty-Second and State, the first federally chartered Negro bank. But he was beginning to think about making another move, this time into real estate.

Owning buildings with rent-paying tenants was a big, lucrative business to be in, bigger than banking. The housing situation on the South Side was desperate. Since Carl's arrival four years earlier, the population of the Black Belt had grown by another twenty-five thousand. Newcomers continued to arrive daily by the hundreds every month. Families were constantly pushing against the imaginary street boundaries of the ghetto. Those who could afford it reached into other communities wherever a breach occurred. "We were denied in years gone by the privilege of owning the roof over our heads," the *Chicago Defender* pointed out; "now we grasp the first opportunity to invest our earnings in property."[31]

The year the Hansberrys' second child, Perry Holloway Hansberry, was born, 1921, Carl Sr. began teaching himself the real estate business. He left the Douglass National Bank and moved his family into a two-story apartment building at 4518 South Champlain Avenue. They had the second floor all to themselves. To learn as much as he could about property values, he worked part-time as a tax appraiser for Cook County. This, in turn, made him valuable to Jesse Binga, president of the Binga State Bank and one of the wealthiest real estate speculators on the South Side. Hansberry apprenticed himself under Binga as his bookkeeper.

In the opinion of some, Jesse Binga—soft-spoken, well-dressed—was a "mean son-of-a-bitch."[32] He had a method for turning up accommodations, though, even in white neighborhoods. If landlords were willing to do business with him, they received a guarantee that under his management the building would be at full occupancy for a year. Once the building was handed over to him, he would evict the white tenants, subdivide the apartments, move in black tenants, and raise the rent anywhere from 25 to 50 percent to get more than what he had promised the owner.

Hansberry needed this kind of street-level education in the real estate market. He took a third job, part-time, as a rent collector for an Irishman named Mulvihill, a landlord having trouble collecting from his black tenants. But Hansberry, who had the quiet demeanor of a minister, was treated differently. After a while, if the tenants had a complaint, or needed more time to come up with their rent, Mulvihill's courtly agent Mr. Hansberry was the man to talk to.[33]

During his rounds, Hansberry noticed something interesting: Mulvihill wasn't using floor space to its maximum advantage. He was letting a three-flat building go cheap in the face of high demand: one family per floor. Binga, for his part, always subdivided the apartments of his buildings to get more families per floor. If Mulvihill would subdivide two rooms into four and install a cookstove in each one, a two-story flat could become an apartment building with individual kitchenettes for seven or eight families. It would be an advance, an answer to the housing crunch—to say nothing of the income potential.

Mulvihill went for the idea. He notified his tenants at 5000 Grand Boulevard, a former mansion in the center of Bronzeville, that they would have to move out. Subdividing the apartments started immediately. One of the residents, surprised at the suddenness of the eviction, found out that Hansberry had "egged on" Mulvihill to do it.[34]

Hansberry, the erstwhile rent collector, realized he was onto something. In 1922, when Nannie was pregnant with their third child, Mamie Louise, he struck out on his own, quitting his association with Binga and Mulvihill. He purchased an older building and began quartering the floors. He used beaverboard, similar to plywood, to serve as walls dividing a pair of twenty-by-twenty-foot rooms into four ten-by-tens. The kitchen in each consisted of an icebox in the closet, a sink in one corner, and a gas stove vented to the outside. No heat. One bathroom would have to serve everyone on that floor. When it was finished, the property stood to generate more than triple the income it had before it was converted.

It was bold—a twenty-seven-year-old black father with a wife and three small children taking on debt, property, lease agreements, and repairs. Just six years earlier, Carl Hansberry had been stocking shelves in a grocery store and taking night school courses. But this was just the beginning.

2

"The King of the Kitchenettes"

The kitchenette is the author of the glad tidings that the new suckers are in town, ready to be cheated, plundered, and put in their places.

—Richard Wright, *12 Million Voices*

Lorraine's earliest memory: waking up from a nap in a darkened room on a summer afternoon and feeling "very, very hot." Through the window came the clattering of the green-and-yellow elevated train shooting past the backyard every twenty minutes. Home was a two-story Greystone at 5330 South Calumet Avenue, her parents' third residence, just barely inside Washington Park, the first of her father's probes as a real estate speculator into a white subdivision on the South Side. In the apartment upstairs, the footfalls of a pair of brothers, hotel waiters, and their sister (all three migrants from Tennessee) made the ceiling creak. It was probably the summer of 1931. Her sister, Mamie, thought Lorraine, awake or asleep, resembled a "beautiful little doll."[1]

Carl Hansberry was now president of Hansberry Enterprises, at 4272 South Indiana Avenue in Bronzeville. "Good homes for good people" was his slogan. Since going out on his own as a speculator, he had been buying deteriorating and foreclosed properties at cut-rate prices. He could take a single six-room apartment on the South Side renting for $50 a month, split it into six "kitchenettes" (one-room apartments) that rented for $8 a week, and realize $192 a month for the same amount of floor space.[2] The flood of black newcomers seeking shelter meant that just about anything habitable would be snapped up. Tenements that formerly held sixty families now held three hundred.[3]

The office staff of Hansberry Enterprises was the Hansberry family. Carl's half sister from his mother's second marriage after the death of his father, Professor Elden Hayes Hansberry, handled the secretarial work; Carl's half brother collected the rents. A pair of maintenance men went out on service calls to a dozen three- and four-floor houses and apartment buildings converted to kitchenettes. Despite the Wall Street crash of 1929, Carl Hansberry was doing quite well—was getting rich, in fact. The newspapers called him "the King of the Kitchenettes," and his wife and children were proud of the title.[4]

Southern migrants had continued to arrive in Chicago for close to twenty years now. If not on the train, then by driving up Highway 61, many of them believing that their exodus from oppression had been ordained by the divine. Those who rode the train sometimes knelt in the aisle as they crossed the Ohio River (the demarcation of the North), stopped their watches, and sang the gospel hymn "I Done Come Out of Egypt with the Good News." Then they rose and let their watches run again, to symbolize that they had entered a new time in their existence.

But most couldn't leave their country ways behind, learned from surviving in destitution down South. They "simply have no use for grass," a disgusted Bronzeville homeowner said. "Down there they plant cotton right up to the doors of the homes and they are taught that grass should be trampled on and destroyed."[5] Backyard shacks and stables on the South Side became coops for chickens and pens for pigs. Junk dealers piled their wares in the yard. Zoning laws were ignored, and city services declined because, officials said, the taxes paid didn't cover the cost of trash collection. Some alleys became so full of muck and garbage that they were impassable. Houses of prostitution, or "buffet flats," began operating without interference by the late 1920s, under the protection of gangsters, black and white, and the police.

Residents concerned about their property values tried to prevent slums from spreading by forming neighborhood improvement associations. The *Chicago Defender* cheered on their efforts to keep the streets free of trash and gave out awards for the "neatest lawn" to disprove the "dirty propaganda" of white property associations and their "rot" about black neighborhoods. Volunteers turned vacant lots into gardens or little parks, purchasing communal tools and sometimes hiring a gardener or landscaper to help keep them looking nice.[6]

But what their grass mowing, sweeping, and pruning couldn't prevent was the proliferation of Carl Hansberry's idea—the kitchenette. It was simple and inexpensive to convert one apartment into four—basements, too. "So many fine houses have been ruined by cutting them up into kitchenettes," lamented one woman. If only, she wished, petitions could somehow keep out "a lower class of people."[7] Competition was quick to come up with more versions of "light housekeeping units." Kitchenettes were gold mines for real estate companies, banks, churches, and universities.[8] In 1941, a city inspector found thirty-one persons sharing two toilets in a vermin-infested three-floor converted mansion. In a smaller house where seven children slept on the floor, he saw rats running in and out of holes in the bathroom wall.[9]

"The kitchenette," wrote Richard Wright, "with its filth and foul air, with its one toilet for thirty or more tenants, kills our black babies so fast that in many cities twice as many of them die as white babies." Wright lived in a kitchenette with his mother, brother, aunt, and grandmother at 3743 Indiana Avenue, five blocks from the offices of Hansberry Enterprises. His bedroom was a closet with a lightbulb. "The kitchenette reaches out with fingers of golden bribes to the officials of the city, persuading them to allow old firetraps to remain standing and occupied long after they should have been torn down. The kitchenette is the funnel through which our pulverized lives flow to ruin and death on the city pavement, at a profit."[10]

During Lorraine's childhood, the South Side went into a steep decline. First, the concerted effort of banks, real estate agents, landlords, and white homeowners to isolate black Chicagoans inside a ghetto caused the community to weaken. Commerce and businesses in Bronzeville couldn't survive, trapped inside a bell jar. Then the crash of 1929, the city's failure to enforce building codes, and landlords like Hansberry brought the Black Belt to its knees.

The first two winters of Lorraine's life were the coldest in Chicago memory. Families crowded into condemned houses without light or heat, and sometimes without water.[11] For warmth, they huddled around oil-filled kerosene lamps and turned the flame as high it would go. There were more than seven hundred fires in six months—more than one hundred a month, three every day—most of them fatal. The whole of the Black Belt seethed with misery. The arrival of June weather brought disease. A tenement was a "hundred delta cabins, plus tuberculosis," said a journalist about the same conditions in parts of Harlem. Death from lung disease for black children in Chicago under twelve was ten to twenty times higher than for white children the same age. Overall, the death rate of black Americans in Chicago was comparable to that of people in Bombay, India.[12]

South Side residents, to escape their loneliness in kitchenettes, to avoid the nighttime noise in tenement buildings, or only to grab a breath of fresh air, found their way (sometimes by the hundreds, even thousands) to Thirty-Fifth and State Streets, where they stood around the intersection greeting one another, talking, sometimes all night long, just to keep the community alive.

Christmas 1935: The Hansberrys' holiday dinners were sumptuous. Sometimes the dishes were supplied by a hired cook, because friends and extended family were expected. Lorraine and family were living at 3803 Giles Avenue now, within walking distance of Hansberry Enterprises. Their former address on South Calumet Avenue, on the edge of Washington Park, had proven to be a sluggish real estate market. Carl hadn't been able to widen the wedge for blacks seeking housing; no one would sell to him, apparently.

Regular guests at the Hansberrys' table included E. Horace Fitchett, a sociologist married to Carl's half sister; he was working on a graduate degree in Negro history at Claflin, a private, historically black college in South Carolina.[13] Also: Graham Perry, Nannie Hansberry's brother, a Chicago attorney; his daughter Shauneille, who was Lorraine's age and her playmate; and Leo Hansberry, Carl's brother, who, having received his master's degree from Harvard, was enrolled in the University of Chicago's Oriental Institute and pursuing a doctorate in ancient African history.[14] Recently, Leo had been delivering a slideshow lecture to South Side civic and church groups about the historic decline of Ethiopia. He concluded his talks by expressing his concerns about Mussolini's invasion of Ethiopia and the Second Italo-Ethiopian War: "The prospect of calamity was just as great for Italy as for Ethiopia," he predicted.[15]

If five-year-old Lorraine had been listening, she may well have been encouraged to share what she knew about Ethiopia. In the Hansberry household, being dull was considered impolite.[16] She had seen a newsreel at the movies with her mother about the war between the Italians and the Ethiopians. On the screen, white soldiers were attacking dark-skinned men who were rushing into battle without helmets or trucks and waving rifles as they rode forward on donkeys. There was loud, harsh music, mixed with the sounds of shouting and explosions. Planes dropped bombs on burning villages.

She was frightened. Her anxiety grew worse when her mother joined the angry murmur in the theater darkness when Pope Pius XI was seen blessing Italian troops.[17] Looking up at the screen again, Lorraine leaped the emotional distance between herself and the dark-skinned people on-screen fighting for their lives. She understood that "somebody somewhere was doing something to hurt black and brown peoples."[18] Whether she could explain to the adults around the Hansberrys' Christmas dinner table why the images frightened her, burned in her so, is hard to say; she was only five.

On Christmas morning, with their guests looking on, Mrs. Hansberry insisted that Lorraine unwrap and show everyone her lovely gift. It was in a large box. Under the wrappings and ribbon, inside the carton, wrapped in tissue paper, was a child-size three-piece ensemble from an exclusive downtown shop: a white ermine coat, hood, and muff. Lorraine was told to stand up, and then the coat was first lovingly shaken and then thrust upon her frame and buttoned to her chin as if she were about to go out into the cold. Next, the muff was placed on her fists, and last, the satin-lined fur hood that made her head look twice as big. She hated being exhibited. She was old enough to know that when something special or expensive entered the house, it was treated much the way as she was being treated now: as something her parents wanted. She was instructed to walk up and down in the outfit so that the grown-ups could ooh and aah at her. Walking past the hall mirror, she saw herself looking like one of the rabbits from her coloring books. She hated those rabbits. Several hot tears spilled down her cheeks and past her tight lips until they dripped onto the ermine.[19] The hateful outfit was not limited to church, either. When the school year resumed after winter break, her mother made her wear the complete ensemble her first day at her new school.

It's generally reported that she began kindergarten in January, at Betsy Ross Elementary. Actually, she started kindergarten in September, at Herman Felsenthal Elementary, in a racially mixed area. The reason she went to two different schools was because, as one historian of Chicago put it, "Local authorities were not lacking in imagination as they constructed a racially separate school system."[20] Starting in January 1936, new attendance boundaries on the South Side changed some schools to majority-black and others to majority-white. Because her address was in a middle-class neighborhood, Lorraine was reassigned to Betsy Ross Elementary, at 6059 South Wabash Avenue, where 80 percent of the students were white. She described it later as a ghetto school, but that doesn't square with the school boundaries. And the building was brand-new and about to receive additional classrooms. In the meantime, however, it was overcrowded with morning and afternoon shifts, the result of the Chicago school board's having redrawn the district lines around color instead of school building size.[21]

Why her parents didn't send her to a private school mystified her as an adult. They were "some peculiar kind of democrats," she later thought.[22] Actually, they were black progressives for their time, and in favor of inclusivity.

Her mother insisted she wear the beautiful ermine outfit on her first day, to demonstrate that "we were better than no one but infinitely superior to everyone."[23] At recess, Lorraine dawdled on the playground because she didn't know anyone. Eventually, a group of children sauntered over to examine this peculiar person standing by herself, a kindergartner in a white fur coat. Though eager to make friends, she knew she was a "serious, odd-talking kid" because her parents insisted she speak properly—no slang.[24] She didn't know the street games for the playground, or the words to the loud, hand-clapping rhymes that went with jump rope, either. The other children studied this newcomer who looked like the Easter Bunny arriving early. The girls twisted back and forth, whispering, hugging themselves, and blowing on their chapped hands. Offended by Lorraine's uppity airs, they pushed her down and smeared mud on her coat. From that moment, she said later, she became a rebel against unfairness.[25]

Being different was painful in the classroom as well. One day, the teacher asked the children to stand up and say what their father did for a living. Each student stood beside his or her desk and announced their dad's job. When her turn came, Lorraine stood and repeated what she had heard at home: "He's a magnet."

"A what?"

"Real estate—a magnet."

The teacher laughed. "You mean, your father is a *maggot*."

Lorraine sat down. Whispers and snickering accompanied her humiliation. Against her will, with the kids watching, she began to cry.[26]

The children at Betsy Ross Elementary were tough and streetwise. Fighting was second nature to them, and they doled out to others what their parents had taught them: to be strong, not to flinch or to seem afraid.

"Who you callin' a lie?" they accused her.

"Calling nobody a lie," she replied.

"Yes, you are. You say you didn't say what I said you said!"

"I didn't," she said, knowing that it was no use.

"See—she just said it again! Hit her!" Then a fist would come flying that blocked out the whole sky. Or, she remembered, she would be "seized in a hostile embrace of fury and thrown to the sidewalk, where the pebbly texture of the concrete cut into the elbows and knees."[27]

She craved the other children's pride and carelessness, the way they shouted with laughter, and cursed, and talked about what their parents did at night. Defiantly, they tossed their chins up and stood, hands on hips because they didn't care what anybody thought. There was something noble about them. Some had a latchkey on a shoestring around their necks because no one would be home after school. Lorraine scrounged for something to wear to show that she understood their talismans, that she was part of their world. She tied a skate key to a string around her neck. But the divide between her and the clan she wanted to join was hard to cross, and appealing to racial solidarity wasn't enough. On Saturdays, as she was being driven to dance lessons—in a recital, she was the "Little Mama Doll," "a beautiful, quiet little girl," her teacher remembered—she looked out the car window at children playing hopscotch, jump rope, and marbles.[28]

Sometimes she brought a playmate home with her, as a way of sharing. Her small visitor would be respectful and shy, gazing at the baby grand piano in the living room, the gleaming china cabinet, the rows of books in the family library. Usually, Mrs. Hansberry could be found seated on the couch, reading, a cigarette at an angle in a long holder between her manicured fingernails. She always put on her high heels first thing in the morning, as if to go shopping.[29] Lorraine's father wore a suit around the house, and her teenage siblings, Mamie, Carl Jr., and Perry, were swank and sophisticated.

A friend of Lorraine's, Carmen Smith, invited her over one day. The Smith family's walk-up flat was bare and had no rugs. Taking Lorraine into the kitchen, Carmen sociably slapped together bologna sandwiches for both of them. Then she "talked to her mother who lay on a mattress on the floor," while Lorraine watched, "with no spring or legs under it, looking very tired or sick, and who had to tell the girls about the chores they would have to do when they came home from school because she would be gone to work by then."[30] Lorraine envied the sympathy between Carmen and her mother, their intimacy—being needed, depended on.

She remembered her sister and brothers treating her tenderly. But after she began kindergarten, they expected her to act more grown-up, less needy. She felt like a "race apart" from them now. "They do not mind diapering you the first two years," Lorraine wrote, looking back, "but by the time you are five you are a pest that has to be attended to in the washroom, taken to the movies and 'sat with' at night. You are not a person—you are a nuisance who is not particular fun anymore." She couldn't remember Mamie ever hugging her. Only when she was sick, physically out of order, did she feel important again. Then her mother waited upon her and brought a tray of soup to her room. To get rid of germs, her mother gave her enemas in a hot, steamy bathroom—like taking something to the dry cleaner. But "of love, there was nothing ever said."[31]

She felt closer to her father. He was quiet and gentle, his serious expressions wrinkling his bald head. His preference for double-breasted suits made him look like the mayor of a town where good people were expected to do good things. Lorraine wanted to get nearer his pleasant bearishness. And he always seemed to be up to something amazing, she thought. He did things with such confidence that she assumed all fathers were like that. She liked him best when he was tinkering in the kitchen with appliances that had gone on the fritz, or explaining to her one of his sketches for an invention such as a pump or a railroad device. He was an idea man; progress inspired him. He had, she said later, an "educated soul."[32]

Sometimes, on a summer night, when it was too hot to be inside any longer, they drove to Midway Plaisance, a parklike strip on the boulevard separating the University of Chicago campus from residential areas, a neutral zone for Negroes and whites, where families could gather to escape the baking heat of the streets. Her father would unfurl a blanket on the grass, and Lorraine would get the privilege of lying beside him. She liked how it was "cool and sweet to be on the grass and there was usually the scent of freshly cut lemons or melons in the air. And Daddy would lie on his back, as fathers must, and explain about how men thought the stars above us came to be and how far away they were." He knew about the stars. "I never did learn to believe that anything could be as far away as *that*," she said. "Especially the stars . . ."[33]

In 1937, her father was working on a plan to break out of the ghetto and pioneer his real estate business into fresh residential areas. Construction had begun on federal housing projects. Plans were underway for high-rise apartments, row houses, and garden apartments in a landscaped setting. Hansberry charged high rents for his kitchenettes—brand-new, rent-subsidized public housing would cut heavily into his market.[34] What he needed was fresh housing stock to attract middle-class blacks, who, like most Americans, equated moving up with a better address.[35] Once he made an inroad somewhere, whites would begin selling out cheap, and he could start chopping floors into kitchenettes. The racist practices of banks aided in tipping neighborhoods into his hands, too. Black homeseekers, eager to get out of the ghetto, made bad bargains. If a bank turned them down for a mortgage, they often signed an agreement with a real estate speculator.[36] For a low down payment, they could acquire a house on installment, followed by huge monthly payments. The danger was that the smallest violation in the contract (a month's delinquency, for instance) could result in eviction. Families who were desperate to keep their homes would rent out rooms to boarders—too many boarders sometimes, the beginning of the property's becoming a slum.[37] The domino effect kicked in after that, and entire blocks flipped.

Like a commander consulting a map showing where the opposing forces were located, Hansberry wanted to choose the point of least white resistance. He put his finger on a subdivision known as South Park: a rectangle comprising twenty-seven blocks between Sixtieth and Sixty-Third and west of Cottage Grove, once occupied by a racetrack. This meant jumping over most of Washington Park, which had proven too hard to break into anyway, and landing in the northwest corner of Woodlawn, where the housing vacancy rate at the border with Washington Park was already 15 percent. Some rental buildings were only half full, and white tenants were demanding lower rents to stay. The "most vulnerable spot to attack," Hansberry decided, "was where the pressure was greatest," where white homeowners and landlords found "themselves with property on their hands which is no longer desirable to the better paying class of whites and because of restrictive covenants, they are not available to the colored occupants."[38] Standing in his way were those restrictive covenants. He would have to bust in: buy a home on a block and then fight for his family to stay in it.

Restrictive property covenants (private contracts legally enforceable between buyers and sellers) had come into use after the Red Summer of 1919 to stop the "Negro invasion." They had spread "like a marvelous delicately woven chain of armor," exulted a Hyde Park newspaper, from "the northern gates of Hyde Park at 35th and Drexel Boulevard to Woodlawn, Park Manor, South Shore, Windsor Park, and all the far-flung white communities of the South Side"—covering about 80 percent of the city.[39]

The Chicago Real Estate Board supplied the legal boilerplate in a deed that appeared as a covenant.[40] Under the covenant, the signer agreed not to sell, rent, or lease the property in question to minority groups, usually blacks, but also sometimes Jews, Chinese, Japanese, Mexicans, Armenians, Persians, or Syrians (Muslims). More accurately, these additions to deeds were also called residential *racial* covenants, because the economic health of a housing market was thought to depend on ensuring white homeownership. Sometimes covenants covered only a few blocks; other times, entire communities. They existed all over the country.

Restrictive covenants were about more than property. They implied a promise: by agreeing to exclude nonwhites from the neighborhood, the signer was endorsing whiteness and claiming it for himself—a bid to belong.

YMCAs, churches, women's clubs, PTAs, Kiwanis clubs, and chambers of commerce all endorsed restrictive covenants as good for the social order. Civic-minded Theresa Capone, Al Capone's mother, signed a covenant to guarantee the respectability of her neighborhood.[41]

However, an unintended consequence of papering over communities with covenants was that, as blocks showed signs of changing, homeowners and landlords were stuck with the provisions of the covenant, unable to sell or rent to interested minority applicants. Saddled with a mortgage on a house or apartment building, the owners knew that the value of their investment was dropping, but they couldn't do anything about it. Adding to their anxiety were real estate agents' warnings that they should sell soon, before it was too late, even if it meant taking a beating.

Hansberry intended to exploit this white fear by "blockbusting" in the South Park subdivision. It "was not a matter of law, evidence, precedence, equity, or justice," he said, "but rather, a matter of the greatest influence fortified by prejudice."[42] In other words, he was going to leverage racism. It could be dangerous, though; it could be fatal. There were an estimated thirty thousand Klansmen living in Chicago in 1922.[43] An armed guard protected Jesse Binga's unattached two-story brick home, on the eastern edge of Washington Park. Seven times, bombs had blown off his front porch. "I will not run," he declared. "The race is at stake and not myself."[44] One black pioneer who managed to buy in a white neighborhood had refused an offer from the Hyde Park and Kenwood Association to purchase his home at a profit. A bomb thrown from a car destroyed the front of his residence while he was away on business and his wife and children were asleep. The police advised him to get "anything from a Mauser [semiautomatic pistol] to a machine gun" and wait for the next assault.[45]

Hansberry could have used a few preemptive strikes to soften up his target. Speculators sometimes hired a black woman to wheel a baby stroller down the sidewalk, startling the white residents. Having cars with black drivers cruising the neighborhood was another tactic. Easier was phoning white-owned residences on a block and asking, with a drawl, "Is Tyrone there?" Also, anonymous calls, warning "They're coming!" could be effective.[46] But Hansberry was impatient. Anticipating trouble, either in court or on the street, he created the Hansberry Foundation "to safeguard the Negro's civil rights and to make additional housing available to them."

He put as much of his own money into the foundation as he could afford, to create a war chest.[47]

Incredibly, the willing seller he found on the other side was the former president of the Woodlawn Property Owners Association, James J. Burke. The owner of several apartment buildings, Burke had been pleading with renters belonging to the association not to move out just because blacks were living nearby.[48] His plea was met with more than just disagreement from his fellow members; they were indignant. They resented what was happening as much as he did, but the handwriting was on the wall. Nothing could stop them from moving wherever they chose. Free country, wasn't it? Burke resigned angrily as president of the association in March 1937, but before he quit the group, his parting shot stunned them all: "I will get even with the Woodlawn Property Owners Association," he said, "by putting niggers in every block."[49]

Hansberry had his man. He went to Supreme Liberty Life Insurance in April for a $4,400 note to purchase one of Burke's properties: a three-flat building at 6140 South Rhodes Avenue, in Woodlawn. His loan application indicated that Hansberry Enterprises owned a dozen apartment buildings. The "overwhelming sentiment" of the bank committee, said Truman K. Gibson Jr., one of the insurance company's attorneys, was to make Hansberry the loan.[50] As a gesture of support, and to make it doubly hard on the Woodlawn Property Owners Association, the black president of Supreme Liberty Life Insurance, Harry H. Pace, purchased another house from Burke, just around the corner from Hansberry's, at 413 East Sixtieth Avenue.

Gibson would later work closely with Hansberry in connection with this property, and he saw Hansberry operate behind the scenes as an entrepreneur in a black business environment where cash was the only thing trusted. Hansberry "yearned," Gibson said, "for the surefire chance to make a killing. He socialized with the policy guys, which served only to feed his appetite for the fast buck."[51] The policy guys ran the numbers racket. They drove the finest cars, wore the most expensive clothes, owned summer homes and private airplanes, and vacationed in Europe and Mexico.

Things moved quickly after that. Burke found a straw buyer for the Hansberry sale: a retired white widower with the melodramatic name of

Jay B. Crook. Crook obtained a mortgage on the Rhodes Avenue address through his bank, the First National Bank of Englewood, "with the distinct understanding," argued the Englewood bank later in court, "that said sale was not to be to a negro [*sic*]." Ignoring this, on May 26, 1937, Crook signed a quitclaim deed and conveyed the property to Hansberry. Then Crook passed along the house keys—through an intermediary probably. Hansberry's personal lawyer, C. Francis Stradford, would have been the natural choice.

It was like stealing or planning a robbery.

3

Stay Where You Belong

The white people fall back bitterly before the black horde; the landlords make a tidy profit by raising the rent, chopping up the rooms, and all but dispensing with the upkeep; and what has once been a neighborhood turns into a "turf."

—James Baldwin, "Fifth Avenue, Uptown"

Can white folks kill you any deader than T.B.? Listen, I'll kill anybody that tries to stop me from getting out of that—that rathole!

—Frank London Brown, *Trumbull Park*

The Hansberrys moved into the house with three apartments on South Rhodes Avenue the evening of May 26, the day that Carl signed the deed. The first-floor apartment was empty, the way that Burke, the disgruntled association president, had left it. The South Park subdivision was quiet and residential, with no stores or businesses. Rows of turn-of-the-century brick residences with roofed porticos in front—"porches" everyone called them—faced each other across the tree-lined street. The Hansberrys didn't bring much from their home at 3803 Giles Avenue, which they still owned, just enough to make do. The rest would follow. The weather had been warmish, with intermittent rain all day. It was dark before eight o'clock. The building belonged to them now, but there were still renters upstairs.

The white people in the second- and third-floor apartments, a Mr. Mooney and a Mrs. Cotsones, threw a fit when they realized what was happening. Hansberry wasn't their landlord, they insisted; Burke was, and they refused to pay rent. They were going to sue before Hansberry could throw them out and rent to Negroes.[1]

A week later, five members of the Woodlawn Property Owners Association, Anna Lee et al., filed suit to evict the Hansberrys and asked that Carl be restrained from collecting the rent or renting other apartments at 6140 Rhodes Avenue to "colored people." *Hansberry v. Lee* named Harry H. Pace and the Supreme Liberty Life Insurance as defendants, as well as the seller, James J. Burke, and the white real estate agent who had facilitated the sale, William I. Sexton. Separately, the association sent a letter to the Chicago Real Estate Board demanding that Sexton's license be revoked for his having violated the covenant.

May became June, and the other residents on Rhodes Avenue gave the Hansberrys the cold shoulder. No one brought over a dessert, or knocked on the front door to say hello. Mornings, when Mrs. Hansberry came out to empty the kitchen garbage pail, people on their porches went inside. No one returned her smile.[2]

School ended, and the neighborhood children began playing outside during the day, but Lorraine was told to stay close to home. She dawdled in the house or sat on the porch. The porch faced west, and as evening came on, a blue-white radiance from a million electric lights a few blocks away erased the stars from the sky. The glare was White City Amusement Park, where Negroes weren't allowed to use the indoor roller rink. The contrast made Rhodes Avenue seem darker somehow, and still, as if holding its breath. The cicadas hadn't started buzzing yet, and it was too early for fireflies. Sometimes, the porch door opened behind Lorraine and the bodyguard her father had hired, a black off-duty policeman, came out to have a look.[3]

One evening, Lorraine was sitting on the porch before bedtime with Mamie and her best friend, Jewel Stradford, the daughter of Carl Hansberry's attorney.[4] It was getting dark, and the weather had been blazing hot all day. The windows of the house were open. The girls could hear Mrs. Hansberry talking to an older woman who was visiting, a relative. Carl was expected home after a trip to the state capital on business related to the Woodlawn association's lawsuit. The Hansberry brothers, Carl Jr. and Perry—"the boys," as they were called in the family—were off somewhere. They were old enough to drive and had their own cars. They preferred top-end chariots from Detroit—Buick, Cadillac, or Lincoln.[5] Although she was only eight, Lorraine thought they were "silly" about their automobiles.[6]

It was Mamie's job to keep an eye on Lorraine, and she wasn't happy about being an unpaid nanny. She was a teenager, popular at Englewood High School, and could think of better things to do. "Mother hardly had anything to do for her," she complained of her sister. "I did it all."[7] Playing the "Little Mama" included Sundays, too. Mrs. Hansberry liked to doll up Lorraine for church. She'd been a hairdresser at one time and expertly twisted Lorraine's hair with a curling iron into sausage curls that waggled above the collar of her starched pinafores. During the service, Mamie doled out pieces of candy from her purse to make Lorraine keep still.[8] Jewel thought Lorraine was a bit of a pill, someone fond of getting attention by saying she was going to be a doctor when she grew up—smart but spoiled, and "born to affluence."[9] Out of loyalty to Mamie, Jewel tolerated her friend's little sister hanging around. But she didn't belong with them.

While the girls sat on the porch killing time waiting for it to get dark, some whites gathered in the street. They started pointing and hooting. When a stone clattered against the brick, Mamie grabbed Lorraine and shooed her inside with Jewel. Mrs. Hansberry told the girls to stay back from the windows. The bodyguard was there, she reminded them, and the maid. But Lorraine was shocked to see her mother take a pistol from a desk drawer and begin patrolling the house, peering through the window shades as if they were under siege.

Outside, the shouting and taunts grew louder. Something tore through the window screen, flew past Lorraine's head, and slammed into the living room wall—a piece of broken brick, fired from a slingshot probably.[10] The bodyguard, gun unholstered, went outside to face down the mob until the police arrived.

After things had calmed down in the street, an officer came inside to make his report. He saw the chunk of brick embedded in the plaster and said he was going to take it for evidence. Mrs. Hansberry said no, she wanted it to stay right where it was—so she could show her husband. "The big cop had his hands on his hips and made his impatience evident," Lorraine remembered. "Look lady," he said, "I don't care about your husband, I've got to take the brick to headquarters. I don't give a damn about none of this, I'm here because I was sent. I don't know what you folks are all excited about anyhow. Some people throw a rock through your window and you act like it was a bomb. Jesus, these people wouldn't have bothered you noways, if you was in your own neighborhood."[11]

Lorraine's mother stood her ground, and the brick was still in the wall when Carl Sr. arrived home late that night. Lorraine listened, lying in bed, to "his voice at the telephone all night, the South was still in it. . . . I went to sleep with his voice in my ears, thinking happily how I would play with the brick in the morning."[12] She felt safe. Her father was good at keeping a grip on himself under pressure. Self-containment and poise, invulnerability— that was the Hansberry way.[13]

A squad car dawdled on Rhodes Avenue until dawn.[14] But no one was arrested for damaging the Hansberrys' property. City and state authorities were apathetic about enforcing the law to protect blacks from white violence.[15] The cop had spoken for everybody, from the officials at city hall, to the average white resident nursing a beer at his corner tap, to the members of the chamber of commerce: stay where you belong.

In the days that followed, nothing about the attack appeared in the downtown newspapers. The Chicago Commission on Race Relations requested that, for the sake of social harmony, the press not publish accounts of race riots, although stories about Negroes accused of crimes ran all the time. But Chicago was the capital of black journalism, with five publications, and was home to the Associated Negro Press. What had happened to the Hansberrys went out from the Associated Negro Press all the way to the *Pittsburgh Courier*. After that, Lorraine noticed black cabbies driving by slowly. They circled the perimeter like sentinels.

School began in October, delayed by a month due to a citywide outbreak of mild infantile paralysis. Lorraine's new address put her in a different attendance area. For the third grade, she switched from Betsy Ross Elementary to A.O. Sexton Elementary, at Sixty-First and Langley, where most of the students were white. The Woodlawn Property Owners Association had gone to lengths to keep black children out of Sexton Elementary and Hyde Park High School because, explained the association's president, it was "hard to get tenants with children who have to be sent to school along with Negroes."[16] Once again, however, because Lorraine lived in a middle-class neighborhood similar to Betsy Ross's attendance area, she slipped through the net and became quite possibly the only black child at her school. Fortunately, she made friends with a red-haired white girl who walked the same way every morning. When the weather turned cold and Lorraine "could smell the paint on hot radiators," the redhead dazzled her by wearing a beautiful plaid snowsuit.[17]

There was a new subject awaiting Lorraine in the third grade, social studies, an hour during the day devoted to learning about life experiences and institutions in America. Her father was an American history buff, and she was interested. But, she discovered, having dark skin canceled one's part in a story that began when the *Mayflower* bumped into Cape Cod in mid-December 1620 carrying 120 half-dead passengers.[18] Whites from England and their descendants, according to the textbook, brought the United States its national language, its laws, its glorious flag, and democratic government. But the origins and history of twelve million black Americans was, by implication, too shameful to discuss. It was taken for granted, Hansberry said later, that "Everything distasteful and painful was associated with Africa." An African was a "savage with a spear, uncivilized, naked, something to laugh at." Children taunted her, "You look like an African."[19] Her father had taught his children to be proud of their family, but she didn't know enough about Africa for it to be useful to her spirit.[20]

Left to her own devices, Lorraine let her love of reading lead her to imagine her history. Her parents had a library of contemporary literature from subscription book clubs—contemporary fiction, nonfiction, and poetry, some by authors of the Harlem Renaissance, such as Langston Hughes, William Waring Cuney, and Countee Cullen. She began dipping into the pages when she was nine. "Beautiful mountains, plateaus, beautiful dark people," she remembered. "I was deeply influenced by them and their images of Africa were marvelous and beautiful."[21] In "Heritage," the poet Cullen wonders, as Lorraine did:

> *What is Africa to me:*
> *Copper sun or scarlet sea,*

Jungle star or jungle track,
Strong bronzed men, or regal black
Women from whose loins I sprang
When the birds of Eden sang?
One three centuries removed
From the scenes his fathers loved,
Spicy grove, cinnamon tree,
What is Africa to me?

The Hansberrys didn't know, week to week, whether they could remain on Rhodes Avenue, an anxiety Mrs. Hansberry tried to keep from Lorraine.[22] They were not demonstrative people, and regardless of what was happening, the default emotional temperature inside the house was set at cool. About this time, Lorraine began having stomach pains from stress.

On July 1, 1937, the plaintiffs in *Hansberry v. Lee* requested immediate relief in Cook County Circuit Court. They wanted the Hansberrys out. The judge, Michael Feinberg, made no secret of his scorn for the defendants. It was plain to him, he said, that they were "engaged in an obvious conspiracy." He granted the eviction and issued a temporary injunction preventing Carl from collecting rent from the building's tenants. Judge Feinberg also fixed a bond on him of five thousand dollars, payable in eight days. The Hansberrys were given until October 1 to vacate. The trial was set for a later date. Pointedly, the judge, who was Jewish, added, "I don't go where I'm not wanted."[23]

At the end of July, Walter White, executive secretary of the NAACP, flew from Washington, DC, to Chicago for a meeting with South Side leaders at the Wabash Avenue YMCA in Bronzeville. White told the group that the NAACP was "backing the fight against these real estate covenants and [that] all its resources would be used."[24] It was imperative to get people out of the slums. A squad of attorneys volunteered to represent Carl Hansberry and his codefendants: Irvin C. Mollison, president of the Illinois State Conference of the NAACP; Earl B. Dickerson, president of the Cook County Bar Association and alderman of Chicago's Second Ward; Loring B. Moore, assistant attorney general of Illinois; C. Francis Stradford, Hansberry's attorney; and Truman K. Gibson Jr., counsel for Supreme Liberty

Life Insurance. The key, they believed, would be invalidating the Wood-lawn covenant; the rest would follow.

But they lost again. Despite receiving a change of venue away from Judge Feinberg, at the end of a ten-day trial in circuit court in April 1938, Judge George W. Bristol ruled that, indeed, the covenant had never legally existed because only 54 percent of the property owners had signed it. But there was a 1932 precedent involving, incredibly again, James J. Burke of the Woodlawn Property Owners Association. In that ruling, *Burke v. Klei-man*, a covenant was still considered binding even if it had fewer than the required number of signatures. Therefore, Judge Bristol upheld the Hans-berrys' eviction from Rhodes Avenue. He ordered them to leave by June 1 or face arrest for "dispossession"—that is, taking property by misusing the law.

Carl told the family to pack only what could fit in one suitcase apiece, "because we want them to know we will be back."[25] Lorraine chose the books, toys, and clothes she thought she would need as the family prepared to return to Giles Avenue. Come September, to begin fourth grade, she would return to Betsy Ross Elementary.

"No man puts his family through that lightly," Truman Gibson said. "The compelling factor for Hansberry that made that bruising turmoil necessary was the goal of busting the covenant."[26]

Mrs. Hansberry wanted to go home. Not to Rhodes Avenue—that was impossible—but home to Tennessee, to see her mother. She had spent a year worried about her family's safety, only to be cast out by her trium-phant, antagonistic neighbors, who, according to one account, jeered at the Hansberrys as they left.[27] Back home with the rest of the Perry family, she could enjoy some peace of mind.

While her father managed Hansberry Enterprises and attended to the lawsuit, Lorraine and her mother, brothers, and sister made plans to drive to Tennessee. It was important that they make it at least into Kentucky on the first day. After they left the South Side, there was only one hotel, according to the *Negro Motorist Green Book*, that would accept black trav-elers: the Dudley, in Springfield, Illinois, and that was out of their way.

Chicago's skyscrapers began falling away behind them as they drove down Halsted Street until, after an hour or so, the road became Dixie Highway and, out the car windows, only farmers' corn and potato fields went rushing by. The warm wind made Lorraine drowsy. She had never been to visit her grandmother, but her cousin Shauneille would be visiting, too, and they could play together.

Usually during the summer months, the Hansberrys went to Michigan for a vacation. The all-day drive went around the southern tip of Lake Michigan, then north from Grand Rapids, past onion fields, lumberyards, and fish hatcheries—three hundred miles to secluded Lake Idlewild, deep inside the Manistee National Forest. Du Bois owned property there; as did Madam C. J. Walker, the cosmetics entrepreneur; and novelist Charles W. Chesnutt. Du Bois praised Lake Idlewild by its nickname, "the Black Eden," extolling it as "the beautifulest stretch I have seen for twenty years, and then to that add fellowship—sweet, strong women and keen-witted men from Canada and Texas, California and New York, Ohio, Missouri and Illinois—all sons and grand-children of Ethiopia, all with the wide leisure of rest and play—can you imagine a more marvelous thing than Idlewild?"[28]

Mamie adored the place. There were dances at the Purple Palace Supper Club, the Flamingo, and the Paradise Club, all crowded on weekends with chic people from Chicago and Detroit, some of them famous. At sixteen, she was becoming quite a stunning young woman, with broad, classic features like her mother, but tall and statuesque.

Lorraine wasn't crazy about vacationing there. The problem was summer: it was too hot, in her opinion; too bright, "light too blinding." Hot weather upset her. Summer was like being in a stark black-and-white movie she couldn't escape. She didn't like the scratchy sand of beaches, either, or the cold water and the "ick-perspiry feeling of bathing caps." She didn't know how to swim—and never would learn. At ten, she was getting chubby and may have felt self-conscious wearing a bathing suit. Summer to her was "too stark and yet too intimate a season."[29]

By the time she woke up in the car from a long nap, they had already crossed the Ohio River and were entering Kentucky, a border state during the Civil War. Her mother was "pointing out the beautiful hills on both sides of the highway" and explaining "how her father had run away and hidden from his master in those very hills when he was a little boy." It was true. Lorraine's Grandfather Perry had escaped slavery in 1860, when he was thirteen. Finding his way to New York City, he had survived by making himself handy around theaters and public entertainments. He was thirty-three when he returned to Tennessee and a seminary graduate. He married Grandmother Perry in 1880, when she was sixteen. She, too, had been born into slavery. Together, the Reverend and Mrs. Perry raised their children to become respectable people.

Lorraine studied the hills "for miles and miles after that[,] wondering who and what a master might be."[30] Apparently, she hadn't heard it before in connection with her family; nor, during the rest of her life, did she ever publicly refer to slavery as part of her family's past. Perhaps she didn't know many details. But a distant cousin of hers, Alton Kelly, a griot in Louisiana, spent years tracing the family back to their earliest-known Hansberry ancestor, William Hansberry, Lorraine's great-grandfather. His story, told here for the first time, is a remarkable one.

William Hansberry was born in 1819 on the 3,200-acre Salubria plantation, in the hills of Virginia's northern Piedmont, between the Blue Ridge Mountains and Culpeper, the county seat. The plantation's name comes from the Latin *salubris*, which suggests a "healthful" or "pleasant" spot. Hansberry's father was the master of Salubria, a forty-year-old white bachelor named William Hansbrough. A close friend described him as a gentleman of "exemplary character, habits, and deportment" who loved horse racing, and "in accomplishment of dancing[,] he was excelled but by few."[31] We know practically nothing about Hansberry's mother, who was also owned by Hansbrough. She might have been a house servant named Betty Packer, but that's not certain. Frederick Douglass, also the son of an enslaved woman and a white plantation owner, remarked drily, "Genealogical trees do not flourish among slaves."[32]

The main house at Salubria is still there, a two-story Georgian mansion open to the public at certain times of the year. Enslaved workers dug the basement in the mid-1700s and used the soil to create the slopes for a terraced garden, a status symbol among wealthy Virginians then, where there would be beautiful plantings, a vegetable garden, and herbs for the kitchen. And, again, slaves, working with local artisans, raised the exterior walls with Flemish bond brickwork, built the fireplaces, framed and glazed the double-hung windows, mitered the doors, laid the wood flooring, and carpentered the paneling and the enclosed winding staircase.

When visitors called on Hansbrough, if the weather was nice, the south door down the main hall would be open, beckoning them out to the gardens, where he would be waiting. The view was expansive, framed by landscaped trees and flowering bushes that hid from the panorama the hogpens, ice barn, slave quarters, and other outbuildings needed for the plantation to run in feudal fashion. Negro headmen supervised field-workers who cultivated two thousand acres of wheat and rye and looked after the sheep, cows, and cattle grazing on a thousand acres of pasture. Negro boys and girls worked on trash gangs, as they were called, sweeping up and carrying water to the people in the fields, or driving cows to pasture—until they were old enough for adult labor. Bill Hansberry was one of those children.

For years, the big house was the scene of weddings, balls, and celebrations. But then, a serious breach opened between Hansbrough and the rest of his family. It was so serious that he became estranged from everyone. In the autumn of 1837, when he was dying at age fifty-eight, he expressed his anger in the most devasting way he could, by depriving his kinsmen of what they expected to receive upon his death: his property. He canceled their financial legacy in his will and pulled Salubria down around him. Everything was sold off, down to the last rake, horse, and wagon.[33]

Not yet twenty years old, Hansberry was chained to other people owned by his father, under the eye of a pair of slavers out of Culpeper, Humphrey Taylor and his son J. Warren Taylor. Their business was driving coffles of men, women, and children overland to Mississippi and Louisiana. Walking at a pace of three miles an hour, the prisoners—for so they were—took about sixty days to reach Clinton, Louisiana, the seat of East Feliciana parish, one of the Taylors' regular auction stops. Buyers were alerted through newspaper advertisements that father and son were on their way and that "those wishing to purchase negroes would do well" not to miss the sale.[34]

Two-thirds of Clinton's fourteen thousand residents were enslaved, most of them picking cotton that was packed into bales and transported southwest by rail to Port Hudson, on the Mississippi River. From there, steamboats carried it a hundred miles downriver to New Orleans, where it was loaded aboard oceangoing ships destined for the textile mills of New England or Great Britain.[35]

On auction day, Hansberry, wearing new clothes given to him by the Taylors, was exhibited on the steps of the copper-domed, Greek Revival Clinton courthouse, which is still there, its massive Doric columns serving as a backdrop for the slave market. In the crowd appraising the Taylors' "likely Negroes" was Joseph M. Young. Young may have thought the asking price for Hansberry was a bit high (double the average[36]), but he paid it and signed his name to a bill of conveyance, a sales receipt. This transaction may have been when the name "Hansbrough" was heard or written as "Hansberry." If Young didn't pay the full amount, he could have taken out a mortgage on Bill, which was a common practice, the way a farmer today borrows money to purchase a piece of machinery.[37]

For the next twenty-seven years, Lorraine's great-grandfather remained the property of another man, disappearing from view. In *A Raisin in the Sun*, Walter Lee Younger, robbed of the life insurance money that his father had amassed by working himself to death, cries out in agony, echoing the pain of labor stolen by slavery, "That money was made out of my father's flesh!"

Stories handed down by Hansberry's descendants attempt to fill in the gaps of his life. A favorite involves the Union raid on Clinton in 1863. Bill Hansberry, it's said, helped Young hide his gold, silver, and jewelry by burying it in the woods. Later, Young attempted to escape through Union lines and was killed. After the war, Hansberry retrieved the treasure and used it to buy land, thus bringing the circle of justice around to a satisfying end.[38]

The truth is more interesting. At end of the Civil War in 1865, Hansberry was in his forties, emancipated from slavery but starting out with nothing. Once he had access to money and credit, however, what he accomplished was astonishing.

Free and on his own, Hansberry worked for Young as a sharecropper. The default rate on sharecropping in that part of Louisiana was high, but Hansberry soon earned a reputation as a good farmer who paid his debts on time.[39] In 1870, he pooled his money with two partners and bought 650 acres of a plantation eight miles north of Clinton. He hired freedmen, who built homes on the place, farmed their own plots, or worked at his brick kiln. To get his goods to market, he organized wagon caravans to

Port Hudson, which was less expensive than paying the railroad's freight charges.[40]

The next step he took had more than symbolic importance. He claimed his rights as a father. In 1872, he formalized his marriage to the mother of his eight children, thirty-eight-year-old Arminda Walker. They had fallen in love while they were enslaved on Young's plantation. Hansberry had his photograph taken, too, a half-length studio portrait that resembled the paintings of Hansbroughs that had hung on the walls at Salubria. He's wearing a black frock coat with velvet lapels. His features are regular and handsome. A dark, heavy mustache, rounding the corners of his mouth, becomes an ivory beard that reaches the second button of his shirt. He looks back at us—husband, father, cotton grower.

Not long after that, he lodged a complaint with the federal government. He had been threatened, he said, by a white Democrat who had tried to turn his vote during the 1876 national election, in violation of the Fifteenth Amendment. He testified in New Orleans before F. A. Woolfley, commissioner of the U.S. Circuit Court, District of Louisiana, appointed by Governor William Pitt Kellogg to gather testimony on voter suppression.[41] After Hansberry described how he had been interfered with, he took a quill pen and made an *X* in the bottom right-hand corner of his transcribed words; unlike his children, he couldn't read or write. His statement was entered in the *Congressional Record* of the Forty-Fourth Congress of the United States.

William Hansberry lived another eighteen years, dying at age seventy-four in 1894. In spite of starting out on his own when many former slaves his age were stooped or ill from overwork, he grew into a man of social standing and honor in his community, to say nothing of his success in business.

As Lorraine, her brothers, sister, and mother reached the end of the long drive to Columbia, Tennessee, she must have been thinking about how her mother had always said that their grandmother Charlotte Perry was a "great beauty." Because when they arrived at a humble house on a rural road, she was momentarily bewildered. A very old woman in a rocker was waiting for them on the porch. Lorraine's grandmother was as "wrinkled as a prune" and could barely see or hear.

Mrs. Perry lived with her son, Lorraine's uncle George, a porter at the town's railroad station. Her other children worked as a seamstress, a laborer, a grave digger, a movie projectionist, a cook, and a practical nurse. Three of her children had gone North—Lorraine's mother, Nannie; Graham Perry, Shauneille's father; and Zelia Perry, who had married Dr. L. H. Johnston, the man murdered in the Elaine Massacre.

Lorraine recalled feeling "startled." Nothing resembled her mother's romanticized descriptions of the rural South. It was plainer, harsher, more beaten down. Mamie had always thought their grandfather was a bishop, but his church was small and nothing out of the ordinary; and the Sunshine School, the Sunday school where their mother had taught before leaving for Chicago, was a little whitewashed building in the rear.[42] While Shauneille and Lorraine stuffed themselves on their grandmother's sweet corn muffins, Grandmother Perry "always seemed to be thinking of other times," as if sustaining herself on the past and what could have been. The window of Reconstruction had opened briefly after the Civil War, giving emancipated people access to a greater world rife with possibilities, and then was gradually lowered again. She talked about slavery as if it were a presence lurking just out of sight. (Du Bois, walking through that part of Tennessee as a young schoolteacher, felt that he, too, "touched the very shadow of slavery."[43]) Perhaps it was then that Lorraine understood how near in time slavery was to her own life and how the pain seemed carried in the blood. Later that year, when she saw *Gone with the Wind* at the movies, the fable of the Old South "didn't sound anything like" what she'd heard from someone who had been enslaved.[44]

Grandmother Perry, as though the twentieth century hadn't arrived, "was captivated by automobiles," Lorraine discovered, "and, even though it was well into the Thirties, I don't think she had ever been in one before we came down and took her driving." On a safe stretch, they let her get behind the wheel. The old lady who could barely see steered determinedly down the road.[45]

Lorraine had a different perspective of her mother after she had seen her against the background of rural Tennessee. Her resentment about the white fur coat on the first day of kindergarten came into sharper focus. Her mother was the "product of robust semi-feudal backwardness." Her "vain and intensely feminine" behavior was of a type "the Southland alone can thrust upon the world." Keeping up appearances and being above reproach were vital to her; added to which, owning things (cars, property, material goods) was supposed to be evidence of self-worth.

So much followed from that. The Hansberrys had to be known as regular church attenders, although Lorraine's mother did not allow God to "intrude" into everyday life.[46] And they had to be members of the right church: African Methodist Episcopal, where there was no joyous shouting, no tambourines, no falling out from ecstasy. Nannie wouldn't permit her family to set foot in a storefront church or rented hall. At African Methodist Episcopal, the Hansberrys filed into pews beside lawyers, insurance executives, high civil servants, and white-collar businesspeople. They listened attentively to a sermon by an ordained minister, not a preacher bent on whipping them up. And as the service concluded, and the organist played a soaring postlude for all to rise, the Hansberrys' chauffeur heard his cue to pull the car around to the front and get ready to greet them as they came down the steps. Sometimes they went for a Sunday drive through the North Side suburbs to appreciate the beautiful homes.[47]

Proper breeding meant practicing emotional reserve, acting sensibly. "My dear daughter," her mother inscribed in a gift book to Lorraine when she graduated from the eighth grade at Betsy Ross Elementary, "use common sense in education, in religion, and in common life."[48] She emphasized that women were most useful as unpaid volunteers—committee chairs, organizers, and so on—especially for charitable causes. "And if they had to work by necessity," she advised, "then they should be teachers and not principals, nurses and not doctors, and secretaries and not managers."[49]

And yet, Lorraine conceded that her mother had virtues worth emulating, chief of which was never "slighting true improvement" in others.[50] She believed in human possibility. She was invariably gracious and considerate of others. Her attitude toward the value of etiquette and keeping up a good front was, at its heart, deeply ethical and humanitarian: she believed that behaving decently would result in being treated decently, no matter who you were.

During that summer, Carl Hansberry found a splendid third-floor, four-bedroom apartment for his family in Chicago, at 5936 South Parkway

Avenue (now South Martin Luther King Jr. Drive). The three-story building made of burgundy brick has a large, tree-shaded courtyard in the middle. The benches beneath the redbuds and elms are there for enjoying the small private park, away from the noise of the street. Passersby can see the courtyard on the other side of a seven-foot-high wrought iron gate.

Hansberry must have been feeling in the chips, because he also invested five thousand dollars in the National Rig Company, a new outfit prospecting for oil in downstate Centralia. He visited the site with executives from Supreme Liberty Life Insurance, and Julian Black, manager for heavyweight boxer Joe Louis. Truman Gibson Jr. was approached but wasn't interested. He heard later that the men had "spent hours gazing at the property, walking around it, and imagining oil derricks pumping black gold out of the ground, their heads filled with visions of oil dollars gushing out of the rich agricultural dirt of central Illinois."[51]

Lorraine's new home on South Parkway was only a quarter mile or so northwest, as the crow flies, from Rhodes Avenue. But because of how the South Side was divided into racial and ethnic segments, just by moving a few blocks in a certain direction, the Hansberrys were in safer territory now. Across the street was 3,200-acre Washington Park. The fieldhouse, open to the public, offered classes in boxing, arts and crafts, dramatics, speech, singing, and dancing. Behind it was an outdoor forum known as the "Bug Club" (after *bughouse*, slang for "mental health asylum"), where speakers "representing every conceivable opinion," according to Richard Wright, debated one another or delivered soapbox speeches to anyone who would listen.[52] The Communist Party used it frequently.

Communists were the bane of landlords. When a family was being evicted, it was not unusual to send the children running to "find the Reds." Once the landlord's men and a city marshal had left, the Reds would break the padlock on the door or jimmy a window and put the renters' belongings back inside again. Neighbors, vicariously enjoying the fruits of the small rebellion, sometimes brought food and beer over for a welcome home party. The landlord might refile the paperwork and pay the marshal's fee again, only to have the same scene repeat itself.

Once, a Communist rally at the Bug Club turned into an eviction protest march. Hundreds made their way to a home on South Dearborn where a seventy-two-year-old woman and her belongings were being put out. A struggle with the police led to a gunfight, and officers killed two black men. That evening, the body of one of the march organizers was found dumped in Washington Park, shot through the head and mutilated.[53]

Lorraine's new route back to Betsy Ross Elementary took her down unfamiliar streets in white neighborhoods. She was "spat at, cursed and pummeled in the daily trek to and from school." Meanwhile, she remembered resentfully, her father "fought the respectable part of the battle" in the courts.[54]

Hansberry v. Lee was argued on appeal before the Illinois Supreme Court in Springfield in February 1939. It was an open secret by now that the University of Chicago in Hyde Park was paying the attorneys' fees for lawsuits such as *Hansberry v. Lee* to preserve a buffer zone of white residential areas around its campus. "It's a matter of economics," Robert M. Hutchins, president of the university, supposedly remarked. "The university has a huge investment in the South Side, and I've got to protect it."[55]

The student newspaper, the *Pulse*, argued that undoing covenants was useless and counterproductive. "Chicago's Black Belt is not a pretty sight. It lies like a gangrenous sore on the city's side, erupting a continuous flow of crimes, small riots, protests and betterment meetings—to say nothing of salvationist revivals." Removing covenants wouldn't do any good because, without them, "chiseling landlords would take over in most cases, returning housing to the previous situation."[56]

The Hansberry defense team returned in October to Springfield to hear the Illinois justices' ruling. They rejected the appeal, using the principle of res judicata: the matter had already been competently decided in the lower court and could not be argued again. Whether segregation was constitutional, or covenants were legal, was not addressed. Nevertheless, the decision was made to keep going, and Hansberry dug deep into the Hansberry Foundation's fund. In spring 1940, petitions were filed with the U.S. Supreme Court.

In the meantime, Carl decided to throw his hat in the ring for national office. The voters of Illinois's First Congressional District, who were primarily Negroes, would recognize his name because of the housing case. If he made it through the Republican primary, his opponent would be the only black congressman, incumbent Democratic representative Arthur W. Mitchell. Quickly, because the election was in April, Hansberry recruited Lorraine, Mamie, Perry, and Carl Jr. to help with the campaign, while he and Nannie canvassed door-to-door. The older Hansberry children left flyers in hallways of kitchenette buildings that smelled dankly of baby milk, fried chicken, and cigarette smoke, observed by small faces peering from doorways. Candidate Hansberry, Republican and stalwart capitalist, called for "Driving out labor goons and racketeers; putting a limit on income tax; subsidizing new industries; exempting all new construction from taxes for several years; and increasing business and employment by improving the relationship between employers and employees."[57] It was Lorraine's first taste of politics.

But he lost the Republican primary. With only weeks to go before the election, Hansberry spent "considerable money," according to the newspapers, to reintroduce himself as an independent. Mitchell was reelected with 52 percent; Hansberry received less than 1 percent. Six weeks after his defeat, he helped pay for the June wedding of his twenty-year-old son, Carl Jr. He was stretched to the limit now. His business, his finances, and his health were suffering.[58]

That summer, the justices of the U.S. Supreme Court voted to hear *Hansberry v. Lee*. The NAACP's magazine, *The Crisis*, rallied its readers' spirits: "There is no right more elemental, nor any liberty more fundamental in a democracy than freedom to move where and when you please." The situation in Chicago's ghetto was unconscionable because "unscrupulous landlords have taken supreme advantage of the situation and 'kitchenettes' are becoming the rule."[59]

On the morning of Friday, October 25, the defense team took its place before the justices. Present in court were Louis Rothschild Mehlinger of the Department of Justice, whose mother had been born enslaved and whose father was a Jewish immigrant; and Ralph Bunche of Howard University's law school, one day to be the first American Negro to receive the Nobel Peace Prize. The court's ushers were black and listened intently from the side as Earl Dickerson, the lead attorney for Hansberry, spoke for sixty minutes. During the question period, the justices focused less on constitutional issues than the legality of the Woodlawn covenant.[60]

Normally, the Court issued its opinion on a case after several months, usually in May. This time the decision was handed down in three weeks. The justices ruled that *Burke v. Kleinman* and *Hansberry v. Lee* were not comparable class action suits because they had conflicting goals. In the former, Burke wanted to sell property; in the latter, Hansberry was not allowed to purchase property. Therefore, the Illinois Supreme Court's decision in *Hansberry* could not be reached by applying *Burke*, and was reversed. Regarding the Woodlawn covenant, it was invalid because it lacked the requisite number of signatures. Whether covenants are constitutional, the court didn't say; in fact, the scope of the victory was limited to the defendant, Hansberry, at that address, 6120 Rhodes Avenue in Woodlawn, only. By its decision, the Supreme Court handed back Carl Hansberry his house.

Hansberry v. Lee had created a chink in the "delicately woven chain of armor" of covenants covering 80 percent of Chicagoland.

Carl Hansberry became famous. The black press heralded the ruling as a "substantial victory for our people who have been huddled into a miserable Black Belt. . . . It means that Negroes henceforth can invade those residential zones in which they were hitherto prohibited from dwelling."[61] Lorraine's parents shared in the bouquets thrown their way. They were photographed together in their living room: the paterfamilias untangling the affairs of the world, and his wife knitting together the home. Mamie was proud of their mother's courage. "Who was it that took charge and ran things when Daddy was involved in his many projects? Mother. Who was it that stood toe to toe with a gang of racists who threatened her children? Our mother."[62] "The Hansberrys of Chicago," *The Crisis* lauded them. "They Join Business Acumen with Social Vision." Mr. and Mrs. Carl Hansberry, said the magazine, "had the distinction not only of conducting one of the largest real estate operations in the country operated by Negroes but they are unique business people because they are spending much of their wealth to safeguard the civil rights of colored citizens in their city, state, and nation."[63]

Soon, the NAACP would be assisted in other discrimination cases by amici curiae briefs filed by the American Jewish Congress, the Japanese American Citizens League, the Congress of Industrial Organizations, the American Civil Liberties Union, and the American Indian Association, among many others. In 1948, the courts would find restrictive racial covenants unconstitutional in *Shelley v. Kraemer*.

The case is important historically for another reason, too. It ignited the first widespread instance in Chicago of white flight, the urban phenomenon that has bedeviled city managers, sociologists, economists, and presidential administrations ever since. Fearing a financial loss if they stayed too long, whites began an exodus from Woodlawn that couldn't have been any more headlong than if they had left by wagon train.

At work was an aspect of human nature: affiliation. People prefer to be around others like them, as a glance at any high school lunchroom will show. Years before, South Side Republican congressman and black real estate speculator Oscar De Priest had warned, "Negroes are going to move anywhere they can pay rent, and if the white people don't like it, we'll run them into the damn lake."[64] No one likes being in the minority, resulting in what Nobel Prize–winning economist Thomas Schelling calls "congregation" in neighborhoods, because "people elect like rather than unlike environments."[65] Mixed-race neighborhoods tend not to be stable, even when everyone desires integration. Meanwhile, segregated neighborhoods are stable and tend to persist. Recognizing this, the Federal Housing Administration aided the exodus by offering whites mortgages in racially restricted suburbs, where the new move-ins had choices of homes galore.[66]

Two years after Carl Hansberry overcame the restrictive covenant covering Woodlawn, a survey by the Chicago Planning Commission showed that the Washington Park/Woodlawn communities averaged more cases of juvenile delinquency, tuberculosis, and infant mortality than the rest of Chicago. The area was 97 percent nonwhite, and fewer than 6 percent of the properties were owner-occupied, meaning the rest were renters.[67]

The Court's decision was a victory for civil rights, but the spoils of the fray went into only a few pockets. Real estate speculators made a killing, including Hansberry, who was named a "Race Achiever" in 1940 by *Ebony* magazine. When a decent return on rental property was 6 percent, Hansberry was making 40.[68] One newly minted landlord, Claude A. Barnett, director of the Associated Negro Press, confided to Truman Gibson Jr. that he had purchased three buildings in Woodlawn at bargain prices and that "they were the best investment he had ever made."[69] Rents went through the roof.

4

American Princess

In speech and action they strove to act as un-Negro as possible, denying the racial and material foundation of their lives, accepting their
class and racial status in ways so oblique that one had the impression
that no difficulties existed for them.

—Richard Wright, *Black Boy (American Hunger)*

February 1945. The end of World War II was within sight, and fourteen-
year-old Lorraine, a freshman at Englewood High School, attended a Saturday night debutante ball on the campus of Tennessee Agricultural &
Industrial College. The guest of honor was Miss Lurelia Hale Freeman,
daughter of Dr. Samuel Freeman, an orthopedic surgeon at Meharry Medical College, in Nashville, and his wife, the former Millie E. Hale. (Mrs.
Freeman, a nurse, had converted the upstairs of their home into the Millie
E. Hale Infirmary for patients turned away by white hospitals. Lorraine's
parents praised that kind of effort, the balancing of wealth with social
improvement.)

The campus banquet hall accommodated hundreds of Miss Freeman's
guests, who danced to the King Kolax Orchestra, the first black orchestra
ever to play on NBC Radio. At the edge of the dance floor was a table displaying compliments to Miss Freeman from well-wishers—115 gifts and
130 congratulatory telegrams.[1]

Early the next morning, Lorraine and nineteen other girls put on their

English riding habits (tailored jackets, jodhpurs, leather boots, and derby caps) for a trail ride led by Miss Freeman at the Couchville Pike Country Club in Nashville. But first, they attended church. The sight of them in their outfits, singing from shared hymnals, must have seemed very British, as if the best of young womanhood were about to be sent off to the war.[2] After the service, a caravan of hired limousines arrived to take everyone to brunch at the Revolutionary War–themed Saratoga Café, inside the country club. Beside each place setting was a small basket filled with Valentine chocolate mints. Finally, after an hour or so, it was time for the ride.

Stable hands brought out the horses, saddled and ready. It was cold, in the forties, but the colors of the girls' riding habits were bright and springlike.[3] The young riders turned their steeds around to line up behind Lurelia. Some of the girls would see each other again, when Lurelia came through Chicago. In April, she was going to visit the city as part of a year-long campaign of teas, parties, and dinners coordinated by Dr. and Mrs. Freeman before she applied to Fisk University, her mother's alma mater.[4] Mrs. Hansberry was having a dinner for eleven young women in Lurelia's honor, and Lorraine would serve as hostess.[5] Very soon, however, Carl and Nannie would be leaving for a two-month vacation in Mexico.

About the time Lorraine entered Englewood High School, she began to take her writing seriously. In the privacy of her third-floor bedroom, from where she could see the green intra-urban buses toiling up and down South Parkway through gusts of gray exhaust, she wrote about "winter landscapes and dust-filled skylines, clouds, elevated trains, being in love, to be sure, and of existence itself." She alluded to "love letters," too, but then added ". . . another's."[6]

She won an award her freshman year for a short story about football. Actually, she'd never been to a game. All the details about how it was played had come from questioning Mamie and one of her boyfriends. (Later, she became "so rah-rah" with school spirit that it "ran my family nuts," she told a friend.[7]) Also, an exciting episode at Englewood became, in her hands, a story about racial pride. Two hundred white students had walked out, protesting, "We're not going to school with Negroes."[8] The school was about 20 percent black, but changing rapidly. Lorraine described other black students from neighboring high schools riding in like the cavalry to scatter the besiegers. They came "pouring out of the bowels of the ghetto, the children of the unqualified oppressed: the black working-class in their costumes of pegged pants and conked heads and tight skirts and almost knee-length sweaters and—worst of all—colored anklets, held up with rubber bands! Yes, they had come and they had fought." But there wasn't any fighting, a disappointing denouement for the young dramatist. "The white kids did nothing. They didn't chant or cry out or look angry or raise their fists or anything."[9] The superintendent threatened to suspend the striking students unless they returned to class.

Lorraine liked stories that packed an emotional punch. Secretly, she read Lillian Smith's novel *Strange Fruit*, a romance between a white doctor's son and a light-skinned young black woman. Banned for its descriptions of sexual intercourse and masturbation, the novel ends with a murder and a lynching. *The Good Earth* impressed her, Pearl S. Buck's grim novel of a Chinese peasant farmer and his family suffering through a famine. From Du Bois's *The Negro*, the work that had inspired her uncle Leo to become an Africanist, she chose two personal heroes: Hannibal, the Carthaginian general who defeated Rome's legions with his African war elephants; and Toussaint Louverture, the leader of the Haitian Revolution against the French in 1791 that emancipated the island's slaves. Which of the two was greater, she couldn't decide.

She was becoming a cosmopolitan young person, with access to quite a bit of cultural capital.[10] Because of her parents' prominence, it was said that anybody who was anybody visited the Hansberrys. Buzzed in through the iron gate at 5936 South Parkway came some of the leading figures in arts, letters, and politics of the day: Paul Robeson, the internationally known actor, athlete, concert artist, and political activist; W. E. B. Du Bois; composer Duke Ellington; boxing champion Joe Louis; and four-time Olympic gold medalist Jesse Owens, among others.[11] Sometimes Uncle Leo brought African students he was mentoring at Howard University.[12] One of these young men, or a composite of them, would become Joseph Asagai, the student from Nigeria in *A Raisin in the Sun*.

It's very likely Lorraine went to the Negro Progress Exposition at the gigantic Chicago Coliseum in the summer of 1940, attended by hundreds of thousands. Truman Gibson Jr. was the executive director. The open-floor, block-long building was twelve stories high. Inside, a thousand-voice choir from local black churches rocked the hall with song. Two hundred thirty Negro newspapers displayed photographs of black Americans from all walks of life. Life-size dioramas re-created historic episodes. In a specially built theater seating four thousand, Lorraine would have seen *The Cavalcade of the Negro Theater*, a pageant combining reenacted scenes from black history with Creole melodies, spirituals, folk songs, blues, and specially written numbers by Duke Ellington and Thomas A. Dorsey, the "father of gospel music." Her first staged productions would be pageants, perhaps drawing on this show for inspiration, which any impressionable child would remember.

In fact, had she been a little older, she might have participated in the high point of the Chicago Black Renaissance. A generation of Negro writers and artists passed her on the streets of Bronzeville while she was young: Richard Wright and his fellow novelists Arna Bontemps, William Attaway, and Willard Motley; playwright Theodore Ward; and poets Margaret Walker, Margaret Esse Danner, Frank Marshall Davis, Langston Hughes, and Gwendolyn Brooks. They were a sociable bunch, too, because, said artist Charles White, "if you were interested in any of the arts[,] you eventually knew everybody else, every other black brother and sister who was interested in the arts."[13]

Most of the cultural workers on the South Side were politically far left. Some were avowed Communists, and the Hansberrys were careful not to allow Lorraine to get too close to the proletariat and their grievances. Theodore Ward's attack on landlords and capitalism, *Big White Fog*, struck too close to home, for example.

The play is about a married couple, Dan and Juanita, who've gotten rich as kitchenette landlords. Dan believes that becoming middle class will eliminate racism from their lives, because racism, he says, is a mere delusion of white people that money gets rid of. Dan tries to convince his brother-in-law Victor to invest in kitchenettes, too, and take advantage of the flood of southern migrants coming into Chicago. But Victor, an idealist and local leader of Marcus Garvey's Back-to-Africa movement, dismisses the idea of capitalizing on poor blacks. In the final scene, Victor resists being evicted and is shot from behind by a sheriff. Before dying, he glimpses the future: His son's white working-class comrades join hands with Victor's family. They pledge to dispel the white man's fog of racism and the black man's air of defeat. When the play premiered in Chicago in 1938, there were fears that the Marxist ending would cause a riot. It didn't.

Regardless, Lorraine's parents were careful not to expose their youngest child to leftist ideas or involve her in things beneath her social class. When Lorraine was in grade school, she begged to take art lessons. The South Side Community Center offered painting and drawing instruction for children, and her father had been on the committee that had welcomed First Lady Eleanor Roosevelt to the center's dedication. Instead, they enrolled her at the Art Institute of Chicago, where she would meet other children who were middle and upper-middle class.[14]

Years after she had allied herself with older leftists in the arts, she titled an essay about Charles White "We Are of the Same Sidewalks," but as a child, Lorraine Hansberry and artists of the Chicago Black Renaissance did not travel the sidewalks of Bronzeville figuratively arm in arm—although, in spirit and outlook, she would always be a Southsider.

The first major step in Lorraine's development as a dramatist came from seeing a folk play. She had been to performances of *Othello* and *The Tempest*. (Her favorite English teacher, Miss Rigby, she nicknamed "Pale Hecate," from *Macbeth*.) And then she went on a date to see *The Dark of the Moon* at the Shubert Theatre, in the Loop, following a nine-month run on Broadway.

The Dark of the Moon, set in the Smoky Mountains, is a supernatural fable based on the Scottish "Ballad of Barbara Allen." The show has singing, poetry, rhythmic dialogue in places, and country dances. The characters speak the vernacular of unlettered Scots-Irish backwoodsmen. The action starts when a witch's son, John, falls in love with a human girl, Barbara, and pleads with a conjure woman to make him appear as an ordinary mortal. She grants his wish, but on the condition that if his beloved is unfaithful within a year, then her life is forfeit, and he will return to his own kind. John, transformed by magic into the shape of a man, woos and marries Barbara. She gives birth to a witch child, and the midwives, horrified, destroy it. During the frenzy of religious revival, Barbara reveals to the townsfolk that John isn't human, instantly breaking the spell on him.

He returns forever to the world of the mountain witches. She dies, having been untrue.

Essentially, *The Dark of the Moon* is a campfire story intended to delight, mystify, shock, and ultimately sadden the audience. Part of the spell is woven by language. The characters' mountain-accented, nonstandard English is colorful, poetic, and creates pictures for the mind's eye that makes the theater space seem vast. John declares his pleasure at being a human in love by shouting, "No more ridin' with my eagle, black against the moonlight, a streak against the sky. No more diggin' in the graveyard, no more yellin' in the night a-screamin' with a long high cry that splashes 'gainst the stars!"

Written by William Berney and Howard Richardson, Alabama and North Carolina natives respectively, *The Dark of the Moon* is a folk drama, a genre that came out of the Little Theatre movement of the 1920s. When films became popular after World War I, small regional theaters offering live performances were hit hard. Rather than try to compete with the likes of Charlie Chaplin or the spectacle of *Ben-Hur*, dramatists experimented with art theater, attempting to raise contemporary American experience to the level of literature. Eugene O'Neill's *Desire Under the Elms* (1924), for example, turns a rural New England love triangle into a Greek tragedy. This new kind of play caught on because the uncommon ways of common people—their beliefs, customs, humor, manner of speaking, and so on— surprised and enlightened. The *American Review of Reviews* predicted, "When every community has its playhouse and its own native group of plays and producers, we shall have a national American theater that will give a richly varied authentic expression of American life."[15]

A parallel effort, the Negro Little Theatre movement, inspired a debate: whether to deliver authentic black folk culture or progressive reform. Alain Locke, the prime mover of the Harlem Renaissance, argued for folk culture as a resource. "Here in the very heart of the folk-spirit are the essential forces of the New Negro." Locke called upon artists to refresh their creative energies and reclaim their identity by embracing folk culture through the blues, dialect, exuberant religiosity, ballads, and lyric expressions of suffering.

Du Bois took a different position. The purpose of black theater, he argued, was to uplift and educate. Instead of presenting Negro characters that met whites' notions and stereotypes, he believed that theater could be a means of changing minds by representing, with truth and genuineness, the full array of black humanity. "Thus all Art is propaganda and ever must be," he wrote, "despite the wailing of the purists."[16]

Lorraine Hansberry would bridge both approaches in *A Raisin in the Sun*. For now, though, the moment when she perceived what drama could encompass, and how inclusive it could be as an art form, began with the evening she was enchanted by, as she said, "all that witch-doctor stuff" in *The Dark of the Moon*.[17] Caught up in the pleasure and excitement of the performance, perhaps she experienced again her fascination with the children she envied when she was little—the tough kids' tribalism, their rituals, their argot and style that made their lives a kind of art. *The Dark of the Moon* justified her obsession with them, and she could reclaim those feelings.

Folk drama is about marginalized people, whether they live beside the rackety elevated tracks in Bronzeville or dwell deep inside the whispering pines of South Carolina. It loses any claim to significance if it strays into caricature by turning unfamiliar people into figures of fun (except as a comment on the playwright). But if it takes the democratic view that every person is an individual, yet deserves equal treatment, folk drama can present the lives of impoverished or unrepresented people in a way that goes beyond "biological" understandings of race and behavior. People, if presented fairly, do as they do, audiences come to realize, because of the circumstances of their lives.

"The honesty of their living is there in the shabbiness," Hansberry thought to herself one day, looking out the window of an elevated train shooting past the backyards of the South Side. "Scrubbed porches that sag and look their danger. Dirty gray wood steps. And always a line of white and pink clothes scrubbed so well, waving in the dirty wind of the city. My people are poor. And they are tired. And they are determined to live."[18]

Her father, meanwhile, having triumphed in *Hansberry v. Lee*, carried on a personal crusade against racism. Having tasted what it was like to win, to be vindicated—and on a national scale, too—he wouldn't tolerate any insults to his self-respect. He didn't have to. He had money, power, and he knew the law.

When a Pennsylvania Railroad ticket agent in Chicago refused to give him the first-class ticket he had ordered by phone, he had a warrant issued for the arrest of the railroad's general manager. After vacationing at the famous Pythian Hotel and Bathhouse for black guests, in Hot Springs, Arkansas, he was angered by a Rock Island agent who refused to sell him a first-class return ticket to Chicago. He telegrammed the president of the railroad, threatening to sue. The reply was immediate: "Regret you had trouble getting a seat. Undoubtedly due to heavy loadings present conditions." A first-class ticket was waiting for him at his convenience. In Chicago's Loop, a bartender tried to give him and Nannie the bum's rush by charging them five dollars for a twenty-five-cent beer. Carl instructed Nannie to wait by the door while he went for a cop, and he had the owner arrested. (In court, the judge admonished the tavern owner for not wanting to serve "nice-looking people." Mrs. Hansberry interrupted: "Not 'nice-looking,' your honor. Anybody has a right to purchase a drink if they're decent and clean and can afford it."[19]) A few times, he used the older children to sting restaurants. If they went inside and the wait seemed unreasonable, he entered and informed the owner that it was illegal to refuse service to Negroes. He'd shut the place down if he had to.

He was so keen to litigate that the Chicago branch of the NAACP began backing away from him, after he threatened to sue Goldblatt's department stores for not hiring black employees.[20] The Goldblatt brothers, immigrants from Poland, were part of a network of wealthy Jewish donors to civil rights causes. The Rosenwald Fund, for instance, founded by Sears and Roebuck chairman Julius Rosenwald, awarded eight hundred fellowships to black intellectuals and artists, singlehandedly bringing about, in the words of literary historian Lawrence P. Jackson, a "dramatic change in the literature produced on the American race problem."[21] The fund also established more than five thousand "Rosenwald Schools" in rural black communities throughout the South.

But Hansberry, unpersuaded that the NAACP had to choose its battles carefully, and growing tired of eagerness to accommodate whites, started his own racial justice organization, the National Negro Progress Association (NNPA). The NNPA, he said, would do for Negro business in America "what the Rockefeller Foundation and the Rosenwald Foundation have done for Negro Literary Education." A handsome booklet published by Hansberry Enterprises, titled *Moving Forward: A Plan for the Negro's Advancement in Business and Industry*, declared that the NNPA would create a one-million-dollar "Foundation Fund" to build and expand "Negro business and enterprises, thus creating thousands of permanent jobs for the race."[22]

To rustle up members, he launched a heavily advertised essay contest, offering up to five thousand dollars in cash prizes. The topic was "What you think about Negro business and how to improve it?" Entrants were required to include the names and addresses of ten sponsors, whom Hansberry then approached in a follow-up letter for donations. "We are asking fifteen million people to raise only one million dollars, not in one year, but in two or three years."

It was an ambitious project. The NNPA would set up "three hundred banks, numerous investment banks, several fire insurance companies, a security exchange with branches in all cities and two thousand industries or enterprises that will employ one million people."[23] There already existed black labor unions and business-minded groups with the same goal—better-paying jobs for Negroes after the war—but Hansberry continued soliciting donations for the Foundation Fund.

Financially, he needed this idea to work. The oil company he had invested in several years earlier, National Rig Company, had turned out to be a swindle. The three promoters behind the scheme were wildcatters from Oklahoma. Once they struck oil in downstate Illinois, they had cut a side deal with a refining company to sell barrels off the books. When Carl and the other partners found out, they filed suit to dissolve the company. But in November 1941, one of the promoters shot the other two, killing one and critically wounding the other. Equipment suppliers came after the company partners for debts, and Carl went to court to prevent having the drilling cranes seized. He had to get his profit out before everything was impounded. At the end of three years of suits and countersuits, the judge ruled that the crooks were judgment proof because they were insolvent and residents of Oklahoma.[24]

Nannie was alarmed. They were going to run out of money at this rate. During a particularly bad argument between them, Lorraine ran to her room and shut the door. Suddenly, Mamie said, her father clambered over the furniture in the living room like an obstacle course, continued down the hallway, into the bedroom he shared with his wife, and stamped violently on their bed until it broke.[25]

In February 1946, when Lorraine was a sophomore at Englewood High School, her parents left for their second vacation in Mexico, accompanied by Perry and Carl Jr. They had a home there now, in Polanco, a suburb of Mexico City. Mr. Hansberry had high blood pressure. While he was south of the border, he said, he felt happy "and free for the first time in his life."[26]

Still, overwork and financial cares were wearing on him, and his square build had settled into the pear shape of a man who eats to relax. He was beginning to think that perhaps the United States was hopeless in its treatment of Negroes.[27] With the war over, black industrial workers were being displaced by returning white veterans, because manpower was no longer in short supply. Returning black soldiers were running into the same discrimination and violence as their fathers had after World War I. The National Negro Progress Association was kaput. Advertisements and news items about it had stopped appearing.

Instead of taking the train to Mexico City as they had the year before, the Hansberrys drove down. When they reached Laredo, on the Texas-Mexico border, it was getting dark, and they were still seven hundred miles from Polanco. Hotels in Texas were segregated, and nothing was available to them. Rather than sleep in the car, they parked and walked across the border, into the town of Nuevo Laredo, where they found accommodation without much difficulty. The next morning, Carl went back through customs to retrieve his car. As he entered the United States again, a white man fell into step with him.

"The good old USA," the man said. "Great to be back, huh?"

"I'm going over here to get my goddamn car," Hansberry said, "and if I never see this country again, it'll be all right with me."[28]

He put the incident behind him. Within a few days, he had settled down to "relaxing in the balmy Mexican air," he told friends. Polanco was a new neighborhood in an upper-class enclave of tree-lined streets and large homes—the center of the good life in Mexico City. He was thinking about living there permanently. The city of Chicago was classifying blocks of deteriorated homes on the South Side as slums and preparing to demolish them to make way for public housing projects with the support of black civic organizations. The Wild West days of housing speculation were behind him.

At the end of February, he was feeling seriously unwell. But Carl Jr. sent Lorraine and Mamie a telegram reassuring them that "Father is feeling much better. Tell all the family." Three days later, a messenger rang the doorbell with a second telegram, this one from Perry:

> Mamie do this without fail get help from doctor Turner Thompson someone send air mail express these tablets at once 4 flasks of mannitol hexanitrate or ½ gram if you can't find this in Chicago send to the William H Rorer Co Drexel Building Independence Square Philadelphia have sent airmail to Dr. Luis Rangel Gurza . . . spare no money do this Dad may depend on this to get well can't get it here something new on market. If you need more information wire get Mrs. Carroway to help rush.

Mannitol hexanitrate, used for treating vascular disease, had been on the market for only three years. Carl had suffered a stroke from high blood pressure and was partially paralyzed. A week passed, and then a third telegram arrived: "Daddy passed will be home as soon as possible with body be brave. Mother."[29] He had died at three in the morning at Concepción Béistegui, a private hospital in Mexico City. The cause of death was hypertension leading to a brain hemorrhage.

Three weeks passed before the body arrived in Chicago. Following a service at African Methodist Episcopal Church, mourners drove in a funeral cortège to Burr Oak Cemetery, a forty-acre memorial park established by Earl Dickerson, one of Hansberry's attorneys, and by the Supreme Liberty Life Insurance Company, to serve families who were part of the Great Migration. The residents of the little town of nearby Alsip didn't want the cemetery there, even though it was in the middle of open Illinois prairie.[30]

During the ceremony beside the grave, Lorraine saw a change come over her family. Her mother had "not fondled, any of us—head held to the breast, fingers about that head." But now "she held her sons that way, and for the first time in my life my sister held me in her arms[,] I think. We were not a loving people: we were passionate in our hostilities and affinities, but the caress embarrassed us."

Her father had died, she said, "a permanently embittered exile in a foreign country." The defeat of a few racists in court and forcing integration in Woodlawn had not resulted in the destruction of racism. Nor had education, refinement, automobiles, or achievement made the Hansberrys invulnerable to it. She was convinced "American racism helped kill him."[31]

For the rest of her life, Lorraine noted the date of her father's death on calendars and in her journal. But she was always off by one year in the sum of how long ago it had been, as if 1946 couldn't be pinned down. It wasn't calculable. It always existed, unfinished.

PART II

Madison,
Wisconsin

5

Entering into a Romance

You did not know the Black continent
that had to be reached
was you.

—Gwendolyn Brooks, "To the Diaspora"

What thou lov'st well shall not be reft from thee
What thou lov'st well is thy true heritage

—Ezra Pound, "Canto LXXXI"

The University of Wisconsin–Madison campus extends for nearly a mile along the crest and wooded slopes of a hilly ridge overlooking the southern shore of Lake Mendota, the largest of Madison's four lakes. The university, Lorraine thought, "lay spread out across the land like a huge rambling feudal estate."[1] The day she arrived, accompanied by Mamie and Perry, everything was deep in snow. The temperature at the end of January 1948 had been below zero for two weeks, but it rose into the twenties for their hundred-mile drive to campus.

They were taking a chance by arriving a week before registration for new students. Lorraine's living arrangements were up in the air. The materials she had received from the admissions office cautioned, "acceptance does not guarantee accommodations. . . . For the past several years there have been twice as many applicants on February 1 than there were accommodations available." The line for lunch at the Memorial Union went up the stairs from the Rathskeller (cafeteria), out the door, and snaked around the building for a hundred yards.

The Hansberrys parked and began hunting for the housing office. Mamie and Perry may have been annoyed with their sister over how inconvenient all this was. If Lorraine had chosen Howard University instead, Mamie would have known everything there was to know, right down to which sororities were the best. But Lorraine wasn't interested in Howard; she preferred Wisconsin for its art and journalism programs. And her mother had taken her side, even against the administration of Englewood High School.

Her guidance counselor had told Lorraine that Wisconsin was out of the question. Applications were due the previous June 20, and she was a midyear graduate. Even if she had submitted her application by the deadline, female high school applicants were required to be in the upper 30 percent of their class.[2] Lorraine was in the upper half: 67th out of 167.

That's when Mrs. Hansberry put her foot down. She made an appointment to meet the counselor and the principal of Englewood High School. She didn't trust tests, grades, or report cards. Outside of class, Lorraine had been president of the one-hundred-member Debate Club, demonstrating a rugged intellect like her uncle Leo's, Atlanta University's top debater his freshman year.[3] She and her team had spent two months preparing to take the affirmative side of the question "Should the federal government require arbitration of all labor disputes in basic American industries?" At a debate tournament, they won. Her class rank by itself might give the impression that she was slightly above average, but it could just as well be an index of something else: how poorly the school engaged black children because it didn't make them curious about themselves. Also, as a parent, Mrs. Hansberry knew her daughter better than anyone else, including what kind of college experience she should have.

Temperamentally, Lorraine was unlike Mamie, who'd been the quintessential 1940s coed at Howard: extroverted, materialistic, and envied— she always seemed to have a beau on a string. Mamie was the glamorous sister. When she had arrived to begin her freshman year at Howard, she had stepped from a chauffeur-driven Cadillac, followed by seven steamer trunks of clothes.[4] After that, she became a regular in the *Chicago Defender*'s society pages, appearing with other coeds in a holiday fashion spread, or seen by the *Defender*'s gossip columnist, Ole Nosey, dancing on New Year's Eve to Roy Eldridge and his band at the Preview Lounge, in the Loop. Her junior year, she transferred to Traphagen School of Fashion, in Manhattan. Typical of the difference between them was the time Mrs. Hansberry had asked Mamie to go downtown with Lorraine and help her choose a new outfit. Lorraine had grown three dress sizes larger during high school, although not much taller; she was falling short of the kind of appearance expected of a Hansberry.[5] But when the sisters reached the department store, Lorraine had told Mamie to pick out something for her and then toddled off to the library.[6]

She preferred solitude—reading, drawing, and daydreaming out her bedroom window. It was her sanctuary, and she would get furious if any of her siblings barged in, oblivious to her demand for privacy.[7] Her circle of friends at Englewood was small. Her two best friends were the daughters of a postal clerk and a chauffeur. She dressed like them, too—that is, not as smartly as Mrs. Hansberry would have preferred.[8] Consequently, the competitive social life of Howard University probably wouldn't be a good fit for a young person like her. All this Mrs. Hansberry understood. But she was not going to watch her youngest child become accustomed to accepting white people's judgment of her—that was a separate issue.

As a result of her mother's intervention, Lorraine's application materials received the necessary signatures, and her transcripts were stamped with the high school's official seal and mailed. A few weeks later, she received an acceptance letter and an unexpected offer of a scholarship that would waive her tuition. Placement exams for new students were February 5 and 6.

Mamie, Lorraine, and Perry found Bascom Hall, where the housing office was located, but they were informed that there was no dormitory space available. The university paired Negro students in the residence halls, but apparently, there was no black female to room with. Worse, the Hansberrys were offended by what sounded like gratuitous advice.

As Lorraine remembered it, the director "took the view that 'our' Jewish students were 'happier' with 'our other' Jewish students and that Negro students would be 'happiest' wherever they could find dormitory space or university approved housing in town that would *accept* [Hansberry's italics] them. And on the post-war, ex-GI jammed campus of 1948 space of any kind was not easy to find."[9] The Hansberrys went back outside into the chilly air with a list of approved off-campus residences.[10]

Three years earlier, the editors of the campus newspaper, the *Daily Cardinal*, had pressured the university to remove from its approved housing list off-campus residences that wouldn't accept Negro, Chinese, or Jewish students. Ninety-five percent of them wouldn't. Some yielded to the unfavorable exposure and agreed to open their doors to minority students; but most, knowing that the university was desperate for housing, refused. Fraternities and sororities had it written into their constitutions that minorities were not allowed to pledge.[11]

Rather than spend hours knocking on doors, Mamie knew a radio disk jockey in town and called him. He recommended a private residence, Langdon Manor, whose black cook might have some ideas.[12]

Langdon Manor was a twenty-minute walk from campus, on Langdon Street, a four-block district of collegiate rooming and fraternity and sorority houses once known as Mansion Hill. Social status started with the sororities and fraternities nearest the Memorial Union and gradually declined the farther down Langdon Street one went. Langdon Manor was at the end. The "manor" was a three-story, turreted Queen Anne–style "dismal old home," according to one of the young women who lived there, "a grotesque error of the era" whose spaces had been cannibalized to provide baths and bedrooms for thirty-two female residents.[13] The cook, however, told the Hansberrys that there happened to be an unoccupied double room upstairs. The housemother, Mrs. Miler, wouldn't return until later. That was all they needed to hear.

Lorraine's luggage was brought in from the car and carried to the third floor—a scene reminiscent of the Hansberrys arriving on Rhodes Avenue at night. Said Mamie, "[I]f you go ahead and do something, and don't meet the opposition—because most white people are only concerned about what other people are going to say—if it's gone smoothly, then that's what's happening." With that finished, Perry and Mamie lingered for bit, the better to describe the place to their mother, who preferred that Lorraine live in a residence hall. There were several Jewish students from New York, two young women from China, one from Australia, and one apiece from Boston, New Orleans, and Hawaii. Most of the housemates were Midwesterners. Lorraine would be the only Negro. Everyone seemed friendly, though—receptive. Satisfied, Perry and Mamie said their farewells, gave Lorraine a check for a week's rent, and left her on her own to meet the housemother.[14]

Mrs. Ann Miler, a thin, chain-smoking Catholic widow, returned shortly before dinner to find herself with something of a fait accompli:[15] a "Miss Hansberry" had arrived. This development was a surprise, and Mrs. Miler had to tread carefully. Several years before her tenure, Langdon Manor had been sued for ten thousand dollars by a university junior who claimed to have been turned away because she was Jewish.[16] If this seventeen-year-old from Chicago who had been left on the doorstep, so to speak, was put by herself in a double room, how would that be interpreted? Would she feel comfortable, and if she didn't, what would be the consequences? Across the street was the Groves Women's Cooperative, established five years earlier to foster interracial and international harmony.[17] But suggesting that Miss Hansberry might want to have a look over there might be taken drastically amiss.

Instead, Mrs. Miler came up with a solution. The girls would vote on whether they wanted Lorraine to stay, like at a sorority. If the vote was in favor, then they would have made a commitment; if not, then the house would continue as it was.

That night, Lorraine came to dinner with everyone. If she knew she was being auditioned, she didn't let on. She had been in situations like this before—the new kindergartner, the new third-grader, the high school freshman at a majority-white school. This was yet another elementary school playground in January, and she was determined to be included. She had an advantage, too. She was practiced in the social arts of sitting pleasantly and making conversation with strangers. In this arena, the Hansberrys were adept.

By the end of dinner, said one of the residents, the "entire group was won over by her warmth and charm." The vote (taken, it's to be hoped, with Lorraine out of the room) was unanimous in her favor. Mrs. Miler was still faced with the implications of her newest resident being left alone in a double room. She asked whether anyone would like to be Miss Hansberry's roommate. Roma Borst, a junior majoring in Spanish, said she would happily trade her single room for the bigger double.[18]

It was settled. And on Valentine's Day at Langdon Manor's open house, with her placement exams behind her and classes starting, Lorraine made small talk with visitors beside a refreshment table of donuts, candy, and a bowl of dark Wisconsin cider. Sometime later, she was "contemptuously amused" by an article in the campus paper: "Experiment in Interracial Living Termed Success, Langdon Manor's World Home."[19]

Mrs. Miler was quoted extensively.

It was Negro History Week when Lorraine registered. Black pianist and nightclub singer Hazel Scott was appearing at the Wisconsin Union Theater. Duke Ellington and his orchestra performed for one night at the Orpheum, downtown. How many nonwhite students were enrolled at Wisconsin at that time is hard to determine, but there were very few, judging from the yearbook and other student publications. A chapter of the NAACP had been founded a year earlier, after Alain Locke, visiting from Howard University, had delivered standing-rooming-only lectures on culture and fine art. Fifty sororities and fraternities sent representatives to attend the monthly Greek Letter Society for Racial Relations—an empty gesture. Nearly all refused to admit minorities. The number of black residents in the city of Madison was less than 1 percent: eight hundred out of ninety thousand.

A decade earlier, playwright Theodore Ward (*Big White Fog*) had been one of the few persons of color at Wisconsin. Although he lacked a high school diploma, it was arranged for him to pursue a degree. Attending on a fellowship, he studied literature and dramatic arts. But he left, disheartened "with the isolation of university life for African Americans."[20]

Lorraine's experience at Langdon Manor was the reverse. She won over her housemates by blossoming into the confident and sociable person her parents had raised her to be. Perhaps it was because she wasn't in Mamie's shadow. (Once, when she was eleven, she had opened the front door to admit one of Mamie's boyfriends and led him silently through the foyer and into the living room, where she announced that her sister would be down soon. Then she went away like a butler. She thought of herself as round and plain.[21]) Or it may have been just an act of will: She was not going to be denied. She went into situations not expecting to be treated differently.

She joined in a game of leaving notes under doors written in shorthand or Spanish. She entertained by playing the piano in the lounge and singing, in a loud falsetto voice, "The Blue Bird of Happiness." ("She seemed fond of this song," remarked one of her housemates drily.) One of the young women Lorraine became close to, JoAnn Beier, said she had "an offhand way of shrugging off any minor problems. . . . She was sly, sagacious and used sarcasm in a most delicious way—never to harm but amuse. She would delight in chiding, gently, humorously, and seemed to relish a giggly, off-guard response." However, beneath her laid-back exterior was an undercurrent of restlessness, Beier suspected, because she was "extremely intelligent (more so than she would let us believe) and perhaps more cultured than some of us."[22] The girls elected her house secretary.

Roma Borst, Lorraine's roommate, could be a real scrapper in arguments with everyone else—"vicious," Lorraine said—but she liked Lorraine because she was easy to talk to and "good at making jokes, especially if they were on herself."[23] Lorraine may have brought a few items from her clown collection to decorate her side of the room. She identified with clowns. They were oddballs, hapless comedians and disturbers of the peace.

When classes started, Lorraine set out over the hilly campus via the icy, shoveled paths. "Have you fallen yet?" was the question everybody seemed to be asking. (Roma noticed that Lorraine had a "friendly amble to her walk.") Sometimes she paused to take in the view. "Beyond, across the lake, mounted on the white hills, were the black trees of the winter countryside." She preferred winter and "cold, clean drifts of sparkling Northern snow" to the closeted, muggy feeling of summer.[24] She wore a heavy, calf-length overcoat when the fashion was shorter. She liked the "feel of her woolen skirt and sweater" on a "blustery gray day," and fireplaces and tea and things that felt "very dry and warm and British." As for summer, "nature had got inexcusably carried away," in her opinion, and "let the whole thing get to be rather much." A summer's day seemed "maddeningly excessive; an utter overstatement."[25]

But there may have been an additional reason she preferred clothes that were serviceable and modest: she was not one who spent time on sex appeal. Later in life, she reflected on how college women (probably those living in Langdon Manor) were treated by their male dates. The perspective and empathy suggest a feminist in the making, one who resented men trespassing on women's bodies like hunters tramping over private land.[26]

> Let us say that in a college dormitory there are about ten women [sitting] in a room, and every one of them, every single one has just come in from a Saturday night date. For three of them, it was the first night out with that particular young man; for four of them the guys were fellows they had been out with every so often in the past but are not "going steady" with. The remaining three have engagement or semi-engagement relationships with their young men. Each of the young women in that room have either been openly asked, subtlety coerced, or had the most pointed kind of verbal or physical hint made toward ending the evening with physical intercourse. In varying degrees, they may comment on it, some are shocked, others disgusted with college men, others think it is college sophistication—others think that men are hopeless anyway, and revolting. It is possible that two out of that ten will have a love affair with a roommate or dormmate before she leaves college, out of sheer disgust with masculinity's preoccupation with sex.

"Perhaps I am too bitter toward men," Hansberry reflected later, "though I doubt it. I cannot help feeling that it is they who commit extreme actions, not I who make them extremists."[27]

She planned to major in journalism, although it was only a "dim notion." Her grades in introductory liberal arts courses for the first quarter were respectable, despite her self-admitted "undisciplined habits."[28] Outside of class, she read Jomo Kenyatta's *Facing Mount Kenya*, which was dedicated to "all the dispossessed youth of Africa: for the perpetuation of communion with ancestral spirits through the fight for African Freedom, and in the firm faith that the dead, the living and the unborn will be united to rebuild the destroyed shrines." She returned to reading Du Bois, with his *Black Folk Then and Now: An Essay in the History and Sociology of the Negro Race*, a survey of the Negro from ancient times to the present. Du Bois argued for a "dynamic and not a static conception" of race. From Africa, humankind spreads outward, he writes, changing in "appearance, and in cultural gift and accomplishment."[29]

Du Bois's concept of humanity evolving, intermixing, and trading advancements is one of the themes of an autobiographical novel Hansberry began writing her first semester: "All the Dark and Beautiful Warriors." It's a self-examination. She would return to it now and then for the rest of her life, but never finish it.

The novel's protagonist is Candace, a multiracial young woman of African, European, and Native American ancestry who attends the University of Wisconsin. Hansberry seems to be thinking about essentialism, the belief that entities must have an underlying reality or true nature, to "make the thing what it is," as one philosopher has explained, "and without which it would not be *that* kind of thing."[30]

Candace wonders what's at her core. "What was it about snow and evergreens: her affinity for it, her love of it? Was the European part of her bloodstream Viking perhaps? She knew nothing of that." She knew more about Africa; she might be southern Zulu, central Pygmy, eastern Watusi, or the "slave-trading Western Ashanti," Kikuyu or Masai. It disturbs her that her European ancestors could include "thin-faced, thin-blooded, watery-eyed [British] decadents in riding boots, pawing noble black women in ripped muslin, their faces turned away in silent, helpless outrage."

Studying herself in the mirror, Candace peers at her face, "searching, searching for a generality" in her features that would place her somewhere on the African continent. But she knows that when she hears African music, it claims her. It invites her to connect with whatever is elemental and instinctual in her. She feels "at one, texture, blood, follicles of the hair, nerve ends, all with the sound of the mighty Congo drum."

Candace, and her creator Hansberry, share the sensibility of the Romantic poets, who aspired, by imagination, to the ideal. The tension forces one to live in two disparate worlds of what *is* and the exciting possibility of what *could be*. Candace spends hours poring over maps of the African continent in "All the Dark and Beautiful Warriors," "postulating and fantasizing: *Ibo, Mandingo, Housa, Yoruba, Ashanti, Dahomean. Who, who were they!*" Finally, she surrenders to her feelings and simply "embraced all Africa as the *homeland*."[31]

Before coming to Madison, Lorraine hadn't yet discovered drama as an avenue of expression. Debate was her forte. During her senior year at

Englewood High School there was a production of A *Midsummer's Night Dream*, but she wasn't a member of the stage crew or the cast of twenty-five. It was true that *The Dark of the Moon* had fascinated her. But how she progressed from an admiring groundling at fifteen into a thespian, she left rather vague. She said she saw "plays by Strindberg and Ibsen for the first time, and they were important to me. I was intrigued by the theatre. Mine was the same old story—sort of hanging around little acting groups, and developing the feeling that the theatre embraces everything I like all at one time." The "k-*pow!*" of theater, as she put it, didn't really happen until a few years later.[32] In fact, practically everything she would become as a dramatist, including her beliefs about the purposes of art, was conceived in her freshman year at the University of Wisconsin.

One evening in early April, she went "by accident" to a play at the Wisconsin Union Theater, which is inside the Memorial Union. Her seat was in the orchestra section, close to the stage. The show going up that night was Irish playwright Seán O'Casey's tragicomedy *Juno and the Paycock*, performed by the Wisconsin Players, an independent troupe made up largely of students and nonprofessional actors from Madison and Milwaukee.

A little background about O'Casey: Born in Dublin in 1880, he grew up in a family that, instead of rising into the middle class, had fallen out of it. His father died when O'Casey was six. To support his mother, he worked as a child laborer and, later, as a "navvy," a road and building digger. The thrust of his plays, as one critic said, is "freedom from landlords, pawn shops, over-priced soiled food, slums, and all the capitalist exploitation visited on the poor," with a kick in the pants to the British government and the Catholic and Protestant Churches for good measure.[33]

O'Casey renders the lives of the working class with a kind of broken-hearted beauty. His impoverished Irish, under the heel of the Protestant Anglo-Irish ruling class, use humor, sentimentality, love—and violence, on occasion—to endure oppression condoned by the Church and the colonial government. (The "gratefully oppressed," James Joyce sardonically calls them.)[34] The remedy, O'Casey argues, is socialism. But he doesn't belabor the point, or deliver sermons at the expense of his drama. His method is more like Dickens's sympathetic portrayal of the poor, instead of that of his fellow Irishman and socialist Bernard Shaw, whose self-professed aim was to "instruct rather than to entertain."[35]

Juno and the Paycock takes place in 1922. In the background is the Irish Civil War between those Irishmen who accept the 1921 Anglo-Irish Treaty with the United Kingdom, giving Ireland the status of a dominion within the British Commonwealth, and the die-hard Republicans, who consider the treaty a betrayal of their ideal of an independent Ireland.

The "paycock" (peacock) is Captain Jack Boyle, usually drunk on liquor and self-delusion. The title of captain is one he's given himself, and he loves to regale anyone who will listen with his hair-raising adventures at sea. But there's more of the blowhard about him than blow-the-man-down. He made a trip on a coal barge across the Irish Sea exactly once. Complementing Boyle is another specimen of male vanity, Charlie Bentham, a young man of twenty-five who thinks very highly of himself, and dresses accordingly. The play begins with Boyle's daughter Mary, Bentham's girlfriend, looking in a mirror and wondering what color ribbon would set off her hair the prettiest. Mary is also being courted by Jerry Devine, whose prospects as a leader of the labor union are excellent.

The stage setting provides powerful but mute dramatic irony: The Boyles live in a slum. There's almost no place to sit, except at the table, which Boyle reserves for himself, storytelling and complaining—a fog meant to hide the reality of the domestic crisis they live in.

Hansberry immediately saw parallels between American blacks and the Irish. "I remember sitting there stunned with a melody that I thought I might have sung in a different meter. . . . [B]ut the melody was one that I had known for a very long while."[36]

The counterweight to masculinist fantasy onstage is "Juno" Boyle, the captain's wife. He gave her that nickname, not knowing that "Juno" was the Roman name for the goddess who presides over family life and safeguards women, marriage, childbirth, and finances. Juno's chariot was said to be drawn by peacocks; but Boyle, deadweight in the family, hinders more than helps his Juno. As the title of the play suggests, Juno is on one side, representing the lot of women in a sexist society, struggling against male entitlement; the paycock, on the other.

This symmetry is carried through in how the action falls into two halves. A slow, upward movement of hope in act 1 continues until it crests in act 2. Boyle is convinced he's going to come into a legacy and that all his financial problems will be solved. The audience is tempted to laugh in spite of itself when, in anticipation of suddenly becoming middle class, Boyle purchases vases, flowers, vulgar bureaus and chairs—an explosive desire for material things, when nothing about his life has changed.

Then, inevitably, comes the falling off. During the celebration of the Boyles' good fortune—everyone's singing "When Irish Eyes Are Smilin'"—a funeral procession passes by on the street below. Robbie Tancred, the son of their neighbor in the tenement, Mrs. Tancred, was an Irish Republican Army diehard, but he was betrayed by someone and executed. The informer, apparently motivated by petty resentment, was Johnny Boyle, Juno and Captain Jack's son.

In act 3, the furniture is repossessed—there was no legacy, it turns out. Mary reveals she's pregnant by Charlie Bentham, who has abandoned her. She renounces her faith in God, but Juno rejects her daughter's self-pity. She stands by Mary, and in an act of love and female solidarity, she says they'll raise the baby together. The child, she says, will "have what's far better [than no father]—it'll have two mothers." This is the only hope before the final disaster: Robbie Tancred's comrades come for Johnny Boyle and drag him away to be shot. Mrs. Tancred enters, crying aloud for a blessing that will stop the suffering and violence, a scene that deeply affected Hansberry: "the shriek of misery fitted to a wail of poetry that consumed all my senses, and all my awareness of human pain, endurance and the pity of it. . . . The wail rose and hummed through the tenement, through Dublin, through Ireland itself and then mingled with the seas and became born of the Irish wail that was in all of us."[37]

In the final scene, drunken Captain Boyle returns with a sycophantic friend, Joxer Daly, to the almost empty room, bereft of everything: hope, happiness, expensive furnishings. Joxer, who's sick of how "Captain" Boyle always plays the great man, rejoices in his comeuppance and tells him what a fraud he is.

Hansberry left the theater that night in a transcendent mood. "I considered my own evolution as a writer in a way I had not heretofore done." Over the next several weeks, she began a "composition in the form of a primitive dramatic narrative. Conceived for reasons I don't understand in the form of individualized spoken parts and climactic events." Later, she was a bit awed by her own presumption, a seventeen-year-old who knew almost nothing about "the near mathematical disciplines and demands of dramaturgy," deciding to write a play. "Just thinking about this I won-der who I was and what I was to make such a transition." She was like Candace, breaking into a spontaneous dance upon hearing African music, "celebrating the purely intuitive." That was Hansberry's muse: "the intel-lectually involuntary, the unbridled, the freely formed." She entered into, as she said, a "romance."[38]

O'Casey's impact on her was "like that on all of us," said black play-wright and director Douglas Turner Ward, whom Hansberry would later meet. The Boyles of Dublin were not only part of an oppressed people liv-ing within a larger nation—a parallel with American Negroes—they also spoke in their own vernacular, used their favorite expressions, and shook their fists at those who were dominating them. They were empathetic char-acters who deserved better. In fact, the correspondence between O'Casey's Irish and American blacks was so close that Ward claimed that many of O'Casey's plays would work better with black actors.[39]

Theatergoing black Americans like Ward and Hansberry also saw their cultural ideals reflected in Irish drama and how it proclaimed "the spirit of the nation." Plays from Dublin's Abbey Theatre toured the United States three times between 1911 and 1914, encouraging Alain Locke and more than a few Harlem Renaissance writers to think that Irish Literary Revival was an example they ought to follow. "Harlem has the same role to play for the New Negro as Dublin," Locke wrote in the opening essay for *The New Negro: An Interpretation*, apart from differences in politics.[40] Irish folk art, he pointed out, expressed through the people's indigenous language, songs, and stories, had produced some of the finest literature in the English language and surpassed Ireland's conquerors in their own tradition, vindi-cating themselves as a race apart and reclaiming their self-respect.

The night Lorraine saw *Juno and the Paycock* at the Wisconsin Union Theater, the Boyles of Dublin stood in for all Ireland; and one day, the Younger family in *A Raisin in the Sun* would represent the black commu-nity amid the American nation.[41]

A reviewer of the Wisconsin Players production remarked that the student who played Mrs. Tancred "has a tiny bit as a grieving mother and handles it quite beautifully."[42] Her name was Edythe Anne Cohen. She lived a few blocks away in the Langdon Hall dormitory, and Lorraine made a point of befriending her. Cohen's blue-green eyes, generous mouth, and abundant dark brown hair somehow justified how she had changed the spelling of her name from the prosaic "Edith" to "Edythe."

Like Lorraine, she was the youngest in her family, with four siblings. The Cohens spoke Yiddish at home. Edythe planned to make a career in journalism or theater—she wasn't sure which—a choice that Lorraine was thinking about, too. Judging from the letters they exchanged over the next few years, Hansberry seems to have developed a crush on the Russian-Jewish girl from Milwaukee.

It may have been only a sentimental attachment. Lorraine was still rather strict with herself, raised as she was in a conservative home. And the amount of time they could spend together was short. Edythe would be graduating in two months. Lorraine, in a letter she shyly left at Edythe's door in June, confided:

> I do not plan to be around when this is read—or I should be embar-rassed silly—but since it the last thing that I may say to you I shall speak honesty—
>
> Of the few people in the world whom I do truly respect, you are one, and I am warmed at the thought of having known Edythe Cohen—when you are home you shall be no more than two hours from me but it is quite likely that I shall never see you again Edythe—which I sup-pose is why I am just a little sad. I can in my life remember no one else who I could speak with as I have on long nights.[43]

Edythe departed with the rest of the graduates, but before Lorraine left cam-pus for the summer of 1948, Roma Borst invited her to attend her brother's high school graduation in the little town of Brooklyn, Wisconsin—very German and Dutch.[44] Lorraine, up for an adventure, accepted.

The half-hour trip aboard the Chicago and Northwestern train took her from the state capital and into the rolling countryside of dairy and crop farms. As the Brooklyn depot came within sight, a trainman stepped out from the station and waved a flag to signal the engineer that he was approaching the village of 450 residents. As the train slowed, tall white letters painted on the side of a bright-red granary slid past the window: "Farmers' Mutual Benefit and Trading Company."

Roma's father owned the feed mill and the farm implement store in Brooklyn, served on the village board, and was one of the wealthiest men in Greene County. As Lorraine entered Brooklyn High School's library to join in celebrating the fifteen graduates of the class of 1948, Roma noticed that "many eyes were on [her], the first Negro, perhaps, ever to visit the village."[45] It was like Lorraine to enter a social situation and not reflect anyone's assumptions that she was different. She reciprocated by inviting Roma to visit her in Chicago for four days that summer.

Borst discovered that the Hansberrys in situ were rather interesting people, although some of the girls in Langdon Manor might have prepared her for that. Four of them had driven Lorraine all the way home for the weekend and met her mother. Mrs. Hansberry had graciously invited her daughter's guests to spend the night. She was a "warming and loving woman," one of them remembered, and she cooked a wonderful breakfast, asking if any of the young ladies would like a glass of wine first. They politely declined, although the gesture somehow "seemed so elegant and right, so gracious and hospitable."[46]

When Roma met her, Mrs. Hansberry happened to be "lying regally on a lovely chaise lounge" when they were introduced. Mamie was there as well: "very beautiful and graceful, very different from Lorraine then." The next morning, Roma listened to Carl Jr. explain the health benefits of drinking raw eggs. She grimaced as he downed a tall glass of six. Then there was a toast-eating contest; Lorraine won.

Nothing was really foreign to Borst, however.[47] She was beginning a lifetime of travel, and she had tales to tell about having just returned from her second trip to Mexico. Lorraine had never been to the land where her father had passed away, and listening to Roma's stories may have given her an idea. Two years of a foreign language were required for Wisconsin undergraduates; a summer course for credit in Mexico would provide intensive practice.

More exciting, though, while she was home for the summer in Chicago, were developments that Lorraine could only vouchsafe to Edythe because of a "new emotion" that "I may tell no one about—indeed not even thee—completely."

I am hopelessly "interested" in one very wonderful young man. (I never thought it possible.) If you are at all interested: he goes to Roosevelt

[College] here, belongs to the [Henry] Wallace group (where I met him), is a thinker, I think, has said nothing at all suggestive of interest *in me to me* (but he does stare at me all through meetings—whatever that may mean)—He has a beautiful body and eyes and a smile that do all sorts of queer things to this one. Forgive me dear Edythe—I know not what I write—I may tell you this however—that nothing shall *ever* come of this—That is why I could not be good company because I should so very much [want] for "something to come of it."

The reason she had met him was because she had "gone one hundred percent Progressive" in support of Henry A. Wallace, the Progressive Party's candidate in the upcoming 1948 presidential election. "I spend my few social hours arguing with 'friends' so I will make no excuses to you! [for not replying]." Being a Wallacite was a big step to the left politically, away from her family's Republicanism. And for her to attend meetings of white Progressives was risky. "Here in Chicago a district police chief made public a statement declaring that *any mixed meetings* (in his eyesight) anywhere in the city *constitute communist gatherings*."[48]

6

The Young Progressives

I was born on the South Side of Chicago. I was born black and female. I was born in a depression after one world war, and came into my adolescence during another. While I was still in my teens the first atom bombs were dropped on human beings at Nagasaki and Hiroshima, and by the time I was twenty-three years old my government and that of the Soviet Union had entered into the worst conflict of nerves in human history—the Cold War.

—Lorraine Hansberry, *The Collected Last Plays*

Nothing came of her infatuation with the beautiful young man. But when she returned to campus in the fall of 1948, she joined four hundred students, mainly Wallace supporters and members of the Young Progressives of America (YPA), who were picketing the Campus Soda Grill carrying Stop Jim Crow signs. The owner had withdrawn the offer of a room above the grill to a black student.

The protest became disorderly at about 10:30 p.m., after the owner threatened to have the Wallacites arrested. Hecklers started pushing and shoving, and the police were called. Lorraine wrote Edythe, "My parents have *forbidden* my attending so much as one more Wallace meeting. I am quite sick about it. They are afraid Little Lorraine will call up one night from the police station and ask for her pajamas or [be] tied to a post [and] a [Communist hammer and sickle] branded on my forehead."[1] She continued attending meetings for the Progressive Party anyway, disregarding what she had been forbidden to do.

The Wallace campaign under the Progressive Party banner galvanized the idealism of college youth like her. She was part of what would become known as "the Silent Generation"—born too young to have participated in World War II and confronted with a postwar era that was a war of nerves between the Soviet Union and the United States. She questioned why good Americans were supposed to be uncritical, even in a time of crisis. "We were ceaselessly told, after all, to be everything which mutilates youth, to be silent, to be safe, to be without unsanctioned opinions, to be compliant and, above all else, obedient to all the ideas which are in fact the dregs of an age."[2] By contrast, a central part of the Progressive Party's platform was its uncompromising language of world peace, social equality, and racial justice.

The campaign of former Vice President Henry Wallace was launched rather late in the contest for president, creating a mad urgency among his supporters. He resigned from the editorship of *The New Republic* and threw himself into the struggle to build a third-party opposition to the Democrat incumbent, President Truman. The new party's strategy was to appeal to outsider groups whose hopes had been raised by wartime social liberalism: union workers angry with inflation, Negroes and Jews fighting discrimination at home, women working for equal rights. He promised to limit the influence of corporations in American civil life, continue many of the New Deal policies, expand the welfare system, enact civil rights legislation, protect and support the new Jewish state in Palestine, guarantee the rights of women in the economy, and implement a foreign policy to protect the lives of Americans from war—a party of peace that could end the Cold War through direct negotiations with the Soviet Union. The Communist Party of America endorsed him, which hindered him in most voters' minds, but he refused to expel its members from his campaign. He said he wanted to "keep the door open."[3]

To his detractors, Henry Wallace's Gideon's army of young people, the disempowered, and the politically disenchanted was more of a fifth column than an authentic progressive alternative. Although his movement was interracial—he had consulted with a group of black leaders before announcing his candidacy—most black voters were leaning toward Truman because they believed he could actually deliver on civil rights. The NAACP fired W. E. B. Du Bois as editor of *The Crisis* because he endorsed Wallace, and Du Bois lost his column in the conservative *Chicago Defender*, too.

Hansberry's joining the Wallace campaign marks the beginning of her thinking about what she was willing to fight for, although nonconformity carried serious risks during the Cold War. She understood that "if you went to the wrong debates on campus, signed the wrong petitions, you simply didn't get the job you wanted[,] and you were forewarned of this early in your college career."[4] But she was reaching an intersection where her desires both to create herself and to explore different identities were converging. She enrolled in a sculpture class in the fall of 1948, and there's a telling description in "All the Dark and Beautiful Warriors" that illustrates feelings of disconnectedness, pieces of oneself becoming but not yet fitting together. In the unpublished novel, Candace walks into a silent studio:[5]

> Across the mammoth floor were scattered armatures which varied from single square rods mounted on small wooden platforms for head studies to life-sized metal skeletons, grotesque in their unfleshed pos-turings. Here and there a piece had been begun and left swathed in wet sacking; things emerging, coming, starting to be; things that had not been. . . . She had stayed, wandering there alone among the pedestals; uncovering work here, touching clay and instruments; noting the room itself with its center platform for the model, the long tables at the rear with plaster-smeared basins; piles of chisels and mallets lay about and everything was dusted with a fine pink and blue powder.

She also enrolled in a freehand drawing class, but she found art majors weren't her kind of people. They seemed to be a rather fey group, "in their uniforms of paint- and plastered-stained jeans," sitting together in the Memorial Union Rathskeller drinking coffee and beer, "all day long with their paint brushes behind their ear," discussing art from "the depth of their superior opinions."[6] They were an exclusive crowd. And she disliked artiness when it was a pose. The students' lassitude and air of world-weariness ran contrary to what she had been taught as a child: "Life was not a struggle—it was something one *did*."[7] Of course, they weren't all like that: she became friends with an oil painter, Kate Weiskopf. Kate was from

South Shore, in Chicago, a middle-class, ethnic community not far from Lorraine's.

Kate had transferred from a small college in Michigan after waiting two months for a room at the Groves Women's Cooperative, across the street from Langdon Manor. The small Michigan college had been too white-bread, and she wanted more variety. The co-op members shared the tasks of running the household together: washing up after meals, sweeping, cleaning the rooms.[8] Kate liked Lorraine because she was open-minded and nonjudgmental. "Lorraine was smart, talented. Never got angry. We weren't petty, actually. Neither one of us. We just did our thing. We were nice to people—we were nice to each other." She recalled an art teacher saying, "'You know, Lorraine could do anything.' And I think he was right."[9]

That fall, they both became members of the Wallace-supporting YPA— "young people working together," said a flyer the group handed out, "to maintain and extend peace, progress and abundance in America and the world."[10] The United States could either go down the path of producing superweapons, and follow "the cold war to its bloody catastrophic end," or settle its differences with the Soviet Union through the United Nations.[11] "We are quite sternly begging for another war," Lorraine wrote to Edythe, "and say what you will against the Reds and their 'violent' tactics of con-trol[,] they *do not advocate a war of any nature* (and I didn't have to read that in the [Communist] *Daily Worker!*)."[12]

Hansberry also supported the Progressive Party's call to end discrim-ination. Wallace's running mate on the Progressive ticket, U.S. senator from Idaho Glen H. Taylor, had been scheduled to speak to the Southern Negro Youth Congress in Birmingham, Alabama, but as he was entering the building, police arrested him for violating segregation laws.

Several of the members of the YPA at Madison were Jewish. Hansberry looked up to Roy M. Mersky, who was five years older and enrolled in law school. When war was declared against Germany, he had memorized the eye exam chart so he could pass the army physical without his glasses. One of his hands was scarred from wounds he received as a machine gunner during the Battle of the Bulge. Some thought he was a little abrasive, but he had been through more than his fellow Progressives.[13] And raised in a Jewish home in the Bronx, he had formed strong opinions, founded on

Hebraic teaching, that the right to be oneself, the right to be different, made a person no less real, worthy, or honorable than anyone else.[14]

Through the YPA, Hansberry entered a new circle of friends. Belonging was important to her. She enjoyed spending time chatting, discussing, and arguing over cigarettes and coffee at the Green Lantern Eating Cooperative, where the leftists on campus congregated. Candace, Hansberry's persona in "All the Dark and Beautiful Warriors," "especially liked it on the weekends, when they all pile into somebody's car and head out to the countryside to talk to the farmers about Henry Wallace. Afterwards they found country inns where they ate hearty German country food and drank strong dark beer and then crowded back into the cars and drove the lovely miles through the countryside back to the campus in the near darkness, singing a little, softly, when they were not too tired, the lovers among them holding hands and nestling. They were the best of times, those."[15]

She had been bitten by the theater bug, too. "I've been to a couple of *Girl Crazy* tryouts," she wrote Edythe; "I don't know when I've had more fun." Trying her best to "look like an accomplished thespian," she auditioned for one of the singing parts. She didn't make the callbacks, but it was the experience she relished. "You know, Dollink," she wrote to Edythe. "I like your 'show people.' They are probably the most self-centered and shop-talkingest bunch I've ever been around."[16]

And then, in mid-October, art and politics converged on the same day. President Truman arrived aboard a sixteen-car train as part of a whistle-stop campaign across the United States. It's quite possible that Hansberry stood with other YPA members waving Vote for Wallace signs as Truman rode past in an open cream-colored convertible on his way to speak to the four thousand supporters waiting inside the university pavilion.

How to control the spread of nuclear arms was a prime campaign issue. Wallace endorsed sharing the United States' atomic secrets with the Soviet Union to avoid an arms race. The Republican nominee, Thomas E. Dewey, combined his anticommunism with a general call for national unity to face the challenges ahead. Truman, speaking from a dais festooned with flags inside the pavilion, advocated giving control and inspection of nuclear weapons to a multinational organization like the United Nations.

That night, Lorraine went to hear Frank Lloyd Wright speak at the

Memorial Union. She stationed herself by the doors of the theater where she had seen *Juno and the Paycock*, to catch a glimpse of him. And then, "finally there they were, [Wright] and his entourage, sweeping in, it seems to me now, in capes and string ties and long hair. Through the corridors of the Union building," like the shock troops of art sent to counterattack the philistines. Every seat was filled. She heard Wright inveigh against everything ordinary, conventional, or expected, "foremost among them, the building he was standing in for its violation of the organic principles of architecture." He attacked materialism, conformity, and the current purpose of education, saying, "[W]e put in so many plums, and get out so many fine prunes, each like the one before." The students laughed and applauded; faculty members, too, but "nervously," Hansberry thought. "Then he went home back to Taliesin East, a set of dark and dramatic rectangles set on a hill which people pointed out from the highways."[17]

In the same theater where O'Casey had inspired her to try playwriting, Hansberry had heard a warning to the young artists, critics, and activists in the audience from one of the most influential architects of the age: not to be satisfied with mediocrity; not to be lukewarm in one's opinions, thoughts, or desires; not to be content with what was acceptable by society but alien to oneself. Instead, dig down into one's own strong, but unarticulated emotions to find truth.

It was enough to rely on one's subjective experience as a guide, Hansberry gathered. What was personal and important to oneself often was universally understood, just as O'Casey's dramatization of poverty in Dublin had reached out and touched her.

"I think that *is* love," she wrote to Edythe, "and people ought to do what they love, they ought to, they ought to, they ought to—Frank Lloyd Wright did."[18]

Following the celebrated architect's visit, Hansberry organized something new on campus: the Progressive Theater. Time was short before the November election, but the idea was to raise money for the YPA and the Wallace campaign. She went looking for the best student talent she could find, starting with Gerald Hiken, a senior who had performed in *Juno and the Paycock*. After he consented to direct, she brought him a stack of plays to choose from. He culled the ones he wanted, but she had something more political in mind than the ones he chose. Maybe, at least, she suggested, they could end with the cast all coming out and singing the Communist anthem, "The Internationale," like in Clifford Odets's *Waiting for Lefty*, when the actors lead the audience in shouting, "Strike! Strike! Strike!"

Hiken said he wouldn't do that. He told her that he "wasn't all that Left."[19]

They compromised on three plays with themes that satisfied both of them: Arthur Laurents's *Home of the Brave*; Federico García Lorca's *Yerma*, set in 1930s Spain, about a young Catholic woman who's afraid she will fail somehow if she doesn't have a child; and Aristophanes's *Lysistrata*, the Greek comedy in which the women of warring city-states withhold sex from their husbands and lovers until they negotiate a peace treaty. There was time enough before the election to perform only one, but Hiken agreed to direct a series into second semester as well.

Rather than post audition notices, Hansberry sought the actors out herself. The university was holding a drama festival to celebrate the one-hundredth anniversary of its founding, and she attended all the performances, making notes about the actors she wanted for the Progressive Theater productions. Remarkably, for *Lysistrata*, she was able to assemble an all-black cast, which included her.

The night the curtain went up for *Lysistrata*, actress Geraldine Page, then a student at the Art Institute of Chicago, was in the audience. She had heard that some very interesting, edgy theater was being performed by students in a rented hall near the Madison campus. Lorraine, she thought, was quite good in her part.[20]

Wallace lost, finishing with 3 percent of the vote, the same as the independent, Dixiecrat candidate, South Carolina governor and segregationist Strom Thurmond. Although many American liberal and radical intellectuals were deeply disaffected with President Truman and his hard-line anti-Soviet foreign policy, his coalition of old New Dealers, labor unionists, and black voters triumphed over Republican Thomas Dewey, who had been heavily favored to win.

The YPA carried on after Wallace's defeat, and Hansberry was elected to the student board. She favored holding even more outdoor rallies focusing on world peace, but the administration put a stop to these because of incidents involving the police. Regardless, the group energetically advertised meetings and social events to the point where the dean of men complained about "their penchant for distributing leaflets."[21]

But really, the excitement of the campaign season was over now, and the November weather turned dry and freezing. Edythe was home in Milwaukee, preoccupied with finding a job and making new friends. Lorraine missed her. To emphasize how sad she felt, she punctuated her thoughts with ellipses in a letter. "It's a lovely, ugly good Wisconsin day. Windswept and clear and so very cold, yet it's a blue day, a crisp blue day . . . however what I want to write to you I don't know . . . I just want to write . . . to you. . . . It is also a very lonely day. . . . I should be used to loneliness, I guess. I've spent a lonely eighteen years. After your last letter you don't deserve anything better than this so I won't apologize for it. . . . [Y]ou are a vain hussy you know." Thanksgiving was in two weeks, but she wasn't looking forward to going home; "yet I know come Thanksgiving I would be a mass of tears if I were any where else . . . damned if I know what is wrong." The darker days of winter were beginning to affect her like this, a problem that seems to have started in late adolescence. Come November, when the days grew noticeably short, she began feeling hopeless and apprehensive. "I envy your wanting *something*," she told Edythe, "unstable or vague as it might be, I envy it of you."[22]

"All the Dark and Beautiful Warriors" has a story line about a young man named Son who's not long in Chicago after migrating from Tennessee. His first Christmas in the city, he buys a "bright plaid heavy mackinaw," a cap with earflaps, a pair of high rubber boots, and he sets off exploring the Loop. The department stores dazzle him with "the wonders that they held." He eats a hot dog while gazing at the displays, like a spectator at a circus. An expensively dressed woman with blue-gray hair casts "amazed eyes on him." When the hurly-burly of goods and bright colors, lights, and music becomes too much, he walks to Lake Shore Drive, "which edged the great and furious winter lake; he would stand there scanning its immensity, wonder[ing] what oceans there might really be in the world more vast. Then he would turn inland suddenly, and surprise his eyes with the city skyline; it always gave him a thrill.

"Still for all its wonders, faithful to a tradition, the season brought its own sudden, smarting, special loneliness."[23]

7

Mexico

The supreme test of technical skill and creative imagination is the depth
of art it requires to render the infinite varieties of the human spirit—
which invariably hangs between despair and joy.

—Lorraine Hansberry, *To Be Young, Gifted and Black*

"See Mexico through the eyes of an Indian villager this summer," the
advertisement read. "The Mexican Workshop combines art study with
the experience of living in a small Tarasan community, Ajijic, which is
one of the most beautiful and exciting regions of Mexico."[1]

The first week of July 1949, while on summer break from college,
Lorraine left home in Chicago for a monthlong stay in the village of Ajijic, on Lake Chapala, on the western side of Mexico. The workshop and
cultural tours offered through the Fine Arts School of the University of
Guadalajara would answer several needs: practice in Spanish, instruction
in modern art, and (perhaps unconsciously for Hansberry) a chance to
be near the spirit of her father.[2] How artists encounter the influences that
shape their perspective happens in different ways. But the key thing is
that they must explore. Whatever it was that encouraged Lorraine to travel
to Mexico—possibly Roma's experiences there—her instincts served her
well. Although her immediate objectives were to practice speaking Spanish and learn more about visual art; in the long run, her monthlong stay

contributed importantly to her development as a dramatist and an intellectual.

Her college plans for the fall were already settled. Come September, she would have a new roommate at Langdon Manor; Roma had graduated. It would be JoAnn Beier, one of the girls who had been welcomed to stay overnight by Mrs. Hansberry. Academically, Lorraine's classes were tending toward a major in art and theater; journalism was never a serious contender. However, her grades were on the low end of average. If they didn't improve, one failing grade would put her on academic probation.

Edythe's letters had been trailing off, which saddened Lorraine. "Something wrong?—if so I apologize—if not—why don't you write?" she pleaded in handwriting that was uncharacteristically small and constrained, instead of displaying the usual exuberant loops and angles, as if she were feeling hurt and defensive. Through mutual friends, she had heard that Edythe was auditioning for local theater in Milwaukee. "Heard you had another nice part—I'm happy *too*—*second hand info*—I don't know why I rate that—I'm not proud—*I wish you would write*. Very much—very soon. Love, Lorraine."[3] Then, as if she were leaning her face against her hand and musing to herself, she wrote in large block letters in the margin, "EDYTHE COHEN," wanting to give that name permanence.

She flew to Guadalajara and, on the morning of July 10, boarded a bus bound for Ajijic, in the Mexican state of Jalisco, along with nineteen other students. On the way, she struck up a conversation with Irma Jonas, the New York director of the program, about her interest in theater.[4]

The advertisement for the workshop hadn't overpromised how lovely the village was. Ajijic was a panoply of red-tile roofs, white adobe walls, cobblestone streets, and blossoming trees against a background of Lake Chapala's blue water, the sky, and the encircling mountains. Out on the lake, there were fishing boats; and on the beach, nets drying in the sun. The aroma of wood smoke came from booths by the water selling roasted corn.

Ms. Jonas had arranged a welcome for them. As the bus pulled in, horsemen in embroidered charro suits spurred their animals, pivoting, and waved their hats and whooped. The Old Posada, a ten-room inn where Lorraine would be staying, run by a pair of British expats, was within sight of the centuries-old great stone pier jutting into the lake. On the inn's menu were dishes collected by the cook, Candelaria, such as "Pork Bone that will Spot your Tablecloth" and "Eggs of a Señora who lived in Tuxcueca but Died."

That evening, Lorraine and the others attended a reception at the home of the abstract expressionist painter Ernesto Linares, a handsome blond man who had, a friend said, the "untroubled face of a good German." In love with him was a beautiful American woman, Zoe Kernick, who had recently left Big Sur, California, following an affair, she said, with Henry Miller.[5] Observing Linares's party for the students that evening, Kernick noticed how, "Everyone came to welcome them. The conglomerate of foreign residents of Ajijic and Chapala, the villagers, the charro lads. Martinis made music[,] and mariachis made noise."[6]

As it grew dark, sunsets over Lake Chapala were purple and gold, and if the sky stayed clear, Lorraine would have been able to see shooting stars streaking over the mountains.

Mexico, as a refuge, was never far from the imagination of black Americans. During the years of American slavery, the Underground Railroad went south as well as north. The southern route crossed into Mexico, where slavery had been abolished in 1829 for economic reasons.[7] The farthest point on the escape route was the "Freedom Station" located in Mazamitla, Jalisco, roughly sixty miles south of Ajijic. Some of the campesinos bringing their farm goods into Ajijic were descendants of escaped slaves from Texas, Louisiana, Mississippi, and Alabama.

The legend of Mexico as a promised land meant that American Negroes were well disposed toward life there. Carl Hansberry's remark that he "felt free for the first time" in Mexico was echoed by many.[8] Langston Hughes had lived with his father on a ranch in the Mexican mountains. Returning there on business in 1934, he said he felt he was home. "Here, nothing is barred from me. I am among my own people for . . . Mexico is a brown man's country." Richard Wright lived in Mexico from 1940 to 1946, and reported to *The Atlantic Monthly* that "people of all races and colors live in harmony and without racial prejudices or theories of racial superiority." Yet it must be said that the desire to get away from Jim Crow generated some descriptions of race relations in Mexico that are too generous and uncomplicated. Mexico attempted to limit black emigration in the 1920s.[9]

There was also a cultural bridge between Mexican folklore and the oral traditions of African storytelling. Ajijic had plenty of the superstitions, legends, and "witch doctor stuff" that had delighted Lorraine about *The Dark of the Moon*. Islands in Lake Chapala were said to be haunted by the spirits of slain conquistadores. Their spirits were supposed to glow in the night in the form of fireflies, rising from the marshes where the white egrets nested. Church bells rang for no reason; electric lights went on and off. The clergy of Guadalajara told parishioners that Ajijic was "an evil village," where people cursed on Sunday. There was a German woman, a *bruja*, "a witch," whom the villagers consulted for fortune-telling, blessings, and cures. People said she was kind.[10]

A style of popular art steeped in protest caught Hansberry's political eye. Part of the workshop in Ajijic included tours of museums and art centers in Guadalajara where works by Mexican social realists made up a significant part of the collections. She saw depictions of indigenous Mexican culture, of *negros y mestizos*, and epic murals about the national Revolution of 1910.

Already by the 1930s, black American painters had become interested in the social realism of Mexican muralists: Diego Rivera, David Alfaro Siqueiros, and José Clemente Orozco, in particular. Their depictions of common people were the subject of lectures and discussions at black community centers, including the South Side Community Art Center in Chicago, near where Lorraine grew up. The Mexican muralists celebrated folk culture as a heritage with dignity—heroic and enduring. A number of midcentury black American artists on the Left, such as Charles Alston, John T. Biggers, Jacob Lawrence, and Hale Woodruff, produced works with themes of racial, ethnic, and class struggle using Mexican mural art as their touchstone.[11]

As Hansberry said about Seán O'Casey, there is a "genuine heroism that must emerge when you tell the truth about people."[12] Social realism, she said later, is about "what is possible . . . because that is part of reality, too. So that you get a much larger potential of what man can do." She believed it was essential to recognize the humanity of the subjects under study, to be a witness to life, and that "you put what you believe *is*."[13]

Hansberry loved the little village. There was time set aside for swimming, climbing the mountains on the back of a burro, and making excursions to neighboring villages. Away from the grind of university classes and the expectations of her family, she reveled in a feeling of "nobody cares."[14] One of her instructors was Carlos Mérida, a Guatemalan artist who had been Diego Rivera's mural-painting assistant. Then in his late fifties, he was integrating European trends—pictorial ideas from Joan Miró, Paul Klee, Pablo Picasso, and Amedeo Modigliani—with pre-Columbian Mayan aesthetics to express his heritage in modern terms. Lorraine admired his work and later was proud to say she had studied under him.

Ernesto Linares, she thought, was a phony. "We literally threw paint on canvas."[15] While his lady friend, Zoe Kernick, gleaming with coconut oil, sunbathed on the big pier, Linares demonstrated how to brush canvases with lacquer normally used on cars to make surrealist or abstract pictures, some of which were purely decorative. Another of Hansberry's teachers, Nicolas Muzenic—who was "tall, haughty, grand," said his lover and co-instructor Tobias Schneebaum—produced somber paintings of dirty yellows and browns: tight, recondite, and convoluted.[16]

Hansberry had no patience with what she considered fooling around. A year of managing the Progressive Theater, and debating with her socialist and Communist friends in Madison, had convinced her that great art had purposes higher than self-expression. The closer she moved to Marxism, the more doctrinaire and purist her opinions became about what was worth doing and what wasn't. In a letter to a friend, she laid out her philosophy about what art should do. "[O]ne either writes, paints, composes or otherwise engages in creative enterprises . . . on behalf of humanity—or against humanity." Abstraction was self-indulgent and elitist, a marker of class. It excluded people who should be welcomed in. The "most unlettered Mexican peasant is quite capable of announcing in full-voiced opinion what he does or does not like in 'art,'" because Mexican art has "maintained a quality of healthy genuine *traditional* development . . . which ours for the most part has completely departed from." Abstractionists, in her opinion, enjoyed being inscrutable. "And so they proceed with the smearing of the canvases and making jackasses of themselves; the public which accepts it out of ignorance, the fraudulent intelligentsia, and the critics who prostitute their function shamefully by pretending that this whole damn thing is anything more than a fraud."[17]

Her views would never change. In 1962, she wrote Hoyt Fuller, the editor of *Negro Digest*, that nothing would endure in art that had "not evolved out the process of communication with the broadest base of 'the people.'"[18]

At the end of her retreat in Mexico, world events were thrust into the foreground of Lorraine's life again. A week or so before she returned to campus, the Soviet Union successfully detonated its first atomic bomb in the steppes of Kazakhstan. The United States was no longer the only nation with a nuclear weapon, and the arms race was on. "The Bomb," as Americans bleakly referred to it, became part of the Soviet Union's and the United States' strategic policy for pursuing peace and social justice.

The Soviets argued that the process of liberating humanity from imperialism would be the inevitable end point of capitalism. Tearing out the system by the roots might be violent, but the final stage would be a peaceful socialist society. To speed this outcome, nuclear weapons were necessary to ensure that the Soviet Union would be able to defend itself.

The terror of such weapons being used would become a reason Lorraine turned toward the Communist Party of America. It argued for, in the interests of the Soviet Union, a worldwide campaign of peace and justice to humanitarians like her; getting "rid of all the little bombs—and the big bombs," as she was still hoping for near the end of her life. One of her last dramatic works, the one-act, *What Use Are Flowers?* (1961–62), is set in a postapocalyptic world. She wanted audiences to come away "with some appreciation of the . . . cumulative processes which created modern man and his greatness and how we ought not go around blowing it up."[19]

The identical words used by the Communists (*peace, freedom*, and *justice*) were repeated by the American government, but the argument was reversed. Patience and fortitude were needed to alleviate want and human misery in the world; and preserving peace and freedom in the meantime depended on containing Soviet-spread communism and, ultimately, defeating it.[20] The strategy of the Truman administration was to maintain a nuclear arsenal that would make world war between the two countries unthinkable, leaving open a space for diplomacy.

During the wait, humanity was threatened daily with the specter of a planetary conflict that beggared the imagination. When the Soviet Union's test bomb "First Lightning" detonated in August 1949, the explosion and heat immolated fifty airplanes, a bridge, a train station, and fifteen hundred animals. Miles away from the blast, the atmosphere imploded, and the windows of schools were sucked out. Students' bodies convulsed from the shock.[21]

In September 1949, when Lorraine returned to Langdon Manor, Mrs. Miler asked to speak to her privately. JoAnn Beier was too ashamed to admit that her mother would not permit her to room with a Negro. Beier later said she "suffered the agony of seeing Lorraine—and giving her the briefest explanation," but the harm was done: the friendship was never the same.

That fall, Lorraine gave a talk to her Langdon Manor housemates about her summer in Mexico. The YPA elected her president. She dated a black football player, later a sports journalist. He wasn't interested in social issues, but he appreciated that she "could whip together a fresh picket sign with her own hands, at a moment's notice, for any cause or occasion."[22] "And then I believe," Beier said, "Lorraine left at the end of the semester."[23]

She did, but not from disappointment over not rooming with Beier. The reason she left, it's routinely reported, is because of something her instructor in Stage Design class said to her. First, he supposedly gave her a failing grade; and then he compounded the shock by explaining that he was doing her a favor. A young black woman wouldn't succeed in the technical side of theater, he allegedly said; it just wasn't in the cards.[24]

But the fact is she didn't receive an F in Stage Design. On her official transcript, she received a C. Her grade in Theater: Antiquity to the Present was a D; she received a D in Animal Biology, and she failed Physical Education. Beginning the spring of her sophomore year in 1949, she was put on final academic probation. On the verge of flunking out, she would have to pass another science course to graduate, because freshman year she had failed Physical Geography.

She decided it was time to "pursue an education of another kind."

Every person has two educations, Carter G. Woodson wrote in *The Mis-Education of the Negro*: "that which is given to him, and the other that which he gives himself. Of the two kinds the latter is by far the more desirable. Indeed all that is most worthy in man he must work out and conquer for himself."[25] Hansberry had become disenchanted with the University of Wisconsin anyway. In "All the Dark and Beautiful Warriors," Candace scoffs at the university's reputation as one of the most liberal in the country. That high-minded aim, it seemed to her, had "long since vanished," leaving instead the "ideal atmosphere for the conservatism, smugness and stasis."[26]

Before she left for home, Lorraine attended a meeting of the Labor Youth League, "a new youth organization dedicated to education in the spirit of socialism." She was already familiar with the LYL; in fact, she may have helped bring a chapter to the University of Wisconsin. The league's first conference of 150 delegates from the YPA had been in May, two months before she went to Mexico, at the Peoples Theater on West Forty-Seventh, an old movie house near the Union Stock Yard, just a fifteen-minute walk from her home on South Parkway. A few days later, she began writing a pageant that was "Dedicated to the fighters of the Illinois Labor Youth League":[27]

> Narrator: We the youth have risen in each age
> To give life and hope to the struggle of men.
> Group: Here we stand now: risen!
> Here we stand now: angered!
> Here we stand now: FOR PEACE!

The LYL national chairman elected at the conference was twenty-eight-year-old Leon Wofsy, who would become a lifelong friend of hers. Formerly the national director of the Communist youth movement, he now had a new mandate: to develop the young Progressives and socialists into Communists by studying Marxism-Leninism and advocating for the working class. Those who joined the LYL would "learn about working class internationalism and how it is indivisible from love of country."[28] Communism was patriotism, and peace was freedom—peace with Stalin's Soviet Union and with Communist China under Mao Zedong.

At the LYL chapter meeting Lorraine attended a few weeks before she left campus in January 1950, she was one of sixteen students. The agenda was aligned perfectly with the kinds of things she cared about. It was announced that the NAACP was planning a march on Washington in mid-January to demand an end to poll taxes and to support passage of an antilynching bill. The LYL would provide transportation. Also discussed was a proposal to form a coalition with other youth groups such as the National Council of Methodist Youth and the National Student Council of the YMCA, to call on Congress to suspend federal aid to public schools that practiced discrimination.[29]

Among those listening to the discussion was an FBI informant. He or she forwarded the names of everyone present to the Bureau's Milwaukee office.

In 1949, the FBI office in Milwaukee had thirty-six agents and eighteen support employees with satellite branches in Green Bay, Superior, and Eau Claire, Wisconsin. Regarding Lorraine Hansberry, the special agent in charge of the Madison area noted, "Will, through informants and other investigation, ascertain the subject's Communist activities or associations."[30]

Actually, the Hansberrys, without their knowledge, had been on the FBI's watch list since 1943, when Lorraine's father established the National Negro Progress Association. An army intelligence colonel supplied FBI director J. Edgar Hoover with a summary of Hansberry's education, his business, and his "ardent" support for the NAACP—anything that might be relevant.[31] Hoover took an interest in prominent American Negroes. He believed that black intellectuals, artists, and some civic leaders such as Carl Hansberry might have connections to dissidents, nonconformists, antiestablishment radicals, and politicians considered unfriendly to law enforcement.

Hoover was less an anticommunist, says a historian of the FBI, than a "reactionary countersubversive."[32] By secretly passing on derogatory information about citizens under surveillance, often illegally, to a private network of congressmen, congressional committees, reporters, and columnists, he made himself the indispensable man, deflecting attention away from the Bureau's shortcomings.

The perception that black militants and Communists were in collusion began sometime in the 1930s. The Reds were for bread-and-butter issues such as better wages and working conditions, and against police brutality and Jim Crow. Liberals of all stripes (socialists, Quakers, progressives, labor organizers), observing how the party organizers could build bridges between "the most despised and dispossessed elements of American society," felt respect bordering on awe.[33] In Chicago, on South Calumet Avenue—Lorraine's street when she was newborn—fifty residents signed election petitions in 1940 for Communist candidates.[34] A five-cent pamphlet sold at Bug Club rallies in Washington Park carried the title *The Negroes in a Soviet America*. On the cover, a smiling young black worker contemplated a future vastly different from the life he was living. By the late 1930s, the Communist Party of America had a membership of about sixty-five thousand and a following that was several times larger.

Lorraine Hansberry was exactly the type of Negro whom J. Edgar Hoover and the Bureau wanted to keep an eye on. She was educated, and she was active in social causes; her participation in the Wallace campaign and the YPA brought her into contact with "Reds." Most troubling, however, was that she was defecting from her privileged background and going over to the other side. She presented the profile of someone who might become, in the language of counterintelligence, a "present danger." It was too early to tell whether she should be added to the Bureau's Security Index, a list of thousands of citizens "who in a time of emergency are in a position to influence others against the national interest." The FBI's Milwaukee office decided to wait and see, because there was as yet no information about Hansberry "specifically indicating membership in the Communist Party."[35] For the time being, a file was started: "Lorraine Vivian Hansberry: Female, Negro, five feet five inches, 130 pounds, medium build, black hair, light brown eyes and light brown complexion."

By the end of her brief life, her dossier would be a thousand pages long.

PART III

Harlem

8

"Flag from a Kitchenette Window"

The intellectual in America is a radically alienated personality, the Negro in common with the white, and both were hungry and seeking, and some of the best of both found food and an identity in communism.

–J. Saunders Redding,
"The Negro Writer and His Relationship to His Roots"

Struggling for a better future, linking arms with one's fellow men and women—Marxism was a civilizing view of the world. For Lorraine Hansberry, it became an instrument she could use to pursue a life of meaning. She had been seeking ways of belonging, waiting for a sign that, in the scheme of things, she was necessary. And now the teachings of the Communist Party had given her insights about herself that she had never considered. Because of it, she had moral authority; she belonged to the brotherhood and sisterhood of humankind. She saw that she already possessed standing.

"It is perhaps hard to understand now," wrote Vivian Gornick, the daughter of working-class immigrant Jews, in *The Romance of Communism*, but "the Marxist vision of world solidarity as translated by the Communist Party induced in the most ordinary of men and women a sense of one's own humanity that made life feel large: large and clarified."

Richard Wright came away from meetings of the Marxist John Reed Club on Chicago's South Side thinking, "There was no agency in the world so capable of making men feel the earth and the people on it than the Communist Party." He pored over the materials he'd been given to read by party members. "It seemed to me that here at last, in the realm of revolutionary expression, Negro experience could find a home, a functioning value and role."[1]

Capitalism was condemned as sanctioning selfishness, hoarding, and appropriating what rightfully belonged to everyone. It was a cynical system that couldn't withstand scrutiny when the cool logic of a Marxist scientism was applied. It fed on people's fears of being deprived in the scramble for what they needed to be self-sufficient, encouraging them to think they couldn't rely on one another—and with good reason: greed and the acquisition of things had skewed the American Dream to benefit the few at the expense of the many.

But it wasn't too late, Hansberry was convinced. Destroying class distinctions and restoring the basic needs of life would enable those who had been existing on their knees, waiting for help, to stand upright again, dignified. The broken promise of American democracy, equality for all, would be truly realized.

As a black woman who knew the pain of being an outsider, she could put her experiences to good use in the roles she would need to play in the coming revolution.[2]

Meanwhile, the city of Chicago was cracking down on kitchenettes. More than eighty thousand conversions had occurred during the 1940s. Kitchenettes were rented by all races, including white veterans and young families on the upscale Near North Side. But on the South Side, ramshackle, rat-infested units occupied hundreds of blocks. They were dim, claustrophobic warrens, said Richard Wright, that forced "desperate and unhappy people into an unbearable closeness of association." Most lacked private bathrooms.[3] Reformers blamed the "evils of the kitchenette apartment system" for high mortality rates, delinquency, illegitimate children, and community deterioration.

In October 1947, fire swept through a South Side kitchenette building, killing ten people.[4] Editorials in Chicago papers called for something to be done, and city officials instructed building inspectors to step up their operations. But many slum landlords found it cheaper to pay the fines than to replace frayed wiring, rebuild staircases, or fix stopped-up toilets. Some avoided paying property taxes altogether because they knew that the amount they owed would eventually exceed the actual value of the building—at which point, under the Neighborhood Redevelopment Corporation Law, the city would seize the property, condemn it, and knock it down, absolving the landlord of responsibility for it. Vacant lots began appearing like toothless gaps in rows of houses.

Carl Jr., president of Hansberry Enterprises, was cited for failing to remove the combustible partitions he had installed without a permit to make a kitchenette; also, for renting an underground basement as a dwelling.[5] But he ignored the summons and the fines.

When at last Carl Jr. was forced to appear in building court, the judge, who began his career working for the Legal Aid Society of Chicago, mused aloud, "What has always been a great mystery to me is the altruism of real estate owners. They suffer untold hardships and great expense just to give someone a place to live." Hansberry explained that he was saddled with paying $750 a month to maintain the building—added to which was the inconvenience of "coming down here all the time." Seeing that His Honor was unmoved by these arguments, thirty-year-old Carl Jr. pleaded, "I'm just a young, little boy."[6]

He was fined fifty dollars and costs.

Lorraine was stuck at home during the spring of 1950. She tried persuading her mother to let her go to New York, the way Mamie had when she dropped out of Howard and enrolled at Traphagen School of Fashion. It would be a fresh start—in New York there was "excitement, theater, everything."[7] But Mrs. Hansberry needed time to think it over. She hadn't invested years of preparing her youngest to become part of the Bronzeville elite only to have her misfire. At twenty, Lorraine was unable to support herself, had no prospects of marriage, and wasn't interested in the family business. How was rushing off to New York an improvement on her situation?

Wearing her mother down would take time, and Lorraine settled in for a long campaign until she got her way. Rather than lounge around the house, though, she enrolled as a student-at-large at Roosevelt College, a stopgap while she waited. She signed up for Introductory German, never having had any success at memorizing Spanish vocabulary.[8]

Roosevelt College, located on South Michigan Avenue, near Grant Park, was the most liberal and diverse institution of higher learning in the city. Its president, Edward J. Sparling, and most of Roosevelt's faculty had resigned five years earlier from Central YMCA College, to protest racial and ethnic quotas in admissions. On the advisory board were contralto Marian Anderson, novelist Thomas Mann, Albert Einstein, and Eleanor Roosevelt, who had given permission to name the college after her late husband. Trade union members took evening courses on collective bargaining and labor law. On "Discrimination Day," a group chosen at random from the student body of four thousand—blonds, people under five and a half feet, those whose last name started with M—were barred from the student library to "highlight the absurdity of racial discrimination."[9] Anticommunists referred to Roosevelt as "the little Red schoolhouse."

Lorraine's German class met on Tuesdays and Thursdays, which left her time to participate in local theater. The Skyloft Players at the Parkway Community House, founded in 1941 by Langston Hughes, wasn't far from her home.[10] The group was a cultural descendent of the Little Theatre movement. Its commitment to the audience, declared by its first director, Helen Spaulding, was to deliver "theater of the people, for the people, by the people." Besides offering dependable audience pleasers such as *Our Town* and *The Emperor Jones*, the players also staged original works with interracial and social justice themes. "Those who abhor the crap-shooting roles given to Negro actors and actresses on stage and screen," Spaulding said, "should use this opportunity to show the true side of our current problems and living conditions, and to portray a more equalized racial representation to the public."[11] The season before Lorraine joined, Roosevelt students had appeared in Hughes's Broadway hit *Mulatto*. So, despite living at home, Hansberry was still in her favorite milieu: theater, ideas, and activism.

She began dating Joe Elbein, the former president of the Communist Club at the University of Chicago. Kate Weiskopf was home for the summer, in South Shore, and met him; she was impressed. Word of the relationship percolated back up to Madison. The social chair of the YPA, Rhoda Winter, wrote to Lorraine wanting to know all about it. "Kate told me about the terrific young man who was with you the Friday night you and several other people went to the rally in Chicago. What goes?"[12]

Twenty-five-year-old Elbein, the only son of working-class Russian-Jewish immigrants, was a navy veteran studying economics and a "fervent Marxist," according to a friend.[13] He had been subpoenaed to appear before the state's Seditious Activities Investigation Commission, which was hunting for Reds at Roosevelt and the University of Chicago. But he ignored the summons, and the commission seems to have forgotten about him. (Asked by a newspaper reporter after a meeting of the Communist Club whether he was a Communist, he said, "You have no right to ask that." And then, "Yes, I am.")[14] Like Lorraine, Elbein advocated for a democratic transition to socialism, not insurrection. Still, he wasn't just a café Communist talking about the means of production to signal that he was in tune with the underclass, either. Marxism, no less than the tenets of the U.S. Constitution, was a theory for building a strong, more equitable nation, in his opinion, and worth fighting for.

In mid-July, Hansberry and Elbein went to a Labor Youth League rally at Washington Park, an event publicized as a "Clarification on the Korean Situation." A few weeks earlier, the UN Security Council had authorized dispatching multinational forces to Korea to counter the Communist invasion from the North. Lorraine was firmly in the peace camp now, opposing war and armaments. The LYL's position was that Americans should refuse induction and not answer "the call of military brass for young killers to slaughter colored Asians."[15] The choice of the word *colored* was intended for the ears of black Americans who were aware of Paul Robeson's remark to a Communist-led convention in Paris: "It is unthinkable that American Negroes would go to war on behalf of those who have oppressed us for generations against the Soviet Union which in one generation has raised our people to the full dignity of mankind."[16]

In August, Mrs. Hansberry gave Lorraine permission to go to New York. What probably persuaded her was that Lorraine had a plan: she would enroll at the New School for Social Research, in Greenwich Village. But her mother would not permit her to take the train alone. Her youngest had never been to New York. They would drive, and Mamie would go along because she was familiar with the city.

This was not the adventure Lorraine had in mind, being chaperoned all the way to New York. She called Kate, who had a boyfriend there. "I'm going to drive. Let's drive." Weiskopf agreed.

Actually, Lorraine scored a double victory, although the second one was a secret. Not only was she extricating herself from her family, but her first poem, "Flag from a Kitchenette Window," would be published in *Masses and Mainstream*, the American Marxist monthly in September.[17] It was a public declaration of being affiliated with the Left. Because her family might be hurt or angry if the Hansberry name were associated with anything communistic, she gave herself a new identity. The author of "Flag from a Kitchenette Window" is "Emily Jones."

The poem's speaker gazes out from a building of the type Hansberry Enterprises might have owned, contemplating an American flag hanging from a window on Memorial Day. The occasion commemorates liberty's defenders, yet twenty million citizens are deprived of their rights.[18]

> *Southside morning*
> *America is crying*
> *In our land: the paycheck taxes to*
> *Somebody's government*
> *Black boy in a window; Algiers and Salerno*
> *The three-colored banner raised to some*
> *Anonymous freedom, we decide*
> *And on the memorial days hang it*
> *From our windows and let it beat the*
> *Steamy jimcrow airs.*

On the appointed morning of the big departure, late in August, Lorraine, Mamie, and their mother pulled up in front of Kate Weiskopf's house. Kate came down the sidewalk carrying her luggage, followed by her mother, who just wanted to say hello to everyone. There was plenty of room for the suitcase in the capacious trunk of the "very large Cadillac," Weiskopf noticed. Then she came around and slid behind the wheel to take her turn sharing the driving. It was 795 miles to their destination. "It was all very exciting," Kate remembered. Farewells were said, and everybody was waving good-bye as Kate eased the eighteen-foot, five-thousand-pound land yacht into the street. She hit the brakes. "I couldn't do it. I was intimidated. I felt like the car was driving me. It was too much. I just couldn't do it. It was terrible. I felt so guilty." A change of drivers was recommended. And with that, the journey continued.

During the trip, Kate had time to get to know Lorraine's sister and mother. Mamie was very beautiful, "a social person, quite a bit different from Lorraine. Lorraine was like her father, and her sister was like their mother." Kate was a little bewildered by Nannie Hansberry. "Very much a lady—reserved, not at all radical, but a little dotty. She kept talking about what it was like when her husband broke the restrictive covenant. She seemed preoccupied with those days."

Roaring along two-lane Lincoln Highway through Indiana and Ohio, they reached Pittsburgh after a day. Fortunately, the car was air-conditioned. About suppertime, a motel advertising "Vacancy" looked like a good candidate for spending the night. Lorraine and Kate went into the office to inquire. "But the desk clerk took one look at us and said, 'No,'" Weiskopf said. They tried another motel down the road. "And that happened over and over again. We could not find a place to stay for the night. And I realized they didn't know who I was. I'm Jewish, so I was used to anti-Semitism. Somebody disliking me for what I am was not entirely unfamiliar to me. But I was black, as far as they were concerned. Two girls come in, black and white, and all they saw was black. Lorraine's mother was tired and getting very, very upset."

Finally, at yet another place whose sign promised vacancies, Mamie instructed everyone to stay in the car while she went in alone. A few minutes later, she opened the car door, smiling. "All set." They unloaded the trunk, and with Mamie leading the way, key in hand, they went down the row of doors until they found their place for the night.

As they were unpacking, Lorraine asked her sister, "What'd you say to the guy?"

Mamie, affecting her best female-in-distress manner, replied in a soft, Southern voice, "Pah-don me, sir, but do you take culluds?"

Lorraine was furious, "You didn't! You *didn't* say that!"

"Sure, I did. What difference does it make? We got the room, didn't we?"[19]

It was a matter of outflanking the whites to get what you wanted. Just as their father had taken possession of the house on Rhodes Avenue at night, and the way Lorraine had landed unannounced in Langdon Manor, Mamie had followed her philosophy that "if you go ahead and do something, and don't meet the opposition—because most white people are only concerned about what other people are going to say—if it's gone smoothly, then that's what's happening." But Lorraine was disgusted. That her sister would perform for the titillation of a desk clerk the "simple, lovable, and glandular Negro" was humiliating—and racist.[20]

The next morning, they set off again, reaching New York City in a few hours. Mrs. Hansberry had reserved a suite at the Waldorf-Astoria, the tallest and most expensive hotel in Manhattan. They pulled up to the hotel's red-canopied Park Avenue entrance, between Forty-Ninth and Fiftieth Streets. A valet took their car keys, and a bellhop hustled to bring in their luggage behind them. At the front desk, Mrs. Hansberry informed the receptionist that there was a reservation under her name, "Mrs. Carl Hansberry." A suite. "He took one look at us," Kate said, "and replied, 'No, it's all gone.'" Lorraine's mother protested—they had a reservation! The receptionist flipped through the pages of his records, scanning all the room numbers. Yes, they did have something available after all.

"And they put us in some crappy place," Kate said. "You know, someplace absolutely all wrong. It was just all wrong. It was terrible."[21]

After that nightmare, and dropping Kate off at her boyfriend's, Mrs. Hansberry and Mamie deposited Lorraine at the Albert Hotel, at 23 East Tenth Street, in Greenwich Village, which was, conveniently, a few blocks from the New School for Social Research. Her mother had given her a list of people to call, in case she needed help. Other than that, she was on her own. When she hewed closely to the Hansberry mode of doing things, that was good; but when she had to have her way, her mother took the attitude that she would simply have to find out for herself.

The Albert is a ponderous-looking, eight-story affair that was built in German Renaissance Revival style at the end of the nineteenth century.

Mark Twain lectured there, and Hart Crane wrote his poem "The Bridge" in one of its rooms. "Meet me in the bar at the Albert Hotel," Jimmy Stewart instructs Raymond Burr in Hitchcock's 1954 thriller *Rear Window*. The chef was a self-declared "genius-in-residence" who had taken over the hotel's French restaurant and changed the cuisine to American fare. "All the steak you can eat for $2.35." The Albert's sidewalk café, next to an eight-foot-tall aluminum model of the Eiffel Tower, was offered to tourists as a spot "where the quaint rubs shoulders with the avant garde . . . where bearded poets still sip wine." The servers wore berets.

Beneath its patina of savoir faire, however, the Albert had become, in fact, a mélange of SRO (single-room occupancy) apartments with meager kitchens and bathrooms down the hall that smelled of disinfectant,[22] a dump that Lorraine couldn't imagine herself living in for long. She wrote a description of where she was, in the third person, as if she weren't really there:

> The Hotel was a dark, musty place. It was old and full of strange old people with staring eyes who appeared and disappeared in doorways and elevators and never spoke. People who seemed frightened of something, nervous of something.
>
> In the nights, she would rise from her bed and go to the windows to listen to their quarreling that echoed in the high, black brick courtyard of the hotel. Sometimes there were other sounds, the quiet and more terrible sounds from the rooms close to her. The hard, frightening laughter of unhappy women at work, the grunts and sighs of matter-of-fact lovemaking. And now and then below, the splash of vomit on concrete, and she imagined somewhere a man leaning feebly against a building in the shadows.
>
> And she would sit thus for hours—feeling great sadness, for all of them—feeling a great wonderment for all of them.

Her stomach began to hurt, the pain brought on usually by stress or loneliness.[23]

With the assistance of the New School's housing office, she found an apartment to share with three other young women: Estelle, Vivian, and Francine. Much to her "total dissatisfaction," it was on the low-rent Lower

East Side, which at one time had been a noisy community of immigrants in tenement buildings. Now it was simply a working-class neighborhood of fish markets and little eateries, where the residents (first-generation Americans, most of them) saved up money until they could go higher on the housing scale. She would have preferred somewhere on a poetic street in the Village.

The apartment, she conceded, was a "modern little four-room job," but there was little privacy for reading or writing. She spent hours away from it, dressed in jeans and a shirt, exploring Midtown, looking at things and writing down her impressions in a pocket-size spiral notebook.[24]

She had already decided she would take courses only in the New School's Advanced Adult Education program, because there were no entrance requirements or exams, and no academic record had to be supplied. Study was self-directed, which was fine with her. Any of fourteen fields could be combined for a diploma. "The mature men and women who come here to study know what they seek. They are responsible only to themselves for the completeness with which they get it. The School does not presume to organize their instruction as the instruction of the young and immature is usually organized."[25] Reinhold Niebuhr would be teaching The Meaning of History; Margaret Mead, Basic Problems in Sociology; Eugene O'Neill Jr., Greek Drama; and Will Maslow (cousin of Abraham Maslow), Current Problems in Race Relations.

From the list of more than a hundred courses, Hansberry chose a salad of offerings: A Beginners' Writing Workshop, Dominant Ideals of Western Civilization, and basic classes in photography and jewelry making.[26] As for introductory courses and examinations—she didn't want to commit to a lot of lectures and coursework; she hadn't come to New York for that. She was there to "pursue an education of another kind," the reason she had left the University of Wisconsin and dropped the German course at Roosevelt College. She had come to live on her own for reasons she could never tell her family. She wanted to reinvent herself in Harlem.

She began taking the subway up to Harlem. A forty-five-minute ride brought her to 125th Street, the chief artery—the "Main Stem," people called it. From there, she could set out in any direction to explore.

Harlem illustrates the great themes in American history of restlessness and replacement. The land was originally inhabited by the Lenape and Weckquaesgeek tribes. Then the Dutch built the town of Haarlem in the early 1600s, named after the city near Amsterdam. The English settlers who came after them farmed the area for two hundred years. During the nineteenth century, the location became a favorite of country squires, who laid out neat roads and estates.

Harlem apartment buildings were originally built for white tenants around 1900. But speculators and developers overestimated. At that time, the subway stopped at 145th Street, and landlords had difficulty renting apartments in the eastern end of Upper Manhattan. They began lowering rents. A black real estate developer, Philip A. Payton, suggested offering apartments to Negroes on 134th Street. Two buildings were filled this way, and soon more. Big private homes were going up between Lenox and Seventh Avenue. By the 1920s, the district was perhaps the only completely cosmopolitan community in the world—black and white, Mexican, European, and African—"another statue of liberty on the landward side of New York," Alain Locke called it. "It stands for a folk movement which can be compared only with the pushing back of the western frontier in the first half of the last century, or the flow of immigration which swept in from overseas in the last half." Harlem, he exulted, "has become none the less the greatest Negro community the world has known—without counterpart either in the South, or in Africa."[27]

The Harlem Renaissance began with a musical comedy in 1921: *Shuffle Along*, a celebration of black life. Prior to its production, black music, blues, and jazz left New York to go on tour. *Shuffle Along* ran for 502 performances on Broadway, and Harlem nightlife flourished. Soon after, the first straight dramas by black playwrights headed for Broadway, too: Willis Richardson's *A Chip Woman's Fortune* and Garland Anderson's *Appearances*.

The cultural ferment in Harlem contributed to the development of negritude in art and literature, an affirmation of African culture and heritage. Shirley Graham's tremendous opera *Tom Tom*, the first commissioned three-act opera by a black female composer, was an epic production. The story spanned the centuries from precolonial West Africa to contemporary Harlem. A baseball stadium in Cleveland became a theater where twenty-five-thousand people saw a performance that featured a chorus of two hundred, a live elephant, and waterfall. A national radio hookup carried the event coast to coast.

Between 1920 and 1930, eighty-seven thousand migrants arrived in Harlem, mainly from the southern United States. "Southern Negroes fled from physical lynchings and West Indians from economic lynchings," observed playwright Lofton Mitchell. "They met in the land north of 110th Street and they brought with them their speech patterns, folkways, mores, and their dogged determination. They brought, too, their religiosity and their gregariousness and they created here a distinct nation that was much like a small town."[28]

But as in Chicago, overcrowding and ghettoization drove up rents in Harlem, stampeding out whites and allowing speculators to purchase their properties cheap and rent them at extortionate rates to black families. After World War II, many middle-class black Harlemites moved to Bedford-Stuyvesant, Brooklyn, and the Bronx; others remained in the Sugar Hill neighborhood where there were stately residences with elevators and doormen. In that enclave, families sent their children to private kindergartens and the Ethical Culture School.[29]

When Lorraine emerged from the A train and stepped onto the platform at 125th Street in September 1950, there were half a million people living in Harlem, about four thousand per block—comparable in concentration to the entire population of the United States living in one half of New York City's five boroughs. She knew as much about Harlem as most Americans. A feature story, "Harlem Gang Leader," had appeared in *Life* magazine in November 1948. With pictures supplied by Gordon Parks, identified as "a young Negro photographer," later one of the originators of blaxploitation films, the ten-page photo essay was a lurid Cook's tour of crime and poverty. "Under the smoke and haze," it begins, "are the crowded tenements and the cluttered dreary streets of Harlem, the US's biggest Negro community." When Parks showed the magazine to Red Jackson, the gang leader profiled in the story, he said, "Damn, Mr. Parks, you made a criminal out of me."[30]

Lorraine remembered feeling "confused and stifled" as she passed soda pop joints, shoeshine parlors, and grocery stores looking for Room to Rent signs. Not only because it was plain that Harlem was "too damn crowded" to readily offer up someplace for a young stranger, but also because of the disparity between her imagined idea of Harlem and the reality of what it was.[31]

She tended to romanticize the poor, observing them in their backyards from a passing elevated train or as they appeared onstage when they knew their lines and when their makeup and costumes were expertly lit. "O'Casey never fools you about the Irish," she insisted. "The Irish drunkard, the Irish braggart, the Irish liar, who is always talking about how he is going to fight the Revolution."[32] From a Marxist point of view, she was guilty of a typically petit bourgeois attitude, of "rotten liberalism," in Soviet parlance, by sentimentalizing the face of class struggle. Yet it was the most direct way of rejecting her family's privileges. She blamed those privileges, at this point in her life, for estranging her from her true heritage.

Perhaps she envied the idea of an existence lived close to the bone because it seemed authentic; there was no place for abstraction. Coming to Harlem, she hoped to identify the source of that spontaneous joy and insouciance that she had envied in her playmates when she was small. Perhaps Harlem was a kind of black Rome of the diaspora, where the full expression of blackness would be all around. She would automatically respond to the vibration in the air, as she had reading poems by Langston Hughes, Claude McKay, and Paul Laurence Dunbar when she was a child. It would just happen.

French novelist and intellectual Simone de Beauvoir had been given a tour of Harlem several years before by Richard Wright. "And on 125th Street," Beauvoir said, "I indeed discover the movie houses, drugstores, stores, bars, and restaurants of Forty-second or Fourteenth Street; but the atmosphere is as different as if I had crossed a chain of mountains or the sea. Suddenly, there's a swarm of black children dressed in bright shirts of red-and-green plaid, students with frizzed hair and brown legs chattering on the sidewalks. Blacks sit daydreaming on the doorsteps, and others stroll with their hands in their pockets. The open faces do not seem fixed on some invisible point in the future but reflect the world as it is given at that moment, under this sky."[33] Harlem was a frame of mind.

Hansberry trudged around until she felt tired. As she walked, Negro and white canvassers sidled up beside her and tried to get her to buy a copy of the *Daily Worker*. "This paper's trying to keep your rent controlled . . .

Make that greedy landlord kill them rats in your apartment. . . . Who do you think fought the hardest to help free those Scottsboro Boys?"[34] She found a diner in which to sit down and took out her spiral notebook.

She had come to Harlem in the spirit of wanting to be with "my people," a term she was beginning to use more frequently, influenced by references to "the people" in Communist circles. But somehow, the desire alone wasn't enough. A young man passed her table, someone she recognized, a weird and prophetic coincidence: Randy—she remembered his name—from the University of Wisconsin, as if giving the lie to the whole idea that she could ever become someone else. Miserably, she wrote in her notebook, "Harlem is cold. Why does Harlem frighten me? (Saddens me I know). But why can it, does it? Frighten me?"[35]

9

Freedom

We will not be satisfied to take one jot or tittle less than our full man-hood rights. We claim for ourselves every single right that belongs to a free-born American, political, civil, and social; and until we get these rights we will never cease to protest and assail the ears of America. The battle we wage is not for ourselves, alone, but for all true Americans.

—W. E. B. Du Bois, *The Souls of Black Folk*

Estelle, Vivian, and Francine (last names unknown), the three women sharing the apartment with Lorraine on the Lower East Side, thought of themselves as progressive. Sometimes, however, incorrect positions taken about housework, groceries, and rent resulted in some frostiness among the roommates. Francine later apologized to Lorraine. "Our apartment in 418, which could have been a jewel in the progressive movement, ended up in an ugly morass because of continued acts of chauvinism on the part of Viv and myself. This, of course, you and Estelle fought bitterly and hard over a long period of time to point out, despite the white chauvinist resistance."[1]

Lorraine seems not to have let Francine's self-admitted "rotten bour-geois ideology" bother her much. She was out of the apartment practically every day. In October, it still felt like summer.

During her hours out and about, she tried seeing things through the eyes of a revolutionary. She despised a "slim woman in a perfect black coat with a bright silk red lining" coming out of Rockefeller Center. "[S]he had blonde hair—pulled back in a perfect bun and perfect white teeth and her head was thrown back in laughter." She felt proprietary about Harlem, wishing that whites would stay away. "And I'm tired—tired of going into the Theresa [Hotel] and Frank's [Restaurant] and seeing them, the white ones, either looking condescending or tolerant as if this is the only decent place in Harlem."[2] The new Lorraine Hansberry was a zealot.

This phase didn't last long. After meeting a leading black Communist, Claudia Jones, she set her sights on bigger things: effecting change instead of talking about it. Jones, who was "tall, elegant, brilliant, and Trinidadian," in the words of her biographer Carole Boyce Davies, was on the lookout for black female protégées who could be trained for leadership.[3]

Claudia Jones, born Claudia Cumberbatch in 1915 in Port-of-Spain, Trinidad, was an official of the Communist Party. "Jones" was an alias to throw off the authorities.

When she was eight, she immigrated to the United States with her parents, three sisters, and an aunt. They lived in a Harlem slum. Five years later, her mother died of spinal meningitis while bent over her sewing machine in a garment shop, exploited to death, Jones said. "I was later to learn that this was not just an individual matter, but that millions of working-class people and Negro people suffered this lot under capitalism—if not identical, in one degree or another."[4] Not long after her mother's death, Jones was hospitalized for a year with tuberculosis, probably because her bedroom was constantly damp from backed-up sewer water.

Her first job after high school was in a laundry, where the women fainted from the summer heat and long hours. The next job, working in a nail factory, was tedious and low-paying. She quit and found a position as a salesperson in a Harlem millinery store. In 1936, she joined the Communist Party and began writing for the *Daily Worker* about, among other things, racial capitalism—the practice of exploiting people of color to get value from them. She was twenty-one then and applied to become a naturalized citizen, but was denied, probably due to J. Edgar Hoover's influence. As a resident alien, she would remain a "deportable subject" under the 1918 Immigration Act, used for getting rid of undesirables and foreign radicals. In 1948, she was arrested under the act and kept in jail on Ellis

Island for a night, then released on bail because the government requested more time to prepare for her deportation hearing.

When Lorraine met her in the fall of 1950 through Leon Wofsy and the Labor Youth League, Jones was the editor of the women's page in the *Daily Worker* and the secretary of the Communist Party's Congress of American Women. In her appearance, she made a point of playing against stereotypes of Reds. If the media expected to see a Communist firebrand, some kind of subversive harridan, what they got instead was an attractive, British-accented woman who spoke like a college instructor. Even when she led protest marches with hundreds in step behind her, she appeared smiling and well put together: purse, coat, heels, and occasionally gloves. It was disarming.

She revamped the *Daily Worker*'s women's page, scrapping the mast-head (a silhouette of a woman in high heels feather dusting) and replacing it with two women's faces smiling, one white and one black. Out went the dress patterns and household hints, too. Instead, there were articles about women's history and profiles of women activists. Jones editorialized about male supremacist practices, such as referring to adult women as "girls" and belittling women's skills.[5] From her post on the Congress of American Women, she urged the party to take a stronger stand on championing black women's rights in industry, because the "capitalists know, far better than many progressives seem to know, that once Negro women undertake action, the militancy of the whole Negro people, and thus of the anti-imperialist coalition, is greatly enhanced."[6]

Although Lorraine probably didn't realize it, she was just the kind of young woman Jones was looking for. She came from an upper-middle-class background and was college educated, interested in Marxism, and seeking to connect with Communists.[7] The party leadership directed officials like Jones to unite all progressives into a national peace front against nuclear weapons that would defeat American conservatives.[8] The heart of this strategy was strengthening the resolve of the progressive bourgeoisie.

Whether Hansberry could be schooled to become a committed member of the party remained to be seen.

Not long after the start of their friendship, Lorraine wrote two or three pages of a story about two characters, Claudia and Sydney; the latter was a

"Negro woman twenty years old"—herself, in other words. This may be her first piece of lesbian-themed fiction, a projection perhaps of what she'd like to happen. Her handwriting looks rushed, and the voice is full of feeling.[9]

> For blocks there were the outdoor fish markets on 1st Avenue and Claudia would take Sydney by the hand and pull her through the shopping people, speaking Italian and Polish and Jewish—. . . . There had been the raucous, challenging spirited meeting at the Garden and the others had waited for Claudia to lead them to a party—But instead she had taken Sydney's hand and they slipped out into the crowds to a fire escape Claudia had found and then they were free in the splendidness of New York at night. They walked together, silent and holding hands—young Communists—they were together—and Sydney could feel it in the other one—she *was* lonely.

It's certainly unlike anything Lorraine submitted to the Beginning Writer's Workshop at the New School. For that, she produced typed, double-spaced, correctly formatted stories that didn't take emotional risks. There was a satirical one about six college girls, for example, in a setting that sounds like Langdon Manor, which included a character named "Gertrude Merchan Lee, the drama major from Atlanta, Georgia, who looked like she weighed an awful lot and spoke with a broad A and said there were some things about the South, she just couldn't stand, really."[10]

The difference in tone and energy must have come from feeling that she was on the cusp of something new and revolutionary; perhaps she felt empowered to throw bourgeois morality to the wind. And that sense of feeling pleased with herself is what comes through in her giddy description of Claudia and Sydney, hand in hand in "splendidness."

Within a few years, Hansberry would be able to write, "The company of women is intellectually as well as emotionally more preferable than that of men."[11] It could be that Jones was a sort of bridge relationship, a way for Lorraine to see if it was safe to proceed.

In October, probably through Jones or someone in her circle, Lorraine heard about an opening at a new monthly newspaper called *Freedom*, funded by Paul Robeson. She had been attending classes at the New School for, as she put it, "about two erratic months," and looking for a way to live in New York permanently.[12] A job would be the answer and would free her from being completely dependent on her mother.

The address she was given was 53 West 125th Street. Climbing the stairs, she found that *Freedom* operated out of "a somewhat bare and harrowed Harlem office overlooking Lenox Avenue." In adjoining rooms were three other organizations: the Civil Rights Congress, the National Negro Labor Council, and the Council on African Affairs—all Communist-affiliated. *Freedom* consisted of two desks, one typewriter, and a "remarkably enthusiastic working staff of two": the office manager, Edith Roberts, and the editor, Louis E. Burnham, a man with a large black moustache.[13] The newspaper had yet to publish a single issue.

Burnham was born in Barbados in 1915 and raised in Harlem. He had studied social science at the City College of New York, where the students (first-generation Jewish Americans, many of them) argued like it was a sport. According to a friend, Burnham developed a consistent source of income by doing papers for classmates. "I would often find him pounding away at the typewriter. He'd ask me if I could wait a few minutes until he finished a few pages of a thirty-page paper. Out of curiosity, I would ask him what he was working on, and he would say nonchalantly, 'Oh, this is a paper on the economics of the period of Henry VIII in England,' or 'This is an analysis of the political role of small farmers and small businessmen during the period of Jacksonian democracy.'"[14] After World War II, Burnham and his wife, Dorothy, went south and became organizers in Birmingham, Alabama, for the Southern Negro Youth Congress, headquartered in Richmond, Virginia. They organized sit-ins, sharecropper protests, and voter registration drives. But harassment and physical attacks, sanctioned by police commissioner Eugene "Bull" Connor, had forced them to shut down the Birmingham branch and return to New York.

Burnham's voice, Hansberry said, "was very deep and his language struck my senses immediately, with its profound literacy, constantly punctuated by deliberate and loving poetic lapses into the beloved color of the speech of the masses of our people." He was a storyteller, and sometimes, in the middle of a tale, "he just opened his mouth and howled for the joy of it."[15] His warmth won her over, and she opened up to him. Perhaps this was the first opportunity since her father's death to talk to someone who, although not old enough to be her father, was fatherly. She was feeling uncertain about the future. "I told him about the novel I had wanted to write when I was eighteen. I told him how I was desperately worried about having become too jaded, at twenty, to retain all the lovely things I had wanted to say in my novel when I was eighteen."

Behind him was a curving window that "allowed one," she said, "to see a lot of Harlem at one time." He swiveled in his chair so he could watch the scene outside while he listened to her talk. "It was part of his genius as a human being that he did not laugh at all or patronize my dilemma, but went on to gently and seriously prod me to consider the possibilities of the remaining time of my life."[16] *Freedom*, he said, would be about justice: challenging racism, imperialism, colonialism, and political repression and advocating for civil rights, labor rights, and world peace.

She was offered a job and accepted it. Beginning November 1, in time for the first issue, she would be *Freedom*'s subscription clerk, receptionist, typist, and editorial assistant, at $31.70 a week. By then, she was going up and down sidewalks in Harlem distributing a handmade flyer: *The Negro People Are a Great People. They Need a Great Newspaper. Read Freedom, Paul Robeson's Newspaper.*[17] Its motto in the masthead would be "Where one is enslaved, all are in chains."

The little building on 125th Street was an intellectual and creative hothouse to work in. Some mornings, Lorraine had to weave between the small crowd blocking the front door because Robeson, six feet, three inches tall, was like a Gulliver in the middle of the children and well-wishers wishing to shake his hand or get his autograph.[18]

Paul Robeson was one of the most famous people alive in 1950. A two-time All-American college football player and the valedictorian at Rutgers University, he had graduated from Columbia Law School in 1923. He quit practicing law after only a year because his firm failed to protect him from racism: white clients refused to be represented by him. His singing career began in nightclubs in black communities. His deep, thunderous voice and charismatic presence enraptured audiences. His concert repertoire included Negro spirituals, favorite standards, folk songs, and classical arrangements. He was praised internationally; his abilities as an actor brought him even more acclaim. His finest performance was as Othello on Broadway during the 1943–44 season.

To the consternation of many Americans, however, Robeson considered the Soviet Union his "second motherland" because, he said, it was free from class hatred and racial animosity and because it was waging an international struggle in "every arena of world conflict for genuine democracy and for peace."[19] When he arrived there on an invitation from the Kremlin in 1934, he was treated like a hero. "Here, I am not a Negro but a human being for the first time in my life," he told reporters. "I walk in full human dignity." His performances were interspersed with praise for the Soviet Union, much to the impatience of audiences and the consternation of black activists. "As far as I can see," Bayard Rustin wrote to a friend in 1947, "he [Robeson] has done a very damaging job in the field of race relations in the past two years." Robeson knew of Stalin's purges and that the great experiment in a classless society had gone terribly wrong.[20] But he could not be persuaded to change his mind. Stalin, he said, "was clearly a man who seemed to embrace all. So kindly—I can never forget that warm feeling of kindliness and also a feeling of sureness. Here was one who was wise and good—the world and especially the socialist world was fortunate indeed to have his daily guidance."[21]

The summer Lorraine arrived in New York, the State Department had suspended Robeson's passport because he had refused to sign an affidavit declaring that he was not a member of the Communist Party and was loyal to the United States. U.S. Border Patrol agents had been instructed to seize him by any means necessary to prevent him from leaving the United States. He filed suit in federal court against the secretary of state, John Foster Dulles, over the passport issue. Unable to travel abroad, he launched *Freedom* as his bully pulpit. It would become nothing less, he said, than "the real voice of the oppressed masses of the Negro people and a true weapon for all progressive Americans."[22]

In the web of offices that *Freedom* shared with the Civil Rights Congress, the National Negro Labor Council, and the Council on African Affairs, ideas and viewpoints cross-pollinated, creating the aura of an ongoing salon. Robeson's wife, Eslanda, encouraged writers, actors, and playwrights to stop by the office. Sometimes egos collided. Theater director Julian Mayfield recalled having "furious exchange of ideas" with people who were "deeply and angrily and sometimes violently concerned about the issues of the day and the world."[23]

Robeson wanted that kind of fire in the air. He escorted visitors from all over the country and other parts of the world through the narrow rooms. Occasionally, he would stop to talk about the struggles of black people, not only in the United States but also in colonial Africa. He was an evangelist for black liberation everywhere. A visitor saw Robeson having an animated discussion, "talkin' and signifyin'" with Burnham and George B. Murphy, editor of the *Washington Afro-American*. Burnham was responding to Robeson's passion by "exploding every now and then with a characteristic, 'Amen, Amen!'" At her desk was Hansberry, "whose lovely brown face was illuminated with a serenity which seemed curiously out of place in a loft on 125th Street."[24]

Lorraine was in her element. She enjoyed a good tournament of ideas. The friction of disagreement rubbed away what was unclear and exposed something that was shiny and true underneath. Having an informed point of view gave her a greater sense of agency; her beliefs began to align with the kind of person she intended to be. Many mornings, she wore a favorite piece of jewelry to work: an African-looking silver medallion on a chain. It was her talisman, her expression of solidarity with her people, just as her pretend latchkey in grade school had once been. Feeling in the mood to crow a bit, she wrote to Edythe:[25]

I do reflect quite often on the wild miscalculations of the Langdon Manor discussions. How far-fetched we all were, the sophisticated and the naïve alike. . . . We used to, all of us chide the hearty leftist amongst us for so carelessly referring to their beloved phrase for the enemy: *fascist*. But dear friend, both of us in whatever our present day thinking must admit, in our America today we can in truth, smell it in the air . . . and how foul it is. Certainly I feel closer to what is happening than you perhaps yet feel. It is true I know many of those who have already been lapped up by this new Reich terror, know about the arrests in the early morning, the shifty eyed ones, who follow, follow, follow . . . and know the people who are the victims: the quiet and the courageous. . . . I am sick of poverty, lynching, stupid wars and the universal maltreatment of my people and obsessed with a rather desperate desire for a new world for me and my brothers. So dear friend, I must perhaps go to jail. Please at the next red-baiting session you hear . . . remember this "Communist!"

Yet, despite that constant talk of liberation and equality, the atmosphere in the office was heavily male and chauvinist, which she doesn't seem to have remarked on. Hansberry "was always trying to think things through," said Julian Mayfield, and thinking things through was considered, by most men, a "distinctly unsweet and unfemale virtue." Because she "looked like a coed" and was given to fits of laughter, the men weren't sure whether she was an intellectual or a Gal Friday who typed speeches for Robeson. They wanted to label her. "She could be so serious and to the point," said Mayfield, "that her enemies would want to give her a sock on the jaw and say 'Shut up, girl, we men are talking about serious things now.'" Novelist Sarah Elizabeth Wright, a member of the Harlem Writers Guild along with Lorraine, said it was as if "a virtual wilderness of the human mind" existed among most black men. They couldn't accept or respect women as thoughtful individuals or as capable of producing "significant and humanly meaningful work."[26]

Lorraine slimmed down, which she attributed, tongue in cheek, to how little she was paid. She took more care about her appearance and stopped "whacking off" her hair. Her face cleared up, as if adolescence were at last behind her. In her spare time, she saw foreign movies but not often plays. She attended meetings almost every night, sampled exotic food, sang in the Harlem Youth Chorus, ushered at rallies, and would go "for long walks in Harlem and talk to my people about everything on the streets."[27] She was at last catching the ineffable spirit of something that had eluded her. "Sometimes in this country maybe just walking down a Southside street, or maybe suddenly up in a Harlem window, or maybe in a flash turning the page of one of those picture books from the South you'll see it—beauty . . . stark and full . . . No part of something like this—but rather, Africa, simply Africa."[28]

Movies with racial themes interested her, and there was a raft of them suddenly: *Intruder in the Dust* (1949), *Home of the Brave* (1949), *Pinky* (1949), *Lost Boundaries* (1949), and *No Way Out* (1950). Victory over fascism during the war had forged a liberal consensus that America was an exceptional society rooted in class harmony, democratic capitalism, individualism, and abundance. Segregation, interracial dating, and biracialism were regarded as problems that Americans were equal to solving. When Walter White, president of the NAACP, saw *Lost Boundaries*, the story of a black family passing for white in New England, he confessed to being profoundly moved. "One thing is certain, Hollywood can never go back to its old portrayal of colored people as witless menials or idiotic buffoons now that *Home of the Brave* and *Lost Boundaries* have been made."[29]

Lorraine, for her part, saw other subtexts in the "race problem" films she watched. It seemed to her that the importance of *Home of the Brave*, in which a black soldier fears that he will forever be an outsider, was that "Hollywood has felt the pressure of the insistent demands of the Negro people for honest representation," an interesting remark given that, as she knew, in the play *Home of the Brave*, the protagonist is Jewish. She dismissed *Pinky*, about a biracial young woman, as an example of "Hollywood's absurd preoccupation with the 'passing' theme—certainly mighty low in importance among the Negro people themselves. . . . For the Negro audiences are, after all, the real critics and experts on the question." She concludes that moviemaking is simply "big business," which it was. Hollywood studios didn't consider black Americans a large enough audience to cater to; it was white audiences they were after. But Hansberry tended to judge something by whether it was good, or right, or moral. Gray areas and abstractions frustrated her; worthwhile purposes should have an end in sight. The demands of the free market, to her mind, should be secondary. That Hollywood would make films for the majority of moviegoers struck her as just typical of "America's major big profit industries."[30]

She was in a good place in her head and in her heart. Coming home on winter nights to the Lower East Side apartment she shared with Estelle, Vivian, and Francine, she would "look for the splinter of light way up there on the 4th floor." And if she saw it, she would walk a little faster, chin lifted because "now was the hour for friendship." She vowed to herself that she would remember being young. "I will remember being excited and realizing the future is mine to do whatever I choose."[31]

10

"A Young Harriet Tubman"

The most striking thing about Lorraine, even at that early age, was her combination of steel will and brilliant intellect. Her demeanor bordered upon arrogance—not the arrogance born of an egotistical temperament, but of one who did not suffer fools lightly or countenance intellectual sloppiness. Yes, her sarcasm could be withering. This formidability was mitigated by an ardent idealism and near romantic sensibility.

—Douglas Turner Ward, "Lorraine Hansberry and the Passion
of Walter Lee," *Freedomways*

Roosevelt Jackson was handsome and charming, said his roommate, Douglas Turner Ward. They lived together in an apartment in Harlem at 680 Saint Nicholas Avenue. "Rosie was a very slick dude," said Ward, "there was a hustler in him. I'm not saying he was insincere. When he got up on the ladder to speak, he meant what he said, but it was all part of a persona."

They were members of the Harlem LYL, and Rosie was a good speaker. He was in his early twenties and a forceful person. Before he became politicized, according to Ward, he had been a gang leader in Harlem.[1]

When he spoke, it was in front of the thirteen-story Hotel Theresa, at 125th Street and Seventh Avenue, the "Waldorf of Harlem." For at least a generation, the intersection had been to Harlem what the Bug Club had been to the South Side of Chicago: a place to preach, persuade, admonish, and inspire. "Hot boiling rhetoric," said actor and activist Ossie Davis, "all meant to free the lazy black man and set him in motion."[2] Across the street from the hotel was the National Memorial African Bookstore, with a sign over the door that read, "Knowledge Is Power; You Need It Every Hour. Read a Book." On Sundays, some people went to listen to the speakers instead of going to church. There were benches to sit on and plenty of room on the sidewalk to listen to what was being delivered. Novelist John O. Killens called it "the University of the Streets."[3]

When Rosie climbed the stepladder to speak, his subject was socialism and how white-controlled capitalism was a trap. Lorraine might have been remembering his style of delivery when she wrote a scene, later omitted, for the film version of *A Raisin in the Sun*, in which a street speaker says:[4]

Well, my brothers, it is time to ask ourselves what the black man is asking himself everywhere in this world today. . . . Everywhere on the African continent today the black man is standing up and telling the white man that there is someplace for him to go . . . back to that small, cold continent where he came from—Europe! . . . How long before this mood of black men everywhere else in the world touches us here? How long! How much has to happen before the black man in the United States is going to understand that God helps those who help themselves? . . . What is the difference, my friends—between the black man here and every other man in the world? It's what every one of you knows. . . . We are the only people in the world who are completely dis-inherited! . . . We are the only people in the world who own nothing, who make nothing! I ask you, my friends, where are your factories? . . . Where are your textile or steel mills? Heh? Where are your mighty houses of finance? . . . Answer me, my brothers—Where are they?

While Jackson was speaking, Ward, the director of the Harlem chapter of the LYL, handed out pamphlets urging people to attend political rallies and meetings. Hansberry was also there many times, distributing subscription blanks for *Freedom*.

Ward developed an affection for her. They were the same age, and both had become "radicalized" (his word) in college by campaigning for Wallace and the Progressives. They held the same political ideology and were involved in the same radical movements. He had written a half-hour play about slave rebellion leader Nat Turner, called *Star of Liberty*—"just to lighten up the heavy political raps"—performed at a rally before about five hundred people, and it was well received, the beginning of his writing for the theater. Perhaps Lorraine saw this.

But Lorraine wasn't romantically interested in Ward; she fell for Roosevelt Jackson. Ward thought that she was attracted to him because Jackson was "a Harlem street dude" and "the epitome of the working class for her."[5] He was the kind of person, Lorraine said, who would stand up in church to talk about housing conditions, or the cost of living, or to protest the latest lynching. "And wise old ladies" in starched dresses would listen to him, she noticed. When he wasn't speaking to crowds, he sold the *Daily Worker*, canvassed for political candidates, collected money for causes, and helped evicted people carry their furniture back into their homes. Lorraine thought he had an inborn nobility about him.[6]

> I would dream of draping you in our robes
> Put an ancient chant upon your lips,
> It is that so much—without being so—
> You are so very much *us*
> And that is why I love you.

Lorraine and Rosie became engaged in July 1951. She wrote to Edythe and shared the big news. "Supposed to get married in September. Spirit: Happy and defiant."

"But Rosie," said Ward, "was too much of a hustler to love anybody."[7]

The month Lorraine became engaged, Ward was arrested on the street by federal marshals. He had registered with the Selective Service when he turned twenty-one, as required by law, but his draft board hadn't received replies to the induction notices they had sent him. After he was arrested, a fundraiser was held for his legal expenses. Claudia Jones and Leon Wofsy spoke in his defense, charging the government with political persecution because Ward had been outspoken about his opposition to the Korean War.

July also happened to be the month Hansberry published "Lynchsong," in *Masses and Mainstream*, a poem about the execution of Willie McGee, accused of raping a white woman, Willette Hawkins, in Laurel, Mississippi. Hawkins claimed that McGee had broken into her home and raped her while her husband was asleep in the next room. The black community was aware that Hawkins had been sleeping with McGee for years. "People who don't know the South don't know what would have happened to Willie if he told her no," McGee's wife said.[8] The trial took a few hours on an afternoon, and the jury deliberated only two and a half minutes before sentencing McGee to death. McGee's trial, the lack of due process, and his death provoked worldwide condemnation.

In September, Louis Burnham assigned Hansberry her first story for *Freedom*: attending the trial of her friend Douglas Ward at the Federal Courthouse in New York's Foley Square. Taking her seat in the courtroom, she found her eyes drawn to the American flag. "In the corner undisturbed stands the flag. The American flag. I study this flag created by men in open rebellion against the tyranny of King George III—I wonder if these men ever notice that flag in this room."[9]

While on the witness stand, Ward was asked by his attorney, by way of background, about the kinds of work the Labor Youth League was involved in. He replied that it had supported the Martinsville Seven, young men who were all between the ages of eighteen and twenty, except one, accused of raping a white woman. They were found guilty and executed, the largest reported mass execution for rape in the United States. Lorraine was taking notes. "He starts to speak of the last hours about the last of the victims, when there is an objection. That word must not be mentioned here, not 'victim.' This must not be a court of propaganda. There mustn't be none of those tales of legal lynching and all that. No, this must be a strictly factual procedure. My mind runs to the word factual. Are the seven workers of Martinsville not dead? What facts does he have in mind?"[10]

Ward was found guilty of draft evasion and sentenced to three years in the Louisiana State Penitentiary. His attorney, John Coe, who had represented Willie McGee, wrote to William Patterson, head of the Communist Party's International Labor Defense, that the jurors must have lied when they were selected, "because no sane jury could have brought this verdict." By comparison, a white musician, Dick Contino had fled the day before he was scheduled to be inducted and was sentenced to only six months in jail.

Lorraine mused in an unpublished poem titled "News Item" about Ward going to the penitentiary, "Three years . . . that's a long time . . . for a guy / For any one . . . but especially a guy / '21.'"[11]

Ward was led in handcuffs through the Pennsylvania Station train terminal by four federal marshals. An elderly black woman confronted them and demanded, "Where are you taking that man?" She was told to mind her own business.

Lorraine continued seeing Rosie, but they didn't marry in September, as she had told Edythe they would, probably because a visit they made to Lorraine's home was a fiasco.[12] By bringing home a Harlemite turned rabble-rouser, Lorraine wanted her family to understand how much she had changed. Not a lot is known about what transpired, except that Mamie remembered, "When Mother heard that Lorraine was moving evicted families' furniture back into their apartments to protest unfair rental rates, I thought she would have a fit."[13] Mrs. Hansberry wanted Lorraine to get married and settle down. But after sizing up Rosie and hearing the tales of what her daughter was doing in Harlem, she regretted consenting to Lorraine's New York adventure.

Rosie, for his part, "fell in love with the Hansberrys," Ward heard later, and was fascinated by the way they lived—the cars, the house, the family business, all of it. "He almost had a romantic notion of the black bourgeoisie. So he was sort of attracted to their position as well-to-do blacks."[14] But he and Lorraine postponed the wedding.

Meanwhile, at *Freedom*, Burnham promoted Hansberry to associate editor. Until then, her bursts of poetry, fiction, and campus journalism had been part of a leisurely output. But her pen responded well to the discipline of producing on deadline, and she began contributing articles of advocacy journalism—feature stories with an editorial slant. After Ward's trial, she traveled to Washington with the "Sojourners for Truth and Justice," a group of 132 black women—"wives, mothers and victims of race hatred." They listened to a speech at a Washington church by legendary civil rights and suffrage activist Mary Church Terrell, then in her nineties. Two spaces in the front pew were left symbolically vacant: one for Claudia Jones, who was still in prison awaiting a deportation hearing, and one for Rosa Ingram, jailed in Georgia for killing a white man who tried to rape her. Next, they went to the Justice Department, to the office of the Civil Rights Division, where a "single white government official stood at first with his arms folded in cold arrogance," Hansberry reported, "as if he had come to watch a show." He listened to their statement. "Our men are lynched, beaten, shot, deprived of jobs, and top of it all, forced to become part of a Jim Crow army and go thousands of miles to Korea to carry war to other colored peoples." One woman wanted to know why a Confederate flag was displayed in Union Station. There was no answer.[15] They made an appointment to see the attorney general.

Their last stop was the home of Frederick Douglass, to listen to concluding remarks. They went by taxis, dozens of them. The drivers were black and didn't charge when they learned the women's reason for coming to the capital. On the way, Lorraine remarked on how exciting it was to make this kind of pilgrimage to the home of one of the "greatest of all Americans." Someone asked if she thought "Mr. Douglass," who had died in 1895, would be home. The woman was sincere, and Hansberry was struck by what it portended for someone like her, who wanted to be a socially conscious writer. "The work of the Negro artist is cut out for him: the vast task of cultural and historical reclamation—to reclaim the past if we would claim the future."[16]

Her work as a reporter for *Freedom* increased her understanding of systemic injustice in American society. After she read that a third of Harlem students were three years behind their academic grade level, she visited Public School 157 in her capacity as a reporter for *Freedom*. The classrooms were overcrowded. Recess was on an asphalted, sunless playground, and lunch was served in a large, cheerless basement. Even though the children were still small, already they were being taught vocational education, instead of learning liberal arts. This, in addition to everything else about the school, she wrote, contributed to children's low self-image. "No skill, no job, bad schools, inadequate recreational facilities, no future (unless atomic war can be called a 'future')—these are among the causes of the disturbing youth crime and delinquency rates which the sensational documentation of the commercial press omits."[17] The same observation about segregation's psychological harm would be made four years later, in *Brown v. Board of Education of Topeka*.

Hansberry applied Marxist utilitarianism to the problems she wrote about, weighing issues in socioeconomic terms about what benefited society and what didn't. Sometimes the effort to be consistent impaired her critical sense when it came to the arts. She was offended by Richard Wright's just-published novel, *The Outsider*. Damon Cross, the protagonist, is psychologically trapped in an existential nightmare of his life as a black man in the United States, and Hansberry castigated Wright, a former Communist living in self-exile in France, for abandoning social realism. In his earlier novels, she wrote, *Black Boy* and *Native Son*, "he had the ability to scoop out the filth and sickness of white supremacy and present it to his readers with a stark and terrible realism." But *The Outsider* "is a story of sheer violence, death and disgusting spectacle written by a man who has seemingly come to despise humanity. . . . He exalts brutality and nothingness. He negates the reality of our struggle for freedom and yet worked energetically on behalf of our oppressors." Instead of focusing on what Wright was trying to accomplish in the novel, she was distressed about the effect she believed the story would have on readers, insisting that Wright had deviated from "literature's social accountability and ethical obligations."[18] Black writers should task themselves with illuminating the way forward, she believed, not flounder in existentialism.

Her writing began sounding doctrinaire. She was becoming "obsessed with a rather desperate desire for a new world for me and my brothers."[19] She chastised in stern language the motives of capitalists, reactionaries, colonialist powers, and indifferent whites. Her moral outrage injected iron into her articles for *Freedom*, making them taut and heated. She was appalled, for instance, that two radio shows caricaturing Negroes from the 1930s, *Beulah* and *Amos 'n' Andy*, had transitioned seamlessly to television, the modern hallmark of postwar middle-class living; and, although only twenty years old, she protested this with a pen dipped in fire. "For years Negroes have been subjected to the shrill or lazy yuk-yuking dialect voices of the radio stereotypes," she reminded the readers of *Freedom*. "These 'characters' are intended to give the nation and the world a distorted and degrading image of the American Negro. . . . The vicious impression of Negroes the TV and radio moguls strive to create and maintain before the people is no accident. The longer the concept of the half-idiot subhuman can be kept up, the easier to justify the economic and other kind of discrimination, so rampant in this country."[20]

Killens noticed her becoming "a one-woman literary warrior for change" and a "Pan-Africanist with a socialist perspective."[21] She took to ascending the stepladder at 125th Street herself and speaking to crowds, a friend said, "with the fierceness of a young Harriet Tubman."[22]

She was late, however, coming to communism, and the day for American communism was nearly over. Her politics were better suited to the "vanished world of the thirties," remarked Harold Cruse, author of *The Crisis of the Negro Intellectual*, who tried to contribute to *Freedom*, but found the staff resistant to his ideas. "Nothing unsettled them and made them bristle self-righteously more than a threat of criticism."[23] If so, it was because they were sensible of falling back in retreat and fighting a rearguard action.

Enthusiasm for communism and socialism had peaked during the Great Depression, when capitalism had collapsed. In those days, there was a passion for reform, which the New Deal had co-opted, stealing the radicals' thunder. Many of Roosevelt's policies had become widely accepted: public work projects, financial reforms, increased worker protections. Black workers in industry, once willing to listen to Communist organizers' talk of unfair practices, couldn't be induced to strike when they had jobs that paid middle-class wages.

And yet, racism remained ubiquitous in American life, which seemed to repudiate the Communist argument that once wealth and material goods were redistributed equitably, racial equality would result. But it didn't work that way, not in the United States. The proletariat was not one giant, undifferentiated mass of workers, like the sloganeering figures on Soviet agitprop posters, proclaiming, "Listen, Country! The Dream of the People Is Calling!" American workers didn't rise together as a class. True, living standards were far higher after the war—almost all adult Americans were generally better off than they had been in the 1930s—but the South was still segregated, "race mixing" was illegal in most states, and racism was routine. The American Communist leadership was trying to reaffirm the party's interest in "the Negro Question" by championing Negroes' right to self-determination, but it was too late by the 1950s. Black leaders on the Left were suspicious of continued involvement by white organizers in black self-determination, having seen the way the Communist-led Popular Front of the Great Depression had petered out after prosperity returned and racism had persisted. Whites' "help" hadn't seemed to make much of a difference.

The final blow to American communism came from U.S. tensions with the Soviet Union. Criticisms of the United States' values and history, real or imagined, came off as disloyal. McCarthyism was making any association with the Reds, no matter how long ago, a serious liability. Almost all middle-class black Americans were becoming anticommunist for the sake of their careers. The NAACP's magazine, *The Crisis*, began attacking its former editor, W. E. B. Du Bois, and Paul Robeson, as troublemakers who endangered the organization's financial support.[24]

There was a sense of the old order being cleared away and of a third way opening up. Playwright Julian Mayfield remembered, "[W]e were beginning to talk about power and to feel the first stirrings of Black Nationalism as we understand it today. We were beginning to question the solidarity of our alliances with our white allies, and I remember distinctly that we bitterly resented that black people were placed second on the Progressive Party tickets."[25]

Black Power as a movement was more than a decade away, but in the early 1950s, there were already over twenty nationalist organizations in New York City, including the Muslim Brotherhood, the African Nationalist Pioneer Movement, the United African Nationalist Movement, and the Universal African Nationalist Movement. From this uprising in consciousness about identity would come Malcolm X.

Hansberry, young, idealistic, was one of those referred to by John O. Killens as "long distance runners." She had received the baton from the past of the 1930s and was carrying it along, straining to hand it forward.[26]

In the fall of 1951, Lorraine went as a reporter to a demonstration at New York University in Greenwich Village, thinking she might find a story for *Freedom*. A group of students was picketing in Washington Square to protest how blacks were excluded from the university's basketball team. There was a "gentlemen's agreement" among many schools in college athletics (from Harvard to Rutgers to the University of Michigan) not to have integrated teams because the southern schools they played in competition had requested it. Some colleges with Negro players left them behind on southern road trips, as a way of being gracious to their hosts.[27]

Lorraine approached a pair on the picket line for an interview: Robert Nemiroff and his wife, Elma Lopez. They were outgoing, so perhaps she felt comfortable speaking to them. Also, interracial couples were uncommon, and she might have wanted to meet them out of curiosity.

Bob Nemiroff, the son of Russian-Jewish immigrants, was a graduate student in English and only six months older than Lorraine. He was also a fellow traveler—he may not have been a member of the Communist Party, but his parents were. For many years, his mother had been a garment worker on the Lower East Side. During the Depression, his father was unemployed until the family managed to get into the restaurant business. They owned, in partnership with Bob's brother, Leo, the Russian Skazka ("Story"), a cellar café on West Forty-Sixth Street, near Times Square, frequented by Soviet diplomats and American Communist Party comrades for its ethnic food and "all Muscovite" floor show. Red Army musicians had performed there during the war to raise money for Russian War Relief.

The Nemiroffs had a gift for self-promotion and reading the public taste. The Russian Skazka did well. But then, with federal scrutiny of immigrants with Communist ties increasing—the FBI characterized the Nemiroffs' mother as a "fanatical Communist"—the family had recently renamed their restaurant "the Habibi Café" and switched the menu and entertainment to native Israeli.[28] "A sign of the times," commented a dining reviewer.

By coincidence, Kate Weiskopf had known Bob Nemiroff when they were both counselors at Camp Woodland, an interracial camp in the Catskills. Children there learned folklore, ethnic folk dances, and Negro spirituals, led in singing sometimes by Pete Seeger. Weiskopf knew Bob to be a "nice guy," not very mature, with a knack for organizing things.[29] At NYU, he was a member of the NAACP and had been a delegate to the Communist-sponsored first World Festival of Youth and Students, in Prague, Czechoslovakia. His wife, Elma Lopez, was a dancer and had been raised in a large Puerto Rican family. She was petite, twenty-one, and resembled Eartha Kitt, a fellow performer in Katherine Dunham's dance troupe.

Interracial romances were new territory for party members in a nation where miscegenation was illegal in twenty states and public disapproval could be anything from a remark to a physical attack. Marriages like Elma and Bob's were unusual, and Nemiroff was rather proud of this. The Communist line encouraged whites to have "comradely and proletarian social relations with Negro comrades." Interracial sex was joked about by some who wanted to seem hip and open-minded, but party purists discouraged that kind of talk because it "suggested a tension that hindered political commitment."[30]

There really wasn't much of a story about the basketball team for Lorraine to write about. Bob invited her to join him, Elma, and a few others at Ratner's, a kosher restaurant on Second Avenue famous for its cheese blintzes, potato pancakes, hot onion rolls, and split-pea soup. It was snugged in beside Yiddish theaters on an avenue that some people called "the Jewish Rialto."

She went along. There weren't many people her age, she found, who liked to discuss books and authors—Bob was writing his master's thesis on Theodore Dreiser. Films and theater were generally outside the ken of most hardened leftists, who regarded that kind of thing as snobbish and bourgeois. Lorraine thought it was a matter of background and what a person had been exposed to.[31]

She enjoyed herself with Bob and Elma, and the three became friends.

The evening of November 1, 1951, was a big night. It was the first time that a scripted work by Lorraine Hansberry would be performed onstage. Rosie Jackson sent a telegram because he couldn't be there, unfortunately. "Thinking of you tonight and wishing you the greatest success expect to be home about the middle of next week I will write you tomorrow explaining further all my love." She'd written a pageant, *In Celebration of the Historic Struggles of the Negro Press*, marking the anniversary of *Freedom*'s first year. The goal was to sell subscriptions to *Freedom* by providing first-class entertainment about black journalism—not an easy theme.

The Rockland Palace in Harlem, at 155th and Frederick Douglass Avenue, was a gilded hall with three tiers of balconies and the sky-blue heavens painted on the ceiling. It was a coup for Hansberry to have her first work appear there. She was starting out ambitiously as a dramatist. She liked the format of pageants, later thinking that social realism and musical theater could be combined to great effect. In early drafts of *A Raisin in the Sun*, the characters alternate between songs and drama. In one scene,

Walter Younger, a chauffeur, adjusts his driver's cap in the mirror, and sings a number, "Yes Sir, No Sir!," about pleasing his white customers.

In Celebration of the Historic Struggles of the Negro Press illustrated in song, dance, and word the history of the Negro newspaper, from the founding of *Freedom's Journal* in New York City in 1827 to the launch of Paul Robeson's *Freedom*. Robeson sang selections from his concert repertoire; jazz trombonist Lawrence Brown played a set; and Asadata Dafora, one of the pioneers in black dance in America, performed numbers accompanied by drums.[32] Lorraine read aloud her poem "Lynchsong" and an untitled free-verse poem, "Sometimes I Dream of Africa."[33]

It was well received, and the following February, she partnered with a contributor to *Freedom*, Alice Childress, to write another one for *Freedom*'s Negro History Festival. It was the first of several collaborations between two eminent black female playwrights of the twentieth century.

Lorraine described Alice Childress in a humorous letter as "a real gift to the theater who knows her onions."[34] This wasn't surprising, given that Childress was fourteen years older than Hansberry and had started as a working actress in the American Negro Theater in 1941. The company's first production was *Anna Lucasta*. Childress received a Tony nomination for Best Supporting Actress. Turning her hand to writing, she would become the first African American woman to have a play professionally produced in New York City (*Gold Through the Trees*, in 1952) and the first woman to win an Obie for Best Play (for *Trouble in Mind*, in 1956). In fact, if *Trouble in Mind* hadn't been plagued with problems between her and the producer, she would have been the first black female playwright to have a show on Broadway, instead of Hansberry.[35] Childress knew theater from the ground up, and Lorraine was quite happy to take instruction from a woman she respected.

Respect was important to Childress; she insisted on it. Perhaps because she had been raised in Harlem by her grandmother, she possessed a view of herself that was more typical of someone older. She had set the playwright Robert Sherwood straight on how he should address a black woman:[36]

Your letter was placed on the bottom of the pile and I think I should tell you why.

You forgot to call me *Miss* on your envelope and sent it to "Alice Childress." Within the letter you greeted me "Dear Alice," you signed it "Robert Sherwood." Your second letter was addressed in the same manner and also began . . . "Dear Alice."

The Southern tradition is to avoid the use of titles when addressing Negro men and women in order to maintain their mythical assumption of white supremacy. I am sure that you and the other members of the Trade Arts Theater do not wish to uphold and perpetuate this kind of tradition. I point this out that you may correct this mistake in dealing with others who may not feel inclined to answer your letters.

Childress wrote her first play, *Florence*, on a dare from Sidney Poitier, a fellow actor in the American Negro Theater, who snorted at the idea that a decent play could be written in a night. The next morning, she had one.

Florence, a one-act performed at St. Mark's Church in Harlem in 1949, is about a southern mother, Mrs. Whitney, who's trying to get to New York by train to rescue her daughter from the poverty and indignity of life on the stage. She clutches her hard-earned savings, which she plans to use to bring Florence home, even if it means not having money for rent. Anticipating *A Raisin in the Sun*, the play has each member of the Whitney family expressing different ideas about how the money should be spent.

A northern white woman waiting on the train platform, Mrs. Carter, has been an actress herself, she says, and is proud that she "eats with Negroes." She offers to help Mrs. Whitney's daughter by recommending her for a job as a maid. As she produces a piece of paper with a phone number on it for Florence to call, Mrs. Whitney forcefully grabs Mrs. Carter's wrist—the "helping hand"—to restrain her. Mrs. Whitney has decided to send Florence the money instead. She wants her daughter to continue looking for acting roles, rather than give up and lower herself to meet the expectations of whites.[37]

As a piece of social realism, *Florence* presented a new "Mama" figure, different from the clichéd black matriarch.[38] For Mrs. Whitney, what is personal is political. Her decision to send Florence the "keep-on-trying" money is an act of resistance. And like Childress herself, Mama doesn't mask her feelings to please whites. "You're hurting my wrist," Mrs. Carter exclaims. "I mustn't hurt you, must I?" Mama replies, doubtless putting emphasis on *you*.

It's said that Hansberry shared an office with Alice Childress at *Freedom*, but Childress came in only to drop off pieces for her column, Conversations from Life, featuring a character named Mildred. Childress and Lorraine knew each other socially outside work, through the network of politically minded women in Harlem, such as the Sojourners; and they had a friend in common: Claudia Jones.

Mildred is worth taking a look at for a moment because of what she represents in the evolution of black feminism. She's a thirty-two-year-old domestic worker who chats over coffee with an invisible listener, Marge. The character was based on Childress's aunt, "a wonderful woman," she said, "who refused to exchange dignity for pay."[39] Mildred talks leftist "man talk" about lynching, McCarthyism, the Cold War, anticolonial struggles in Africa, Negro History Month, and labor rights for black working-class women—all topics that Hansberry wrote about in *Freedom*.

It required ingenuity for Hansberry and Childress to get women the space they deserved in *Freedom*. The premise of journalism was that men generated the real news and, furthermore, that only black, male issues were central to racial problems.[40] Childress made Mildred a shrewd critic of current events. Lorraine looked for opportunities to accompany news stories with photographs of women—in one of hers about the Kikuyu people's anticolonial protests against the British, the photograph in the article isn't of the male leaders imprisoned, but of the Kikuyu women marching on the prison compound. "Obviously," Lorraine later said, "the most oppressed group of any oppressed group will be its women, who are twice oppressed."[41]

Hansberry and Childress began working together on a script for the Negro History Festival, to be held in late February 1952. It was a celebration pageant, beginning with the Negro spiritual "Oh, Freedom."

In theater terms, Lorraine understudied Childress and was learning on the fly.

11

The Passport

It matters so much *how* we die, and for *what*, and we like to *choose*.
—Lorraine Hansberry

Paul Robeson's passport was still in limbo by the spring of 1952, and the State Department intended to let it languish there indefinitely. Without it, he had been unable to travel outside the United States for eighteen months.

Restoring his passport had become a cause célèbre around the Western world, beyond the issue of whether the government had the right to confiscate his passport. Robeson himself was a flashpoint. Speaking at a Civil Rights Congress rally at Madison Square Garden, he had called on President Truman to stop sending troops to Korea. "I have said it before and I say it again, that the place for the Negro people to fight for their freedom is here at home."[1] There were widespread allegations that Robeson was a traitor. "Mr. Robeson is as worthy of internment as any Jap who got penned away in the last war," declared Robert C. Ruark in his syndicated newspaper column, "since by his own lusty baritone he is an enemy of his own country and a passionate espouser of those people who are now declared enemies." J. Edgar Hoover agreed, and wrote across the top of his copy of the article, "Certainly well said."[2]

Walter White, director of the NAACP, blamed Robeson for hampering civil rights efforts by praising the Soviets' supposed commitment to racial equality. Anything the Communists did was perceived as somehow against

American interests—and certain to persuade many as the sole reason *not* to do it. White suggested that Robeson might have mental problems. Writing in *Ebony* magazine, he described Robeson as a "bewildered man, who is more to be pitied than damned" with "innumerable contradictions . . . which are only understandable to himself and possibly a psychologist."[3]

On the Left, Robeson's defenders framed the dispute over his passport as a challenge to American imperialist power. "This was, from the outset, more than a fight for a passport," said Ossie Davis, who supported Robeson. "[A] state of war existed between us and the status quo—those men of means and power who correctly felt that Paul was a danger to them, and to their postwar effort to reconstruct the world."[4] When Robeson's attorneys pressed the State Department for specific reasons as to why his passport had been suspended, it turned out that his endorsing communism had been only one factor in the decision; the other was that he had been "extremely active on behalf of the independence for the colonial peoples of Africa."[5] Robeson was a thorn in the side of American foreign policy makers.

Hansberry defended him unconditionally; she was as committed to him as she was to *Freedom*'s stances against racism and colonialism. Like Robeson, she had no interest in creating an American soviet. She believed in creating a society in which privilege and classism could not exist, in which the guarantees of the Constitution would be manifested throughout the land. Women were freer in Russia, she suspected, than they were in the United States.[6]

Consequently, she leaped at the opportunity to represent Robeson at the Intercontinental Peace Congress in Montevideo, Uruguay, in March 1952. She would be one of several delegates traveling from the United States. The conference would be about topics that fit *Freedom*'s agenda perfectly: nuclear disarmament and social and economic justice for the people of the Americas.

It was an honor representing Paul Robeson, one that Hansberry couldn't have imagined coming her way at twenty-one. With less than a week to spare, she applied for a passport, stating that she was going on vacation for two months to England, Scotland, France, and Italy. The address she supplied was a friend's, not hers, making it harder for the authorities—"the shifty-eyed ones who follow, follow, follow," she called them—to find her. She needed the passport immediately, and it was granted on the spot. In her rush, she had barely enough time to gather the "necessities of shortly notified travel."[7] Things had been happening to her so fast recently. Louis Burnham had promoted her to associate editor, and she wanted to be worthy of the trust he had put in her to carry out an international assignment. She could "smell it [fascism] in the air."[8]

At Idlewild Airport, she found the gate where the Boeing 377 Stratocruiser was waiting on the tarmac. The plane was as big as a B-29 Superfortress, which it was, essentially—the same big-bellied aircraft that had dropped atomic bombs on Hiroshima and Nagasaki—now converted for one hundred passengers with state-of-the-art appointments inside. The air-conditioned cabin was done in sea blue and snow white, with twenty-eight full-length sleeping berths in first class that folded down from the ceiling. On the lower deck, accessible by stairs, was a lounge with an open bar. And there would be a three-course dinner on china and linens that, the airline said, "any housewife would be proud to serve." Actually, the meal was prepared by Maxim's of Paris: cocktails, canapés, consommé, boeuf bourgeois, white or red wine, with a choice of cheese and coffee and cognac for dessert. The air route was New York, Trinidad, Rio de Janeiro, and finally Buenos Aires, Argentina—the closest she could get to her ultimate destination, Montevideo, Uruguay.

At their first stop, in Port of Spain, Trinidad, she left the plane to stretch her legs and went into the terminal. In the washroom, the attendant came over to the sink and sat down beside her "intently," Lorraine noticed. "It is clear she would like to talk to me." The woman asked what the United States was like because it was her dream to go there someday.[9]

In Buenos Aires, Hansberry checked into the Florida Hotel in the old quarter of the city, a sedate twenty-room hotel in Spanish Colonial style. Then she went outside to wait for the car being sent to pick her up. Standing beside her, a woman in a colorful cotton dress studied her wool suit, low-heel pumps, and shoulder strap bag. It was hot outside. "*Ah, la norteamericana tipica!*" the woman said. She spoke "from the reaches of her shawls and earrings and long, flowing hair." She was an Argentinian attorney and a delegate to the peace conference, too. Her comment, Hansberry decided, was "neither a compliment nor altogether an insult; it was a remark of wonder." The conservative wool outfit was "the mark of the fashion-indifferent woman who desires freedom and utility of movement." It made Lorraine think about whether femaleness should be celebrated with clothes and hairstyles that expressed womanhood. Was her neutral look—understated, businesslike—really a choice that she had freely made, or was she conforming to the way a *norteamericana tipica* was expected to dress, regardless of how she wanted to present herself?[10]

The drive was long, and Hansberry was the only passenger—the beginning of an air of secrecy that was necessary to evade the forces of oppression, she was told by the driver. The U.S. government didn't want the conference to be held at all, which was why Lorraine had to be taken alone to the location. As she entered the plenary session, she was handed a plate of food "and instructed to be prepared to get up and dance in the event the police should arrive. A pianist was posted at the piano to provide light music immediately if need be."[11] There were nearly 250 delegates waiting. The blinds were drawn, and reports were delivered quickly and without applause.

At first, the speakers addressed abuses in Paraguay: martial law in cities, resources used to make war, families with loved ones in political exile. Then the focus shifted to the "stranglehold" of the United States, beginning with the "US government demands troops for murder" in the Korean War. As Lorraine listened, a Chilean representative "told of the robbery of their copper, which can be exported only to the United States." A member of the Women's International Democratic Federation, whose headquarters were in East Berlin, described the horrors she had seen on a fact-finding mission to Korea. She accused the U.S., South Korean, and UN troops of committing war crimes against women and children—"the extermination of a people," was how Hansberry described it.[12]

After such terrible indictments of U.S. foreign policy, she was humbled by what happened at the next session, reserved for women only. She was presented, as a representative of the American Negro people, with "a beautiful bouquet of red carnations by the women of Brazil; a lovely handmade handkerchief from the women of Paraguay; and a traditionally costumed doll from the women of Uruguay." And she continued to be treated as special, an honored guest: "When I entered the meeting of the youth, the entire gathering stood and applauded." She was unanimously elected to sit on the presidium with the organizers. Although she had been sent as only a delegate, she found herself immediately raised to the center of attention.

After that, "Everywhere[,] I spent hours signing autographs and being interviewed by the press. Everywhere[,] I was warmly embraced and asked to bring greetings to my people, and to tell them how great was the admiration of the people of the Americas for their struggles." She was photographed with María Rosa Oliver, special assistant to former assistant secretary of state Nelson Rockefeller for improving relations with Argentina. A few years later, Oliver would be awarded the Lenin Prize by the Kremlin for those who had "strengthened peace among comrades."

The final evening of the conference was a personal triumph and put the cap on Hansberry's serving the Soviet-funded organizers as a "useful innocent," a phrase used by Communists for misguided, liberal sympathizers. All pretense of secrecy was dropped. Before a throng of five thousand in the main square of Montevideo, she was asked to speak. Behind her was a huge blue-and-white banner proclaiming, "Peace!" Loudspeakers boomed her every word "through the heart" of the city. As photographers' flashbulbs popped around her, she began, "In my hand I hold a message from a man whose name in our country is synonymous with the word 'peace.'" The crowd instantly started roaring, "Viva Robeson! Viva Robeson!" and "*Imperialismo Yanqui!*" This, Hansberry thought, "was the final victory."[13]

Before she left for home, she dashed off a telegram to Rosie. "Can you meet me," she wrote at first, but then she scratched this out and started over: "Arrive 1 am Thurs. Meet me." She signed it with her middle name, "Vivian," in case prying eyes should intercept it. She had to leave before she received a reply.[14]

Everything about the event—the vitality of the protests in the name of the people, the gifts she had been given, the adulation that had been accorded her, a stranger—was so affirming. Looking out the airplane window, she gazed down at the Caribbean Sea far below and at the green, tree-canopied islands ringed in white sand. She thought "Of smelling the earth—and loving life. Long live good life! And beauty . . . and love!"[15]

When she landed at Idlewild, Rosie wasn't there to meet her. She was already back in her apartment when a telegram from him arrived, although he could just as easily have called: "Leaving today at two pm. Can't get along without you. Love Roosevelt Jackson."

It wasn't long before the truth came out—why he was unavailable when she needed him, why his responses to things were late and his behavior hard to understand. It had been a ruse; she'd been hustled. He was married with a child. "He also had buddies and they wrote to him for narcotics while they were away. That was how I found out that he took heroin, sniffed it, they say. And I, who knew nothing of such things, found this out."[16]

She went to his apartment—the one he had been sharing with Douglas Turner Ward—and saw that his belongings, including Ward's, were being put out on the sidewalk. They'd been evicted because Jackson hadn't been paying the rent. Hansberry wrote to Ward, warning him that his "stuff was being lost" because there was no place to store it, which came as a shock to him. "I was out on bail making my appeal," he said, "but I was forced to stay in New Orleans and couldn't do anything about it."[17] For her part, Lorraine washed her hands of the situation.

Judging from a cold letter she sent to Rosie, her feelings for him weren't deep—or perhaps she didn't want to give him the satisfaction of thinking that they were. "I am angry, disgusted, and a little outraged. But I am glad there is no hurt here, you seem to have lost your ability to do that. Now you simply anger me, beyond telling." He had already made the usual offer—to divorce his wife—but Lorraine was finished with him. "I do not want to and will not marry you. I do not want to see you again . . . ever." She ended with a piece of advice: "For your own benefit, I will share my most prominent thought with you and that is: You should fall out of love with Rosie Jackson . . . I have."[18]

Years later, she remembered the whole scenario bitterly in her journal: "People say to me, what makes you so suspicious? Ha! In this world to think that some even dare ask! I was twenty when I came to this city, twenty. I met a boy then, girls do. He was twenty-three or something like that, I think[,] and he had already been married and already had a child but not divorced. It had not occurred to me that young men could already have wives and children when they came to call. . . . Now I am thirty-two and it is impossible when people say to me, 'Why are you so suspicious?' I am suspicious because this world is a pig trough!'"[19]

She threw herself into her work. Now that she was the associate editor at *Freedom*, she wrote more than ever; in fact, she contributed more copy than anyone else. Her bylines were aliases, perhaps because her real name was appearing almost as often as Paul Robeson's. In a candid snapshot taken of her at her desk, she looks embarrassed, frumpy, and tired.

In *Freedom*'s eight pages, she would have a mix of three or four articles about colonialism in Africa, the arts in Harlem, trade unionism, or the struggle for racial justice. This was in addition to her monthly feature, Stories for Children, about black history. She worked hard because she knew she was in a position of influence. She felt sure that appeals made to people's consciences would persuade them to agree—not only because she was certain that Marxist-inspired reporting would improve society, but also because, at heart, she was a humanist. "[O]ne cannot live with sighted eyes and feeling heart and not know about and react to the miseries which afflict this world."[20] She believed that people were, by nature, good. "I don't think people start out in this world to be bad, they start out to be happy."[21] If individuals engaged in behaviors that were harmful to themselves or others, it was because their actions were condoned, encouraged, or compelled by immoral social structures that should be reformed—not by fire and sword, but rationally and democratically.

There were several items about Robeson in every issue now, which hadn't been the case at first. The passport controversy had awakened in him a defiant, publicity-seeking response.

Robeson's determination to keep his name in the news led to a change in *Freedom*'s editorial direction. Louis Burnham met with the others who worked in the small offices on 125th Street: the Civil Rights Congress, the National Negro Labor Council, and the Council on African Affairs. It was decided that they would join forces to create the United Freedom Fund, the purpose of which would be to support the cultural and political work of Paul Robeson. From then on, Robeson was shown in *Freedom* as often as possible, greeting supporters, marching on picket lines, conferring with black leaders, or preparing for his concerts. There was always a list of the cities where he would be appearing and when.

When Lorraine's full-page story about her Uruguay trip appeared in April, it was accompanied by a four-page special supplement, "Happy Birthday, Paul Robeson," written by colleagues and family members, "honoring this great people's artist and fighter for peace and freedom."[22]

In the spring of 1952, in addition to her work for *Freedom*, Hansberry began teaching at the Jefferson School of Social Science, at 575 Sixth Street, in Lower Manhattan. The Communist-backed "Jeff School," as it was called, had opened during the war in a nine-story former furniture warehouse, its motto a remark by Thomas Jefferson, the school's namesake, in a letter to James Madison: "Educate and inform the whole mass of the people, they are the only sure reliance for the preservation of our liberty."

The Jeff School was a combination grassroots socialist movement and adult education program. There were one-night, one-week, or semester-long courses to accommodate every person's schedule. Enrollment was open to everyone "except known enemies of the working class."[23] Some courses were reading and discussion classes on Marxist approaches to racism, male chauvinism, and the state. Self-improvement classes included creative writing taught by novelist Dashiell Hammett or Howard Fast; art appreciation by Charles White; acting and drama by Alice Childress; and for homemakers, interior decorating and personal beauty on a budget. Hansberry team-taught "Working Class Poets of the Negro People" with Yvonne Gregory, a contributor to *Freedom*. The students liked her. "Lorraine had such a deep and profound interest in her people," remembered one. "She seemed to get the very essence of the depth and beauty of the Negro. . . . She was so full of life, interest and ideas, to say nothing of her sense of humor," making the class "'crack up' every night about one thing or the other."[24]

The Saturday Evening Post saw the purpose of the Jefferson School differently, warning its readers, "Here's Where Our Commies Are Trained"; it was an "open conspiracy." Students participated in an "appalling" number of "picket lines, mass demonstrations, political rallies" when McCarthyism and the Red Scare were at a fever pitch. The FBI, to keep an eye on things, had informants enrolled in classes, many of whom were black, so as not to arouse suspicion.[25]

There were two annexes in addition to the main campus in Lower

Manhattan, one in Brooklyn and the other in the Bronx. Hansberry volunteered to assist in opening a third branch, in Harlem, at the Frederick Douglass Educational Center, located in the Elks Lodge building on West 124th Street. The kickoff for the center was a music-and-dance festival celebrating West Indian, Negro, and Puerto Rican culture, held at the Golden Gate Ballroom, a former showcase for jazz greats. The largest auditorium in Harlem could be rented for almost nothing because it was about to close.

In July, an FBI agent from the Chicago office pressed the gate buzzer at 5936 South Parkway, the second address Lorraine had listed on her passport application, the first one being a decoy.

Hearing the buzzer, Mrs. Hansberry might have debated whether to admit her visitor after the voice on the intercom identified himself as an FBI agent: the Hansberrys were defendants in a civil suit that summer, brought against them by the Department of Justice for violating the 1947 federal Housing and Rent Act by allegedly overcharging rent from a Negro tenant in an apartment building.[26] Perhaps the agent added that his visit concerned Mrs. Hansberry's daughter in New York.

The Bureau's discovery that Lorraine had given it the slip by applying for a passport for a vacation in England and then writing articles for *Freedom* and the *Daily Worker* about participating in a Communist-sponsored event in Uruguay had triggered an investigation.[27] An informant—someone close to the Hansberrys, evidently—had tipped off the Bureau to the fact that the family was wealthy and owned considerable real estate in Chicago.[28] The Chicago office was instructed "to institute an investigation of the subject to determine whether or not her activities warrant her inclusion in the Security Index," meaning she might have to be upgraded to the level of a threat.[29]

No doubt, the agent was there to find out if Mrs. Hansberry knew where her daughter was. Providing false information on a passport application was a crime punishable by a fine and up to twenty-five years in prison.[30] It so happened that Lorraine had been there a few days earlier, and she had left her passport with her mother. Mrs. Hansberry retrieved it and gave it to the agent. She also supplied him with Lorraine's address. Her daughter could be found residing with a "Jones family" at 504 West 143rd Street.[31]

The Hansberrys were solid Republicans. They had been involved in many civic programs for the betterment of the community, and Mrs. Hansberry and her late husband had held important posts in politics and business. The implication that they were not good Americans because Lorraine was associating with Communists, which had brought the FBI to their door, was the last straw. Mrs. Hansberry made plans to travel to Harlem to see for herself what was going on. What she wanted "more than anything," Mamie said, was for "Lorraine to settle down and get married," the way respectable people did.[32]

Salubria, the 3,200-acre plantation in northern Virginia where Lorraine Hansberry's great-grandfather was born in 1819.

Despite being in his forties when he was emancipated in 1865, William Hansberry became one of the most successful planters in East Feliciana parish, Louisiana. He hired freedmen, who built homes on the place, farmed their own plots, or worked at his brick kiln.

Lorraine's parents, Carl Augustus and Nannie Hansberry, went to Chicago around the time of World War I and met while working in a black-owned bank.

Carl Hansberry capitalized on the idea of kitchenettes, tiny apartments created by subdividing existing apartments into smaller units with a shared bathroom. The "King of the Kitchenettes," as the Chicago press called him, was a civil rights activist and one of the largest slumlords in the city.

Lorraine (second row, second from left) was president of the hundred-member debate club at Englewood High School and a classmate of James Forman, later secretary of the Student Nonviolent Coordinating Committee. Hansberry told a friend that she was "so rah-rah" with school spirit that it "ran my family nuts."

Hansberry became an associate editor of *Freedom*, founded in Harlem by Paul Robeson, seen here attending a birthday party in 1950 for Joseph Stalin at the Soviet embassy in Washington, DC. No U.S. government representatives attended.

Bob Nemiroff was a married graduate student at New York University and a member of the NAACP when Hansberry met him at a campus protest.

Hansberry attended a Communist-sponsored peace conference in Montevideo, Uruguay, to represent Paul Robeson. Her mother surrendered Lorraine's passport afterward to the FBI.

A reading of Douglas Turner Ward's first play inspired Hansberry to try her hand at playwriting. "The most striking thing about Lorraine," Ward said, "even at that early age, was her combination of steel will and brilliant intellect."

On Whitman Avenue by Maxine Wood, about a veteran (Canada Lee) and his family denied housing in a white neighborhood, played on Broadway in 1946. Hansberry met Wood while she was writing *A Raisin in the Sun*.

Charles R. Swibel, a Chicago real estate developer and advocate of public housing, heard that the producers of *A Raisin in the Sun* "needed money badly." Anonymously, he made the largest investment, equal to the amount Sidney Poitier demanded up front for starring in the lead.

Bob and Lorraine looking exhausted a week before the premier at the Ethel Barrymore Theatre in New York City. The *Christian Science Monitor* objected to how Hansberry was routinely referred to as a Negro playwright. "There is something double-edged about the fact that recognition of Negro talent is in itself still considered particularly newsworthy."

Hansberry dancing with director Lloyd Richards at Sardi's restaurant after the premiere. She told him, "Where the play stop[ped] being mine and became yours—it became a larger and more powerful play."

Nelson Algren, novelist of the dispossessed, emphasized in a review of *A Raisin in the Sun* its theme of material aspiration over human dignity. "As a social study it is a good drama about real estate," he wrote, angering Hansberry.

Bob Nemiroff, promoter and impresario, at a recording session in the Brill Building with Carole King and Paul Simon in 1959. *A Raisin in the Sun* had premiered on Broadway a few months earlier.

Very quickly, *A Raisin in the Sun* turned Hansberry into a sought-after spokesperson about integration, housing, black families, social reform, and theater. Here, with Nemiroff on her left, she speaks to students at Brandeis University.

Hansberry purchased and moved into an apartment building on Waverly Place in Greenwich Village, where she met Dorothy Secules, who was one of her tenants. They became lovers.

After the Chicago Hansberrys fled to Los Angeles under threat of arrest, they continued to remain active in the Republican Party. Here, Mamie Hansberry (white suit) meets Richard Nixon, candidate for California governor in 1962.

At Bob's urging, Lorraine purchased a house in Croton-on-Hudson, New York, where she could write without distraction. She worked at her desk "at all costs until five" and then she downed "two brave sized scotches," followed by talking her "fool head off" to Bob. It was her last home.

12

"I Do Love You"

We could see he was very attentive, and in fact, he was overly attentive, for our money.

—Mamie Mitchell Hansberry[1]

The "Jones family" that Lorraine was living with was only Claudia Jones. It's hard to tell exactly when the two began living together, but judging from letters, it seems to have been during the fall of 1951, before the Uruguay trip and before the FBI paid a visit to Mrs. Hansberry.

After Jones's release from prison for the second time—her deportation order was still pending—she had been very active in the Congress of American Women and the National Council of Negro Women, traveling to forty-three states to organize black and working-class women against the Korean War. Writing in the Marxist magazine *Political Affairs*, Jones called upon women "to unite lest their children, like those in Korea, suffer the fate of Hiroshima's atomic destruction."[2]

While Jones was traveling, Lorraine had the apartment to herself. Their shared space resembled a workshop, a place of study and of things in development. "There were stacks of books and newspapers everywhere," remembered Esther Cooper Jackson. Jackson had spent the mid-1940s in Alabama with Louis and Dorothy Burnham, working for the Southern Negro Youth Congress. "The three of us—Lorraine, Claudia, and I—would discuss politics and what we were reading, and I was so impressed by these two brilliant women. I participated some, but I listened more than I talked. I knew they were going to make great contributions because of their self-confidence."[3]

What Lorraine's life in Harlem was actually like, the work she was doing and who her friends were, was going to be a shock to her mother. And Mrs. Hansberry and Mamie would be coming to New York on an inspection visit in October. The ground had to be prepared for their arrival, because there was another aspect of Lorraine's life that her family knew nothing about: she was dating a recently divorced white man, Robert Nemiroff. This would come as another surprise. The Hansberrys "hadn't done anything interracial really with someone immediately in our family," Mamie said.[4]

Bobby and Elma Nemiroff had been married for fourteen months, but they were having problems. After they met Lorraine during the picket line demonstration in Washington Park, they turned to her for advice, because she "had great insights about life," Bobby said.[5] Then, about the time that Lorraine broke off her engagement with Rosie, in March 1952, the Nemiroffs split up, and Elma filed a petition with the Catholic Church to have the marriage annulled.[6] It was granted. The most common reasons for a declaration of nullity at that time were for deceit, psychological incapacity, or failure of the couple to "become one flesh." In June, the day after the civil divorce was legally finalized, Bobby called Lorraine for a date. They went to a museum and, afterward, to Ratner's. It was the start of a codependent relationship from which neither of them would ever break free.

Bobby Nemiroff was polite and boyish looking, with a light, high voice that came unexpectedly from a man on the tallish side. In his FBI file, notes on his physical description—brown eyes, brown hair, medium build—include the remark "effeminate."[7] No one, at first, glance, would have taken him as an antiestablishment type. At eighteen, he had been an American delegate to the first World Youth Festival, in Prague, Czechoslovakia, organized by the Soviet Union and the Eastern Bloc countries to commemorate events of October and November 1939, when thousands of young Czechs protested Nazi occupation.[8] Like Lorraine, Nemiroff had campaigned for Henry Wallace and had joined a Communist youth group.

He had supported Wallace's opposition to the draft. At a rally of two thousand students at Turner's Arena, in Washington, DC, he had warned, "From the minute we entered the army, the Bill of Rights would be suspended, and we would know democracy 'brass-hat style.'"[9]

Lorraine had her own story about the draft, if she cared to tell Bobby about it. Her brother Perry had refused to be inducted during the war, based on what Carl Jr. had told him about his experiences serving in Patton's army. The moment Carl had arrived for boot camp in the South, Jim Crow was the order of the day. White southern officers were put in charge of black recruits, because they "understood" Negroes. Black troops were given low-status jobs such as driving trucks, cooking in the mess tents, and, when it came to fighting, digging graves.

When Perry received his draft notice in June 1944, he had informed his family that he wasn't going to report for duty. Lorraine's father was outraged—his name was in the newspapers as a fundraiser for the war effort. The Carl A. Hansberry chapter of the Women's Defense Corps of America had been throwing dances to sell war bonds. Father and son fought "like two Titans clashing," and Lorraine, frightened, had run to her room.[10]

The day before he was supposed to be inducted, Perry filed a lawsuit, saying he was:

> willing and able as well as anxious to join any branch of the military service of the United States of America where he can best serve the interest of his country, but feels it would be the height of folly to enlist or be inducted in to a Jim Crow, segregated, discriminated army and be subjected to all manners of humiliation, disadvantages, segregation and other forms of limited privileges in order to fight for the reserve [sic] of these things and liberating people from humiliation, oppression and other disadvantages that he has never seen.

Named as defendants were President Franklin Roosevelt, the national and Illinois state directors of the Selective Service, the secretaries of the navy and war, and the members of Perry's local draft board.[11] A federal judge dismissed the suit, ruling that only Congress had jurisdiction over the president. Moreover, the Supreme Court had already upheld the Selective Service Act. Perry had reported for duty and served for two years.

Something else Lorraine and Bob had in common: as Communists—he was a card-carrying member now, she wasn't—they were aware that the party encouraged "real black-Jewish intellectual and artistic collaboration." This came easily to Hansberry: many of her friends in college had been Jewish.[12] She believed the only difference between human beings was skin color and other physical differences; all else was environment.[13] "Our beliefs were shared," Nemiroff said. "Lorraine was a militant, but that had nothing do with being anti-white. We were both radicals and believed that radical changes would have to take place in this country. She was very proud and very black, but the one special thing about her was that she was a profoundly humanistic writer. She was equally touched by the Irish or Jewish condition."[14]

They both knew what it felt like to be outside the American mainstream. Jews and blacks began meeting in northern urban centers at the turn of the century, sometimes in the same neighborhoods, as two major migration streams flowed into one another. Blacks were leaving violence in the South; Eastern European Jews were fleeing persecution. The two groups had been making common cause since the 1920s, when the Ku Klux Klan had reemerged, terrorizing Jews, progressives, Negroes, and Catholics. Black socialist labor leader A. Philip Randolph considered Jews among his most reliable supporters.[15]

On the street level, however, the relationship between Jews and blacks was tense. Writing in the Jewish magazine *Commentary* in 1948, James Baldwin attempted to explain that "Negroes Are Anti-Semitic Because They're Anti-White" and made a mess of it by trying to justify hatred of Jews as deserved. "Jews in Harlem," he wrote, "are small tradesmen, rent collectors, real estate agents, and pawnbrokers; they operate in accordance with the American business tradition of exploiting Negroes, and they are therefore identified with oppression and are hated for it. . . . The Jew has been taught—and, too often, accepts—the legend of Negro inferiority; and the Negro, on the other hand, has found nothing in his experience with Jews to counteract the legend of Semitic greed."[16]

What Baldwin failed to understand was that Judaism's goal of fulfilling human potential to the utmost includes making a living. Exploiting people is indefensible, but getting rich through commerce has never been regarded in any way by Jews as sinful, degrading, or morally dubious. This attitude is part of Jewish moral realism, which tries to build a good society for human beings as they are. Seen this way, capitalism proved to be the best economic system for fulfilling Jewish aspirations, which must have been evident even to Nemiroff, Communist that he was, every time he walked into his parents' restaurant in Times Square.[17]

This was something else Lorraine and Bob shared. Despite their involvement with the Left, they were from entrepreneurial families that had both hoisted themselves into the middle and upper-middle class, and greater acceptability, via capitalistic business practices. Lorraine, however, had seen how the love of money had affected her family, and the consequences. Yet, had she repudiated them for that? No. Her position on socialism was intellectual and humanistic. Socialism was a better system, in her opinion, because it would, in Claudia Jones's words, abolish "class divisions and human exploitation."[18] Nowhere in her writings does she talk about political economy—although she owned a copy of Bernard Shaw's *The Intelligent Woman's Guide to Socialism and Capitalism*—or wealth distribution, or government's responsibility regarding property, and so on. In principle, she and Nemiroff were for fairness and "the people" in the abstract.[19]

Lorraine and Bob started seeing each other regularly. They went for walks in the country and often to Washington Square Park, where they had met a year before. Bobby would lie down in the grass, and Lorraine would sit beside him reading poetry aloud. Dan Wakefield, author of *New York in the Fifties*, recalled meeting them one day for coffee at the Limelight, in Sheridan Square. "I remember the intensity of them, the sense of commitment and camaraderie, the feeling that we were part of the same grand effort of art and language to communicate, to break down barriers, to make people see each other as individuals, as we did in the Village, where the arch above Washington Square said, 'Let us raise a standard to which the wise and the honest can repair.'"[20]

By the end of the summer of 1952, Bobby was in love with Lorraine. And he told her so in September.[21]

I realize of course that you are not in any way in love with me, that what these past months have been for me they haven't been at all for you; you made that amply clear. At best they were pleasant, refreshing friendship—I only hoped permanent from your point of view. I understand that with all the uncertainties of your own life at this crucial time, all the hurts and disillusions of the recent past, the uncertainty of what lies ahead—what and how and precisely why you want to do with your life—you were in no position to think seriously about any one person—or, at any rate, about me. And yet you did say many times that the friendship was real, stimulating—that when you thought new thoughts or encountered fresh experience you looked forward to sharing them. And that is why I was so unprepared for, and do not understand, your apparent reluctance to get together at all now. . . .

Perhaps I *should* understand. Perhaps I am just dodging the obvious that this is a way of telling me gently we had been seeing too much of each other altogether, that I was building on a thing that could have no future and that there you think it wiser to call a halt. Or maybe it is simpler than that: Maybe I am not just that interesting a person at all and whatever stimulation I offered has worn off.

. . . there is no person at whose side I would so desire to struggle, from whom I might learn so much, to whom I would give more freely of whatever there is in me to give and for whom, if need be, I would so willingly sacrifice. No person, Lorraine, with whom I should so like to build and share this great gift of life in our times.

In the letter—part declaration of love, part negotiation—Nemiroff says he appreciates what she went through with Rosie and understands her feelings. He reminds her of a few things she said that gave him hope. Then he asks, in so many words, "Am I uninteresting?" a question to which she can only reasonably answer "no." He proposes a kind of payment, a quid pro quo. For what he learns from her, he would willingly sacrifice everything. He asks for nothing except her time. He invites trust . . . and a deal.

One more point worth bringing out: he doesn't ask for deference or respect because he's a man. No chauvinism here. He speaks of creating parity between them—a desexed partnership. In fact, the lack of physical yearning on his part is noticeable by its absence. He speaks directly to her mind, without a single reference to the catalogue of qualities that lovers usually use: her eyes, her mouth, her laughter, or anything of that nature. In this he was being ideologically proper. Communists were on their guard against male-supremacist behavior and were encouraged to live out gender equality in their day-to-day-lives.[22]

For Lorraine's part, she had thought they were seeing too much of each other, but winning her back in slow motion worked. They continued dating.

There still remained the problem of her mother and sister coming to town in a few weeks. And the topic of marriage would be high on the list of her mother's priorities. "Mother was bugging her about coming home after she had been in New York a couple of years or so," Mamie remembered. "She said, 'Well, any middle-class lady shouldn't be in New York so long, because you know it is time for you to think about getting married.'" Lorraine had assured her that she had "met a very nice person," and her mother would expect to meet him.[23] To set the stage, Lorraine found an intermediary. She asked a colleague at *Freedom*, George B. Murphy Jr., to do her a favor: while he was in Chicago on business, to pay a call on her mother and prime her for the event.

As an ambassador of goodwill, forty-five-year-old George Murphy had the ideal portfolio. Born into one of Maryland's most influential families— his brother would soon be elected a Maryland district court judge—he was the grandson of the founder of the *Baltimore Afro-American* and had risen to editor in chief of one of his family's newspapers, the *Washington Afro-American*. Added to this, he was a staunch activist with the NAACP and the National Negro Congress. In every respect, he was on a par with the Hansberrys. His mission, Lorraine made it clear, was to report favorably on her life in New York. He should speak well of *Freedom* and of her boss, Louis Burnham. To make sure he covered everything, she supplied him with a list of talking points—because, if her mother arrived in New York already in a good frame of mind about Lorraine's situation, meeting Bob might go smoother. A lot depended on this, including the check that Mrs. Hansberry was sending her every month.

On a warm, breezy autumn morning in 1952, just a few days before Mrs. Hansberry and Mamie were to depart for New York, Murphy knocked on their door. His letter to Lorraine about what transpired is worth quoting at length. Apparently, Mrs. Hansberry left the door on the chain at first, having been surprised by the FBI once already.[24]

Well, I stopped by your mother's home the other day and took the first step in making myself known to your family. It was a bit awkward as I certainly had not been properly introduced, but I managed to get her to understand, as she peeped shyly from behind the door, with the door catch on, that I was not a thief come to rob her or kidnap her, but just a friend of her daughter's who wanted to talk to mother about how daughter was faring in New York among the wolves, etc. and all the various and sundry characters that infest that great Metropolis. With this small chat accomplished, I was given to understand that I might return at 11 am the following morning.

True to my word, and accompanied by Mr. Gene Braxton, my real estate broker and patron while I am in this town, I sallied forth and this time the door was opened, first, somewhat timidly, and then after certain checks with the "Lady of the House" had been made by a perfectly gorgeous maiden [Mamie], all demure etc. (You'll just have to wait until I get back to New York to rap male supremacy, sister, I'ahm telling you like it is) we were ushered into the Hansberry living room and in a moment or two, a winsome, pert and stylish-looking lady, with flashing eyes, came in and then introductions were made all around.

We sat down and had coffee, and I was literally fascinated by these two women (I said to myself, Murphy, I thought you put down this ogle-eyed stuff years ago, but tw'ont so, I was almost impolite) and then I caught hold of myself and started the Murphy talkathon, but no soap; very gently and very positively I learned that the Lady who heads Hansberry House, knows exactly what she wants to say and no coaching please! So, I sat back and listened for as long as Murphy can listen without bursting, because he wanted to get a little special part of the story in, until she (Mrs. Hansberry) had given me a picture of herself, Paul's [Robeson] visit, the role of God in society (and sister, I agree with her; you'd better catch up on your understanding), and how to smoke an Old Gold with aplomb. . . .

Meantime, I was getting cross-eyed watching Sister Mamie Hansberry (Oh, I didn't call her Mamie; don't get me wrong; it is still "Miss Hansberry") and listening to her voice. All I can say is that Pop and Mom Hansberry sure got some fine brown-frame daughters. . . .

Well, to make a long story short, it was a really rewarding visit and your mother was really gracious. She left the details of discussing a monthly contribution with your sister Mamie, who gave me and Gene her cards and we are going to see her at the office [in Chicago] the early part of next week.

I got in all the points you advised me about, and even brought in Lou's [Burnham] mother, as well as my own, to make her see that you are surrounded by quite a few people whose parents think like she does, only she should be head of a school for mothers of the Negro bourgeoisie . . .

I have the feeling that your sister will help, and although she can do her own thinking on the matter, I felt that she and your mother appreciated that *Freedom* has the highest regard for Sister Hansberry . . .

Well, anyway, that is the sum and substance, or at least, most of the sum and substance of our interview with your mother and sister. So we went out into the October sunshine, walking on air and trying not to mention too self-consciously that this was a most pleasant interlude in the day-to-day fight for freedom, with all the possibilities of blooming into something great.

In mid-October, Lorraine's mother and sister arrived in New York. They met Bob and "went to the theater and stuff like that," Mamie said. "We could see he was very attentive, and in fact, he was overly attentive, for our money. . . . Sometimes we would walk a little bit ahead. But, you know, we could see that he was just an adorable person, and he was completely open and free."[25] They may have attended a panel that Lorraine was moderating—a *Freedom*-sponsored forum at the United Mutual Auditorium about social justice issues. That would have been acceptable to her mother. The Hansberrys had long been involved with those concerns.

But then Lorraine pushed her luck too far. She escorted her mother and sister to a rally sponsored by the New York Council and Youth Committee to Abolish the House Un-American Activities Committee. When it was her turn to speak, Lorraine forcefully denounced the HUAC investigations. "Mother and I just looked at each other," Mamie said.[26] The Hansberrys were donating heavily to the 1952 presidential campaign of

Republican Dwight Eisenhower. One of his planks was countering the Communist threat.

Mrs. Hansberry did not deliver her verdict before she left for home. It arrived via telegram on November 10: "Lorraine times are very troubled. You are causing me much worry. I think you owe me more respect and you should not do anything to cause me more worry. I want you to pack and come home immediately. Mother."[27]

The result of the dread visit was worse than Lorraine had expected, and she scrambled to make some concessions. To start with, her mother had never liked the idea of her living unchaperoned with other women: "it wasn't safe."[28] So she moved out of the apartment she shared with Claudia Jones, but rather than return to Chicago, she bought herself extra time by moving in with a friend from the University of Wisconsin and her husband—newlyweds Loretta and David Pauker. They lived on a quiet section on West 180th Street, in Washington Heights, the kind of neighborhood where people raise a family. Second, she agreed to come home for Christmas. If she didn't, it would be the third time in a row.

She boarded the New York Central Railroad's overnight Fifth Avenue Special, arriving in time for Christmas Eve. It was overcast and snowing a little in "dirty, dismal, Dreiseresque" Chicago, she wrote Bob. This "homecoming was a blip more than anything else, an extended series of political arguments." Instead of making her nostalgic, the whole business made her determined to get away once and for all. She had reached a decision. "I *do* love you, you wide-eyed, immature, unsophisticated revolutionary," she told Nemiroff. To which she added, "I have a terrific, no, exciting idea for a play," juxtaposing, with equal emphasis, two halves of the kind of relationship she wanted. She loved him, but "I shan't ever have the courage to say that face-to-face (except under certain conditions which I also will discuss with you). I thought certain things through to some basic conclusions. They go thusly: *First*, about 'my work': I am a writer. I am going to write. . . . I can paint. I am going to paint." She was going to "become a worker. . . . I am going to institute discipline in my life." Then, in order of importance, apparently, "*Second*, about *you*: I love you, problems be damned. I need you. I am right about those things about you which I have said must change. And I am going to struggle *with* you. That you are what

I want in a man (even if I couldn't realize it for six to seven, how many months?)."

She would be leaving in a few days, arriving on the morning of New Year's Eve, and wanted him to meet her at the station, "but *only* if you let me know you can really meet me," remembering, perhaps, her disappointment when Rosie didn't greet her at Idlewild. She wanted to make love with Bob that day and left it up to him where they could be alone. "Really, there ought to be someplace in that whole big city where it is possible to be alone." Nemiroff telegrammed her back, "Will be the happiest New Year and many more how could I not meet you?"[29]

With everything between them settled, they announced their engagement after the first of the year and set a wedding date for June 1953. As a married woman, she would no longer be under her mother's influence. "She went even further," pointed out a writer who interviewed her later for *Phylon*, the black journal about race and culture: "marrying a non-Negro added to her vision of the far future and the ultimate end of all troubling race distinctions."[30]

After Lorraine's obligatory visit ended and she went back to New York, the Chicago Hansberrys returned to their routine. In January, "Mamie Hansberry, Chicago heiress, blew in looking breathlessly radiant" to the invitation-only inaugural ball for Dwight D. Eisenhower.[31] The parade for the first Republican administration in twenty years was the largest in history. It lasted three and a half hours, with three quarters of a million people lining the route, the start of an era of centrist governance that Eisenhower called "the Middle Way."

That spring, Lorraine enrolled in a one-semester seminar at the Jefferson School taught by W. E. B. Du Bois. The subject was not Pan-Africanism, as some scholars have said. According to the syllabus, Du Bois covered "the government of Africa; the economic organization of the continent, including the Stalinist theory of colonial liberation; African art expression in painting, sculpture and literature; and the probable future of Africa."[32] Lorraine was particularly interested in the Muslim and Christian slave trade, which, she noted from one of his lectures, "cost 'Negro Africa well over one hundred million souls.'" Until then, she reflected, she hadn't been aware of "what must have been one of the primary causes for the decline, decay and the collapse of the cultures, kingdoms and empires which had flourished in black Africa in earlier times."[33]

Du Bois's cardinal principle for studying people was putting the focus on their humanity. What Lorraine learned from him about colonialism in Africa—her final paper was an overview of the atrocities perpetrated in the Congo Free State by King Leopold of Belgium—contributed a sharp, informed thrust to the articles she was writing for *Freedom* about African liberation movements. She treated politics lightly and reported personal costs to people. Her never-finished play *Les Blancs*, about white colonialists in Africa failing to meet their own "enlightened" Western standards about governance and justice, was inspired by this seminar.

Du Bois was eighty-five years old when he taught the seminar and was becoming discouraged by racism in the United States. Two years earlier, he had been put in handcuffs, charged with refusing to register as a foreign agent because he advocated nuclear disarmament and peaceful relations with the Soviet Union. There was no roar of outrage. He "was taken aback when those he had touted—the Talented Tenth—generally headed for the exits when they were asked to support him," wrote his biographer David Levering Lewis.[34] At Du Bois's trial, the judge tossed out the case. But for one of the greatest scholars of the age—he had spent his life disproving Negro "inferiority" through books, lectures, national conferences, studies, and every respected intellectual platform available—being treated as a felon was an unimaginable humiliation.

Hansberry regarded Du Bois as a father figure—more than that, a prophetic figure like Frederick Douglass. "People spoke of him as they did the church or the nation. He was an institution in our lives, a bulwark of our culture."[35] For the seminar, he assigned one of his most popular works, *Black Folk Then and Now*. Lorraine wrote on the inside cover of her copy[36]:

—Imagine then what it is for me a young Negro sprung from all the unrest and fervent searching and anxiety to sit before him.

His back against the sunlight of May afternoons. Blue suit, lined shirt, bow tie, pince-nez, goatee and moustache—Relaxing back leisurely, full and confident in his vast knowledge and his splendid sense of interpretation of history—

His voice coming always perfectly measured. His upper lip curling
now and again in appreciation of his wit—

Freedom's passion, refined and organized, sits there.

In June 1953, Lorraine returned to Chicago by herself to help her mother
and Mamie with the wedding arrangements; one hundred guests had
been invited. Bob was driving out with his best friend and best man, Burt
D'Lugoff, whom he'd known since they were boys together at Camp Woodland. D'Lugoff, a sweet-tempered, lumbering man who was careless about
looking uncombed and rumpled, had worked for a time at the socialist
newspaper the *Compass* before enrolling in premed at New York University.
Growing up in Brighton Beach, he had belonged to the Jewish Center also
used by the American Communist Party. "They were always vying for our
souls," his brother, Art, said of the rabbi and the rabble-rousers.[37]

On the train to Chicago, as night was coming on, Hansberry went into
the women's lounge for a cigarette. Across the aisle, a small child was asleep
on the seat cushions. Lorraine was fond of children, and the Paukers had
enjoyed her staying with them for six months in part because she loved
to play with theirs. A young black woman entered the car and sat down.
Lorraine thought she looked like someone she knew, but couldn't think of
who it was. The conversation turned to marriage[38]:

"I was to have got married the 20th of April."
    I wait.
"But I just upped a week before the wedding and called it off."
"You did?"
"Yep—I just decided I couldn't see m'self married, no sir. So I just
myself called it off. M'dad is old-fashioned. He don't understand. I like
to have a good time and everything. I got three girlfriends. They are
girls who work with me at my job—just as soon as we finish, we finish
at five—why we go right home, have supper and get dressed—and we're
gone. Anywheres. It don't matter. No telling wheres. But the way life is
you got have a good time while you can . . ."
"Yeah." Something in my voice sounds strange to me.
"My dad don't understand that though. He just don't see it. He's

always telling me I ought to get married and settle down. But I wouldn't marry no fella now. Why my girlfriend she got married in January . . . was a month pregnant when he was boom! Shipped to Korea . . . killed on July 16th . . . she's twenty. . . . Fella wanted to marry me. He's supposed to go into the army in about six months, so I just told him to his face . . ."

Lorraine looked out the window, listening. They were passing through Rochester, New York, on the shore of Lake Ontario. It was very late, getting on toward midnight, and the locomotive was beginning its gradual, portentous turn toward the Midwest.

Mrs. Hansberry had recently moved to a smaller, though still very spacious, apartment at 1145 South Hyde Park Boulevard, a ten-minute walk from Lake Michigan, at the end of the eastward, decades-long trek of black Southsiders, first up from the South, then out of the ghetto, and finally toward the vista of the open shore.

The day before Bobby and Lorraine's wedding was a Friday, June 19. They spent the afternoon checking the arrangements in the apartment for the ceremony and reception. They were interrupted by a phone call. A friend of theirs confirmed that the execution of Julius and Ethel Rosenberg, convicted of spying for the Soviet Union, would go forward. Their last appeal had been denied, although, out of respect for the Jewish Sabbath, which begins at sundown, their deaths at Sing Sing Prison, in upstate New York, would be delayed until 8 p.m. They would die, as it happened, on their fourteenth wedding anniversary.

Lorraine, in a short story she left uncompleted, contrasts her repressed terror about the finality of the Rosenbergs' being put to death against images of marital rites and domesticity. Her mother's apartment is heavy with oppressive summer weather, her old enemy, one that makes her flesh crawl. The withering heat and the Rosenbergs' death by electrocution on their anniversary occurring on the eve of Lorraine's wedding make her want to run into the street and scream.[39]

And we spoke of it quietly to one another—our voices soft under the discussion of where the cake would be placed and when the photographers would arrive, and who must adjust the bridal train. Our voices above the champagne glasses, our eyes questioning one another between the fresh fragrant flowers in their gleaming pots on the coffee tables of the wedding house, festive house. The Chicago heat in the vast living room suddenly overpowering the senses, some grim terrible fire within suddenly making it more awful, more stifling—the desire to fling the glass into the flowers, to thrust one's arms into the air and run out of the house screaming at one's countrymen to come down out of the apartments, down from the houses, to get up from the television sets, from the dinner tables, from the kitchens where the dishes are being washed with the evening time conversation. . . . And what shall I say to my children? And how shall I explain such a thing to them?

That evening, Bob and Lorraine left the early arriving relatives and guests at Mrs. Hansberry's apartment, and drove to Chicago's Federal Building to join a candlelight vigil in front of the courthouse. "I watch the line, the tall, thin Negro who walks at the head of these four hundred who understand—at the head, walks a Negro."[40]

The following evening, June 20, Lorraine's pastor and friend of the family, the Reverend Archibald Carey Jr., officiated her marriage to Robert Nemiroff.[41] Bob's side was well represented. His parents, Mae and Max Nemiroff, and his brother, Leo, attended, as well as several friends. Two women from Langdon Manor were there: Lorraine Fuchs and Evelyn Goldwasser. Edythe Cohen didn't attend, if she was invited. Lorraine wore Mamie's wedding dress from her brief marriage to an army private, a marriage that had ended in divorce. The off-the-shoulder gown with a deep neckline revealed that Lorraine was so thin that her collarbones and ribs were visible. Perhaps, since she was going secondhand, Bob did, too, and stood up in the tuxedo from his wedding to Elma two years earlier. They said their vows in front of the fireplace.

They would be moving into Bob's childhood home in Greenwich Village, a two-story walk-up at 337 Bleecker Street, between Tenth and Christopher Streets. The gifts they received were intended to speed their entry into the middle class: a flower vase, an electric clock, personalized pillowcases, a carving set, a luncheon set, bowls, ashtrays, frosted glassware, a rainbow-colored towel ensemble, a silver tray, a gold tea service, and a three-piece relish set. Lorraine's family topped it all, however, with a twenty-inch tabletop Philco television. Only 50 percent of American homes had televisions in 1953— fewer, probably, in Greenwich Village. Bob, Perry, and Carl Jr. struggled to get it on the train because it wouldn't fit in Burt D'Lugoff's car.[42]

Soon after setting up housekeeping, Lorraine made an appointment to see a doctor. The office was in a Greenwich Village basement. "The waiting room is in new shades of pink and blue, modern. The room is cut in two places by those new floor-to-ceiling solid plate glass partitions in shiny, black lacquered wooden frames," she noted, "and it is all modern, very modern. It is a nice room to wait in."[43]

She thought she could write a story about her conversation about marriage with the young black woman on the train and the wedding plans interrupted by news of the Rosenbergs' execution, and the visit to the pink-and-blue doctor's office. Her working title was "Reflections During a Season of Murder: A Memorial in Three Parts."

PART IV

Greenwich Village

13

Camp Unity

No other resort provided the best in contemporary jazz and theater, the stimulation of some of the nation's leading intellectuals, and the sense of being part of a social equality vanguard—all at a price that working people could afford.[1]

> —Robert Steck, Camp Unity director

Lorraine's new husband as of June 1953, "my gentle husband," belonged to the category of "corduroy-wearing, chukka-booted, Bergman film–loving, non–cold water flat living, New School lecture[-]attending, Washington Square concert–going, middle-class and usually Jewish argument[-]loving Greenwich Village intellectual[s]." He played the guitar and wrote songs, although he demurred that "music was never my field." He wanted to turn his master's thesis on Theodore Dreiser into a book, and he wrote poetry.[2]

They resided on the top floor of a three-story brick residence built before the Civil War. Lorraine liked it very much. There was a fireplace in the apartment. Downstairs, on the street level, was a hand laundry owned by a Chinese American man named Joe, and a shoe repair shop. "Ours is a very old Village building," she said, "and the lore of the region inclines one to believe that every other structure in the neighborhood has hidden recesses, that is, covered trap doors and the like, which were the passageways of ancient rum-runners or underground railway agents."

She liked the romance of the "twisty little narrow streets" wandering off by themselves and of the houses "with the squared panes of glass" in wood-mullioned windows that made her think of Dickens's London. Tourists perused the Village "in search of ghosts and painters, poets and music makers who did in fact live and work and agonize in these lofts and streets; but equally in search of the ghosts of those, equally famed, who never set foot in this district but whose names the legends have incorporated anyhow." The presence of Italian Americans was strong in the neighborhood. Some summer evenings, Lorraine could lift the window "and hear the mandolin seemingly everywhere."[3]

Bob guided her through the "curling lost avenues" to the hangouts of artists and writers—"a wonderful little, fizzy sort of world," as poet Kenneth Koch put it—the Cedar Tavern; Reinzi, a popular coffeehouse; and Minetta Tavern.

Some establishments refused to serve gays. "If You're Gay, Stay Away," read a sign in one. On the wall of another was a fireman's axe, with the caption, "For Use on Queers." As Hansberry remarked, "[H]uman beings, being as splendidly human as they are[,] do not necessarily come to love one another simply by virtue of living next door to each other."[4] Bars for lesbians were located by the elevated train that ran along West Third Street: the Bagatelle, the Laurels, Provincetown Landing, the Sea Colony, Page Three, Seven Steps, and Lonnie's Hideaway. "Most of these little joints," novelist Ann Bannon remembered, "were owned and run by organized crime in cahoots with the cops. It was scary to be there if they hadn't been raided by the police in a while. It meant the restaurant might be overdue for a raid, and you could end up in a paddy wagon on your way to the police station."[5] The names of those arrested appeared in newspapers the following day.

For an interracial couple, however, the Village was a safe place to live, safer than Harlem. In black neighborhoods, race mingling was commonly regarded as "disgraceful" and assumed to be sexually exploitive because of class differences.[6] Communists demonstrating racial equality in their friendships weren't given a waiver, either, according to Julian Mayfield. "We were usually traveling in mixed company, and this has always been a suspicious thing to the blacks of Harlem. By mixed company, I mean that it was usually large numbers of black men and white women."[7] In Harlem, equality stopped at the bedroom door. Not that the Village was beyond the reach of racial competition for sex. "Being an interracial couple, anywhere, was difficult," said Hettie Jones, who lived with her husband, Amiri Baraka, in Greenwich Village at the same time as Lorraine and Bob. "It was a little bit easier in the Village because people were looser about that, but it was still so unusual that people would look."[8] There were incidents, not many, of black and white men fighting. The Greenwich Village chapter of the interracial Civil Rights Congress circulated petitions calling for the police to do something about it.

Becoming Mrs. Nemiroff coincided with another important change in Hansberry's life: she no longer worked at *Freedom* full-time, although she would remain a contributor. Robeson's enterprise, after three years, hadn't caught on. Paid subscriptions peaked at around eight thousand. Part of the problem was that *Freedom* was a monthly digest of national and international news of interest to cosmopolitan Negroes, but it wasn't timely. Black readers wanting the weather, fashion, baseball scores, current events, and so on could pick up a copy of the *Pittsburgh Courier* from newsstands; or, if they were looking for more pizzazz, the *Amsterdam Star-News*, which was "gleefully devoted to murder, rapes, raids on love-nests, interracial wars," said James Baldwin; "any item, however meaningless, concerning prominent Negroes, and whatever racial gains can be reported for the week—all in just about that order."[9] *Freedom* was interested in everything but the interests of the lower economic and educated class of Harlem.

To begin her job hunt, Lorraine tailored her résumé to the market. She claimed that she was twenty-four, not twenty-two, and had a degree from the University of Wisconsin. She referred to Freedom Associates as "F.A. Publishing," to downplay her Communist connections. The change in the wording was actually a gesture of protest. As James Smethurst said about other radicals living in the shadow of McCarthyism, "This was not cowardice but a sense that they had no obligation to make the Red hunters' jobs easier."[10]

She checked the want ads in city newspapers, circling ones that looked promising.[11] Being in the arts, as always, was an unpredictable way to make a living. Advertisements for actors, for example, appeared in the same Help Wanted column as openings for dishwashers. But things weren't dire—she wasn't facing what most black artists confronted: "hunger" and "aloneness," remembered Amiri Baraka, or the prospect of New York winters in a cold-water flat "without a job and very little money."[12] (Baraka read and wrote in the kitchen while he was wrapped in blanket, his feet propped up inside the warm oven.) Bob Nemiroff had a white-collar job to cover the rent. While he completed his master's in English literature at NYU, he was working part-time at Ethyl Corporation, a chemical manufacturing company, running the lithograph machine for in-house communications. Also, Lorraine, upon turning twenty-one, had inherited two kitchenette buildings from her father and become a partner in Hansberry Enterprises. Soon, she would begin receiving her share of the profits in the form of annual checks for about $1,200—the equivalent of $11,500 in today's money.[13]

In July 1953, her response to an advertisement placed by *Gourmet* magazine brought an encouraging reply from the executive editor: "If you care to call for an appointment next week, we shall be glad to see you in reference to an editorial position on our staff."[14] The theme of the July issue was "The Semi-Rugged Life," about making preserves and jellies from scratch. *Gourmet*'s offices were located in the exclusive Plaza Hotel, on Fifth Avenue, across from Central Park, not far from the Waldorf-Astoria, where Mrs. Hansberry had been shunted into a "crappy" room, despite having a reservation. Lorraine's appointment was for 11:15 a.m. on a Tuesday. Evidently, she wasn't offered the job.

She was already committed anyway that July to something else—working at progressive summer camp Camp Unity, located ninety miles north of New York City, on 242 acres of woods in the foothills of the Berkshires, beside Lake Ellis. Camp Unity was like Camp Woodland, the one that Bob and Burt D'Lugoff had attended when they were boys. In fact, Lorraine's spending part of the summer at the progressive camp seems to have been Bob's idea. She had been hired to be the "lawn program director," providing entertainment for the guests. Bob planned to come up on weekends with his guitar for the sing-alongs.

Camp Unity had been founded in 1927 as the "first proletarian summer colony" for trade unionists and their families. After World War II, it became the first integrated resort in the United States. But race mixing suggested social leveling and, consequently, raised alarms with the House

Un-American Activities Committee. "This camp is operated by the Communist party," the committee reported, "even though this fact is kept from the general public." Its purpose, the committee maintained, was to bring "submission to Communist party membership and discipline."[15]

Camp Unity was, indeed, operated by the American Communist Party, one of several "Red diaper" family camps, as critics called them, in the Northeast. But Camp Unity's primary aim was to provide enjoyable social and cultural programs for working-class families through "progressive entertainment" offered all summer long. There was folksinging by the Weavers, Woody Guthrie, or Lead Belly, for instance, dances and intramural sports, poetry readings, and speakers on current events. On Saturday nights, there were plays with social themes performed in Freedom Theater. The idea was to inspire campers with the desire to work for a better world.[16] Participation in planned activities wasn't mandatory. Some campers preferred doing their own thing—getting up early and going fishing, taking a snooze before breakfast, and then spending the rest of the day relaxing, which might include playing basketball or tennis. In the evening, there was always the choice to skip the campfire and take a romantic stroll up to a place called Lenin's Rock.

The camp strove to be a good neighbor to the nearby country towns of Webatuck and Wingdale, but occasionally there was friction. When a barber refused to give a black camper a haircut, a delegation from the camp went to his shop and "persuaded him to change his mind."[17]

So, in mid-July 1953, after she'd been married for only a month, Lorraine took the New York Central up to Wingdale. At the train station, an old school bus picked her up for the drive down back roads, deep into the countryside. "Weren't we all so good and pure while all the world was black and evil?" a camper reminisced to Unity's director, Robert Steck. "Wasn't the camp an island in protected waters and weren't the busses like barges swaying along country roads, gliding under tree arches, making dust waves as they headed farther and farther away from the mainland where all the 'Reactionaries' lived and ruled."[18]

The bus rolled up beside the main office, where Lorraine received two towels, two sheets, a pillowcase, and two blankets. Her bungalow was one of those reserved for married couples—albeit with bunk beds, she discovered. On Friday night, Bob arrived and joined her in leading campfire songs, accompanied on the banjo by Guy Carawan, later the arranger of the Negro spiritual that became the anthem for the civil rights movement, "We Shall Overcome." Before Nemiroff returned to the city on Sunday evening, he left a note under Lorraine's pillow with instructions: "Darling, A good good creative summer. I know it will be because you have much to give to the job and much to take away from it. So make the most of it, as I know you will."[19]

Among the guests, there was "little specifically political talk," an FBI informant reported, but Hansberry discovered that most of her fellow members on the staff council were smitten with being social justice warriors, which she found rather tiresome. The "one who remains the sanest," she wrote Bob, was Margaret Burroughs, also alumna of Englewood High and later cofounder of the DuSable Museum of African American History, in Chicago's Washington Park.[20] A major topic of discussion was race relations and white guilt, at meetings conducted Soviet-style, during which, Lorraine said, "amends and self-criticisms are to be rendered." The American Communist Party had renewed a campaign against white chauvinism, spurred by an article in *Political Affairs* by a Harlem Communist, Pettis Perry. Perry had accused white members of the party's New York section of signing restricted covenants in order to get better apartments and of refusing to promote black comrades into leadership positions within the organization—typical chicanery, Perry said, of the "imperialist offensive of the bourgeoisie."[21]

Hansberry was cautious about finger-pointing, which put her at odds with some of the camp's militants. She agreed "that white chauvinism is one of the foremost devices of the white ruling class to separate Negro and white workers"; but it was sowing disunion, she said, when "comrades are made to feel that they are an 'enemy.'" Too much time, she complained, was being spent at meetings discussing petty interactions between white and black campers. "I cannot agree that to dispute, disagree, decide against, or dislike a Negro person is automatically 'white chauvinist.'" She tried reminding council members that Camp Unity was an "opportunity of living democratically" and experiencing "genuine social collectivity" and fraternity and love. Regardless, a group of black waiters continued to meet nightly to share examples of racism they'd witnessed and to discuss how to mete out punishment by castigating the offenders.[22]

Sparing Hansberry from getting too angry—she could be "a furious lady, half-kid, half-queen," said a friend—was her ironic sense of humor. "One hot summer afternoon," remembered a fellow staffer, "we were sitting on the steps of her cabin . . . We weren't really talking—just smoking and sitting—then she turned to me very gravely, 'Do you suppose ol' Massa will *ever* let us have a stomp?'"[23]

She became friends with Doris Belack, an actress, and her husband, Philip Rose. A concert baritone, Rose was born on the Lower East Side to immigrant Jews. He and Doris had met while performing together in a Gilbert and Sullivan opera company. Recently, he had given up that career to start a business producing and distributing "race records"—blues, jazz, gospel music, and also comedy—in New York City's black neighborhoods. Like Lorraine, Rose had a droll sense of humor. He asked her, with an air of concern, whether she planned to pursue a career as a waitress, after she served him in the dining hall, because she was terrible at it. She thought he was a "genuinely worthwhile human being and a lot of fun."[24]

During one of Bob's weekend visits, Lorraine introduced him to Doris and Phil. That friendship, begun at a summer camp between four young people involved in the arts, would lead to *A Raisin in the Sun.*

In the autumn, Lorraine's job hunt resumed. The work she found was never satisfactory or equal to her skills. She sewed clothing labels inside coats for a furrier and applied to be a secretary at Macy's department store. For that, she was required to take an intelligence exam, which, she was informed, she hadn't passed. She was excited when she was hired as a production secretary on a Broadway play. But her chief responsibility, it turned out, was serving coffee. She quit at the end of her first day.

To keep her writing muscles limber, she submitted articles for left-wing newspapers and "all the little journals of the working-class."[25] She made a proposal to the *Chicago Defender* to write a series of profiles of black artists and applied to be a reporter for the *New York Times.* But nothing came of either one.

In the meantime, her friend Douglas Turner Ward had returned to New York. His conviction for draft evasion had been overturned by the U.S. Supreme Court. (Rosie Jackson, his erstwhile roommate and Lorraine's married fiancé, had disappeared. Ward never saw Rosie again.) During his confinement, Ward had written a play, *The Trial of Willie*

McGee. The play was Ward's first attempt at writing drama, and he asked Lorraine if she'd participate in a reading of his script. To give the occasion a professional feel, he rented a meeting room at the Theresa Hotel. His new roommate, Lonne Elder, would be there, a twenty-six-year-old actor who hadn't thought of himself as a playwright until friends at the Harlem Writers Guild began encouraging him.

Lorraine agreed to take part in the reading, not only out of friendship, but also because she'd been working on a play herself, a three-act called *The Final Glory*, based on the arrest and trial of black union leader Harold Ward (no relation to Douglas), in Chicago. A front-page story about the case had appeared in the November 1952 issue of *Freedom*. Ward had been accused of killing a Negro strikebreaker during a walkout at the International Harvester Company. After the strike ended, he was acquitted of all charges. The murder charge had been a frame-up to turn public opinion against the union's demands.

The Final Glory is Hansberry's first attempt at dramatizing the world and characters of *A Raisin in the Sun*. She renames the Ward family "the Freemans." As the curtain rises[26]:

> It is late afternoon in the Freeman apartment on Chicago's Southside. Visible to the audience is the living room furnished with a couch; some commercial paintings on the wall behind; a small table with a phonograph atop it; a coffee table. One corner of the living room is furnished as a kitchenette. . . . After a few seconds, the door to the outer hall opens and a small boy, about nine-years-old, stands in the doorway with school books in his arms. He has used a door key which is tied to a long string around his neck and has not removed it to open the door.

The social message of Ward's *The Trial of Willie McGee* and Hansberry's *The Final Glory* was well timed and reflects a postwar development in New York theater. The energies of the Little Theatre movement of the 1920s and '30s were finding renewal on Off-Broadway stages, especially in the playhouses of Greenwich Village. The ambition of these smaller theaters was not to rival the commercial successes of the big shows on Forty-Second Street, but to open a performance space for dramatizing cultural, social, or political issues—plays in which outsiders fight for independence and dignity, such as George Tabori's *The Emperor's Clothes* (1953), William Branch's *In Splendid Error* (1954), and Alice Childress's *Trouble in Mind* (1955).

Lorraine arrived for the reading of *The Trial of Willie McGee*—his "opus," Ward called it. And indeed, it was four and a half hours long. But it was so good that Elder remembered being "amazed."[27] Hansberry felt the same. If Ward could write a full-length drama like that on his first try, why couldn't they?

That afternoon at the Theresa Hotel in 1953, three new lights of the theater flickered into being. *The Trial of Willie McGee* would never be performed (too long), but Douglas Ward would go on to win a Drama Desk Award in 1966 for playwriting and would become cofounder of the Negro Ensemble Company. Lonne Elder's 1969 play *Ceremonies in Dark Old Men* would be nominated for the Pulitzer Prize. And Hansberry decided she would finish *The Final Glory*—her first step toward becoming a playwright.[28]

Hansberry's second stay at Camp Unity during the summer of 1954 started badly. "My own dear husband," Lorraine began a letter to Bob. "I am sitting here in this miserable little bungalow, in this miserable camp that I once loved so much, feeling cold, useless, frustrated, helpless, disillusioned, and angry and tired. . . . I want to come home—I am coming home. I am sorry. I am sorry for us that it didn't work out, there are some things that could have been wonderful about my being here."[29]

She was disenchanted for several reasons. There was a new director, and he was a butt pincher—something he hadn't tried on her, but his male chauvinism was contemptible. She had performed, poorly she thought, in a play at Freedom Theater. "I don't know what on earth made me think I ever wanted to be an actress. I am so awkward and sound so terrible in my little lines. I don't seem to know how to interpret the most simple things, they sound so silly when I say them."[30] She was glad that Alice Childress was there as the camp's cultural director, but something was wrong with their friendship. Lorraine had looked forward to working with Childress on original material to augment Freedom Theater's offerings of summer stock plays. But she was unable to break through Childress's reserve, for some reason. "Alice and her unlimited dimensions, whom I know no better than I did in the city, but I continue to respect."[31] Unknown to her, Childress was having trouble in her marriage to actor Alvin Childress, a respected alumnus of the American Negro Theater, who played Amos in the popular vaudevillian television series *Amos 'n' Andy*. Alice was adamant that the role was humiliating, and she and Alvin had fought about it. They divorced in 1957.

Most upsetting to Hansberry, however, was how the staff council's ideological purity and mea culpas with regard to "the people," and "chauvinism" and "white supremacy" had increased, percolating out of the meetings, spilling over into the camp, and creating a pernicious atmosphere. She voiced her objections to the council. "The management has to all purposes adopted a vague, inconsistent and ambiguous political policy which reflects a panic-stricken, opportunist retreat." Progressive ideas about equality had somehow been twisted into an obsession with correct thinking that was enforced by the staff. This, Lorraine attributed to hiring "politically underdeveloped department heads," radical poseurs who were making everyone miserable with their sanctimony and power seeking.[32] The last straw was a Soviet-style show trial involving actor Herschel Bernardi, who had been performing at the camp for four years for room and board.

A little background to Bernardi's trial is needed: Prior to Hansberry's working at the camp, the camp baker's wife had been put on "trial" after she was overheard making a racist remark at dinner. An offended waiter summoned her to a meeting on the lawn. While she sat in front of everyone, pilloried, she was accused of "trying to destroy the Negro people." No one came to her defense. Director Steck said it was because she was an unsympathetic figure, "full of the pretensions[,] and expressed the type of status-seeking[,] associated with lily-white, middle-class Queens neighborhoods," a surprisingly anti-Semitic description coming from Camp Unity's leader, but proof that Hansberry was right about the Stalinist parody that the resort was becoming.

In an unpublished memoir, Steck describes what happened when it was Bernardi's turn to confront his accusers, and how Lorraine reacted[33]:

The orchestra leader, a black man, asked Bernardi to make sure nobody touched the drums in his absence. When a black actor came in and began playing the drums, Bernardi told him to stop. The actor replied, "I just ran into him. He said it's all right." Bernardi insisted, "No, this was two minutes ago. He told me not to let anybody play." The actor asked him, "Are you calling me a liar?" Knowing the tenor of the times, Bernardi thought to himself, "I gotta make a big decision. Yes. You're a liar." That night he was charged with chauvinist behavior. If found guilty, Bernardi would be expelled from the camp. He was saved by Lorraine Hansberry who acted as his defense attorney, without meaning to be. She just got up and said, "You're all assholes."

Lorraine felt bad about leaving the camp; she thought she was letting Bob down. He had a way of quietly making it clear that he had expectations for her. "So make the most of it," he'd written in the note he left under her pillow the previous summer, "as I know you will." She was prone to thinking that she was never doing enough, despite participating in protests, picket lines, and causes so often that the FBI had taken a special interest in her.

"I seem to be a woman of crisis," she said miserably when she told him she was coming home. When she arrived in the apartment, there was a note from Bob replying to her letter. He loved her, he said. "Even in a letter such as this[,] where you are so obviously grappling with yourself, uncertain, unresolved about many things. Yes, this was a difficult summer, raising so many questions. You've got the talent, you've got the depth, the inner artistry to give something free and fresh and important to this world. . . . All that you need now, darling . . . is a little more self-confidence; a little more self-honesty and self-criticism . . . and finally, a little less of the feeling that you alone can think all things thru by yourself."[34]

The tone was indulgent. He acknowledged that she was upset without saying she was right and patiently suggested that perhaps some self-examination was in order and that she needed to rely more on him.

14

"One Becomes a Woman"

This is of course why I don't produce a thing—I am too full of dreams!
—Lorraine Hansberry, letter to Bob Nemiroff, 1954

By the second year of her marriage, Lorraine's domestic life resembled that of a middle-class woman. Bob was now an editor in the promotions department for Avon Books, a romance publisher. They had a small dog named Spice who trotted around the apartment—a sort of Sheltie-Corgi mix. In the room where the fireplace was, bookshelves stood from floor to ceiling. And above the mantelpiece was a framed print of Michelangelo's *Adam and Eve*. In one corner sat a Danish modern chair—a good place for listening to music.[1]

Lorraine and Bob were self-admitted "folk music addicts." They went to cellar clubs where the door charge was whatever you could afford, tossed into a basket by the entrance. Lorraine worked part-time handling subscriptions for *Sing Out!*, the magazine covering the folk scene. As a favor to Burt D'Lugoff's brother, Art, she posted flyers all around the Village about a benefit concert Art was producing for Pete Seeger, blacklisted as a Red. Art had rented the Circle in the Square Theatre for a midnight show, getting the venue for practically nothing. The concert was a sellout, despite the hour, and the first professionally produced folk music concert. Bob and Burt D'Lugoff, who was in medical school at New York University, started thinking about how to cash in.[2]

Phil Rose had his finger in the wind, too. Long-playing, high-fidelity, 33 rpm vinyl records sounded richer and mellower than the old 78 rpm platters. There was a market of young audiophiles just waiting to be served. Rose launched his own label, Glory Records, and began building a catalogue of jazz, rhythm and blues, and doo-wop—and, of course, the ubiquitous folk music. Lorraine was pleased when he asked her to write the liner notes for *The Poetry of the Negro*, read by Sidney Poitier.

The essay she delivered for the album's back cover is notable for its fresh insights about black American literature. She disagrees with critics about Paul Laurence Dunbar, for example. They had excoriated his verse as self-hating and embarrassing. "Seen my lady home las' night, / Jump back, honey, jump back. / Hel' huh han' an' sque'z it tight, / Jump back, honey, jump back."[3] Hansberry drew a distinction between dialect and vernacular. "Dialect," she later said, "is the traditional product and device of careless or indifferent artists who are preoccupied with stereotypes rather than true characterizations."[4] Vernacular, such as Dunbar's, has nuances that express an encoded language of resistance, a way of saying no to complete assimilation. Perhaps she was remembering the way the mountain folk in *Dark of the Moon* spun a world of witches and superstition into being with their rustic language; or how O'Casey's characters used certain expressions and flights of speech that distinguished them as Irish. In the same way, black vernacular, she argued, expressed the racial spirit from within.

Hansberry fought against the idea that the ways of ordinary people were inferior. Beginning in college, she noticed, "there was virtually no field in the arts where 'fashion' did not find the vigorous emotions of common folk 'sentimental'; where the wonder of their speech as they actually spoke it and made it work for them was not held 'crude'; where the lively assertion of their mannerisms and clothes was not found 'quaint.'"[5] This attitude, in her opinion, sneered at people's differences and individuality. Personally, she liked to use colloquialisms because they were picturesque. "Youse is a good boy, Denny," she said approvingly to Bob, a catchphrase from her favorite comic strip.[6]

But when she used black expressions in her conversation—often for humorous effect—Bob upbraided her for it, as if she were, paradoxically, appropriating herself. "I utterly loathe to hear the way you colored intellectuals are always affecting the speech and inflections of the Negro masses!"

In turn, she pointed out that his own "first-generation self" often added Yiddish to "colorless standard English." Their disagreement became an essay that she cleverly titled, with puns, "Images and Essences: Dialogue with an Uncolored Egg-Head."[7]

At the end of the summer of 1954, Bob became an entrepreneur with a start-up idea. For the Labor Youth League, he would bring back a 1930s Communist magazine for youth called *Challenge*. Its reincarnation would be rechristened, appropriately enough, *New Challenge*.[8] He might have put some money into it; if so, that decision probably accounts for a plot point in Lorraine's second play, *The Sign in Sidney Brustein's Window*. ("A newspaper? Oh, Sidney, Sidney, Sidney! When are you going to grow up? A *newspaper*?!")

New Challenge would be compact, like *Reader's Digest*: a pocket-size, staple-bound, photo-illustrated publication of around forty pages, priced at fifteen cents. Its mission statement would appear in the masthead: "We take our stand on every issue with the working people of our land, with the small farmer, with the Negro people and the minorities. We interest ourselves in Marxism, which offers a scientific view of society and the hope of a bright future for youth."

Lorraine agreed to support Bob as one of four contributors to the magazine; the other three were LYL friends of his. Bob would be the editor in chief. The work was divvied up. Everyone would write stories covering the magazine's general theme: activism among world youth. Lorraine's bailiwick would be young people's involvement in anticolonial movements in Africa and efforts in the United States to secure equal rights. And Bob, under the pen name "Robert Rolfe," would supply self-help columns on relationships and marriage aimed at their target readership. Bob liked to give advice on interpersonal matters, especially those having to do with meeting the needs of others. One column was "Boy Meets Girl—and Then What?" Another was "Behind the Battle of the Sexes."

In "Is Wedlock a Padlock?," he urged husbands to adopt a feminist point of view: "Like most of us, Sue and Jim had looked on marriage as a chance to start out in life on their own: to set up a home, start a family, fulfill all the normal healthy needs of every young person." But in marriages in which both people work, wives are "dependent because they are considered inferior, can't get as good jobs, get paid less for the same work. . . . [I]t means cold cash to the owners of industry to *keep* women dependent and underpaid!" This is a result of a "'man's world' way of life—and for attitudes spread by the few who profit from it."[9] A husband's responsibility is "to reject all ideas that women are inferior" and to assist his wife in becoming independent.

In September 1954, Lorraine went by train to Chicago to meet Mamie's new husband, Vincent Tubbs. Mamie was thirty-one, and Vincent was thirty-eight; they had married in August, in a small ceremony in Baltimore. During the war, Tubbs had been one of seven correspondents for the *Baltimore Afro-American*, assigned to cover Gen. Douglas MacArthur's campaigns in the South West Pacific.[10] The newlyweds would be living in Chicago because Vincent had joined Johnson Publishing Company as an associate editor of *Ebony* magazine.

Lorraine was not impressed by him. She thought he was "a fizzle" and a "drip in his race and politics thinking." She had only one serious political discussion with him, and "I am sure there are no doubts in his little mind as to what I am and what I believe in." He seemed like "a card-carrying 'Uncle Tom'" to her brother Perry, and she agreed.[11]

Otherwise, the Hansberry way of life continued. Lorraine noted that Perry and Carl Jr. were "full of investment talk," despite being in legal trouble.[12] The State of Illinois had taken them to court for again violating the Rent Control Act of 1947 by overcharging three Negro households. The judge had levied a fine on Hansberry Enterprises of over three thousand dollars—treble the amount the brothers had collected from the tenants. But Carl Jr. and Perry weren't going to pay it, on the grounds that the plaintiffs had lied.[13]

Mamie had been asked to model in a fashion show for charity at the Club DeLisa, the most prestigious black nightclub in the city. For "Dripping in Mink," organized by the Chicago chapter of the National Council of Negro Women, she would promenade down the runway in a full-length pastel mink coat lined in rose-colored statin with straight sleeves and a shawl collar.[14]

One night, after returning from Mamie and Vincent's "ultra-modern apartment," off Lake Shore Drive, Lorraine called Bob. It was late, and

"cool and blowy, in a way that only this Chicago of mine can be blowy."
They talked, but afterward, Lorraine couldn't sleep. She got up and tried to
explain to him in a letter what was really on her mind.

The gist was she was feeling sexually on edge. "I am a little nervous,
smoking too much and remarkably restless and fidgety as I indicated on
the phone. . . . I do wish we were closer in some matters so that there were
no aspects of my problems that we could not share—and yet this is not
the case. We are really terribly different kinds of people. I miss you rather
keenly as a matter of fact—a great deal more than I imagined I would this
time—and apparently my capacity for physical—attention—is showing."
She blamed her anxiety partly on wanting to be too many things—"Lorraine
the Journalist," or "Lorraine the Actress." She was giving "All the Dark and
Beautiful Warriors," the novel she'd started in college, another revision, but
she also had a good idea for a libretto for an opera about John Henry. "This
is of course why I don't produce a thing—I am too full of dreams!"

Tired out finally, she finished up her five-page letter where she had
started: "Honey, it is time for me to go to bed. I wish you were here—
surely there is nothing remotely obscene about a woman specifying why
she wishes for her husband specifically at the bed hour—perhaps I shall
come home tonight—by plane. There *are* things that do trouble me about
our marriage—most of the serious ones have to do with me. But some
have to do with you—we shall discuss them all. Who knows, by the time I
come home perhaps they won't exist at all."

In the margin beside her name, she added, "Baby—maybe this here
earth doan never move—but it sho' do tremble powerful."[15]

Freedom was pretty much finished as a viable newspaper by late 1954. Robeson closed the offices at 53 West 125th Street and moved to smaller quarters in Harlem. The decision to downsize was driven not only by money
problems, but also by signs that the high point of American communism
had passed. The Committee for the Negro in the Arts, the National Negro
Labor Council, the Council on African Affairs—all would fold by the mid-
to late 1950s.

It was the tenor of the times, Julian Mayfield said. "Gone generally
were all of the economic and social factors which had brought about some
small degree of unity between blacks and whites during the Depression. In

the thirties young Communists . . . fought with city marshals who sought to evict tenants from their apartments for non-payment of rent. Gone were the days when Communists had been involved very deeply in the boycotts of the slums along 125th Street, which would accept black money but would not hire black employees."[16]

Robeson had attended a meeting at the YMCA in Harlem organized by the New York NAACP because the topic was getting more jobs for Negroes in radio and television. The chairman announced that anyone who wasn't anticommunist wasn't welcome. When Robeson rose from the floor to speak, he was booed and shouted down. "Paul is no more interested in getting justice than I am in jumping off the Empire State Building," said the chapter's vice president. "We have no intention of being identified with him. I told him three times to sit down. He was recognized for a question and he was going to make a speech."[17]

Freedom, by addressing mainly national and international issues, had missed the big story at its feet: the one that mattered to Harlemites. The ghettoization of blacks at that end of the city was beginning to be laid down in concrete. Urban redevelopment plans for expressways and revitalized business centers were sending bulldozers rumbling into slums. One-third of East Harlem was being razed to create "the Projects"—public housing with seventy-five thousand low-income units, for more than half a million people. "There were too many people full of hate and bitterness crowded into a dirty, stinky, uncared-for closet-size section of a great city," Claude Brown wrote in *Manchild in the Promised Land*. "The children of these disillusioned colored pioneers inherited the total lot of their parents—the disappointments, the anger. To add to their misery, they had little hope of deliverance. For where does one run to when he's already in the promised land?"[18] For some, nothing short of armed revolution would change any-thing.

Malcolm X had arrived in Harlem in 1954 as a minister of the Nation of Islam, and black Muslims were tapping into the community's craving for pride and personal dignity with great success. Even the artists and activists who had once frequented the *Freedom* offices—Julian Mayfield, John O. Killens, Alice Childress, and Esther Cooper Jackson—were beginning to identify "first" as black people, in Mayfield's words, rather than "as mere workers in the class structure of the United States."[19]

"How true it is, we cannot say," reported the *New York Age Defender*, "but we are informed that Robeson is a lonely man when he walks the streets. The once enthusiastic crowds . . . are no longer enthusiastic or curious. They pass him, look at him, but pass him."[20] The terrible irony of his life was that he had given unyielding support to a totalitarian regime that was the enemy of the very goals in which he believed.

FBI agents, picking through the paper trash left behind in the abandoned *Freedom* offices, selected items that looked interesting. Ones that seemed worthwhile or informative were added to the files on black activists with Communist ties, including Lorraine.[21]

On her desk in the apartment was a framed photograph of Robeson. He was an inspiration to her, a hero, but a cautionary lesson, too. He had told the American public what it didn't want to hear, and as a result, it had turned on him.

The choice of subjects for him to speak about had always been limited. To be listened to, he could address the "Negro problem," because that was what whites expected of him: to view all social, economic, and political issues from the Negro angle. He could speak with moral certitude as a "race man," defending Negro interests; he could protest conflicts in his life as a Negro. These were roles permitted him. But when he questioned the sincerity of the American creed regarding freedom of speech, racial equality, and so on, he offended Middle America.

Lorraine, being a generation younger than Robeson, was entering life when the stakes were higher for black intellectuals. Mass media (national television and radio broadcasts) meant that a single voice could be heard by millions, internationally, too. But the media spotlight could just as easily be switched off for those who didn't present an optimistic view of America and race relations, as had happened to Robeson. The microphone was available to the "representative Negro." Mass media could be a new frontier for achieving equity in the public eye or a device for magnifying misperceptions about black Americans.

Lorraine was reminded how deeply embedded were white paternalistic notions when, in October 1954, she happened to read a column in the *New York Times* by film critic Bosley Crowther. Crowther took a rather scholarly approach to film, and wrote as if he were conducting a seminar at his alma mater, Princeton. Thus, when he devoted a column to "Negroes in Film," he took the same plummy tone, even when voicing racist attitudes.

"It has long been a gripe of this reviewer," he began, "that a race of people as wholesomely endowed with talents for singing and dancing as the Negro people are should be so infrequently given opportunities to perform on the screen."[22] He wondered why there weren't more Hollywood black musicals to showcase their natural abilities, like *Stormy Weather*, with Fats Waller and Bill "Bojangles" Robinson, for instance.

Lorraine was incredulous. She fired off a rebuttal, which she intended as a letter to the editor. "It is a sad feature of our American life that those persons like yourself, who appear to have any degree of consciousness with regard to the Negro people in this country, must themselves out of ignorance and misguided beliefs aid in the perpetuation of some of the most outmoded and even vicious notions about Negroes and our culture. . . . We despair of and despise all materials which persist in presenting us as a carefree, irresponsible, childlike people." There are no biological differences between human beings, she argued, "there is no special gift among our people for these talents [singing and dancing]—simply because such gifts are not and cannot be 'racial.'" What black audiences wanted to see on the screen was "reality. We want to see films about a people who live and work like everybody else, but who currently must battle fierce oppression to do so . . . [W]e want employment for our young writers and actors, who can best give expression to our sorrow, songs and laughter, and our blues and our poetry—and the very drama of our lives. After all," she said, "three hundred years of oppression have given us a mighty song to sing."[23]

Crowther replied, thanking her and expressing his wish that more readers would take his criticism as seriously, but regretting that her letter would not be published because of space limitations.

Like all serious beginning writers, Hansberry realized that developing craft is part of the process. "Before the gates of excellence the high gods have placed sweat," warned the Greek poet Hesiod; "long is the road thereto and rough and steep at first." Athena may have leaped fully formed from the forehead of Zeus, but that's not how it works for mortals. Lorraine collected books that she hoped would help her with playwriting. She outlined

Aristotle's theory of tragedy. She kept a file of index cards with ideas and advice from her extensive reading. In a biography of Leonardo da Vinci, she discovered a passage on "how to make an imaginary animal appear real," which she thought applied to drama. The trick was to make sure that each part has some basis in reality—the legs might come from a turtle, the body from a dog, and the head from a parrot. This was useful for, as she noted to herself, creating the illusion of real people on the stage. They should be made up of identifiable components.[24]

She found books about playwriting, however, "rather unrewarding." Better for developing her muscles as a dramatist was analyzing individual plays—scene by scene, line by line, to find out what made them tick, "to dissect the great ones—from Euripides to Shakespeare, from Ibsen through Sean O'Casey. I spent endless hours at this by myself and, of course, I went to the theater and carefully analyzed the best production."[25]

She completed the *Final Glory*, the play about the Chicago union leader accused of murder. Then, her next two scripts, *The Apples of Autumn* and *Flowers for the General*, were a complete change of direction: the conflicts for these came from inside her. The difference was the result of reading a particular book, a "*great* book"—one that had nothing to do with playwriting. She devoted "months of study" to it, and she gave it a prominent place on her reference shelf. It was Simone de Beauvoir's *The Second Sex*, just translated into English, the "work which has excited and agitated me," Hansberry said, "more than any other single book that I can recall out of my adult experience."[26]

Simone de Beauvoir was born in Paris in 1908, to a wealthy, bourgeois family like Hansberry's. One day, while drying the dishes her mother was washing, she caught sight of the wives in the windows opposite doing the same thing, and she had a vision of domestic life as an endless hall of mirrors, reflecting the same image to the vanishing point. "There *had* been people who had done things," Beauvoir said to herself. "I, too, would do things."[27] She studied philosophy at the Sorbonne and took the highly competitive philosophy *agrégation* exam, coming in second behind Jean-Paul Sartre. (He had flunked it the year before.) She became Sartre's lifelong companion.

The implication that *she* accompanied *him* is deliberate. She regarded herself as his disciple, always in second place, and only much later would her reputation as a philosopher and public intellectual pull even with his. Perhaps to explore why she subordinated herself was the impetus for her writing *The Second Sex*, at the heart of which is the nature of patriarchy and how "One is not born, but rather becomes, a woman."

After World War II ended—she had lived in Paris during the German occupation—Beauvoir became intrigued with Americans and racial issues, perhaps because she had met American soldiers, or possibly because it was hard for her to reconcile that the liberators had come from a land where segregation was enforced, despite the national rhetoric and claims of equality. In 1947, she traveled around the United States for four months, often by Greyhound bus, visiting small universities such as Smith and Vassar (women-only colleges at the time) and Oberlin. During her trip, she read Gunnar Myrdal's *An American Dilemma: The Negro Problem and Modern Democracy*. She became friends with Richard Wright. In Chicago, she met a "rather tall young man, his chest stiffened by a leather jacket"— the novelist Nelson Algren—and they became lovers.[28]

Beauvoir sensed that the American story was suffused with themes of power and domination. The master-slave relationship was not at all limited to the antebellum South: in modern American life, there was also the gender divide between the Subject, men, and the Other, women. The Subject is absolute; the Other is inessential.

Yet gender in the natural world, as she argues at length in *The Second Sex*, is not an eternal, inescapable metaphysical or even biological essence; it's only a social construct that robs women of their freedom and power to determine their own destinies and identities. To justify patriarchal domination as normal, Western literary, social, political, and religious traditions have woven a tight, cultural web to reinforce an ideology of women's "natural" inferiority. In many ways, women are treated as if they were members of a racial minority. With males of European descent solidly in the position of master, and with superiority equated with power, the economic oppression of colonized, enslaved, and other exploited nonwhite people also "naturally" follows. When this oppression is challenged, however, when "one fails to adhere to an accepted code, one becomes an insurgent."[29]

Beauvoir's description of women's compulsory status didn't surprise

Hansberry. She agreed with the book's premise, which was basically, in her words, what "woman desires is freedom. She is a subjective being like man[,] and like man she must pursue her transcendence forever. That is the nature of the human race. . . . The station of woman is hardly one that she would assume by choice, any more than man would. It must necessarily be imposed on her—by force."

In her own life, Lorraine had resisted accepting the program her mother had set out for Mamie, which was making herself desirable to men and dependent on them. Marriage should be enough for women, her mother insisted. Beauvoir, Hansberry was heartened to read, "does not anywhere accept the traditional views of its sacred place in the scheme of human development."[30] Nor was having children sufficient inducement to marry, either, Lorraine thought. "They are 'the future of the race,'" of course, she conceded; "they are lovely; they are quick and bright and full of experience from the observing adult—*but they are only children*. One may spend from fourteen to eighteen hours a day with a human being of five[,] and the occasion simply will not arrive when one may discuss the meaning of strontium with that person."[31] Hansberry also objected to the commodifying of women, including the presumption that women giving sex to men was something that made them worthwhile in "this precious society where all women are reduced to the status of home furnishings to be appraised like something to buy on billboards, calendars, theater marquees and in their own bedrooms."[32]

She did not dislike men (and neither did Beauvoir). In fact, she didn't subscribe at all to the notion that men lacked deep feelings. Men should be "supremely insulted" that women were considered essentially superior in "compassion, understanding—and of all things love." This "great slander of the ages" discourages men from feeling empathy, which is crucial for seeing the Other in his or her own right. She was convinced that if "by some miracle women should not ever utter a single protest against their condition there would still exist among men those who could not endure in peace until her liberation could be achieved." If this happened, society would be transformed by women's energies and sorrows: "Freed—who can only guess what stores, what wealth she can give humanity: wealth which will be the product of her centuries of humiliation, exploitation, degradation and sheer slavery."[33]

Sometimes, when she was feeling anxious about herself or the state of the world, Hansberry took down *The Second Sex* and reread parts of it. "It is as if I can hear my whole generation crying out: what is to become of us . . . and humanity around us? . . . And then I read Simone in frustration again and slept. And then I arose and sat and stared and read Simone again and wished that I could drink when it is this bad."[34] Her stomach gave her trouble when she was upset.

One aspect of Beauvoir that gave Lorraine no comfort, however, was the Frenchwoman's embrace of existentialism. Beauvoir's partner, Sartre, had worked out his original existentialist ideas as a deliberate challenge to Marxism. Yet Lorraine, as a Marxist wedded to empirical arguments about how to improve humankind's lot, could not abide the existentialist view that free and conscious human beings had been hurled into an irrational, meaningless world in which they would always feel estranged from themselves and others—a cataclysmic personal experience. Nor could they undo their melancholy fate through religion, artistic creation, good works, liberalism, or social revolution. They could hold on to their dignity only by inventing ways, suitable to them, to endure.

Hansberry had no patience with the argument. "The 'why' of why we are here is an intrigue for adolescents; the 'how' is what must command the living." Consistent with her contempt for abstract art, she did not like anything that seemed nihilistic, which she had made clear when she reviewed Wright's novel *Outsider* for *Freedom* and vilified him for how, in her words, he "exalts brutality and nothingness."[35] The morally mature person, she argued, should be up and at the barricades to defend *liberté, égalité, fraternité*—one of her favorite phrases. Her conviction on this point brought her into fierce debate for the rest of her life with the work of Albert Camus, Samuel Beckett, Edward Albee, Jean Genet, and Norman Mailer over the meanings of human existence, responsibility, and freedom.[36]

As for Beauvoir, Hansberry decided she would not forsake this author whose work meant so much to her over a difference of philosophy. "It remains for the writer who can with superior theories to attack and demolish the forlorn roots of some of the existentialist thought of Mlle. Beauvoir," she said. Besides, even if she disagreed with practically everything else between the covers of *The Second Sex*, there was still the impact on her of, in her words, the "startling chapter on lesbianism."[37]

One night, when she and Bob were out socializing, Lorraine felt uneasy when "a young woman disengaged herself from her party, walked over to our table," she said, "and made flattering and embarrassing" remarks to her.[38] In a short story Hansberry published a few years later, a woman at a nightclub stares past her husband at another woman[39]:

> She was exquisite. The gown was a plain white sheath. The body beneath, one long shimmering river of movement; restrained and delicate. . . . It had happened before in life. On the street; parties; in classes in school years back; the thing of being surrounded by many people and suddenly finding another girl's or woman's eyes, commanding one, holding one's own. . . . Why had pleasure frightened her in the past? Why must one constantly run from it? Control it?

If Hansberry is speaking of herself through the character, she thought she shouldn't have such urges. She was afraid of things getting out of control suddenly. She was "uncommonly possessed of fear," Bob noticed. She didn't like "heights, bridges, tunnels, water, boats, planes . . . For this woman, who spoke so often of 'embracing the stars,' it was literally a small physical ordeal, involving a catching of the breath and tightening of the muscles, simply to get on an elevator." Yet, whatever the cost to her, she preferred facing "down her hobgoblins in silence."[40]

In the "startling chapter on lesbianism" in *The Second Sex*, Beauvoir claims there is freedom in acting on desire. "In truth," says Beauvoir, "homosexuality is no more a deliberate perversion than a fatal curse. It is an attitude that is *chosen in situation* [her emphasis]; it is both motivated and freely adopted." To act on erotic feelings for another woman, for Beauvoir, was a choice, perhaps only for the moment, leaving open the possibility to have relationships with men as well. "Woman is defined neither by her hormones nor by some mysterious instincts, but by the manner in which she reclaims her body and her relation with the world."[41]

Lorraine had recently seen Federico Fellini's *La Strada*, and she identified strongly with the waiflike Gelsomina, an innocent and asexual female clown controlled by men.[42] She decided that in *The Apples of Autumn* and

Flowers for the General, she would experiment with women attempting to act on their desires freely. Would it be as simple as Beauvoir reassuringly said? By putting the question into the mouths of characters, Hansberry would preserve the anonymity she needed, behind the mask of a married woman, and let the story work itself out. In her notes for *The Apples of Autumn* and *Flowers for the General*, she came at lesbianism as a Marxist: it was a "social problem" like "alcoholism or dope addiction or prostitution or any number of things" that show how "the brutality of our lives can hammer perfectly good decent human beings . . . into the depths of degradation."[43] This allowed her to believe that something had happened to her, she was a victim, and that maybe, rationally, she could work herself out of her condition.

The Apples of Autumn is a melancholy play. The protagonist is Julia Bernstein, a poet who will "be among the first to tell [the world] about what [women] really feel—about wars; and work;—and love." Julia breaks off her with her boyfriend because he makes a pass at another girl the same day he proposes to her. Although Hansberry claimed that she "did not want it to become a play about homosexuality"—she wanted it to be about the limitations placed on women by men—the person we care about is Connie, a gay woman who desperately confesses to Julia that she's in love with her.[44] Connie tells Julia a bizarre lie: she was raped by Julia's boyfriend—proof of what men are capable of. But her bid for pity jolts Julia into realizing that she's not attracted to Connie, or any woman. Connie leaves, like Cain banished, while Julia looks forward to the promise of marrying a man who'll make a good, respectable intellectual partner.

Flowers for the General turns up the heat. The main character, Maxine, is confronted with the "problem" of a close female friend, Marcia, who is in love with her. Marcia, mocked as "Sappho" by another character, tries unsuccessfully to commit suicide—the trope of the tragic lesbian. As Maxine comforts her, Marcia reveals that she knows that Maxine is in love with Elly, who's engaged to a soldier. Elly is going to be a contestant in an ROTC beauty pageant; the winner will present a war hero with a bouquet. Marcia condemns the whole affair as a masculine celebration of war and violence, with women lined up like trophies. Maxine agrees that it's obscene, but she eventually gives in to peer pressure and supports the pageant and the ceremony. She compromises her principles still further by vowing to repress her same-sex desire and marry her boyfriend. Marcia, however, refuses to deny the truth about herself, that she loves women. She echoes Beauvoir's view of homosexuality as a choice that can be authentic or inauthentic: "There must be millions who live like that," Marcia says, thinking of Maxine's future; "most people in fact. How very ugly. I don't know that I care very much for such a world."[45]

At the apartment on Bleecker Street, Lorraine held a reading of *The Apples of Autumn* with some of the staff from *New Challenge*. Bob was there, listening, smoking a pipe thoughtfully, a new custom of his. Lorraine wasn't happy with the comments afterward: "Felt the problems of the people weren't very important. . . . Contrived and extreme. No real resolution, no real people. . . . Felt homo theme did not dominate. Thought Connie shadowy." One of her critics, she thought, was "Something of an idiot, who understood absolutely nothing." Bob frustrated her the most, though, because his opinion mattered to her: "Absolutely pig-headed. . . . Did not feel that he understood a single thing—least of all the implications of the play."[46] But what implications did she want him to understand?

On December 9, 1955, Claudia Jones was deported. Almost exactly a year before, she had been tried, along with twelve other defendants, at Manhattan's Foley Square courthouse and found guilty of subversion under the 1940 Smith Act, which made it a crime to advocate overthrowing the government of the United States by force or violence. The defendants were allowed to address the court before sentencing.

Jones rose when it was her turn and attacked the conviction as punishment for her Communist beliefs and for daring to fight for "unequivocal equality for my people." She was "morally free," she said, while the prosecution had violated both the Constitution and the free expression of ideas. She and her codefendants had been tried because of their commitment to Marxism-Leninism, which rejected racist ideas and posed a threat to "white supremacist prejudice." One day, she predicted, the "decadent" Smith Act would be swept from the "scene of history."[47]

The judge sentenced her to a year in prison and fined her two thousand dollars. After three weeks in confinement, she offered to leave the United States because of a serious heart condition. She was placed on parole and advised to end her association with the Communist Party, but she maintained that she would not "desist in the fight for peace." To serve out her term, she was sent to the Federal Reformatory for Women, a minimum-security prison in Alderson, West Virginia.

When she was released in October after ten months, she was served with a deportation order and voluntarily agreed to leave the country. She had applied for residency in Trinidad, where she was born, and in Tobago, because it was another member of the British Commonwealth, but both had refused to accept her. The United Kingdom offered her residency on humanitarian grounds. Before she left, the New York Fire Department was called to her building on West 143rd Street in Harlem. She refused to let them in, and firefighters broke in through a window. She was burning her personal papers in the fireplace, the stove, and the bathtub.[48]

At a farewell party at Hotel Theresa, 350 people said good-bye, among them likely Hansberry. Or perhaps she was at the pier two days later, with dozens of well-wishers, when Jones set sail aboard the RMS *Queen Elizabeth*. During her first transatlantic crossing, Claudia wrote to her father excitedly about the "magnificent ship" and the meal she was served: "English lamb roast, mint juice or sauce, iced pineapple, salad, a fat baked potato, vanilla ice cream."[49] But she was unwell with hypertension, cardiac disease, and coronary arteriosclerosis. When she arrived in London, she was admitted to a hospital, where she stayed for several months. She settled in London and took on the roles of protector and advocate for its Caribbean community. Over the years, Lorraine wrote to a mutual friend, Halois Robinson, a former Sojourner, inquiring about Claudia, and would send money when it was needed.[50] Jones died in 1964, at age forty-nine, from complications of heart disease and tuberculosis. She was laid to rest in Highgate Cemetery in North London, to the left of the tomb of Karl Marx.

It's hard to say with certainty what influence Jones had on Hansberry, beyond offering friendship and schooling her in thought and politics. It's worth remembering, however, how strongly Jones felt about black women. She praised them, fought for them, and put them at the center of black life. "From the days of the slave traders down to the present," she said, "the

Negro woman has had the responsibility of caring for the needs of the family. . . . [T]he Negro woman fights against the wiping out of the Negro family, against the Jim-Crow ghetto existence, which destroys the health, morale and very life of millions of her sisters, brothers and children."[51]

In *A Raisin in the Sun*, the character Lena, the mother, radiates strength. She takes courage in herself and seizes on authority without asking; she must, for the sake of love. Love is empowering, ennobling. "In the United States, a seamstress refuses one day, simply refuses, to move from her chosen place on a bus," Hansberry wrote, "while an equally remarkable sister of hers ushers children past bayonets in Little Rock. It is indeed a single march, a unified destiny, and the prize is the future. . . . On behalf of an ailing world which surely needs our defiance, may we, as Negroes or women never accept the notion of 'our place.'"[52]

The Nemiroffs—for so Lorraine signed her name: "Lorraine Hansberry Nemiroff"—went to Chicago for Christmas 1955. It was unusually warm for December, in the low fifties, but the temperature dropped on Christmas Day. A few desultory snow flurries fell past the Hansberrys' windows. Lake Michigan, gigantic and flat, was slate gray, like the sky.

Bob brought along his guitar. He and Burt D'Lugoff had written a folk song they were trying to get published: "Cindy, Oh Cindy." The melody was from a stevedore song, "Pay Me My Money Down," in the book *Slave Songs of the Georgia Sea Islands*, a collection of African survival songs, dance and fiddle songs, and religious and work songs from the Gullah culture, gathered by ethnologist Lydia Parrish, wife of artist Maxfield Parrish. Mamie had friends over for holiday drinks, and they listened to Bob "plunking" to a calypso rhythm and singing. "We were sniggering and giggling," she said.[53]

Lorraine was deeply depressed. "My unhappiness has become a steady, calm, quiet sort of misery," she wrote late Christmas night, presumably when everyone else was in bed. She typed her thoughts in a combination letter to Bob/journal entry. "It is curious how intellectual I have become about the whole thing—I don't mean about you. I mean about me—and what I apparently am. . . . All these marvelous creatures whom I love! Family! Husband! Comrades! Friends! . . . Then too—there is my work. It is only here on paper that I dare say it like that: 'My Work!'—All which I feel I must write has become obsessive. . . . Oh what I think I must tell this world. Oh, the time that I crave—and the peace—and the *power* . . .

"Fame. It has become a sweet promise, hiding, whispering to me daily . . . fame! I shock myself with such thought and shake my head with embarrassment—fame!"[54]

15

"I Ain't Sick"

There's liable to be confusion
when a dream gets kicked around.

—Langston Hughes, "Same in Blues"

The spring of 1956 found Lorraine Hansberry waitressing at her in-laws'
new cellar restaurant, Potpourri, located at 104 Washington Street, just west
of Sixth Avenue. A reviewer called it an "engaging little grotto" serving "the
best soup I've ever had. Bar none."[1] Bob's parents, Max and Mae Nemiroff,
owners of several eateries at different times during their forty-year marriage, were getting along in years, but this was their last venture. Their previous establishment, Habibi Café, in Midtown, with floor shows and spicy
dishes, had proven to be too much for them, and now they were content to
catch the tourists during the day; and at night, the Villagers who nursed a
cup of coffee until closing time at 10 p.m. Max peeled potatoes and supervised the kitchen; Mae handled the books. Bob brought in hard-up artists,
singers, actors, and playwrights for a meal, and his mother fed them.

Lorraine swung between the tables delivering chocolate egg creams,
homemade orangeade, steak-cut pizza fries, patty melts smothered in
grilled onions, and grilled cheese sandwiches fried in butter. Spaghetti
was available for breakfast.[2] About forty people could squeeze in when
the place was packed. She empathized with the dishwashers in the steamy
kitchen who came and went. "I would stand in my window waiting orders

and watch a new one singing and flinging the scraps into the great garbage vat, his wrists flashing like a dancer's. Then, the other stage, when he
was no longer new. When there was soberness and no singing and little
talking and much staring into space during the cigarette breaks. With the
final stage, I came to see, there was silent anger and restlessness." Mae would
scold the man for being careless, and Lorraine would think, "He will not
come in tomorrow. Tomorrow there will be a new one."[3] Perhaps she envied
him when he hung up his apron and didn't return.

This was not the existence she had pined for when she begged her
mother to let her go to New York. She had felt like she was running away
the first time she arrived alone by overnight train from Chicago. "And the
train came out of the tunnel, and rose up above Harlem. . . . [M]y eyes
stung with sleeplessness in anticipation of The City. I remembered how I
lifted the shade next to my berth on the eastbound train and looked out to
see them flying past—one after the other—the narrow cement and brick
valleys."[4] Having freed herself from the undertow of her family, she surfaced in Harlem as a new person, a different Lorraine. Making herself felt
in the world was important to her. She liked the image of herself speaking
from a stepladder on 125th Street. And the moment when, in Montevideo,
five thousand voices had roared up at her from the public square, "Viva
Robeson!"

Since her marriage, however, she had felt a gentle but persistent pressure to contour her life to fit Bob's. She had moved into his childhood
home, enrolled in a leftist summer camp—his rite of passage into social
action when he was a boy—and worked at his parents' restaurant. They still
picketed for causes in their "spare time," as Bob put it, or attended all-night
vigils, bringing candles, blankets, and snacks—but less frequently.[5] She had
declared, when they were first engaged, "I am a writer. I am going to write."
But without *Freedom* to write for, or an editorial job somewhere, she was
getting out of the habit of regularly or daily putting words on paper.

Sometimes, after she had finished with the breakfast/lunch shift at Potpourri, she walked over to the office of the *Village Voice*, two blocks away,
on Greenwich Avenue. Her excuse for dropping in was that her upstairs
neighbor worked there—Virginia (Ginn) Briggs, a freelance photographer. Through Briggs, Lorraine became friends with another female photographer who sold pictures to the *Voice*, Molly Malone Cook.[6]

Jerry Tallmer, the paper's drama critic, became accustomed to "many, many" visits from Hansberry, the "beautiful coffee-colored silent young woman who was a waitress in a tiny restaurant full of crazy Russian Jews." She came by to talk about "anything and everything in the world" because she read the *Voice* "religiously front page to back."[7] She was hungry for interesting conversation, and the alternative weekly attracted colorful personalities. Nate Hentoff covered jazz and politics; Andrew Harris reviewed films. The house cartoonist was Jules Feiffer. Norman Mailer was supposed to be a silent partner, but had a reputation for being anything but.

One day, Hansberry surprised Tallmer by handing him a critique of an Off-Broadway production he had praised in a review—Strindberg's *Comrades*. She thought it was awful. "An insufferably awkward, social travesty, which has no reason taking up the time of actors anywhere—including the Village. The playwright clearly hated women with a depth and passion which defies reason or a mere expression of the cute 'Battle of the Sexes: Male Point of View.'"[8] Tallmer was impressed: "who knew that this wordless wisp of a waitress could even talk, much less write."[9] He didn't run it, though.

And so, having refreshed her mind with something to think about anyway, she would go home to Bleecker Street because she had to wash off the odor of the restaurant, walk the dog, and make dinner for Bob.

She was in a funk and purchased a copy of Simone de Beauvoir's novel *The Mandarins*, winner of the 1954 Prix Goncourt, France's highest literary prize, perhaps hoping that it would be as illuminating as *The Second Sex*.

The Mandarins is a lightly fictionalized account of Beauvoir's life after the war, a roman à clef about her and four men in her intellectual circle: Sartre (Robert Dubreuilh), Albert Camus (Henri Perron), Arthur Koestler (Victor Scriassine), and Nelson Algren (Lewis Brogan). The landscape of the novel is highly politically charged. Postwar France is trapped between the giant forces of the United States and the Soviet Union. Alliances become the focus. The characters clash over ideology, love, and the future. Sartre believes his protégé Camus has betrayed him. Beauvoir falls in love with Algren, but she can't leave Sartre. While they choose sides and lovers, each privately fears their role as an artist or intellectual following the war's devastation might be useless. They produce essays, novels, reviews, and political tracts for the creative class, people like them. How does this "work" bring about justice, or reform society? Perhaps they are refusing to admit that they're only part of an elite who just happened to have survived the war—the lucky aristocrats of belles lettres. Real activists would be concerning themselves with decisions, direct action, and outcomes.[10]

For an American leftist like Hansberry, the timing of the English translation of *The Mandarins* was "uncanny in its application to the Stalin situation."[11] In February 1956, Soviet prime minister Nikita Khrushchev had denounced his predecessor, Joseph Stalin, during a closed session of the Twentieth Congress of the Communist Party. Two thousand delegates listened in shock and fear as Khrushchev began pulling down the colossus of Stalin, the patriarch, the hero of World War II. He enumerated Stalin's crimes against the people: torture, slave labor, execution, false imprisonment, mass murder. Disturbances broke out on the floor as some delegates shouted, "Shame on you!"—frightened that they would be held to account. Others looked down, and a few wept, as Khrushchev reached the climax of his speech: "Why is it that we see the truth of this affair only now, and why did we not do something earlier, during Stalin's life, in order to prevent the loss of innocent lives?"[12]

With Khrushchev's speech reverberating worldwide, the coincidence of Hansberry's reading *The Mandarins* marked the beginning of her turning away from the Communist Party. Beauvoir, she said, "might have written it for me or rather to me."[13] Hansberry found it "heartbreaking" how Robert Dubreuilh, an old-line party member, struggles to defend the ideals of the Soviet Union despite having known about the slave labor camps for years. She identified with his younger, idealistic colleague Henri Perron. He "is me . . . an honest, militant leftist, who . . . understands what he sees and cannot be fooled or misled" any longer. "For a long time I have known I was unhappy about being unhappy about the 'new' USSR. Now all of a sudden I know why."[14]

She never explained her disenchantment with the Soviet Union, but even the most stalwart American believers in Stalinism were drifting away. For Lorraine, it meant joining a "furious search" with other black leftist intellectuals, said Julian Mayfield, "for identification and literary and political objectives."[15] She would be forced to chart her own way from then on.

In retrospect, one sees that it was necessary if she was to become an artist. Writing to suit the Communist Party and its front organizations had meant bowing to certain impositions. It was almost obligatory in left-wing theaters, for example, for a play to have scenes of black-white unity. It became a trope, a mantra: a better tomorrow depends on interracial cooperation. Genuine analyses of racism and oppression weren't encouraged. "There was always a 'good' white who helped the Negro solve his problem," said playwright Loften Mitchell. However it's "difficult to recall," he said, "an instance of an Englishman 'helping' the Irish in one of Sean O'Casey's plays."[16]

Some dramatists who were party-affiliated refused to go along. Staging *Alice in Wonder* in 1952 became a "memorable experience," said Mayfield, who cowrote the play with Ossie Davis, partly because "the Communist Party did not want us to put it on." It was a one-act about a black television actor who risks his career by not cooperating with HUAC. The party didn't approve—too negative. Without money for promotion, Mayfield and Davis hired local boys to advertise the performance dates on subway walls using crayon and grease pencils. At *Freedom*, Lorraine argued for supporting the production, over the objections of Robeson and Louis Burnham. In the end, she negotiated a win for Mayfield and Davis. The script of *Alice in Wonder* remained as it was, and *Freedom* agreed to give the authors publicity and cut-rate advertising.[17]

Now, four years later, in the spring of 1956, without weekly meetings and political events to absorb her interests, Hansberry found the scope of her life becoming suddenly smaller. The Jefferson School, where she had taught, would close soon; most of the faculty had resigned following Khrushchev's speech. The Labor Youth League was on the point of disbanding as well. And there would be no more article deadlines to meet for *New Challenge*, either. Bob and LYL director Leon Wofsy had decided the June/July issue would be the final one.

Lorraine felt restless and uneasy. The warm, reassuring feeling of collective solidarity from belonging to an international brotherhood embracing the whole globe was fading. Her waking hours consisted of getting through the week: waitressing at the restaurant, mooning around the writers at the *Village Voice*, and making feints at writing drama—"exercises," she called them. To stay sharp, she continued sending letters and commentaries to the editors of mainstream publications. Responding to an article in the *New York Times Magazine* about the Montgomery Bus Boycott, she supplied a perspective on Dr. Martin Luther King that white journalists were missing. His "greatness is overwhelming," she said, "but he is hardly a miracle. He may personally and reasonably choose to draw upon Hegel and Gandhi and Jesus for his ideological sustenance but he is in fact, whatever his methods, founded upon historical traditions of . . . Negro leaders like Frederick Douglass and W. E. B. DuBois, who have been among the most remarkable products of this American nation."[18] Her submission wasn't published.

One day, while she was daydreaming at her desk, she felt a moment of intense yearning just to express what moved her. Looking out the window, she watched as a "woman lifts a window across the street and rests on the sill for a moment. Her hands are white against the dark blue of the working woman's sweater. She is full-bodied and strong looking—even from here I can see that it is a strong body. The hands do know that they are especially beautiful. . . . She cannot know that in this moment she is sprung from Michelangelo."[19]

For her twentieth-sixth birthday, in May 1956, Bob gave her an anthology of plays. The free-verse inscription he wrote on the inside was a bit bullying—playful, teasing, supportive, but also implying that it was her fault, not his, that she wasn't what she wanted to be. "[O]ne day / if you work hard enough at / it (and cut out the nonsense) / You may be up there among / them—if not Shakespeare / then at least Shaw / Love, Bobby." Lorraine was sensitive about being criticized for wasting time. Bob knew she blamed herself for not working hard enough. His little barb sent her to her desk.

Over the weekend of her birthday, from Friday evening through Sunday, she wrote the entire first act of a new play she titled "The Crystal Stair."[20] The image comes from Langston Hughes's poem "Mother to Son."

> *Well, son, I'll tell you:*
> *Life for me ain't been no crystal stair.*
> *It's had tacks in it,*
> *And splinters,*

> *And boards torn up,*
> *And places with no carpet on the floor—*
> *Bare.*
> *But all the time*
> *I'se been a-climbin' on,*
> *And reachin' landin's,*
> *And turnin' corners,*
> *And sometimes goin' in the dark*
> *Where there ain't been no light.*
> *So boy, don't you turn back.*
> *Don't you set down on the steps*
> *'Cause you finds it's kinder hard.*
> *Don't you fall now—*
> *For I'se still goin', honey,*
> *I'se still climbin',*
> *And life for me ain't been no crystal stair.*

Recently, she had seen a play with black characters and "suddenly became disgusted with a whole body of material about Negroes. Cardboard characters. Cute dialect bits. Or hip-swinging musicals from exotic scores."[21] This time, instead of trying to fashion an argument into a play, such as she'd done in *The Apples of Autumn* and *Flowers for the General*, she would correct misportrayals of black families. She wanted to dramatize the limited choices of black Americans in the middle of the twentieth century. She wanted to show how people of courage could transcend their limitations. And she knew she had to involve her audience with the characters, and only after with ideas. She had to tell a believable human story about people the audience would recognize and root for.

She may have had other motives as well. She later said she couldn't write about coal miners: "I don't know how coal miners live. I don't know anything about the life of a General Motors executive." And the black middle class didn't interest her. Yet, she didn't really know much about the circumstances or lived experiences of poor black Americans, either—not like the woman who speaks in Hughes's poem. "I have never wanted for anything," Hansberry admitted. "This, however, was not the situation with the overwhelming majority of the children that I went to school with."[22] Why then did she choose to write about folks who lived in tenements where there were "splinters, / And boards torn up, / And places with no carpet on the floor"? To write about, as she later said, "an American family's conflict with certain of the mercenary values of its society"? Is it *her* family's mercenary values she's atoning for by humanizing the people whom Hansberry Enterprises dehumanized in kitchenettes?

She continued working on "The Crystal Stair" for a few weeks, but was interrupted at the end of June. She was needed in Chicago because the Hansberry family was in crisis. She took the overnight train as usual by herself. When she arrived, Mamie was concerned about her sister's appearance. "I always regret that I didn't have her physically checked then because I noted that she was really thin, and . . . I suspect maybe she was ill even then."[23]

Vincent Tubbs, Mamie's husband, had been arrested, posted a ten-thousand-dollar bail, and was standing trial on charges of raping a sixteen-year-old girl. The teenager had told the police that she was selling items for a school fundraiser and had knocked on his apartment door. He was home alone, and he had attacked her, she said.

Because of the publicity, Vincent was fired from his job as an editor for *Jet* magazine. Fortunately for the Hansberrys, they weren't mentioned in the small item that ran on page 7 of the *Chicago Tribune*: "Ex-Editor Will Face Rape Trial on May 24." Still, the terrible affair threatened their standing in the community and Carl Augustus Hansberry's legacy. "Mama can't stand him," Lorraine told Bob of Vincent.[24]

Carl Jr. and Perry felt a certain amount of schadenfreude about this disaster happening to Mr. Tubbs from Baltimore, although they wouldn't say this in front of Mamie. Tubbs was different from them—a corporate man with a degree from Morehouse College. Not long after he had married their sister, he had been promoted by publisher John H. Johnson from reporter for *Ebony* to managing editor of *Jet* magazine. Following the murder of fourteen-year-old Emmett Till in Mississippi, he had cofounded the interracial Windy City Press Club to bring more attention to news on the South Side, where Till had been raised. The members of the club had elected him its president; and at a black-tie affair hosted by singer Harry Belafonte, Mayor Richard J. Daley had sworn in Tubbs's fellow officers.

This was the kind "Uncle Tom" behavior that Carl Jr. and Perry disliked about their brother-in-law. He had the inside track with the downtown crowd; he schmoozed with the Democrats in city hall. But none of that glad-handing had helped the Hansberrys. Hansberry Enterprises had been cited by city hall's building department for thirteen code violations so far that year, and eight the year before. The Hansberry brothers had been written up for everything from rats and roaches to rotten floors and fire hazards.[25] And they were sure it was because their father had broken through the housing barriers on the South Side and exposed the city's shame before the Supreme Court. From the mayor on down, the establishment had a grudge against them. White real estate agents were colluding with the Mayor's office to put them out of business. Tubbs was going to find out the hard way about justice in the Windy City.

Regardless, Lorraine felt sorry for Vincent and his "troubles." She wanted to argue in his defense, but her brothers were too busy and barely "willing to tolerate him," she wrote to Bob, provided "Mamie is quiet about it."[26] Finally, she couldn't stand the pall hanging over everyone any longer. "My days here are like a Chekhovian nightmare." She decided to speak to her mother about how Carl Jr. and Perry, quick to condemn Vincent, engaged in business practices that made them poor judges of what was right. Perhaps thoughts about "The Crystal Stair" and families living in tenements were on her mind. Some kind of frustration was building up in her, that's for certain. She was so angry she couldn't keep from lashing out at her mother.

"Tonight in a thoughtless moment I bitterly attacked the morality of my brothers to my mother," she wrote Bob. "I was immediately sorry; desperately sorry. Every living word was true and my passion was justified but it hurt her horribly. She chooses to see her sons in one way. Which is more ethical: to denounce false illusions or to encourage an aging and good human being to enjoy peace of mind? For me it is no longer a question. I will never say such things to her again. And yet here is the truth."[27]

Part of her outburst stemmed from frustrations over her marriage. "Everyone asks about you. I have told them nothing. It is all very difficult."[28] She said she was beginning wonder about her "ability to go on living in this fucking world. Literally. (I mean both about the living and the fucking part.)"[29] She had been trying to explain her feelings for women to Bob, but he took it to mean she'd been unfaithful.[30]

> I am easily indignant and hurt and even mystified if you suggest that I—well, what you suggested (damn you, I am still mad about it!) because to the depths of my being I am incapable of actually committing a truly deceptive act—nonetheless what about the things that pass through [your] mind. There is the old saw about between the act and the thought. . . . I suppose I really need you. But you really don't need me. Then too, to be honest, I want one or two things which you simply cannot give. And the particular things that I want—I want desperately . . . I guess it's that that is my particular sickness—oh damn that—I ain't sick—peculiarity. I can't get enough. No one gives me enough. Least of all you. Love, I mean. I should like to be suffocated with it until I no longer feel that kind of need. I doubt very much if it is possible.

It wasn't easy for her to talk about sex. She found Beauvoir's descriptions of sex with Algren in *The Mandarins* "embarrassing. I suppose I am too young and too American and too unintellectual to appreciate[,] or be anything but revolted or at least embarrassed by[,] intimate descriptions of sexual love as made by the advanced middle-aged."[31] (Beauvoir and Algren were in their early forties.) She was more conventional than she cared to admit, and still a product of her proper upbringing in many ways, despite having progressive opinions on just about everything else.

She wasn't prepared for a personal, sexual revolution, despite being assured by Marxism that transcending all the old conformist attachments would bring fulfillment. She accepted that moral codes and conduct were based on class and social circumstances—there were no absolute standards. She was free to choose, theoretically, but being true to her nature was likely to cause others pain. She wasn't quite sure what would happen if she didn't have the approval of people she loved.

She wasn't sure what to do. In the meantime, a strange feeling of being alienated from herself left her "terribly lonely, almost to the point of madness. I know that I shall be as lonely if I return to New York, but somehow it is different. At least you talk to me sometimes. Here all these normal people are much too involved in living to talk about living."[32]

As for Vincent, his trial was delayed for six months. He was found not guilty.

That summer, Lorraine imposed a schedule on herself for making progress on "The Crystal Stair." Breakfast was at eight thirty, and she tried to be at her desk by nine. Two mornings a week she worked at People's Artists, on West Twenty-First Street, a booking agency for performers who sang about peace, civil liberties, and civil rights.[33] By twelve thirty, she was home again for lunch, with dinner ready around six. Afternoons she spent developing the play. Sometimes, however, her plans were interrupted because she was needed at the restaurant.

She hadn't written anything for *Masses and Mainstream* or the *Daily Worker* for months. And except for speaking at a rally for International Workers Day, in May, she was less involved with leftist events. However, the New York office of the FBI noted that she had recently canvassed for the American Labor Party, a socialist organization. Moreover, according to one of its informants, People's Artists was a Communist outfit that was "trying to indoctrinate youth through folk-dancing and ballad singing in Washington Square."[34] To be prudent, the Bureau decided it was time to review whether Hansberry should be added to the Security Index of dangerous individuals. And so, like scheduling an annual physical exam, it ran a check on her at the end of July. The owner of the Chinese hand laundry on Bleecker Street, Joe, was a dependable source for the FBI about his neighbors' comings and goings.[35] But for this review, an eyewitness report was required, so early one morning, an agent parked across the street from Lorraine's building to observe her.

She came down at 7:50 a.m. with her dog. She was wearing a yellow shirt, black toreadors, and flats: a slim young woman with a short, "unruly Italian haircut." At 8:25 a.m., she returned, took the dog upstairs, and then came down again and continued on her way down the street alone. Later, a pretext call to People's Artists established that she was there working. Around noon, she arrived home again. A few minutes later, another pretext call was put through to the apartment. She answered and told whoever it was—someone she knew, probably—that she was "just back from shopping."[36]

She seemed predictable. She had been observed going about her business on a warm, sunny morning in Greenwich Village, the shady quarter of kooks, painters, poets, and tourists. She wasn't a higher-up in an organization considered an enemy to freedom. She wasn't a known agitator in the pay of the Kremlin, or a black leader militating for civil rights and desegregation. From the external evidence, nothing radical seemed to be going on with her.

For the time being, it was decided not to add Mrs. Lorraine Vivian Hansberry Nemiroff to the index of subversives. Whatever she was thinking about, whatever might be going on in her personal life, she wasn't a demonstrable threat to the status quo. The G-men in the New York office turned their attention elsewhere.

In August 1956, the calypso song Bob cowrote with Burt D'Lugoff, "Cindy, Oh Cindy," made the local music charts. It had been recorded by a folk group, Vince Martin with the Tarriers. Phil Rose had issued it as a single on his Glory Records label, and New York disc jockeys were playing it. The old, slow melody sung by Georgia Island slaves could be heard coming from cars, echoing above the boardwalk of Coney Island, and through open windows in all the boroughs of the city. Rose could hardly keep up with the demand in record stores. There was talk of big-name artists making a cover.

The calypso craze had begun earlier in the year, when Harry Belafonte, the Harlem-born actor, had repackaged himself as an open-shirted, exotic West Indian with tigerish sexuality.[37] Calypso was "a new guise for an old character: Jim Crow in a Caribbean mask," writes cultural historian Shane Vogel. Belafonte's version of the Jamaican folk song "Day-O (The Banana Boat Song)" was a cut from his album *Calypso*, the first long-playing album to sell a million copies. Bar owners, riding the wave, bedecked their establishments with fish nets and palm trees and concocted fruity rum drinks. During the summer of 1956, it was beginning to look as if bongos and barefoot sirens like "Miss Calypso" Maya Angelou, star of the film *Calypso Heat Wave*, would become more popular than Elvis Presley and rock and roll.[38]

Philip Rose was impressed with how Nemiroff had caught the craze at the flood. "Cindy, Oh Cindy" was reaching the niche market he had in mind for Glory Records. He made Bob an offer: he could have his own label, Blyden Records—named after the Pan-Africanist educator, Edward Wilmot Blyden—and scout for minority artists and unknown talent. Writing songs with D'Lugoff, who was doing his medical residency at Johns Hopkins, would be part of the deal as well.

Nemiroff had to weigh this against leaving his job in the promotions department of Avon romances. But an opportunity in the music business wasn't too far out of his skill set, either. His parents were self-taught impresarios and had booked performers for their restaurants for years—from belly dancers to dancing Cossacks. Also, Nemiroff, being an antiestablishment type, was comfortable with the idea of promoting outsider music, particularly if it carried overtures of social justice. Financially, he had seen how Burt's brother, Art, could fill an empty theater at midnight with blacklisted folkies like Pete Seeger. He decided that, rather than quit Avon outright, he would go in part-time with Rose.

In October, Lorraine submitted her final article to the *Daily Worker*, under the pen name "John Henry." She stopped after Soviet tanks rolled into Budapest at the end of the month to suppress the student uprising there. Twenty-five hundred Hungarians were killed. The *Daily Worker's* editor, John Gates, turned the newspaper into a forum to discuss the crackdown, a novel event for a party-line paper. The Kremlin demanded that Gates reverse course and justify Moscow's invasion. Gates and many of the staff resigned. From that point on, the *Daily Worker* became only one of dozens of leftist publications, having lost its place, and its subscriber base, as the national print propagandist of communism in the United States.

Lorraine felt numb, anesthetized by loneliness and depression. Without the excitement of meetings to attend and causes of social betterment to support, she was a twenty-six-year-old housewife who worked part-time waiting tables and contributing to small publications. Or she sent hectoring letters to the *New York Times*, which never ran them. She wasn't engaged with the world as she had been before her marriage to Bob. In her journal, she wrote, "I waited for Robert to come home and let the chicken thaw in the kitchen. He did not—I had forgotten that he would not. I called a friend . . . she came and was very dull, and wore shoes such as old women wear. . . . We talked about nothing and she ate. . . . I could not and smoked cigarettes and longed to be quite dead. . . . Today I could not wake until it was almost two and I despised the sleeping and could not stop until it was almost two. . . . Outside it is already deep autumn again and I am twenty-six and somehow there are leaves, the brown unhappy, useless ones on the sidewalks of the streets outside—even though there are no trees. . . . If such emptiness only had a shape."[39]

She applied herself to "The Crystal Stair," but it was hard to concentrate. She doodled the words of a children's song that kept going through her head: "Sweetly sings the donkey at the break of day. / If you do not feed him that is what he'll say: / Hee-haw! Hee-haw! Hee-haw! Hee-haw! Hee-haw!" On a scrap of paper, she drew a sketch in pen of Bob and wrote above it, "I don't like you *at all*." He replied in pencil beside it, "Why? Just relax."[40]

In early 1957, after months of writing and revising, she gathered up everything she'd written and threw it at the fireplace. She went to get a broom, meaning to sweep it all into the grate and burn it, but Bob knelt down, picked up the pages of dialogue, and put them back in order. Without a word, he took the script away. He kept it for several days, out of sight, until one night, while she was "moping around the apartment," he put the script down in front of her. She took it over to her desk and began working again.[41]

16

"Cindy, Oh Cindy"

Be not deceived, wealth is strength, wealth is power, wealth is influence, wealth is justice, is liberty, is real human rights.

—Marcus Garvey[1]

And then, suddenly, in the spring of 1957, Lorraine and Bob were rich, because teen idol and lounge singer Eddie Fisher had released a cover version of "Cindy, Oh Cindy." Not only did Fisher's swinging version become one of the top twenty songs on the radio, but the Tarriers' folksong rendition did, too, and both stayed on the national charts for weeks. In the United Kingdom, a third version by an English singer also became a hit. Bob and Burt D'Lugoff split one hundred thousand dollars in royalties, the equivalent of about a million dollars today. Overnight, Lorraine became one of wealthiest women in Greenwich Village, due to her husband's hustle as an entrepreneur in the evanescent, get-rich-quick free market of American pop culture.

This development encouraged the Hansberrys to revise their opinion of Bob, last seen plunking his guitar and crooning a slave melody at their Christmas party. He had the Midas touch. "And that little song made a hundred thousand dollars," Mamie said. "And we started hearing it on the radio. So we soon stopped laughing about that."[2] On a visit to Chicago, Lorraine purchased a brand-new station wagon and got an Illinois driver's license. She took the car for a spin and pronounced it "a dream," she told Bob. "I shall teach you to drive."[3]

The image is a bit surreal: Lorraine Hansberry, Marxist, pro-Communist, at the wheel of the symbol of suburban aplomb. But it stands as a metaphor for her inconsistent attitude toward money and wealth.

What she wanted, she said, was economic justice for black Americans that would give them access to better opportunities and a standard of living consistent with the pursuit of happiness. To accomplish this, she had "a fierce commitment to the destruction of capitalism," said John O. Killens.[4] Yet she never seemed to understand the complex ways in which aspiration, democracy, and an advanced market economy can go hand in hand, particularly in her own family. She was wealthy because her entrepreneurial husband had ridden a trend at the most consumeristic end of the music business—teen records. She was a partner in Hansberry Enterprises and a part owner of slums, which would eventually cause her unhappiness and embarrassment. But she preferred to skip the moral ambiguities involved in actually realizing the dream and seemed oblivious to them even in her own life.

Having money changed everything. She didn't need nickel-and-dime jobs anymore: she was free to write full-time. In fact, she would never have to work for anyone else again, outside of working with Bob.

At the beginning of the summer of 1957, she traveled by train to Provincetown, Massachusetts, to stay at a seaside inn and continue writing "The Crystal Stair." Bob encouraged her to go like he had urged her to sign up for Camp Unity. It seems to have been his idea of what she should be doing. Provincetown was where American theater had entered the modern era at the turn of the twentieth century, with Eugene O'Neill and others at the Provincetown Playhouse—a propitious location for a young dramatist like Lorraine. "I am *very* grateful for the trip," she wrote to him as soon as she arrived. "The setting is quite beyond anything you or anyone else (including the various and assorted writers) had described." It reminded her of Ajijic. "Same people, same circumstances, scenery, art shows and cocktail parties and I have been advised about six times already by different people that 'one either likes it—or one doesn't.'"[5]

She wanted to avoid socializing too much, however: she was there to make progress on the play. Also, Provincetown was an artists' colony, with published authors and sought-after painters and sculptors. She didn't want to be compared, didn't want to be sized up and excluded—the way she had felt being around University of Wisconsin art students discussing art from "the depth of their superior opinions."[6] But Bob was not to be denied. As a way of getting her into the swim, he had arranged for her to have dinner on her first night with a couple of Nemiroff family friends: Joseph R. Starobin, formerly foreign editor of the *Daily Worker*, and his wife, Norma. Rather reluctantly, she trudged off to meet them.

Joe Starobin was looking forward to meeting the daughter-in-law of his old friends, Max and Mae Nemiroff. He'd known the Nemiroff family since he was a child. He and Norma were in their mid-forties and had a son, Robert, about to graduate from the Bronx High School of Science.[7] Lorraine was part of the younger generation. They welcomed her by taking her out to their terrace, where it was sunny and they could sit and get to know one another.

Starobin recalled his first impressions of their guest. She was "something of a tomboy in appearance," he said, and "she seemed to have a strange quiet and calm about her, contrasting with all the activity of walking on the beach, skipping into town, etc." She didn't offer much about herself. "She said she had been working on a play which would be ready soon, but she did not volunteer much more than that: it was her private affair. I had the feeling of a person capable of privacy, which in the vacation setting was indeed rare. Most vacationers have a need to talk about themselves and to involve others in their affairs. Lorraine was not like that."[8]

After dinner, the Starobins invited her to attend an opening at a gallery owned by friends of theirs, Ed Wiener, a jewelry designer, and his wife, Doris Levin, a specialist in Asian antiquities. Lorraine agreed to tag along, although this was precisely the kind of thing she had hoped to avoid. "What a horror this place is!" she complained to Bob.[9] At the gallery, the Starobins ran into another couple they knew: sixty-two-year-old Edwin Berry Burgum, a literary critic and formerly an associate professor of English at NYU, and his wife, Mildred, a psychotherapist.

Burgum was at the end of a four-year-long, very public crisis that was about to become personally tragic. He was the founding editor of the Marxist journal *Science and Society*, the former president of the New York College Teachers Union, and had been on the national committee to free the Rosenbergs. In October 1952, he had been subpoenaed by the McCarran subcommittee of the Senate to testify about teaching communism in American schools and universities. As he and four other educators, including a New York high school teacher, climbed the steps of the U.S. Federal Courthouse at Foley Square, two hundred students and picketers cheered for them.

Before the committee, Burgum refused to answer questions about his political beliefs, invoking the First and Fifth Amendments in defense of his right to free speech. Two hours after returning home, he received a telegram from the chancellor of the university informing him that he was suspended from teaching. The decision about the "Commie Front Prof" made national headlines. Six months later, the NYU Faculty Committee found Burgum "unfit to be a teacher," and he was dismissed after twenty-eight years at the university. Despite campaigns by lawyers, teachers, and unions, he would never be reinstated.

What happened to Professor Burgum and those who had been fellow travelers of American communism since the 1930s adds perspective to Hansberry. She didn't pay a price for her beliefs, and thousands did. She wasn't as influential as people in Burgum's generation.[10] Other than being under surveillance—a nuisance, in her case—she did not see her career and reputation ruined. She was never called to testify, nor is there any evidence that her participation in the party interfered with her rise to prominence.[11] Just the opposite: her association with communism, limited to writing for small-circulation leftist publications and speaking at rallies, has been used as evidence of her radicalness.[12] Yet, unlike Edwin Burgum, Paul Robeson, Claudia Jones, and Joe Starobin, who had fled the country in the early 1950s to avoid prosecution, she didn't suffer for her convictions. Burgum's wife, Mildred, crushed by the pressure and public disgrace of her husband being reviled, committed suicide three months after Lorraine met her.[13]

As for the art that evening in the Wieners' gallery, there were many examples of abstract expressionism, a movement that was then at its height. "It was, of course, what I expected," Lorraine wrote to Bob, "smeary, sick, meaningless, contemptible *trash*. Naturally this in itself did not frighten or offend me—since I expected it. (Even though I couldn't keep being just a little depressed at the sight of all those people standing around being so serious about such vomit.)" Indoctrinated by Marxism to believe that each piece of art must convey a social message, Lorraine rejected the idea of art for art's sake. To her, it was the product of an elite, this reification of the subconscious into paint and stain—deliberately obscure, private, even condescending to the viewer. Jazz, though, which she was getting into, was her ideal—with jazz, social artists introduced innovation to build an interracial community around their art.[14]

Everyone went out for coffee afterward, during which Hansberry let it be known what she thought of the show. Doris Levin, offended, told her, "rather curtly," to shut up. Back at the Starobins for drinks, Joe and Norma, with the Burgums mainly listening, tried to persuade Lorraine that there was "'more than *one* way to look at reality'—which is the worst of all bullshit when it comes to art," in Lorraine's opinion. She thought they were patronizing her, because she was young, "a bit of a sectarian who will outgrow it all." Norma Starobin, she had a feeling, "has already decided that I am among the dull."[15]

She vowed to herself and to Bob that she would start writing the next day—"To hell with 'the atmosphere.'"[16] She was beginning the third act of "The Crystal Stair," and if all went well, she would finish the play by her twenty-seventh birthday in May: one year exactly, start to finish.

The play was about a family, the Youngers, living on Chicago's South Side in 1953. As a setting, Chicago is as important to Hansberry as Ireland is to O'Casey—Ireland, "grey and cold in weather and in feeling," he said.[17] What Lorraine would later write about artist Charles White could be said of her: "One feels that the memories of that crucible, the Chicago South Side, must live deep within the breast of this artist."[18]

In black literature, Chicago is a place of lost dreams. Losing one's grip on them means slipping down into a "spiritual, emotional, and actual sepulcher," in the words of literary critic Keith Clark. August Wilson's *Ma Rainey's Black Bottom* depicts Chicago as "the black man's dystopia," where soulfulness is not to be found except in music.[19] There is a pervading sense of paralysis—a loss of passion for life. Gwendolyn Brooks speaks of the weariness of South Side women in "Kitchenette Building" (1945):

> We are things of dry hours and the involuntary plan,
> Grayed in, and gray. "Dream" makes a giddy sound, not strong
> Like "rent," "feeding a wife," "satisfying a man."

Despite the article of faith among Americans that upward mobility is possible for everyone, three generations of the Younger family are crowded into the same space. Like the Catholic Boyles of Dublin, held down by the Protestant Anglo-Irish ruling class, discrimination crushes the Youngers like a vise. With fewer resources available to them, money has more significance to the Youngers and stands for more. "These people live here," Hansberry later wrote about the Youngers, "because rents in their ghetto are proportionately higher than in any other place in the city; therefore even slight improvement would be of a nature to exhaust them financially since the hard-earned combined wages of the three income-making members must feed, clothe and house five people."[20]

This is a different approach for her: developing characters in a setting before treating an issue. And she had arrived at it, as apprentice writers must, through trial and error. Previously, in *The Apples of Autumn* and *Flowers for the General*, her intention had been to shine a light on a controversial topic, such as gay love or war, for example, a stark method she later called "putting picket signs on the stage."[21]

How this failed to sustain people's interest she learned from her friends' reactions to *The Apples of Autumn*. "None of the people who read this play got anything out of it," she said in her notes, "therefore it is a literary failure."[22] And it was perceptive of her to qualify it as a *literary* failure. On the emotional level, she hadn't touched them or made them reflect. Instead of making them care, they were figuratively sitting with their arms crossed, trying to make sense of a lot of information. They were being lectured to. This time, she would begin with individuals, offering what she loved about Shakespeare: how he presented, she said, the "human personality and its totality."[23]

As she imagined it, the curtain would rise on "The Crystal Stair," and the audience would recognize a working-class family immediately. The

Youngers are the common denominator in the American experience. The stage directions specify that they're living in a kitchenette; it "slopes backward to provide a small kitchen area, where the family prepares the meals that are eaten in the living room proper, which must also serve as dining room. The single window that has been provided for these 'two' rooms is located in this kitchen area. The sole natural light the family may enjoy in the course of a day is only that which fights its way through this little window."

The first half of the play would be taken up with their excitement after arriving at the new house; the second half would be about them resisting attempts to force them out—a testament to black Americans' doggedness in defending their rights: what social critic and novelist Albert Murray called "the impromptu heroism" of Negroes "as *normal procedure!*" A similar plot hook about a black family and restrictive covenants had been used for Maxine Wood's 1946 Broadway play *On Whitman Avenue.*[24]

The fact that the Youngers are ordinary and therefore might pose a challenge as dramatic material didn't discourage Lorraine. "Virtually every human being is dramatically interesting," she believed. "Not only is he dramatically interesting, he is a creature of stature whoever he is." In addition, despite the story's being about "a Negro family, specifically and culturally," and even more, about a South Side Chicago family in particular, she was betting that their humanity as they loved, dreamed, rose, fell, and then rose again would capture audiences' interest.[25]

Hansberry was not, it must be said, attempting to pioneer new directions with "The Crystal Stair," away from Western conventions of storytelling. Avant-garde productions left her cold. She saw Samuel Beckett's *Waiting for Godot* ("puzzling," the *New York Times* critic said), and she despised it.[26] "People come out of the theatre today, young people like myself," she said, "and they are either pleased or utterly indifferent enough to say, 'Well I don't know what it was about but it was very theatrical. I mean it was *theatre.*' Well, so is the circus. . . . I think that we have been taught it is childish or superficial to probe life as it is."[27]

Nor would she accept the premise of absurdism that life is chaotic and senseless and that humanity is in despair. The character Pozzo in *Godot,* observes gloomily, "That's how it is on this bitch of an earth." Hansberry's rebuttal was the Negro experience. "Despair? Did someone say despair was a question in the world? Well then, listen to the sons of those who have known little else if you wish to know the resiliency of this thing you would so quickly resign to mythhood, this thing called the human spirit." Moreover, defeatism, she insisted, even when logically justified, was morally and artistically wrong. "The task of the thoughtful," she said, "is to try to help impose purposefulness on the absurdity" of contemporary life.[28]

As her models for "The Crystal Stair," Hansberry looked to the domestic dramas of the 1930s and '40s, ones about family stability, morality, economic hardship, and the distance between dreams and reality. She was going against the grain of postwar American theater by looking back to plays of her childhood, produced while the country was in the midst of the worst economic downturn in its history. In Clifford Odets's *Awake and Sing!* (1937), for example, the impoverished Berger family all live under one roof in the Bronx. Bessie, the mother, has high hopes and dreams for her family, but she's haunted by the fear that they will lose their home and all their possessions.

In the 1950s, as opposed to the Great Depression, with the American economy improving at a galloping rate, postwar dramas tended to present characters chafing under interfering rules and authority, such as Tennessee Williams's *Cat on a Hot Tin Roof*, or characters going headlong into what they expected would be a bright future and material success. Arthur Miller makes a tragic hero out of Willy Loman and his hopes in *Death of a Salesman*, about an American Dreamer, "a man way out there in the blue riding on a smile and a shoeshine."[29]

But Hansberry admired the earlier genre for the same reasons she revered O'Casey. The settings are humble, the characters use everyday speech to reveal what they want, and the stories are about someone you might know. "I regard myself, and ever will do so, as a 'popular' writer," she said. "I am aware that the 'artistes' in the world will hold that as an epithet; to me it is the supreme tribute, as I know of no achievement or development in the history of world literature, drama, painting, film that was not evolved out of the process of communication with the broadest base of 'the people.'"[30]

When she returned home from Provincetown at the end of the summer of 1957, she hadn't finished the third act yet; she wasn't even sure what the final scene should be. But she was eager to give the play a sounding and find out whether, after months of writing, she had something at last.

She and Bob invited over Phil Rose, Doris Belack, and Burt D'Lugoff one Saturday evening for a dinner of spaghetti and banana cream pie, after which everyone settled in to listen to Lorraine's work in progress. She started out reading her manuscript while seated in a chair and then ended up sprawled down on the floor with the pages scattered around her. "We started discussing it, and found ourselves arguing about the characters as people."[31] Rose went home after midnight, thinking how "The Crystal Stair," even unfinished, "had an enormous effect" on him.[32]

Early the next morning, he phoned her. He said he wanted to produce her play. And for formality's sake, he wanted to option it, meaning he would have the exclusive rights, giving him time to stir up interest. He offered her fifty dollars as consideration. She laughed and teased him about her cooking, telling him to call back when his stomach felt better. But he was serious, and when she realized he was, she accepted.

Rose had no experience in the practical and legal aspects of theater—no understanding of the papers that had to be filed in order to raise money, how to reserve a legitimate space for an engagement, or the bonds for unions and the fees of a press agent or a company manager. He was a record producer. But first, before he invested more than his fifty dollars, he went looking for a second opinion. He arranged to have a reading at his apartment on Central Park West for Sidney Poitier, who had recorded *The Poetry of the Negro* for Glory Records. Anything Poitier might say would be free advice; more important, if he liked it, he might even consider being in it.

Poitier was due in Los Angeles in a couple of days to begin starring in *The Defiant Ones*, a Hollywood film about two prisoners shackled together, one white and one black, who make a run for it. Rose invited him to "a very private reading in my living room." There were drinks and small talk; then Lorraine was asked to read a work in progress that Rose was interested in. Hansberry hadn't met Poitier before, and she started out a little nervously, joking that she would try to be all the different characters. But after a while, said Rose, "we seemed to forget that Lorraine was reading, and we were removed from Central Park West to a small apartment in Chicago." Rose glanced at Poitier now and then out of the corner of his eye. The young actor seemed both "affected and entertained."

At the end of the second act, Rose suggested an intermission, leaving an opening for Poitier to comment. He wanted to know who the playwright was. No one would say. He tried to guess. "He began by naming the many black writers we mutually knew, starting with Alice Childress, going on to John Killens, followed by Langston Hughes. And as Lorraine and I progressed from shaking our heads, to broadening our smiles, to laughing loudly, he shouted with us, simultaneously and incredulously, 'Lorraine Hansberry?!'"[33] He wished he could stay to hear more, but he had another appointment—luckily, because Hansberry had only a few pages of script before the play stopped, unresolved.

In the days that followed, Rose began his education about the theater business by reading *Variety*, the weekly newspaper covering the entertainment industry. Some of his friends were surprised when he told them he didn't intend to produce Hansberry's play "as a political statement about the civil rights struggle." He saw it "as a potential profit-making production."[34] All that stood in the way of getting "The Crystal Stair" up and running was, first, that it wasn't finished, and second, that they had no investors.

17

The Invisible Lesbian

What would happen if one woman told the truth about her life?
The world would split open.

—Muriel Rukeyser, from "Käthe Kollwitz"

Lorraine's emotional needs had stubbornly evolved into a desire that couldn't be satisfied through her marriage to Bob. She didn't want to deceive him, but she was past the point of being able to deny what she wanted—which was love and physical affection. Yet, even though she admitted in her long, late-night letters to him that they weren't compatible sexually—"you don't really need me . . . I want one or two things which you simply cannot give"—she wasn't ready to leave him, or to cheat on him, either. She said as much in the letter to him about Beauvoir's *The Mandarins*—but indirectly, under the guise of discussing the novel:

The morality of the French intelligentsia as presented is a question in itself. Frankly, I found it shocking. With regard to sex apparently, there is no morality. It simply does not exist. According to the book, one loves for the sake of the soul; one has intercourse for the sake of pleasure; and if the twain should meet—well, *c'est bon*. Otherwise why even make an issue of it in fact—they just do it and think about whether they liked it or not. I am shocked. Me. I disapprove. But what have I to offer by way of a superior morality—of any morality? Absolutely nothing. I know things now that I couldn't possibly have known about human beings when one's morality begins to take shape. I know for instance that one does not go on loving people because one says meaningless vows (meaningless as far as a higher being, of course); nor is one immune to being sexually attracted because one says the same vows. To think otherwise is madness and achieves severe neuroses. What then? Promiscuity? Revolting. But what then, what?[1]

She wondered whether something was wrong with her, if she herself suffered from "severe neuroses." Psychoanalysis was all the rage among sophisticates. Freud was talked about glibly, and labeling people's behavior carried the same kind of cultural cachet as talking knowingly about jazz. Bob seemed to hint that something about her did need fixing, by his remarks that she could be a Shakespeare or a Shaw, if only . . .

Aside from that, she couldn't help but worry that a broken marriage would be a moral failure. Americans' fears of sexual chaos and moral decline were deeply embedded in the national culture. Monogamous heterosexual relationships were equated with the American Way. Being man and wife in a free, prosperous country was something to aspire to. Even if she could push aside all standard notions about what a heterosexual marriage should be (the only kind recognized), Lorraine felt loyal to Bob as her best friend and partner. He had endured her tantrums and her depressions, always returning to his role as counselor, advocate, and gentle critic, no matter what she dished out. In the scales of relationships, didn't his fidelity to her deserve the same thing in return from her?

But she couldn't deny to herself that she found "well-dressed women" attractive, and those who were "deeply intelligent," very appealing. She liked "the eyes, the voice, the legs and the music of Eartha Kitt," and the uninhibited, almost wolfish sexuality of Italian actress Anna Magnani in the 1955 film version of Tennessee Williams's play *The Rose Tattoo*.[2]

There was a book released in 1955 called *We Walk Alone*, about the lesbian scene in New York City, written by Marijane Meaker under the pen name "Ann Aldrich." It wouldn't be surprising if Hansberry read it. A lot of people did; it was a bestseller. The Kinsey Reports of 1948 and 1953, also widely read and debated, had illuminated the range of sexual identities and behaviors among young adults.

Meaker, in *We Walk Alone*, guides the reader through bars and coffee-houses, serving as Ariadne in the gay labyrinth. The McCarthy period of homophobic persecution and gay-baiting had driven much of New York City's gay and lesbian subculture underground.[3] But Meaker, after cruising for fifteen years in this shadowy world, knows where she's going. She beckons the reader into the Blue Room, for instance, "a homosexual haunt off Third Street in the heart of Greenwich Village." It caters "primarily to the gay crowd, male and female, but 'straight' customers are not excluded." She points out the differences among the lesbian clientele by plumage: butches prefer short hair and plain, masculine attire; femmes wear dresses, high heels, and makeup; and college girls outfitted in sweaters, pleated skirts, and saddle shoes hang around to vamp the older women.

Reading the signals right in the gay world was important, said Audre Lorde, who described herself as "black, lesbian, mother, warrior, poet." Although she and Hansberry lived in the Village at the same time, they don't seem to have met. "If you asked the wrong woman to dance," said Lorde, "you could get your nose broken in the alley down the street by her butch, who had followed you out of the [bar] for exactly that purpose. It was safer to keep to yourself. And you were never supposed to ask who was who, which is why there was such heavy emphasis upon correct garb. The well-dressed gay-girl was supposed to give you enough cues for you to know."[4]

Meaker, an armchair Freudian, reckons in *We Walk Alone* that lesbianism is a case of arrested sexual development—maybe an artifact of penis envy or caused by a domineering mother. Psychoanalysts could address the condition, she thinks; still, she says, "the 'incurable' lesbian as I have known her is not usually the tragic heroine of a lesbian novel who lives in abject misery, nor is she the psychotic case material in some psychiatrists' files." Overall, "I hesitate to say that she is a thoroughly happy person, at the same time I cannot in all honesty judge her to be an unhappy person."[5]

Lorraine, pausing to mull this over, might think that a lukewarm existence was the only kind available to her, if she was "incurable." But she refused to settle for that. She wanted to be in love.

About the time she returned home from Provincetown in the summer of 1957, a package arrived wrapped in plain brown paper. She had been waiting for it. Inside were copies of *One: The Homosexual Magazine*. *One* was sold mainly by subscription, because not many newsagents would have dared sell it, and even fewer people would have dared buy it. It was considered "obscene material" by the U.S. Post Office; hence the nondescript wrapping.

One was produced every month in a small loft office in Los Angeles by several men who had been members of the Mattachine Society. The name "Mattachine" comes from a secret medieval French society of unmarried men who satirized oppressive social conventions with masked dances. In that spirit, *One* challenged the view that homosexuality was abnormal. In San Francisco, the Daughters of Bilitis, the first lesbian civil and political rights organization in the United States, published *The Ladder*. Lorraine wanted to assemble a complete run of both. "Would you please send me as many back issues of your publication as the enclosed check will stand for?" Signed, "Mrs. L. Nemiroff."[6]

The Daughters of Bilitis began in 1955, when Del Martin and Phyllis Lyon, who had been partners for several years, started a social club "with the vague idea that something should be done about the problems of lesbians, both within their own group and with the public." The name they chose, "Bilitis"—without knowing what it meant exactly—was a fictional lesbian contemporary of Sappho created by the French poet Pierre Louÿs in his 1894 work, *The Songs of Bilitis*, a collection of erotic, essentially lesbian poetry. The advantage of the name, said Martin, was that "You could be fairly anonymous when asked about it. You could say it was an organization interested in Greek poetry or whatever."[7] A year after the club started, "the DOB," as members began calling it, began publishing *The Ladder*, the first national lesbian publication. Early issues included essays, book reviews, fiction, poetry, letters from readers, and summaries of public discussions held by the DOB and the Mattachine Society. There were articles about raising children in "a deviant relationship," psychotherapy versus public opinion, lesbians and fear, job hunting, criticism of mainstream media depictions of homosexuality, and the psychological dimensions of self-acceptance.

At first, *The Ladder* was typed, illustrated, and laid out by hand. The covers were of construction paper. It was rather high schoolish looking. (It was "laughable," Meaker sniffed. "While they were very brave people, like many pioneers they weren't the chicest people.")[8] No matter. The four hundred or so who subscribed read *The Ladder* to find out where the girls were.

For Lorraine, figuring that out was more difficult than it was for white women. "During the fifties in the Village," Lorde said, "I didn't know the few other black women who were visibly gay at all well." Most black lesbians were closeted because "It was hard enough to be black, to be black and female, to be black, female, and gay. To be black, female, gay, and out of the closet in a white environment, even to the extent of dancing in the Bagatelle, was considered by many black lesbians to be simply suicidal."

It was lonely and furtive, living that way. "There were no mothers, no sisters, no heroes," according to Lorde. "We had to do it alone, like our sister Amazons, the riders on the loneliest outposts of the kingdom of Dahomey. We, young and black and fine and gay, sweated out our first heartbreaks with no school nor office chums to share that confidence over lunch hour."[9] Lorde would pass black women on Eighth Street, "the invisible but visible sisters," and they would acknowledge each other with "that telltale flick of the eye, that certain otherwise prohibited openness of expression, that definiteness of voice which would suggest, I think she's gay. *After all, doesn't it take one to know one?*"[10]

But the editors of *The Ladder* believed that conforming and keeping a very low profile was how it should be, out of necessity. Lesbians wanted to get along like everyone else; they were "saleswomen, dental technicians, photographers, stenographers, teachers, traffic management people. Some are home-owners, some are saving for a home, some are just living. . . . We aren't 'bar-hoppers' but people with steady jobs, most of them good positions." To gain acceptance, they should try to assimilate as much as possible with heterosexual culture, to blend in.

The homophile Mattachine Society agreed. Although the organization had roots in Communist activism, the leadership thought it more prudent, and more productive in the long run, to defuse social hostility rather than agitate for change. In the meantime, camouflage on the street provided self-protection. "In those days we didn't 'out' one another," Meaker said. "There were all sorts of ways we hid our connections to each other so that people who knew we were homosexuals wouldn't know others were."

Lorraine, after she read a few issues of *The Ladder*, questioned whether repressing and effacing oneself was ever the best strategy. Her father and mother had never stopped insisting on equal treatment for themselves, without trying to conceal that they were different. To her, homosexuals were clearly an oppressed minority, akin to other repressed minorities, and the freedom to be a gay woman was a civil rights issue. "What ought to be clear is that one is oppressed or discriminated against because one is different, not 'wrong' or 'bad' somehow."

"I'm glad as heck you exist," she began her letter to the editor, published in the May 1957 issue of *The Ladder*. She just wanted to share some "off-the-top-of-the-head reactions" to what she had been reading in the magazine. To start with, she was cheered that the Daughters of Bilitis were "serious people and I feel that women, without wishing to foster any strict separatist notions, homo or hetero, indeed have a need for their own publications and organizations." She recognized the need for a "room of one's own," so to speak, but she didn't endorse isolation. Moreover, feminism and lesbianism were connected, she maintained—an insight twenty years in advance of the Combahee River Collective's landmark "Black Feminist Statement" and thirty years before feminist critical inquiry into how race, class, gender, and sexuality overlap. But as a Marxist, she was trained to see the bigger picture.

What she wanted to talk about was a recent discussion in *The Ladder* about how lesbians should dress and act. She, for one, could certainty appreciate the wish to fit in with "a mode of behavior and dress acceptable to society." As a Negro, she says, she was raised hearing about the importance of appearing acceptable to whites, and "I know something about the shallowness of such a view as an end in itself." Lesbians can, if they're willing, bow to the "dominant social group" because they think it prevents trouble, but it won't change their being ostracized. Even Ralph Bunche, she points out, the first American Negro to win the Nobel Peace Prize, "with all his clean fingernails, degrees, and, of course, undeniable service to the human race, could still be insulted, denied a hotel room or meal in many parts of our country." The oppressor can never be appeased. To be fair, she does concede that "the sight of the 'butch' strolling hand in hand with her friend in their trousers and definitive haircuts" was red meat to bigots. Currently, that's just how things were and, she implies, would stay, unless those who were different stood up for themselves.

She ends with a friendly appeal: she would like to be included in the discussion; she was looking for community.[11] All the gay organizations, she writes, "seem to be cropping up on the West Coast rather than here, where a vigorous and active gay set almost bump one another off the streets—what is in the air out there? Pioneers still? Or a tougher circumstance which inspires battle? Would like to hear speculation, light-hearted or otherwise."

In accordance with *The Ladder*'s policy about remaining anonymous in print, she signed her letter with her initials only, "L.H.N."[12]

In the June 1957 issue, responses to her letter proved that she had guessed correctly that DOB members and readers questioned the wisdom of abiding by a "dress code." Freedom of choice about appearance, the right to be oneself—women's rights—sparked a spirited discussion. Lesbian feminism wouldn't become a cultural movement and critical perspective for another twenty years, yet Hansberry was already reasoning her way there.[13]

The vigorous opinions inspired by her letter sent her to her desk again, where she wrote two insightful pieces on activism that, unfortunately, weren't published during her lifetime.

The first was an essay intended for *One*, "On Homophobia," in which she points out the moral peril of acquiescing to a political or social zeitgeist that shows signs of being wrong. "[W]hile our understanding of a trial in Israel [of former Nazi commandant Adolf Eichmann] or an execution in Vietnam may not momentarily be rapid-fire, life has a way of showing us why we should have cared all along." Keeping one's head down in response to injustice, going one's own way, quietism, isn't being neutral; it's being complicit. "Men continue to misinterpret the second-rate status of women as implying a privileged status for themselves; heterosexuals think the same way about homosexuals; gentiles about Jews; whites about blacks; haves about havenots." How she describes the routinization of prejudice and oppression through personal relations—not via institutions or official policy—connects with Hannah Arendt's observation six years later in *Eichmann in Jerusalem: A Report on the Banality of Evil* about the "terrifyingly normal" failure of human beings "to think from the standpoint of somebody else."

Also about this time, she penned an unfinished essay on Beauvoir's

The Second Sex. As has already been mentioned, *The Second Sex* was a critical book in Hansberry's life, first, because it introduced her to feminism and, second, because it builds the bridge between feminism and lesbianism that she describes in her first letter to *The Ladder*. Sexual identity, Beauvoir argues, is a social construct that robs women of their freedom to determine their own destinies and identities. "One is not born," she famously said, "but rather becomes, a woman."

Beauvoir's influence on Hansberry was still strong two years after Lorraine read *The Second Sex*. In "Simone de Beauvoir and 'The Second Sex': An American Commentary," Hansberry wonders why such a radical work—"seven hundred thirty-two pages of revolutionary treatment of the 'woman question'"—had failed to incite a women's movement. If this essay is read in tandem with an earlier one she wrote in 1955, also unpublished during her lifetime and later titled "Notes on Women's Liberation," the two pieces inspire an appreciation for how Hansberry is developing, on her own, the analytical power of intersectionality.[14] In "Notes," she had described her frustration in trying to get friends of hers to understand that the oppression of women and blacks was related. "Immediately there is a really admirable roar of protest that 'These are entirely different questions!'"

She argues in "Simone de Beauvoir and 'The Second Sex'" that they are in fact the same issue. Beauvoir asserts that the "feminine" world is a controlling, male fantasy. Hansberry underscores this by pointing to the popularity of *Playboy*, still new in those days. The appropriation of women's bodies as property in a sex magazine for men put a woman on par with "a slave prior to the Civil War," Hansberry says. As if a female—doe-eyed, passive, and obedient—were incapable of understanding (as was assumed about a slave) that she didn't grasp "intellectually the nature of [her] bondage." The oppression of women and blacks was indeed related, she contends.[15] Yet the keys to freedom had always been in American women's hands. "It is woman herself who has wrought the changes in her condition . . . she has demonstrated and gone to jail; chained herself to the capitol gates . . . for the right to vote, own property," and to divorce, if she chose.

Hansberry joins Beauvoir in insisting that what women want is freedom. "Freed—who can only guess," she imagines "what wealth she can

give humanity, wealth which will be the product of her centuries of humiliation, exploitation, degradation and sheer slavery."[16]

How did a young woman in her mid-twenties learn to think so far in
advance of her own times? Hansberry had good teachers. Sojourners for
Truth and Justice, the organization she joined while she was working at
Freedom, was run by black leftist feminists. They linked racism in America
to U.S. wars against foreign nonwhites, a global violation of human rights
on the basis of race, which the Sojourners had attempted to bring before
the United Nations. When there was, as yet, no national feminist discourse
coming from any quarter, Hansberry was schooled in woman-centered
intersectional thinking by some of the most progressive black women of
her day, such as Alice Childress, Shirley Du Bois, Esther Cooper Jackson,
Claudia Jones, Louise Thompson Patterson, and Mary Church Terrell. It
gave her a far-reaching outlook. That's why, for example, she never cared
for the term *sexual revolution*—it was narrow, always confused with "free
love," and time-limited.[17] The greater object, she understood, was universal
justice.

She gave the readers of *The Ladder* more to think about in the August 1957
issue. In the June issue, the main article had been about lesbians married to men: "One Facet of Fear," by Nancy Osbourne. And then, in July,
Marion Zimmer Bradley responded to Osbourne with "Some Remarks on
Marriage."

Osbourne had recommended that a married gay woman "keep her
secret" from her husband. Bradley, for her part, said divorce was the only
option, unless a married lesbian could say to herself, if not to her husband,
"I find other women interesting; that does not in any way affect our relationship." This exchange raised the kinds of ethical choices Hansberry was
struggling with.

First, identifying herself as "a lesbian heterosexually married," Hansberry says she can't get her mind around Bradley's idea of having it both
ways. Finding other women "interesting," Hansberry says, does not begin
to describe "the homosexual impulse," which she defines as having the
"most intense emotional and physical reactions toward other women."
Second, she cannot condone violating marital vows with one spouse by
secretly practicing open marriage. "Not so much because of any sacredness

of our dubious social morality, but rather because it involves the deception of another human being—and that, as always, is intolerable." She thinks Bradley's suggestion that lesbianism is a "psychosexual orientation" understates the reality, too. "I am afraid that homosexuality, whatever its origins, is far more real than that, far more profound in the demands it makes."

One day perhaps—she writes, returning once more to the interrelatedness in society of lesbianism and feminism—women will "emerge who will be able to formulate a new and possible concept that homosexual persecution and condemnation has at its roots not only social ignorance, but a philosophically active anti-feminist dogma." In the meantime, "I think it is about time that equipped women began to take on some of the ethical questions which a male-dominated culture has produced and dissect and analyze them quite to pieces in a serious fashion. It is time that 'half the human race' had something to say about the nature of its existence." Signed, "L.N."[18]

It's worth pointing out that regardless of how Lorraine wanted to join and be accepted by the lesbian community, she wasn't willing to trot out problems in her marriage for the readers of *The Ladder*, like a pitiable sob sister, to impress them. As Bob Nemiroff's best friend, if not his wife in the traditional sense, she protected his privacy and his feelings.[19]

Outside her letters to *The Ladder*, she never again returned publicly to issues of sexuality and sexism. Why she didn't, as will be seen, had to do with a personal decision about choosing her battles. In the meantime, she continued to weigh Beauvoir's momentous statement in *The Second Sex*, that lesbianism is a "choice, arrived at in a complex total situation and based on a free decision."[20]

PART V

The Great White Way

18

"Go the Way Your Blood Beats"

One writes out of one thing only—one's own experience. Everything depends on how relentlessly one forces from this experience the last drop, sweet or bitter, it can possibly give.

—James Baldwin, *Notes of a Native Son*

Boy, if plays didn't have to make sense, I'd be a genius.

—Lorraine Hansberry[1]

On Easter Sunday, April 6, 1958, Lorraine got up from bed sometime after one o'clock in the afternoon. Her old enemy, depression, had returned. It usually did around holidays. Added to which, Saturday had been a day of heavy celebration, with Scotch, because Langston Hughes had given her permission to use a line from his poem "Harlem" as the new title of her play in progress, "The Crystal Stair." She had been waiting to hear from him since February, when she completed the first draft. Now it could be rechristened *A Raisin in the Sun*.[2]

What happens to a dream deferred? Does it dry up
Like a raisin in the sun?

Where Bob was, she probably didn't know. They were drifting apart as husband and wife, though they remained devoted friends. "Do have a good time. Of course I miss you," she wrote to him when he went to San Francisco on music business.[3] She sometimes saw him by appointment, noting the day and time in her pocket datebook. A melancholy ballad he'd written with Burt D'Lugoff, "You're Everywhere," was going to be recorded by Phil Rose's Glory Records.

Outside her window, it was dark and rainy, but she got dressed and went to Prexy's, a diner on the corner of Christopher Street and Greenwich Avenue, for an afternoon breakfast. She ordered pancakes and coffee. While she waited, she smoked and read the *New York Times*. A woman tried to strike up a conversation with her about travel, but Lorraine wanted to catch a 3:25 p.m. showing of *Sayonara*, and there were fewer trains running on Sunday. The pancakes and coffee came to eighty cents. She got to the movie theater on time and paid sixty-eight cents at the box-office window.

Set during the Korean War, *Sayonara*, starring Marlon Brando, was about a love affair in Kyoto between an American fighter pilot and a famous Japanese dancer. The scenes in the Imperial Gardens were gorgeous, splashed across the screen in 75 mm Technicolor, and Lorraine was "much moved"—something that didn't happen very often when she went to the movies.

It was 6:30 p.m., and still gloomy and drizzling, when she came out of the theater. The streetlights were coming on. Rather than get a bite of supper somewhere, she went home and put a dish in the oven. She turned on the radio and sat at the kitchen table. It was 7:15 p.m., and the apartment was quiet except for Spice, "the sort of collie." She was lonely.[4]

For about two months, she'd been meeting with Lloyd Richards on Saturday afternoons to revise her first complete draft of *A Raisin in the Sun*. The first act was still pretty much as she had written it during that furious birthday weekend in May almost a year before. But she was stuck, dangling somewhere in the third act with two possible endings, unsure of which one she should write toward. She imagined having the Younger family hunkered down inside their home, preparing to defend themselves against rioters, poised with bats and kitchen utensils.[5] A sort of stop-action tableau, perhaps, then go to dark. Or maybe, Walter Lee could undergo a religious conversion and see the light. Peace would reign with a larger message for humanity. But that would be the worst kind of deus ex machina. She was also unsure about using a fantasy ballet she had in mind to express the characters' hopes.[6]

She was fortunate to work with Richards, who later directed nearly all of August Wilson's work on Broadway.[7] Her collaborating with him illustrates how a dramatic work, from script to stage, becomes a palimpsest— revised, rewritten, and reinterpreted. And this was not just a development of the modern stage: it's estimated that during London's spring–summer theater season of 1598, over 80 percent of the plays performed were works of collaboration.[8]

In most literary genres, the word *author* is taken to mean a single person. Not so in theater, where the director, performers, designers, and technicians challenge the creative authority of the playwright. There is no correct meaning of the text.[9] "Ready for the stage," Richards said, "doesn't necessarily mean ready for an audience or ready to be a hit or ready in any other component. Ready for the stage, to me, means that there is a true line to the dramatic action in the play, that the characters are relatively clear, that they speak with an individual voice, and that they interact with one another with some degree of reality. Then they can begin to explore questions that may exist within the piece as you work on it."[10]

Richards was thirty-eight; Hansberry, twenty-seven. He had been born in Toronto, Canada, in 1919. When he was four, his family moved to Detroit, where his father, a Jamaican "Garveyite" master carpenter, had worked for better wages on the assembly line at Ford Motor Company's River Rouge Plant. After high school, Lloyd enrolled in prelaw at Wayne State University, but he fell in love with performance. When he was a teenager, he had delivered Bible readings in church in his fine, warm voice. Seeing how his college classmates responded to his rendering of a speech from *Macbeth*, he knew he had found his calling.

His father had died a few years earlier, and Richards's mother was adamantly against his switching from prelaw to speech and theater. As it happened, World War II intervened, and in 1943, Richards enlisted in the Army Air Corps, training to be a Tuskegee Airman. But before he could earn his wings, peace was declared. Returning to Detroit, he joined a troupe of student actors. They rented a large, empty house and turned the living room into a theater-in-the-round, with concentric rows of folding chairs. They made stage lights using three-hundred-watt lightbulbs and slipped Quaker Oats containers over them to focus the beam. His apprenticeship in community theater lasted two years.

In 1947, he moved to New York City and lived at the YMCA at 135th Street off Lenox Avenue, in Harlem. At an audition for nonprofessional actors held by the Equity Library Theater, he met actor Paul Mann, who offered him a job as an assistant in his Actors Workshop. Richards was a dependable character actor, but he wanted to be "a meaningful storyteller," he said, because theater deals with things "that people are concerned about."[11] He took the job.

One of his classmates was Edwin Sherin, later a television producer, who remembered that Mann's Actors Workshop "was the place to be" in the early 1950s. Located in an old building at Forty-Third Street and Sixth Avenue, it "was a mecca for eager, idealistic theatre professionals." Several days every week, actors climbed four flights of dusty stairs, Sherin said, "to satisfy their craving, to do it 'right.'" Among them were Cicely Tyson, Sidney Poitier, Hal Linden, Paul Mazursky, Faye Dunaway, Ossie Davis, Barbara Ann Teer, Ruby Dee, and Douglas Turner Ward. According to Ward, Paul Mann had "committed himself to teaching and dealing with non-majority, non-white students, without paternalism during a time when other acting teachers were just not interested in the minority students" because there weren't enough parts for them in theater.[12]

One afternoon, Richards and Poitier went out for lunch together. They couldn't each afford a hot dog, so they bought one and split it. "If I ever do a major show," Richards recalled Poitier saying, "I'd like you to direct it." Richards returned the compliment. Poitier would be his first choice, too, as an actor.

Several years passed. Then, in the spring of 1958, Poitier phoned Richards excitedly. "I got it—I got the play I want to do on Broadway." He mailed a copy of the unfinished draft of *A Raisin in the Sun*. Richards and his wife, Barbara Davenport, a dancer in the original production of *The King and I*, divided the parts and began a cold reading. Despite the play's length, which was almost four hours, they "howled, and we cried, we had a wonderful time reading it," Richards said. "I told him I was interested."[13] Next, Poitier arranged for Richards to meet Phil Rose at the office of Glory

Records, on West Fifty-Seventh Street. Rose was frank about the financial situation: there were no backers yet. But before Richards made a decision, Rose recommended that he meet the playwright, Lorraine Hansberry—hoping, probably, that Richards would want to work with her.

He met Hansberry for coffee one afternoon and they got to know each other. "And I had great respect for that woman," Richards remembered. "We liked the same people: Chekhov, O'Casey, and Robeson, whom she had worked for." About her play, he recalled her saying, "I'm not doing it to be the first black anything."[14] *A Raisin in the Sun* was about her family.

His impression was that she had "felt diminished and destroyed by the real estate powers in Chicago," and she blamed them for her father's death. *A Raisin in the Sun* was her wish for her brother Perry, the more entrepreneurial of the two brothers, to have a better life than their father. Perry and Walter Lee Younger were alike, she said, because "the drive which impelled them both is the same."[15] (When Douglas Turner Ward later met Perry, he was "shocked," he said. "Her brother was Walter Lee in the play!"[16]) Walter Lee would start out convinced that a combination of making big plans, cutting corners, and getting money was the way to seize the American Dream. By the final act, Hansberry wanted him to show signs of maturing and living up to his responsibilities as a father and husband, instead of believing that money would make him a man.

Richards had the whole picture now: Hansberry was an unknown playwright; this was her first play, and it didn't have out-of-the-box commercial appeal. Nevertheless, he agreed to direct, because getting involved didn't pose much of a risk, really—there wasn't a lot at stake, except his time. "It was no big deal."[17] Besides, he needed the experience directing.

There was another hurdle to be cleared, however, which was Hansberry's first draft. The way she had written it, the main conflict in *A Raisin in the Sun* was the mother's (Lena Younger's) decision over how to make the best use of her late husband's life insurance money to help the next generation. In the first act, all the characters speak to Mama Younger and then leave, clearly establishing her as the person around whom the play revolves. Gradually, Lorraine "bought into the idea," Richards said, "that the play was really about Walter Lee Younger's coming-of-age. Learning to deal with the past, his father, and the present, which is what he was living through. And what was being imposed on him by social circumstances." But to switch protagonists wouldn't be easy.[18] The entire play would have to be restructured.

Every Saturday afternoon, they met. Lorraine would wait while Lloyd read over her pages, still fresh from the typewriter, for what had been added, eliminated, or revised. He would challenge her with new ideas, and then "she would top me in what she wrote."[19] They went scene by scene. During the week, she rebuilt the play, using, she said, "as a model, as a point of departure," Seán O'Casey's *Juno and the Paycock*.[20] How much of *A Raisin in the Sun* was Hansberry and how much Richards is unknown; the original manuscript was lost.

During that year of intense writing and rewriting, Hansberry became friends with James Baldwin. They met in April, at a workshop reading at the Actors Studio of his novel *Giovanni's Room*, which he had adapted into a play. The work is about an interracial love affair. In America, Baldwin said, "the sexual question and the racial question have always been intertwined."[21] Lorraine went out of curiosity.

David, the narrator—"a good white Protestant" and heterosexual—lives in a mansion in the South of France. He describes what it was like falling in love with a darkly beautiful Italian bartender, Giovanni. But then David sees another young man and feels the same keen desire. Overwhelmed by this impulse, he finds his excitement leading to faithlessness, and the situation turns violent. David blames Giovanni, "the other," for tricking him and damaging his manhood. "There opened in me a hatred for Giovanni which was as powerful as my love and which was nourished by the same roots."[22]

This is how David recalls events, but then, no one remembers things reliably because of their need for self-preservation and their perception of who they are. An important metaphor occurs when David studies himself in a mirror. Proud of his masculine appeal, he tells himself that he's not like other people—not like Giovanni, who's dark, instinctual, and lower-class. Being white provides David with a mythology about superiority. "My reflection is tall, perhaps rather like an arrow. My blond hair gleams. My face is like a face you have seen many times. My ancestors conquered a continent, pushing across death-laden plains, until they came to an ocean which faced away from Europe into a darker past."[23] *Giovanni's Room*, Baldwin said, is not so much about homosexuality as it is about the sadness of convincing ourselves that we're incapable of loving others.

As the reading at the Actors Workshop ended and the discussion began, most of the reactions to the play were negative. Baldwin sat listening to his work faulted again and again. Only one attendee defended what she had heard: "a young black woman at the back of the small workshop audience," Baldwin said. "She had liked the play, she had liked it a lot, she said firmly. I was enormously grateful to her, she seemed to speak for me." Afterward, he went over to introduce himself to Lorraine; his impression was that she was a shy but determined person. "She talked to me with a gentleness and generosity never to be forgotten."[24]

As it happened, they lived not far from each other—he was on Horatio Street, a ten-minute walk from Bleecker Street—and they began spending time together, usually at her apartment having drinks and listening to the Modern Jazz Quartet, one of their favorite groups. She was twenty-eight; he was thirty-four.

Hansberry tended to be reserved around people at first, which some took to mean that she was cold. Harold Cruse, from the moment he met her at *Freedom*, decided she was "demonstrably anti-male, especially towards those she considered socially beneath her."[25] She tended to speak carefully, which could give the impression that she was unemotional. To her, conversation was supposed to move toward something, in pursuit of a point, or to clarify an issue. You could see her thinking hard when she was feeling serious. An acquaintance said, "You had to know her pretty well to feel the great warmth she possessed. But there was great joy in this girl. She loved music, the dance, everything. And when she felt relaxed, in an environment where she could let herself go—she was a lively one—a lively one."[26]

Baldwin found this to be true. Hanging out at Lorraine's apartment, the two enjoyed arguing and teasing. He was the eldest in his family, and she was the youngest. The way she picked on him affectionately, like a sister, tickled him. "Just when I was certain that she was about to throw me out, as being too rowdy a type, she would stand up, her hands on her hips (for these downhome sessions she always wore slacks) and pick up my empty glass as though she intended to throw it at me. Then she would walk into the kitchen, saying with a haughty toss of her head, 'Really, Jimmy, you ain't *right*, child!'"[27]

They argued about Langston Hughes. Baldwin blamed him for wasting his talents on minor efforts. Hansberry defended him and cautioned Jimmy not to air his criticisms about Hughes in public, or about Richard Wright, either. It gave racists ammunition. Baldwin insisted that he had to say what he thought, especially when speaking to an audience. To "witness" meant telling people not what they wanted to hear, but what they *needed* to hear. "Relations between Negroes and whites demand honesty and insight. They must be based on the assumption that there is one race and that we are all a part of it."[28]

Lorraine knew that some of Jimmy's feud with Langston was personal. Hughes resented what he considered Baldwin's complicity in encouraging white people's assumptions about black life—"the fakelore of black pathology," writer Albert Murray called it. Harlem was home to Hughes; he accused Baldwin of capitalizing on it as a place to collect material, the grittier and uglier the better, for making dire prophesies about America's future.[29]

Hansberry also disagreed with Baldwin about Malcolm X and the Nation of Islam. He insisted that Malcolm's was "the only movement in the country that you can call grassroots. When Malcolm talks or the Muslim ministers talk, they articulate for all the Negro people who hear them, who listen to them. They articulate their suffering, the suffering which has been in this country so long denied. That's Malcolm's great authority over any of his audiences. He corroborates their reality; he tells them that they really exist." Lorraine refused to give Malcom X, or the Muslims, that much intellectual credit. To her, as she later wrote, black nationalism "was a potluck nationalism that looks backward, not to the wonderful black African civilization of medieval and antique periods, but to Arabic cultures. Muslim 'separation' is not a program, but an accommodation to American racism."[30]

She and Baldwin were of one mind, however, about Norman Mailer's essay "The White Negro: Superficial Reflections on the Hipster," which had appeared in *Dissent* the previous fall. Mailer, writing in jazz-inspired bop prosody, riffs on the Beats, who aspire to a kind of Zen-like mindfulness. They wanted to be aware, Buddha-like, without judgment, of every moment and feeling in a world that was seeking to depersonalize humanity. Human skin had been made into lampshades in Nazi death camps, and an atomic bomb nicknamed "Little Boy" had vaporized forty-five thousand Japanese in a flash. To be Beat, wrote Mailer, was to channel all that madness, to "encourage the psychopath in oneself, to explore the domain of experience where security is boredom and therefore sickness, and exist . . . in that enormous present which is without past or future, memory or planned intention, the life where a man must go until he is beat."[31]

Lorraine dismissed the Beats as puerile and useless. They were disciples of "nothingism. . . . They are a failure. They disturb no one because they attack everything and nothing. . . . They serve no significant purpose, neither to art nor society." They made bohemia seem clownish. She would later tell a college audience, "I am ashamed of the Beat Generation. They have made a crummy revolt, a revolt that has not added up to a hill of beans."[32] White, college-educated hipsters experiencing an existential crisis were one thing. But they appropriated black pain in an effort to feel authentic. Allen Ginsberg declaimed in the Beat panegyric *Howl*, "I saw the best minds of my generation, destroyed by madness, starving hysterical naked, dragging themselves through the negro streets at dawn looking for an angry fix, angelheaded hipsters burning for the ancient heavenly connection to the starry dynamo in the machinery of night . . ."

"Perhaps they are angry young men," Hansberry said, "but insofar as they do not make it clear with whom or *at what* they are angry, they can be said only to add bedlam to this already chaotic house."[33]

Mailer, for his part, a Harvard graduate in aeronautical engineering, could, Beat-wise, dig the Negro scene. He scratched his goatee, analyzed where the Negro was coming from metaphysically, and found him an enviable, fellow cat[34]:

. . . the Negro (all exceptions admitted) could rarely afford the sophisticated inhibitions of civilization, and so he kept for his survival the art of the primitive, he lived in the enormous present, he subsisted for his Saturday night kicks, relinquishing the pleasures of the mind for the more obligatory pleasures of the body, and in his music he gave voice to the character and quality of his existence, to his rage and the infinite variations of joy, lust, languor, growl, cramp, pinch, scream and despair of his orgasm. For jazz is orgasm, it is the music of orgasm, good orgasm and bad, and so it spoke across a nation, it had the communication of art even where it was watered, perverted, corrupted, and almost killed, it spoke in no matter what laundered popular way of instantaneous existential states to which some whites could respond.

For Mailer, the power of black music lay in a presumably savage strain inside the black people who had invented it.[35] A black jazz musician had told Baldwin that Mailer was "a real sweet ofay cat, but a little frantic." Lorraine was less generous. She summarized Mailer's and the Beats' ideas about black people as "look over there coming down from the trees is a Negro" who knows none of the soul-killing constraints of civilization, "and wouldn't it be marvelous if I could be my naked, brutal, savage self again?"[36]

Baldwin loved her caustic wit. "I would often stagger down her stairs as the sun came up, usually in the middle of a paragraph and always in the middle of a laugh."[37]

Hansberry learned important things from Baldwin, beginning with how unafraid he was to share deep intimacies. "Baldwin reveals so much about himself that the embarrassed reader cannot help feeling he has stumbled upon a person performing a private act," Julian Mayfield wrote; "certainly no writer since Gide has written with such naked honesty."[38]

She also took a lesson from him about sexuality. Baldwin preferred to leave his own undefined, without labels. He liked to pass along advice given to him by "an old friend of mine, a black friend, who said you have to go the way your blood beats." Don't be afraid to listen to your feelings. "Those terms, homosexual, bisexual, heterosexual," Baldwin said, "are 20th century terms which, for me, have very little meaning. I've never, myself, in watching myself and other people, been able to discern exactly where the barriers were."[39]

Baldwin's matter-of-fact attitude about love and sexuality tended to unsettle black and white audiences.[40] He came before them sometimes as a black man on a particular topic, but always as a human being, inviting them to treat him, and themselves, compassionately. "Everybody's hurt," he wrote. "What is important, what corrals you, what bullwhips you, what drives you, torments you, is that you must find some way of using this to connect you with everyone else alive." Hansberry admired his "gentle, if impassioned" appeal to try to really "'talk to one another'" across racial borders.[41]

She, too, in *A Raisin in the Sun*, was trying to enter restricted areas. Her dialogue for the Younger family contained unruly, disquieting talk about injustice, moral choices, racism, male supremacy, deferred dreams, colonialism in Africa, and seeking to control one's own destiny. Unlike the men of the emerging Black Theater movement, Hansberry was against breaking off communication with Western culture and creating a separate, Afrocentric identity. Nor was she an assimilationist. She believed, as did Baldwin, that there existed a space in between, where a change of consciousness would leave common ground for peace and equity.

Baldwin lived in this space. He had arrived in Paris in 1948 with forty dollars in his pocket. "I began to see this country [the United States] for the first time. If I hadn't gone away, I would never have been able to see it." The longer he stayed away, the clearer something became to him, writes Harold R. Isaacs in his essay "Five Writers and Their African Ancestors"[42]:

> He came to see, for one thing, that his sense of lostness, far from distinguishing him from white Americans, made him kin with them, that they were just as lost and alienated as he was, and that "this depthless alienation from oneself and one's people is, in sum, the American experience." Baldwin also resolved, with a reassertion of his intelligence, the problem of his sense of divorcement from the stream of culture.... He had stopped seeing himself as waiting, empty-handed and empty-minded, for the white conqueror in Africa while Western man created his glories. Now he saw that in all time all people had exchanged and appropriated cultures and in doing so reshaped them.... Thus Baldwin regained a sense of American identity by realizing that it is the search for an identity that makes all Americans kin, and he won his way through to share in Rembrandt and Bach by striking out from his remote African shore and making his own path through the great sea of the common human experience.

A few weeks after Hansberry met Baldwin, Phil Rose received a certified offering circular from his attorney, meaning he could legally raise investment capital for *A Raisin in the Sun*. It surprised him that trade publications such as *Billboard*, *Variety*, and *Cash Box* made available lists of the investors in all the Broadway shows, and their addresses. With a needed budget of one hundred thousand dollars (a million dollars, today) he started with the most generous angels.

But as the spring of 1958 turned to summer, it became clear that the smart money on Broadway "was not involved and would not be involved," as Lloyd Richards put it.[43] Musicals such as *Porgy and Bess* could turn a profit; or revivals of the Harlem classic *Shuffle Along*; or folk comedies like *Simply Heavenly*, based on Langston Hughes's already famous character Jesse B. Semple. But a straight drama about a black family didn't have the panache to fill the big venues on Forty-Second Street—it was a matter of economics. Producers and investors relied on middle- and upper-class white New Yorkers who were regular theatergoers, on tourists who were in town to enjoy themselves, and on businesspeople with expense accounts. In surveys conducted by *Playbill*, only about 10 percent of Broadway audiences identified themselves as working class.[44]

Rose pitched the show to professionals up and down Manhattan. They "were respectful, even admiring," because they agreed that *A Raisin in the Sun* was definitely a play that should be done. Talk show host David Susskind told Rose he was all for his daring, "but he could not be involved because it wasn't 'commercial.' To be involved in a Broadway production, he had to be sure it would be a hit. He could not stake his reputation on such a risky venture."[45] According to Rose, *A Raisin in the Sun* was turned down by every established name in the theater business. W. E. B. Du Bois was sent a partial script, but he wasn't interested.[46]

With the lists of potential investors turned to ashes, Rose recruited Richards, Nemiroff, and D'Lugoff to help give readings in people's homes. Lorraine, to protect her writing time, didn't participate. The four men, like political candidates holding living room coffees, spoke to groups of half a dozen people usually. They read excerpts from *A Raisin in the Sun* and asked for volunteers to take parts, assuring their listeners that while the play was still a work in progress, it would be finished soon. A share in the production cost $5; checks were generally written for amounts of $250 or $500.

Most of the investors were Jewish, partly because the story of the

Youngers was their story, too. The movement of Jews out of settlement neighborhoods in Manhattan at the end of the 1950s was becoming a tidal wave headed toward Queens, Long Island, Westchester County, Scarsdale, Purchase, and White Plains—"comfortable ghettoes," historian Howard Morley Sachar called them, "enjoying all the physical amenities, even their own ethnic snobberies and eccentricities."[47] That a family like the Youngers should want to live better, happier lives without sacrificing their identity was the goal of Jews who had come through Ellis Island—except that people of African descent had been in America for 350 years, not two generations.

At first, there were no black investors, a fact later lamented by civil rights leader and politician Anna Arnold Hedgeman. "It is tragic that this, the first play which has given us both our universal quality and our special agony, should not have been paid for by us. It is also tragic that poor as we are we didn't make some money on it. One wonders how many dreams could become reality if all of us were determined to help some dream forward each day."[48]

But lack of interest on the part of the black community for such a venture was not unusual, said Douglas Turner Ward, who later sought start-up money for his theater, the Negro Ensemble Company. "It had nothing to do with ideology. Theater was not, especially for the black bourgeoisie, or the black monied class, something they saw as profitable for them. They preferred more dependable ventures to get a return."[49] Lorraine was blunter. The conventional wisdom, she said, was "nobody was going to pay those prices to see a bunch of Negroes emoting."[50]

In fact, though, it was a favorable time to take on race issues. The theater seasons 1956 to 1957 were "remarkable" for black playwrights and actors, according to playwright and theater historian Loften Mitchell, "and once again[,] people started talking about the millennium" arriving for black American drama.[51] Alice Childress was the first woman to win an Obie, for *Trouble in Mind*, her play about white paternalism and racial stereotypes in American theater. The play was optioned for the 1957 Broadway season until her backers insisted that she tone down her indictment of the very institution audiences were paying to see. She withdrew it from consideration. A revival of Louis S. Peterson's *Take a Giant Step*, a coming-of-age drama about a black teenager living in a white neighborhood, which

Hansberry saw and admired, drew larger audiences than when it was on Broadway three years earlier.[52] And Loften Mitchell's *A Land Beyond the River*, about pastor Joseph DeLaine's court case in 1952 to end school segregation in South Carolina, filled the Greenwich Mews Theatre for eight months and earned Mitchell a Guggenheim Fellowship. "The crown jewel of protest drama," one critic later pronounced it.[53]

More likely, the reason that investors for *Raisin* were scarce was because Rose and the others had no experience in theater, no credits to their names, and yet they were certain they could get to Broadway. Some of the play's backers probably put up front money out of respect for the producers' gumption. Perhaps even a few contributed because they felt sorry for this quixotic band of young people with a commendable dream, so they chipped in, never expecting to see a cent come out of it—a mitzvah.

19

"Something Urgently on Its Way"

The Girls, of a Friday night, gather
In fast cruising clusters, gather
To the bars
Sharing their contempt,
Booted and trousered and barbered as it is,
With the moon and marquee light of
The [Theatre] De Lys . . .

—Lorraine Hansberry

In May 1958, a month after meeting Baldwin, Lorraine opened her journal and wrote, "As for this homosexuality thing (how long since I have thought or written of it in that way—as some kind of entity!) am committed to it. But its childhood is over. From now on—I actively look for women of accomplishment—no matter what they look like. How free I feel today. I will create my life—not just accept it." At twenty-eight, Hansberry began seeking romances with women.[1]

It's often repeated, for the sake of keeping the narrative of her life consistent as a black bisexual feminist, that she and Bob separated in 1957. Some chroniclers imply that the union never should have happened because Robert Nemiroff was a "white Jewish man." But the two continued to live together through to the end of her life. They were in each other's lives constantly and still in love, although they weren't man and wife any longer. They were two devoted friends who needed each other in many ways.

Marie Rupert, a theater colleague and college friend of Hansberry's, thought she knew what kept them together: it was the work. "What was the nature of this intimate bond that she and Bobby had? It produced the plays, the 'children' that they had."[2] He was also her business manager and promoter, acting as Willy to her Colette, to use Elise Harris's felicitous comparison in "The Double Life of Lorraine Hansberry." Bob kept scrapbooks of Lorraine's published articles and expertly typed her manuscripts. Gradually, he would evolve from her first critic and manager to her dramaturge and, finally, following *A Raisin in the Sun*, her coplaywright on *The Sign in Sidney Brustein's Window*.

"On the surface it appeared that Bobby was so easygoing that he would do whatever he could for her," Rupert said, "and he didn't make demands, but that was a demand. The access. What he wouldn't accept was no relationship. What was important was that no one take Lorraine away from him. Not necessarily sexually, but just starting a whole other life without Bobby."[3]

Hansberry's gay women friends didn't like Nemiroff, or her attachment to him, and found their relationship incomprehensible. They wanted a clear break. "He was a nebbish," said one of her lovers. "His life revolved around Lorraine and who she was. I have no idea why she married him. She didn't abuse him in any way, but she treated him in a very offhand fashion. There were too many other things that were more important to her in life than Bobby, and she made it abundantly clear. And yet he was always there, he was always around."[4]

Perhaps Lorraine didn't love women for themselves—it's possible, despite Audre Lorde's remark that "When you see the plays and read the words of Lorraine Hansberry, you are reading the words of a woman who loved women deeply."[5] Claudia Card, a scholar of feminist ethics, draws a distinction between authentic and inauthentic lesbian relationships. The latter are practiced by women who are "basically heterosexually oriented" and use women lovers for "consolation and regeneration" in support of their relationships with men.[6] She cites Beauvoir's relationships with female students as an example: those affairs were passionate and possibly sexual, but Sartre remained central in her life. What he offered her by way of "regeneration," intellectually and creatively, mattered more to her than the sympathetic excitement of a same-sex romance.

In any case, Nemiroff seems to have accepted Lorraine's extramarital life, for reasons of his own. What his wife did on her own time was her own business, so long as she came home to him.

The Village's sexual geography as a territory to explore was open and varied in the late 1950s, and had been so at least since the 1920s, when Eve Adams posted a sign on her tearoom door declaring, "Men Are Admitted but Not Welcome." Her establishment, said the *Greenwich Village Quill*, was a place where "ladies prefer each other."[7] Lorraine would have fit in beautifully with the ethos of Miss Adams's tearoom: she preferred not to take a walk on the wild side, in keeping with her upper-middle-class background.

Most of Lorraine's gay relationships were with preppy, cardigan-wearing young women who might have been seen on the campuses of Vassar or Bryn Mawr. She had been introduced to this circle by Helen Leeds, a law student at NYU. Few of her new friends, however, were her intellectual equals. "These were not," in Elise Harris's words, "serious ladies talking about existentialist philosophy."[8] They were nice to look at. Hansberry would have met saltier types at bars, but this didn't appeal to a woman of her sensibilities.

Had she ventured into the gay bars of 1950s Greenwich Village, it would have felt like moving into an all-white neighborhood—not that gays would have admitted to being racists. "After all," said Audre Lorde, "didn't they know what it was like to be oppressed?" Lorde describes her experience as a newcomer at the Bagatelle, on University Place between Tenth and Eleventh Streets[9]:

> There was an inner door, guarded by a male bouncer, ostensibly to keep out the straight male intruders come to gawk at the "lezzies," but in reality, to keep out those women deemed "undesirable." All too frequently, undesirable meant black. . . . When I moved through the bunches of women cruising each other in the front room, or doing a slow fish on the dance floor in the back, with the smells of cigarette smoke and the music and the hair pomade whirling together like incense through

charged air, it was hard for me to believe that my being an outsider had anything to do with being a lesbian. But when I, a black woman, saw no reflection in any of the faces there week after week, I knew perfectly well that being an outsider in the Bagatelle had everything to do with being black.

Likening lesbian groups to neighborhoods isn't far-fetched. Lesbianism was a subculture, according to Lillian Faderman in *Odd Girls and Twilight Lovers*, but it was also divided into groups of women preferring other women who belonged to their group—the purpose of Miss Adams's tearoom. Working-class lesbians in 1950s New York socialized with other working-class lesbians; middle-class professionals (teachers, librarians, and saleswomen) mingled with their own; and the wealthy were off by themselves. Because of differences in class, Faderman said, "mixing was extremely rare."[10]

Similar to how neighborhoods can rapidly change, there was also "gay flight" from self-segregating bars in Greenwich Village during the 1950s. The "'unraveling' process," in economist Thomas Schelling's phrase, is similar in neighborhoods. "Everybody who selects a new environment affects the environments of those he leaves and those he moves among. There is a chain reaction."[11] Some alteration in the community that might not seem important to an outsider would be to the insider. As a resident of a suburb was overheard to say, "When the tricycles start being left out on the sidewalk overnight, it's time to move." The life span of "most gay bars was under a year," Lorde estimated. "Laurel's went the way of all the other gay bars—like the Swing and Snooky's and the Grapevine, the Sea Colony and the Pony Stable Inn. Each closed after a year or so, while another opened and caught on somewhere else."[12]

In *A Raisin in the Sun*, Karl Lindner, the white man from the Clybourne Park Improvement Association, is tasked with explaining the bald truth about why people affiliate: "people get along a lot better, take more of a common interest in the life of the community, when they share a common background." To which Lorde could add, as she said, "community must not mean a shedding of our differences, nor the pathetic pretense that these differences do not exist."[13]

Hansberry was unsure about how presenting herself as queer would affect her—what it described, what it required—similar to Baldwin resisting labels for his sexuality. In *The Apples of Autumn*, she portrays lesbianism as "a limited, even perverse rebellion," meaning perhaps that she saw it, in her case, as a reaction to her unsatisfying heterosexual marriage. In her journal, she reflected on whether it was a "social problem," comparing it to addiction and prostitution. Yet, in *Flowers for the General*, she makes a lesbian character into a visionary poet.

Her desire for women was the only thing she could be certain of, and she looked to Beauvoir for guidance. Beauvoir counseled in *The Second Sex* that lesbianism should be nuanced and individualized—"this will involve playacting, imbalance, failure, or lies, or, on the other hand, it will be the source of fruitful experiences, depending on whether it is lived in bad faith, laziness, and inauthenticity, or in lucidity, generosity, and freedom." There was no right way to conduct oneself. As Baldwin said, "Love is where you find it."[14]

Lorraine was excited by what reinventing herself might bring. In an unpublished article, she quotes an "intimate friend," herself probably, who says she's "a Negro; a woman; an artist; a communist and a lesbian." Being multifaceted could provide inspiration, she hoped. "I am, in one, all the world's most oppressed—or . . . despised—divisions. Jesus!—what I could tell the world!"[15]

One of Hansberry's biographers believes she had an affair with Molly Malone Cook, the *Village Voice* photographer who later became the partner of poet Mary Oliver.[16] It may have begun as a flirtation during the summer of 1957, when Hansberry went to Provincetown. According to Oliver, Cook had a romance about this time "that struck deeply," in which she "loved totally and was loved totally." Oliver adds that it's only "supposition," but it fits that the affair was with Lorraine.[17] Cook frequented the arts scene in Provincetown and eventually opened a photography gallery on Commercial Street. Her candid photographs of Lorraine capture her affectionately—when she is at peace with herself, singing or just daydreaming—a boyish-looking woman, tousled-haired and wearing a loose, rumpled white shirt with unevenly rolled sleeves. Cook and Hansberry shared a passion for Edna St. Vincent Millay, the bisexual, feminist poet of the 1920s whose *Collected Poems* had just been published. Hansberry, in a dedicatory ode to Millay, called her, "Lone woman of the autumns, beautiful St. Vincent."

Sometime in 1958, Lorraine went to East Blue Hill, Maine, perhaps in the company of Cook, who liked taking long driving trips. They met playwright Maxine Wood, whose 1946 Broadway production, *On Whitman Avenue*, dealt with a black World War II veteran encountering housing discrimination. Wood recalled Hansberry telling her "shyly" that she was working on a play.[18] It was while staying "at a beautiful lodge built right into the rocky cliffs of a bay on the Maine coast," Hansberry said, that she met a woman she respected. Her description deserves to be quoted at length, because of the parallels with the end of Lorraine's life.[19]

> We met a woman there who had lived a purposeful and courageous life and who was then dying of cancer. She had, characteristically, just written a book and taken up painting. She had also been of radical viewpoint all her life; one of those people who energetically believe that the world can be changed for the better and [who] spend their lives trying to do just that. And that was the way she thought of cancer; she absolutely refused to award it the stature of tragedy, a devastating instance of the brooding doom and inexplicability of the absurdity of human destiny, etc., etc. The kind of characterization given, lately, as we all know, to far less formidable foes in life than cancer.
>
> But for this remarkable woman it was a matter of nature in imperfection, implying, as always, work for man to do. It was an enemy, but a palpable one with shape and effect and source; and if it existed, it could be destroyed. She saluted it accordingly, without despondency, but with a lively, beautiful and delightfully ribald anger. There was one thing, she felt, which would prove equal to its relentless ravages and that was the genius of man. Not his mysticism, but man with tubes and slides and the stubborn human notion that the stars are very much within our reach. . . .
>
> Every now and then her jaw set in anger as we spoke of things people should be angry about. And then, for relief, she would look out at the lovely bay at a mellow sunset settling on the water. Her face softened with love of all that beauty and, watching her, I wished with all my

power what I knew that she was wishing: that she might live to see at least one more summer.

That summer of 1958, in mid-July, Lorraine took a quick break from investor readings of *A Raisin in the Sun* and from her Saturday revision meetings with Lloyd Richards to spend a weekend on New York's Fire Island. People connected with theater (dressers, performers, dancers, directors, choreographers, set directors, and the like) had been coming out as guests of the residents for a number of years. She took the ferry across Great South Bay and stayed in Cherry Grove, which was then a hamlet of three hundred or so homes. Many of the original families and their descendants were living there with no telephones, electricity, or running water. It was a corny place, gay-friendly, where getting an ice-cream cone and watching the sun go down was a treat. The joke that summer was "A flying saucer lands at Cherry Grove. A space alien steps out, looks the boys over, and says, 'Take me to your queen.'"[20] Not long after Lorraine visited, in 1962, against the wishes of many residents, installing utility lines and sewers became mandatory. After that, the rough and the rural character of the area quickly disappeared, and the old settlers moved on, displaced by the tourism industry promoting Cherry Gove as a lesbian, gay, bisexual, and transgender resort town.

As her circle of women friends grew, Lorraine was invited to parties in the Village and on the Upper East Side. Her female friends were white, and some of them were writers—*Harriet the Spy*'s Louise Fitzhugh, and Patricia Highsmith, for example. The difference between white and black parties was as stark as the light and dark sides of the moon, according to Audre Lorde. Black parties "were always full of food and dancing and reefer and laughter and high-jinks." The get-togethers hosted by white women, meanwhile, resembled faculty meetings with refreshments. "The feeling in the room was subdued. Mostly, women sat around in little groups and talked quietly, the sound of moderation thick and heavy as smoke in the air. I noticed the absence of laughter only because I always thought parties were supposed to be fun. . . . I busied myself looking through the bookshelves lining the room."[21]

At one of those cocktail gatherings, Lorraine met Marijane Meaker, author of *We Walk Alone*. "I didn't know who she was," Meaker said. "All I knew was she was black, and I started to talk about how much I liked Ruth Brown and all these [black] singers. She was polite; she tolerated me. She asked me what I did. I said I was a writer. What do you do? 'Well, actually, I'm having my play produced.' I said, 'Where?' Because I thought it was going to be some dinky little thing. And I was amazed to hear it was going to be on Broadway! And then I felt mortified." Later, when they knew each other better, Meaker teased Hansberry because Lorraine "had a new white convertible and this white girl with blond hair." Meaker remembered her saying, "'I've got to get another color [car] if I'm going to have her with me!'"[22]

Meaker's expectations were typical of what Hansberry's gay women friends thought a black lesbian would be like: not as accomplished as white women in the arts and stepping out of her lane a bit by dating white girls. But Hansberry was only taking instruction on freedom from her hero, Beauvoir, who said, "Woman is defined neither by her hormones nor by some mysterious instincts, but by the manner in which she reclaims her body and her relation with the world."[23]

Without waving placards, without relying on doctrine, she truly made the personal political. Radicalness starts with the self, rather than telling other people what *they* ought to be doing. She wasn't sure where she belonged on the sexual continuum. But like Beauvoir, she refused to deny herself any relationships—male or female, white or black—because of the exclusionary practices of identity politics. Beauvoir rejected a compulsory lesbian identity as a condition of women's liberation: "To emancipate woman is to refuse to enclose her in the relations that she sustains with man, but not to deny them to her." Hansberry would not conform to anyone's notions of a "correct" sex life.

In August 1958, she was called home to attend a family meeting. On the train, she read *The Double Bed*, by Eve Merriam, a collection of seventy-six poems about a marriage that doesn't last. She was saddened by them. Arriving at her mother's home reminded her of being there five summers earlier, when she'd taken her wedding vows.

"My Own Sweet Husband," she began a letter to Bob[24]:

So. I am here in "our" little room in Chicago . . . and I am curiously reminded of you and the times we have spent here and, naturally, all that has, good and bad, come to pass since then. Rather a lot. Far more than we could have possibly imagined five years ago and all that— . . . Do you know that I miss you? I don't understand it. I do not understand my entire relationship to you at this point. . . . Darling, I haven't been able to tell you something because it would sound stupid and beside the point— But I am sorry about the holes this marriage turned out to have in it. Because it was so nice in the solid places. So very nice. Love, Lorraine

The family had been convened because there were important issues afoot. To be in attendance, Perry had flown all the way from Monrovia, Liberia, where he was starting a business importing monkeys for scientific research.

To begin with, Lorraine was being audited by the Internal Revenue Service for failing to pay taxes on rental income she had received from Hansberry Enterprises properties inherited from her father. Mamie suggested their attorney be instructed to have a "conference" with the IRS. Maybe something could be worked out. More serious was the threat of jail for Carl Jr. and Perry as the principals of Hansberry Enterprises. Over the past three years, they had been cited for more than one hundred housing and fire code violations in thirteen of their buildings. There were forty-two lawsuits pending against them for violating the Municipal Code of Chicago. Fines totaled forty thousand dollars (ten times that amount in today's dollars).[25]

One of Hansberry's biographers, Anne Cheney—again wanting the narrative of Lorraine's life to be consistent, this time in regard to civil rights—portrays the family as victims of racial oppression. "Carl, Jr., Perry, and Mamie were carrying on the family business that their father had worked so hard to build. They had acquired new properties and maintained the respect of the families who rented from them. Perry was especially popular for helping renters with unreasonable creditors and merchants. Nevertheless, they had problems with the white political machine. Once Mamie went with her brother Carl to pay off a corrupt city official with hardearned black money—$1,500."[26]

The truth is, the Hansberrys were notorious in Chicago. The newspapers had reported Carl Augustus Hansberry's move to Mexico as "flight."[27] He had left Chicago following the dissolution of the National Negro Progress Association, with its essay contests promising five thousand dollars in prizes and campaigns to recruit dues-paying members. Perhaps there had been more to his hegira to the land where he felt free than met the eye.

At a news conference, journalists had asked Mayor Richard J. Daley why the city had dropped six of the forty-two lawsuits against Hansberry Enterprises. Daley, after meeting with city attorneys and the building commissioner, admitted that "a mistake was made and it will not be repeated."[28] He reinstated all six lawsuits, including one naming Lorraine, along with her mother, brothers, sister, and sister-in-law Juanita Hansberry, for serving fifty eviction notices on families in two adjacent properties, supposedly so the apartments could be repaired and upgraded. All six cases, Daley announced, would be brought to trial.

The Hansberrys decided to stay the course: they wouldn't pay fines or appear in court. Taking the offensive, Carl Jr. retaliated by filing a million-dollar lawsuit against Daley and his officers, accusing the mayor of injuring his reputation by calling him a "slum landlord." The city's "capricious inspections" were due to "personal hostility of defendants to plaintiffs, principally to Carl and Perry."[29] In response, the city agreed not to refer to Hansberry properties as slums; also, city officials would not start any new litigation against Hansberry Enterprises provided there was proof that repairs were underway.

It was a temporary truce. Regardless, Lorraine and her family were convinced that the city held a twenty-year-old grudge against them for their father's Supreme Court victory in *Hansberry v. Lee*. They would not be pressured into changing their method of doing business.

From childhood, Lorraine said, she had been instructed by her parents that "there were two things which were never to be betrayed: the family and the race."[30] She defended her father as someone who "had simply become a reasonably successful businessman of the middle class."[31] He had built up the family's property holdings, patiently, over decades. Her brothers had begun collecting weekly rent while they were still teenagers. If their properties were in poor condition, it was the renters' fault. Their father, too softhearted to do otherwise, had let himself be taken advantage of by tenants who had moved in, torn the place up, never paid rent, and then left in the middle of the night. "Daddy," said Mamie, "lost more money than he ever earned."[32] He was selfless, in their eyes, in trying to find places for black families to live.

At bottom, though, they didn't want things to change, not really. They wanted the status quo to remain as it was. They were rich, and capitalism had enabled them to reach their highest aspirations. They were on easy street, as countless people before and since have wanted to be. As for being called to account about how they made their money and what their responsibilities were, that didn't enter in. The nation had much bigger fish to fry than persecuting them. They were fighting racism and doing their best under a system designed to keep them from achieving their dreams.

At the end of the summer of 1958, Hansberry took the last page of *A Raisin in the Sun* out of the typewriter, patted the script into a neat pile, and then went into the living room to lie down full length on the floor. "I had finished a play; a play I had no reason to think would ever be done; a play that I was sure no one would quite understand."[33]

Yet, after close to eighty readings of *A Raisin in the Sun*, and well over one hundred investors purchasing shares, Rose was beginning to think that he wouldn't be able to produce the show after all. The largest stake was $1,500, from playwright William Gibson, whose *Two for the Seesaw*, with Anne Bancroft and Henry Fonda, had been a hit on Broadway. Still, the production was underfunded. And now Poitier wanted to be paid in advance to play Walter Lee Younger Jr. (Baldwin was later of the opinion that the play wouldn't have been produced without him.)[34] The film Poitier was currently starring in, *The Defiant Ones*, had been nominated for several Academy Awards, and offers of leading roles were pouring in. Had it not been for his friendship with Lloyd Richards, he might have bowed out of the project altogether.

But then the gods intervened. In Hollywood, where Poitier was filming *Porgy and Bess*, the set burned down under mysterious circumstances, which included rumors of arson. The delay meant that Sidney wouldn't be available to begin rehearsals for *Raisin* in September, as planned. Rose, Richards, and Hansberry quietly rejoiced at their good luck: now they would have more time to raise money to pay him.

Meanwhile, Richards had been delegated to begin talking to theater owners about reserving a stage. It wasn't going well. "I remember spending hours and hours sitting in the anterooms of the Shubert Organization, trying to get a theater. There were no theaters."[35] It was the same problem: money. The Shuberts owned most of the best venues in New York, on and Off-Broadway, and they weren't convinced that they should make room on their stages for a production handled, to be frank, by amateurs in the business.

What seemed like the final blow for Richards professionally came from Rose, in a telephone call. Kermit Bloomgarden, a powerful Broadway producer, wanted to take over the show. With a slew of Broadway hits to his name, such as *The Diary of Anne Frank*, *The Crucible*, and *Death of a Salesman*, he had credibility and capital. When Richards heard this, he was crestfallen. He was Lorraine and Phil's third musketeer; without his friends to defend him, he would probably be released for lack of experience.

Rose and Hansberry met with Bloomgarden to hear his proposal. He said he could take their show up to the top, but under two conditions: first, he needed the right to fire Richards, at any time; second, he wanted Claudia McNeil, who had been engaged to play Mama Lena Younger, replaced with singer Ethel Waters; Waters was the bigger star. Bloomgarden gave them a couple of days to decide.[36]

After the meeting, Hansberry and Rose went out for coffee and talked. The reasonable option was to accept Bloomgarden's offer. They didn't have enough money, and the actors they had signed would have other opportunities soon. With that settled, they went their separate ways. A few hours later, Hansberry called Rose. "Look," he remembered her saying "when I first met you, we were going to do it in a church. So, let's go ahead and do it that way," meaning that if playing in a small theater space was the price of retaining control, then that was the better choice.[37] But the budget would have to be expertly handled. Rose brought aboard David Cogan as coproducer, a tax account in the entertainment business.

It was around this time that Hansberry began experiencing the first intimations of the fame she had wished for. She received a phone call in September from someone who was interested in her play and wanted to know how it was coming. She said it would have the usual out-of-town trials as a run-up to Broadway. Then, as the person grew more curious, Lorraine became suspicious and refused to answer any more questions. A few days later, a memo reached the New York office of the FBI, instructing the special agent in charge to establish whether the play "is controlled or influenced by the Communist Party and whether it in any way follows the communist line."[38]

From the editor of *Ebony* magazine came a request to write a profile of Hansberry: "I don't recall having seen your photo anywhere or read anything about you anywhere."[39] It was the first of an incoming tide of such requests inviting Lorraine to be a spokesperson. "Every Negro celebrity is, according to white America, an authority on race relations," wrote Loften Mitchell.[40] But the same is true of black America, too. W. E. B. Du Bois and Paul Robeson had both passed out of the scene as leaders of national influence. Hansberry, not yet thirty, seemed a likely choice as a new voice, a younger voice, to speak about racial issues. From Thurgood Marshall came an invitation for Lorraine and Bob to attend a small supper party hosted by the NAACP Legal Defense and Educational Fund. There would be about fifty guests, and Hansberry would be the guest of honor. "We will not ask you to make a speech but hope you will join me and other friends in an informal discussion of some of the problems that concern us."[41]

Word of the play and the playwright reached Chicago, and it was then that the angel who rescued *A Raisin in the Sun* appeared. He preferred to remain anonymous, and has remained so until now. His investment of five thousand dollars, when the average amount invested was one hundred, was the largest among the show's 145 backers.[42] Who was he?

At age thirty, Charles R. Swibel was a handsome, faultlessly dressed millionaire real estate developer and one of seven on the board of the Chicago Housing Authority, the second-largest public housing program in the United States. He was known to be "no great liberal" among Chicago politicos, but Swibel became Mayor Daley's ambassador to the city's progressive community and managed to cultivate ties with leading civil rights activists in the Chicago Urban League. Through a journalist, Ruth Moore, who covered urban affairs for the *Chicago Sun-Times*, Swibel had learned that the producers of a play about a black family on the South Side "needed money badly." His investment, said his son, Howard, enabled Rose to pay Poitier's fee up front.[43]

With Swibel's investment, things were well in hand financially, but Rose was advised to scuttle the production anyway. He couldn't get a Broadway theater to commit, and his backers had been pep-talked into expecting no less. Instead, he booked the Shubert Theatre in New Haven, Connecticut, for a four-night engagement early in January 1959, followed by a two-week run at the Walnut Street Theatre in Philadelphia—venues traditionally used for out-of-town tryouts. His bet was that "we had something so spectacular, Broadway couldn't ignore us."[44]

Meanwhile, Hansberry took steps to close off areas of her private life to the public. In November, there was a knock on her apartment door at 7 a.m. The Daughters of Bilitis cofounders, Phyllis Lyon and Del Martin, and DOB national president, Shirley Willer, had traveled from California to inaugurate a new chapter of the organization in New York City. They'd written to Lorraine in advance, and she had invited them to stop by. She was not pleased at being up with the birds, but she welcomed them in. Despite the hour, her visitors thought she was "smart, pretty, and gracious." They asked if she would "come out openly, admit to being a lesbian." She told them she had to choose "which of the closets was most important to her." And at that point in her life, Willer recalled her saying, "it was more important for her to be a black woman who had written a great play and book than to come out as a lesbian." They were disappointed, but they understood.[45]

"Like many a closeted black celebrity," wrote Elise Harris, "Hansberry created a role-model version of herself for the media stage. It's the image of Hansberry still familiar to many of us from eighth-grade English class: the noble civil rights crusader; dignified, articulate, controlled. While her plays showed characters wrestling with their demons, her own inner conflict and complexity were kept private."[46]

Continuing to share the apartment with Bob also perpetuated the perception that Hansberry was straight. In her thousand-page FBI file, there's no indication the Bureau knew she was gay. And Nemiroff kept Lorraine's sexuality hidden for years, long after he had heavily edited her writings, collected as *To Be Young, Gifted and Black*.

Rehearsals began two days after Christmas 1958, in the rooftop Frolic Theater, on Forty-Second Street, which had been converted into a rehearsal space. Show business was in the very bones of the building. On the street level was the former New Amsterdam Theatre, the venue for lavish productions of the Ziegfeld Follies with Al Jolson, Fanny Brice, W. C. Fields, and the brother-and-sister dance team, Fred and Adele Astaire.

Rose paid for *Raisin*'s stage sets and costumes, but he concealed the cost from Hansberry, so she wouldn't fret about money while she polished the final script. Lloyd Richards likened the situation to starting down a snow-covered hill in a toboggan: "[Y]ou can resist up to a certain point, but once you go over that first hump, you're going to the bottom, one way or another, whether you smash up in a tree or turn over. You are going all the way, once you make that commitment." There was no time to waste. Equity, the actors' union, allowed reduced salaries for four weeks only, considered sufficient for rehearsing. Never enough, in most directors' estimation.[47] Starting the fifth week, full salaries were required. Rose and Cogan, with their eyes on the bottom line, invited not only *Raisin*'s now 147 backers to sit in on rehearsals, but they opened the set to potential investors as well, a common practice, in the hope of rustling up more money.

During the first week of rehearsals, Richards's method was to foster an ensemble feeling among the cast during table readings. Don't play for the audience, he told them—entertain the person you're speaking to at the table. Storytelling was encouraged. When Richards later directed August Wilson's *Seven Guitars* in 1996, a cast member recalled how "Lloyd and the actors were just anecdoting all over the place. Having fun laughing and jesting. Head into script, and reading the page, and then coming up and, 'You know what? that reminds me of the time we were . . .' and before you know it, we were in a major story."[48]

When the *Raisin* cast began taking their approximate positions onstage, there was as yet no blocking (where to be onstage at any given point). Richards urged them to trust their instincts and move where they felt they belonged, leaving the stage manager to watch their gestures and take notes. "Turn it loose," Richards was fond of saying, "and let it take you where it wants to go. Out of that, you may find the physical self of this character." When he needed to speak to an actor, he would whisper into the person's ear. "Intense" but "light-footed" is how Ruby Dee, as Ruth Younger, remembered his direction.[49]

During an early rehearsal, Lorraine felt the script beginning to stir and awaken. "The first laugh, when people laughed when they were supposed to, I nearly swooned. All I could think was: They dig me, they really dig me."[50] By the end of rehearsals, forty-five minutes had been cut out of the play, and one character had been eliminated to save money—Mrs. Johnson, a jealous neighbor who tries to undercut the Youngers' hopes: "Mmmmm mmmm. The Youngers is too much for me! . . . You sure one proud-acting bunch of colored folks."[51]

Poitier, however, objected to the way his character was developing. "I believed from the first day I went into rehearsal that the play should not unfold from the mother's point of view . . . [F]or maximum effect, A Raisin in the Sun should unfold from the point of view of the son, Walter Lee Younger. . . . I kept insisting that the mother shouldn't be the focus of the play. They accused me of 'star' behavior. Of wanting to be the top dog on stage."[52]

Poitier disagreed with Richards, Hansberry, and the rest of the cast, arguing that Walter reflected badly on the black male. Ruby Dee, playing Walter's wife, Ruth, suggested that he play against Claudia McNeil's character, the mother, who was, Poitier admitted privately, "a tower of strength as a stage personality."[53] He was satisfied that he could raise the temperature of Walter's character, but he groused that commercial concerns were getting in the way—"a bonanza whose aroma was already creeping over the horizon."[54] Hansberry took offense at his fault-finding. On top of which, she detested Porgy and Bess—"anti-Negro slander," she called it—and criticized him for taking the male lead in the film version of the musical.[55] They stopped speaking.

Later, she regretted splitting the baby between Mama Younger and Walter Lee, convinced that it was the play's dramatic flaw. "Fine plays tend to utilize one big fat character who runs right through the middle of the structure, by action or implication, with whom we rise or fall. A central character is certainly lacking from Raisin. I should be delighted to pretend that it was inventiveness, as some suggest for me, but it is craft inadequacy and indecision. . . . I consider it an enormous fault if no one else does."[56] She criticized herself, as a student of Aristotle and O'Casey, for breaking from a time-honored structure. But what she called her "craft inadequacy"—probably arising from trusting her creative instincts—has two strong characters vying for power and centrality, adding another level of struggle, this one primal: mother against son.

The cast and crew arrived in New Haven the second week of January. The Nemiroffs—for so they seemed to be, outwardly anyway—stayed at the Hotel Taft, adjacent to the Yale campus and overlooking New Haven Green, white with snow. Next door was the Shubert Theatre.

Having a tryout in New Haven helped avoid the embarrassment and financial catastrophe of bringing a flop to Broadway, where reviewers, daggers drawn, would put a stinker out of its misery. At the New Haven premiere of the musical *Oklahoma!*, in 1943, audiences were obviously underwhelmed. Richard Rodgers and Oscar Hammerstein secluded themselves at the Taft for a heavy rewrite. Under pressure, a hit was born.

"Dear Mother," Lorraine wrote on Monday evening, two days before *A Raisin in the Sun* opened on January 21. "Well—here we are. I am sitting alone in a nice hotel room in New Haven, Conn. Downstairs, next door, in the Shubert Theatre, technicians are putting the finishing touches on a living room that is supposed to be a Chicago living room. . . . Mama, it is a play that tells the truth about people, Negroes and life[,] and I think it will help a lot of people to understand how we are just as complicated as they are—and just as mixed up—but above all, that we have among our miserable and downtrodden ranks—people who are the very essence of human dignity." Her mother replied by telegram: "Dear Baby, Our thoughts are with you, the actors, co-producers, and the director."[57]

On the first night, Hansberry and Nemiroff sat together in the front of the audience. The house was half empty.[58] There was no curtain, and the stage set of the South Side kitchen stood silent. The house lights came down, and Lloyd Richards walked out into a single spotlight to introduce the first scene. Hansberry shuddered violently.[59] The play began. As Walter Lee circled the kitchen table, complaining that a man has dreams, his unsympathetic wife said, "Eat your eggs!" and the audience burst into laughter. Poitier and Ruby Dee were thrown off and glanced at Richards in the wings. He seemed unfazed; after the action resumed, he added to his notes to leave space in the dialogue for laughter as a way of underscoring the characters' wit.[60]

In the audience was Leon Wofsy, formerly the national director of the

Youth Labor League, now pursuing a PhD at Yale in immunology. The following morning, he picked up a copy of the *Hartford Times* and read the review. "The play was a hit, a gem," he remembered. "More than that, it was the stuff of history—not just theater history, but social history."[61] The cast, reading another review, "was reduced to mirth and tears" said Hansberry, by the critic remarking on how pleasurable it was seeing the way "our dusky brethren" could "come up with a song and hum their troubles away."[62]

A headline in the *New Haven Register* was typical of the racially tinged sense of novelty that accompanied Hansberry's achievement: "Unknown Negro Writer Scores Hit with Play Here." As news about the play gathered momentum, the *Christian Science Monitor* was alone in questioning why Hansberry was routinely referred to as a Negro playwright. "Yet is this the most important point? What counts is that *A Raisin in the Sun* is a vibrant, hard-hitting account of real humans beings. . . . There is something double-edged about the fact that recognition of Negro talent is in itself still considered particularly newsworthy."[63] Sixty years later, artists are still identified as black, but never as white.

The morning after the premiere, a hotel housekeeper announced herself by knocking on Lorraine's door. She was an Irish immigrant and had seen the performance. She was so impressed—the Youngers could have been her family. Hansberry, because her favorite playwright was O'Casey, was especially pleased by the compliment.[64] Many people in theater are superstitious and might have seen such a coincidence as blessing the set.

Sometime during the run of *A Raisin in the Sun* at the Walnut Street Theatre in Philadelphia, FBI agent Carl E. Hennrich found his seat in the audience and settled in to watch. No one had been available from the New Haven office to report on the show when it was at the Shubert. Attending a play on overtime was good duty to pull for the forty-nine-year-old Hennrich— much different from the official paperwork that occupied most of his day. To prepare, he had been reading some postwar literary criticism.[65]

Hennrich was a calm, steady man whose administrative work was usually rated by his superiors as "Satisfactory" or "Good." Most of his career had been spent in the Domestic Intelligence Branch in Washington, DC, until Hoover had transferred him to the Philadelphia office because it needed better supervision. He had just passed the twenty-five-year mark with the Bureau and was planning to retire soon to practice law.

He appears to have been a bit amused by the concern over determining whether *A Raisin in the Sun* "followed the communist line." Each time he encountered that phrase in a memo from Hansberry's file, he circled it and penciled "*??!!*" in the margin. It would be hard to conceive of someone with any commercial sense producing a play that was pro-Communist when the Soviet Empire covered one-third of the earth and Premier Khrushchev could boast, "Who is encircling whom now?"[66]

But if anyone was capable of determining whether the production was a bit "pink" in the middle, Hennrich was. He was an American history buff and proud of being a direct descendent of a Revolutionary War veteran. His son was a junior at the U.S. Air Force Academy.[67] It's easy to imagine Hennrich polishing the glasses he used for reading, taking out a pen from his breast pocket, and steadying his notepad on his knee as he waited for the play to begin.

The four-page analysis he submitted on February 5 is surprising. The writing, though stolid and objective, is nevertheless lively, even admiring in places, and skillful at sussing out what the characters want—not unexpected from someone trained to study human behavior. The mother, Lena Younger, is a "firm-minded dominating matriarch," Hennrich wrote, "with very strong feeling for family unity." Her son, Walter, "wants to make 'big deals.' He has no ethics or honesty of his deals but is willing to sell liquor to other Negroes against his mother's wishes." Walter's sister, Beneatha, "reviles him as an 'entrepreneur.'" Her goal is "self-expression and self-identification. She passes from hobby to hobby, generally expensive . . ." The African student, Asagai, one of Beneatha's two suitors, wants "to educate himself so that he can return to teach and raise the level of the people of his village" so that they can "overthrow the rule of European nations."

Hennrich concludes that *A Raisin in the Sun* "contains no comments of any nature about Communism as such but deals essentially with Negro aspirations, the problem inherent in efforts to advance themselves, and varied attempts at arriving at solutions." Glancing at the audience during the performance, he observed that some characters' lines were applauded by blacks, others by everyone. In the lobby, he heard people praising the acting, but few were dwelling on "the propaganda messages."[68]

Backstage, Rose had gotten the news he'd been waiting for. A representative from the Shubert Organization told him that currently they didn't have a theater for him in New York, but if the play went to Chicago for eight weeks at the Blackstone Theatre, the organization would underwrite the loss incurred by the delay, and in March, the Ethel Barrymore Theatre in Manhattan would be available. The cast and crew prepared immediately.

Carl Jr. and Perry implored Lorraine by phone not to go through with it. They begged her to cancel the run in Chicago. There were dozens of fines outstanding, and court bailiffs were looking for Carl. The publicity was sure to bring the cops down on them.[69] But it was out of her hands, and the cast and crew arrived the first week of February. Mamie, wanting Lorraine to look her best and not rebuffed by her sister's indifference about looking soignée, "got [her] a lovely black dress with floating panels."[70]

Hansberry attended the premiere on February 10. As her brothers had feared, warrants for her arrest were issued immediately, and she had to leave town, following a reception at her mother's home. Historian Lerone Bennett remembered that "she was in the middle of a media volcano right then; she was being transformed from an anonymous person into a celebrity, and so there wasn't much time to talk."[71] She departed from Union Station on the train to New York, leaving Bob behind to troubleshoot.

In her wake, a review in the *Chicago Tribune* by Claudia Cassidy—known as "Acidy Cassidy" in the theater world—raved about the play, saying it had the "fresh impact of something urgently on its way." Cassidy's heart went out to Mama Younger. "And as she stands there you suddenly realize that this ratty apartment, without sun, or a private bathroom, or enough bedrooms, with cockroaches, is her home."[72] The day after Cassidy's review appeared, the *Tribune* carried a headline about the Hansberry family, "Fine Slum Owner, Kin $11,750." Mayor Daley's administration was trying to embarrass them into paying up. The Hansberrys instructed their lawyer to dissolve Lorraine's partnership in Hansberry Enterprises because the adverse publicity was injuring her reputation.[73]

With Lorraine self-exiled from Chicago, "We did our work on that play over the phone for eight weeks," Richards said. "I would work on the play, it would perform at night, and I would talk to Lorraine, make suggestions. She never saw that work, during that period, until we got back to New York."[74]

Langston Hughes was in the audience at the Blackstone and alerted the readers of the *Chicago Defender* that *A Raisin in the Sun* "bids fair to become a milestone in Negro dramatic art." He regarded Claudia McNeil as "my discovery" because he had put her on Broadway in *Simply Heaven*. Now he was going to New York to see Hansberry's play at the Ethel Barrymore, and he said, "I intend to holler REAL loud!"[75]

20

Dismantling the Master's House

I can't really allow the limitations of white supremacist thinking to condition my attitude towards life. That would strangle me to death. I have never thought in terms of "will I write about Negroes?" anyway. I intend to write about characters as they emerge in my mind, and those I don't adequately know will be poor characters, and those I do know will be good ones. I don't think in terms of Negro and white.

—Lorraine Hansberry[1]

Two weeks before *A Raisin in the Sun* premiered in New York, an opportunity of consequence came Hansberry's way. At the beginning of March 1959, she spoke at the First Conference of Negro Writers, hosted by the American Society of African Culture. The theme was "The American Negro Writer and His Roots."

Modeled on the Présence Africaine conference in Paris of the year before, the event drew many of the best-known black American writers of the era to the Henry Hudson Hotel on West Fifty-Seventh Street to discuss the future of black literature—among them, Langston Hughes, John Henrik Clarke, Alice Childress, Arna Bontemps, Julian Mayfield, John O. Killens, and James Baldwin. For Hansberry, who was new on the literary scene, addressing hundreds of professional and aspiring writers, along with publishers and agents, was a sign that she was regarded as a young playwright of promise, a talent who should be heard from.

The decade of the 1950s was closing, and not since Reconstruction had there been so many legal advances recognizing the rights of black Americans. In 1954, the Supreme Court had struck down school segregation. The following year, the Montgomery Bus Boycott, in Alabama, had resulted in the Court ruling that segregation was unconstitutional. In September 1957, nine black students had enrolled at formerly all-white Central High School in Little Rock, Arkansas, escorted by federal troops to their first day of class. Also that month, President Eisenhower signed into law the Civil Rights Act of 1957, the first major civil rights legislation since Reconstruction, authorizing the U.S. attorney general to seek federal court injunctions to protect the voting rights of Negroes.

And yet, the country was far from color-blind. Black literature was "arguing over black representation," writes Mary Helen Washington in *The Other Blacklist*, "over the nature and future of protest literature and the politics of form, over gender and sexuality, over communism and anti-communism, over integration versus black civil rights militancy."

At the conference, there was a robust lack of consensus among the speakers and panelists about how to answer the question "Whither black literature?" J. Saunders Redding, often called the "dean of African American scholars," urged writers to seek "common identity" among Americans who were "hungry for personal fulfillment, for a sense of community with others." Historian John Henrik Clarke called for reclaiming lost African heritage for inspiration. Loften Mitchell wondered whether there existed "a psychological barrier that makes white audiences refuse to identify" with a central Negro character in a play, and what this portended for black dramatists trying to become commercially successful. Killens condemned the attitude that "you must deny any relationship to your roots; you must not go to your frame of reference for your artistic inspiration." Langston Hughes insisted, "Color has nothing to do with writing as such. So I would say, and in your mind don't be a colored writer even when dealing in racial material. Be a writer first."[2]

To Lorraine the job was given of delivering the closing address, which she titled, "The Negro Writer and His Roots: Toward a New Romanticism." Though she was only twenty-nine, her experience as a pro-Communist activist, left-wing journalist, soapbox speaker, and feminist gave her more authority than most of her colleagues. And she was prepared to go full-out.

The week before, she had said in an interview, "We have been suffering from an imposed intellectual impoverishment in the last decade. We were told there were areas of life we were not to examine, problems we dare not investigate."[3] She was going to talk about them. She had prepared a kind of manifesto—a personal artistic statement, a call to conscience, and a summons to support Pan-African unity.

The theme of her speech was something she had long believed: the need for black writers and intellectuals to grapple with the issues of the age in which they lived. "There is a desperate need in our time for the Negro writer to assume a partisanship in what I believe has been the traditional battleground of writers of stature for centuries, namely the war against one's time and culture." There could be no hanging back, no dodge about being only a commercial writer, because "all art is ultimately social: that which agitates and that which prepares the mind for slumber." She contrasted her hero Seán O'Casey, "warrior against despair and lover of mankind," with absurdist playwrights—she had a draft of a play at home called *Up Yours, Edward Albee*—Beat poets, and others whom she accused of giving up. Artists must not simply look for the meaning of the universe and then, not finding it, despair, but should also "*impose* the reason for a life on life."

She had discarded adolescent, sentimental ideas about the poor. She was an ally of truth now. "I believe in the truth of art and the art of truth and the most painful exigency of cultural and social life will not be exempt from exploration by my mind or pen."[4]

> ... let the Negro writer begin to examine much that has formerly been romanticized about Negro urban life in particular. If "the numbers" are basically a prey upon our people, then it should be inconceivable that that particular aspect of gambling should emerge as a folksy and harmless pastime in our novels. The evils of the ghetto, whatever they are, must emerge as evils—not as the romantic and exotic offshoots of a hilarious people who can simply endure anything. Dope addiction, alcoholism, prostitution—all deserve this kind of treatment. In the effort to make the people beautiful we must not beautify the disease... [T]he artist who participates in programs of apology, of distortion, of camouflage in the depiction of the life and trials of our people,

behaves as the paid agent of the enemies of Negro freedom. . . . [A] presentation of the full-scale nature of all the complexities and confusions and backwardnesses of our people will, in the end, only heighten and make more real the inescapable image of their greatness and courage.

I cannot allow the devious purposes of white supremacy to lead me to any conclusion other than what may be the most robust and important one of our time: that the ultimate destiny and aspirations of the African people and twenty million American Negroes are inextricably and magnificently bound up together forever.

For those who were debating a choice between separatism and assimilation, Hansberry proposed a third way: exercising a dynamic U.S. citizenship. Not rejecting America, but using freedom to advocate for global emancipation from imperialism and racialized colonialism—the same position taken by some of the leading black intellectuals of the day: W. E. B. Du Bois, Richard Wright, E. Franklin Frazier, Julian Mayfield, and then later Malcolm X.

Hansberry's speech was of such a different caliber by its audacious, prophetic tone, and it struck so many notes of revolution compared with musings about how to sell books or whether to court a white readership, that it wasn't included in the published collection of prepared remarks from the conference. Also left out was a panel discussion about social protest as a theme, which included remarks by Alice Childress and Frank London Brown. Brown had just published *Trumbull Park*, a novel about race riots, death threats, brick throwing, and nightly bombings and window breakings in a Chicago public housing project.

Perhaps the editor, John A. Davis, the president of the American Society of African Culture, was concerned that Hansberry, Childress, and Brown had gone too far off-script. After all, the event had been funded with grant money from the CIA.[5]

On the night *A Raisin in the Sun* premiered, March 11, 1959, at the Ethel Barrymore Theatre, on West Forty-Seventh Street, Lorraine sat in the third row with Bob. Before she left the apartment, a telegram had been delivered from Phil Rose: "Whatever happens tonight we have been, we have become, we will be inextricably a part of each other's lives." At the theater, she caught sight of him and Doris at the back, watching everything. Lorraine took out a pen and found a scrap of paper. Her hand was shaking. "They can't write anything tonight to take this particular love affair away from me. . . . I knew that you would be as you are when I first fell in love with you both, long, long ago."[6] She passed him the note.

A Broadway first night in those days was a black-tie affair, and it looked as if a huge wedding party of a thousand people were filling the theater. Friends of the Hansberrys had flown in from Chicago. Louis Burnham, from Lorraine's *Freedom* days, and his wife, Dorothy, were in attendance. "*Everybody* was at the *Raisin* opening," Langston Hughes noted happily.[7]

The Nemiroffs continued to act as a married couple—a small piece of theater in its own way. Lorraine had been asked about Bob by a reporter visiting the apartment. She shook her head, bemused. "For a born New Yorker, he's the biggest yokel I know. He finds every item ever published about the play and gets excited anew about every one. But he's a swell guy, though. And if it hadn't been for him, this play would never have hit the boards." She and Bob had watched together, standing outside the Barrymore, as the big black letters on the marquee were changed by hand to announce the opening of *A Raisin in the Sun*.[8] Now he was sitting beside her waiting for it to begin, enjoying the payoff of six years of partnering with her as manager, publicist, first critic, and friend.

Bob, the supernumerary in the public performance of his marriage, was always around. He was there during rehearsals, ready to be the gofer, message taker, and caterer, too, showing up with an armload of take-out coffee and hamburgers.[9] One night after a New Haven performance, Douglas Turner Ward, who was understudying Poitier, had stopped Lorraine backstage to mention something. A certain line didn't sound convincing to him. Behind her was Bob, listening. As Ward began to explain, Nemiroff's face fell. "I got the feeling that I didn't have *permission*," Ward said, "so I backed off. It was unmistakable, and from then on, I didn't bother."[10]

An aisle over from the Nemiroffs was Lorraine's friend Helen Leeds and her male date. Leeds, a law student at NYU, had introduced Lorraine to a circle of Village gay girls. Lorraine glanced over in that direction now and then, because sitting next to Helen was Renee Kaplan, and Lorraine was infatuated with her. She wanted to make a pass at Kaplan when the time was right.[11]

A few rows back were Nannie Hansberry and Mamie, there to savor this triumph. Lorraine had been sending her sister clippings about the play. One was from the *New York Age Defender*, a "cullud [colored] type newspaper, therefore the *mistakes* in the thing are enormous—so I include the copy of what I actually wrote so you can see how it should have read."[12] She was getting drawn by interviewers into questions about what the play really meant or what she intended to say—a trap that writers learn to avoid. Critics will tell you what it means, even if you wrote it. The year before, George Plimpton, interviewing Ernest Hemingway for the *Paris Review*, had asked him if "he would admit to there being symbols" in his novels. "I suppose there are symbols since critics keep finding them," Hemingway replied. "If you do not mind I dislike talking about them and being questioned about them. . . . The fact that I am interrupting serious work to answer these questions proves that I am so stupid that I should be penalized severely. I will be. Don't worry."[13]

Hansberry had been angered by a *New York Times* interview published three days before the Broadway opening. In it, she came off sounding, she thought, as if she were promoting assimilation. The reporter, Nan Robertson, quoted her as saying, "I told [potential backers] this wasn't a 'Negro play.' It was a play about honest-to-God, believable, many-sided people who happened to be Negroes." Based on that remark, Harold Cruse, who disliked not only Hansberry but also the "left-wing interracial" clique at *Freedom*, practically hooted that Lorraine had admitted to selling out with a "quasi-white orientation" to make the play popular.[14] In her scrapbook, she wrote beside the *New York Times* article, "Never said NO such thing. Miss Robertson goofed—letter sent post-haste—Tune in next week."[15]

Lorraine did indeed lodge a complaint with the *New York Times* editor, but then thought better of it and apologized to Robertson. "I was horrified to learn that my letter about your perfectly fine interview had made waves in the ranks. I guess I didn't think of all the implications or something. . . . If I have been the villain in this minor confusion, please accept my sincere apologies. If I have been the victim, please have some sensation of sympathy."[16]

Yet she continued to downplay the racial aspects of *A Raisin in the*

Sun. Three weeks after the Robertson squabble, she said in an interview with Ted Poston, a respected black journalist, that she had written the play with white theatergoers in mind. "I felt that if I could take a group of Negroes and successfully involve them in life, I could get the audience to accept them as people with whom they share common ground. Then I could introduce any question at all—not just the Negro-white conflict. We have plenty of problems besides that one." Months later, long after the premiere, in an interview with Cecil Smith, the drama critic for the *Los Angeles Times*, she repeated that race in *A Raisin in the Sun* didn't matter. Smith wrote, "[S]he believes that the racial quality is completely irrelevant—'like O'Casey's Irish, they belong to everybody.' The play touches its audience because 'it cuts across race lines,' she believes."[17]

But rather than go down the garden path of what the young artist was trying to explain in off-the-cuff interviews, what does *A Raisin in the Sun* say about the playwright? What was "the intent that came hurtling across the footlights," in her words, from her life and thought as the house lights came down on opening night at the Ethel Barrymore Theatre?[18]

A Raisin in the Sun is a protest that the American Dream—spelled out in the Constitution as life, liberty, and the pursuit of happiness—is being withheld from black Americans. Hansberry's play isn't mainly about Negro aspirations, racism, or integration by "moving into 'white folks neighborhoods,'" as playwright Amiri Baraka, for example, thought it was. It's a parable, written from a Marxist perspective, attacking class oppression. Oppression was a universal problem, not "a unique question where white people do not like black people," Hansberry wrote.[19] Her aim was to depict the humanity of the people under an economic system she wanted to overturn, capitalism, to replace it with socialism. FBI agent Hennrich had the wool pulled over his eyes when he reported that the play contained nothing revolutionary.

But because Hansberry wanted to reach the greatest number of eyes and ears, having learned her lesson about the mistake of "putting picket signs on the stage" and boring people, she wrapped her ideology inside an engaging story.[20] She fused W. E. B. Du Bois's protest theater, which was supposed to educate the masses, with Alain Locke's art theater honoring Negro folk culture. The result was a play that has dramatic heft, with well-developed characters who give voice to important, contradictory, and radical ideas. And yet, they are only themselves, not perfect, not paragons of anything. Audiences have been charmed ever since.

The story in *A Raisin in the Sun* unfolds in an easily recognized way, even to those who seldom visit the theater—"Four dollars and eighty cents!" exclaimed a woman at the box office in Philadelphia. "I can see Sidney Poitier around the corner in a movie for ninety-five cents."[21] We can tell immediately where the Younger family stands on the economic ladder. Their threadbare furniture fills a kitchenette. The little boy, Travis, sleeps in a made-up bed on the couch. There's a bathroom down the hall, and trying to get a turn in it adds to the stress of getting ready for work and school every morning. Nothing about the beginning of *A Raisin in the Sun* suggests that something avant-garde or hard to understand is approaching. It's an "old-fashioned play," Harold Clurman later said in a review for *The Nation*: a socially relevant domestic drama in the vein of Clifford Odets's *Awake and Sing!*, from the mid-1930s.[22] And he was right, although Clurman, a distinguished man of the theater, meant this as a criticism.

In fact, at least one man in the audience of *A Raisin in the Sun* was startled by a sense of déjà vu. In a letter to the *New York Times*, he complained that from the first scene, when Ruth Younger commands Walter Lee, "Eat your eggs, they gonna be cold," he was reminded of Seán O'Casey's *Juno and the Paycock*. The parallel line in *Juno* is "Eat up your sassidge." And that was just one of several similarities he'd seen. Bob clipped this item, too, and pasted it into Lorraine's scrapbook. Merrily, she annotated it, "Plagiarist! At last!!!"

Even Seán O'Casey himself was notified that his play had been stolen. A black theater critic named Samuel A. Boyea informed eighty-year-old O'Casey in Dublin that Lorraine Hansberry was guilty of appropriation. "I can swear on a stack of *Juno and the Paycock* [scripts] that her debt is at this moment a huge monetary one . . . that is, unless you gave her permission to adapt your play." O'Casey replied that he was not unhappy if his influence was noticeable on the other side of the Atlantic, and he wished his correspondent well. And because Boyea's children had Irish names, some of them, O'Casey sent them all a kiss.[23]

As the Youngers rush through their morning routine, the inciting incident, the fuse that lights the major conflict, concerns money. The plot revolves around it. A death benefit, a ten-thousand-dollar life insurance check is on its way to Walter Sr.'s widow, Mama (Lena) Younger. Evidently, the son, Walter Lee Jr., a married man with responsibilities of his own, was not considered mature enough by his late father to be named the beneficiary.

Receiving a legacy as a plot device is central to *Juno*, too. Actually, it's a nineteenth-century cliché in Western literature. (What would Dickens have done without it?) But among working-class black Americans, owning a life insurance policy was putting aside money for the future; and so, it has, culturally, a legitimate place in *Raisin*. For a few pennies a week, a man like Big Walter could be assured of a decent burial and a small inheritance for his loved ones. Big Walter worked "hisself to death" after the death of their child Claude, says Mama Younger, "fighting his own war with this here world that took his baby from him." Big Walter's ten-grand payoff, when many men made two thousand dollars a year, could be seen as his atoning for having been too poor to save his son.

Money, or not having enough of it, preoccupies the Youngers. O'Casey believed that lack of money was the root of all evil; that impoverished people were misled, tricked, lied to, and would ultimately act against their own interests unless money ceased to count for so much in their existence and in the ways that they perceived themselves. Walter Lee tries to persuade his mother that money is more important than anything else. It is food, shelter, and even love: "It is life, Mama!" She replies, "Oh—(*Very quietly*) So now it's life. Money is life. Once upon a time freedom used to be life—now it's money."

In the ghetto, said Hansberry, "Our spiritual affirmation of life rests on a most materialistic base."[24] A handful of loose change sparks a quarrel between Walter Lee and his wife, Ruth. When Travis whines for fifty cents, his mother says they can't afford it. But Walter Lee, to show that he has stature as man and a father, gives his son a couple of quarters and then defiantly digs into his pocket for more. "In fact, here's another fifty cents . . . Buy yourself some fruit today—or take a taxicab to school or something!"

Hansberry wants the audience to stay focused on all the economic harms that are taking a toll on the Youngers. A number of people in the audience, especially middle-class blacks, would have been familiar with

Gunnar Myrdal's landmark book published in 1944, *An American Dilemma*, devoted to a study of the color line and its effect on the social and economic status of black Americans. It was one of the most impactful books of the twentieth century—study groups were formed to discuss it—and Hansberry is determined to refute its conclusion.

The "Negro problem," according to Myrdal, had nothing to do with the unequal distribution of resources. It was a moral problem, a failure by the nation to live up to its creed of equality for all. White Americans had perpetuated a caste system to maintain segregation. Organizations such as the NAACP—fighting in the courts for material gains such as equal housing and equal schools—were stunned, when *An American Dilemma* was published, that Myrdal would, in the words of one critic, lay "the whole meaning of racial exploitation" at "the altar of caste."[25] As a solution, Myrdal urged white Americans to discover their own guilt, a shibboleth that's back again with Isabel Wilkerson's *Caste: The Origins of Our Discontents* (2020).

Hansberry rejects caste as "the cornerstone of the social, political, and economic system in America," as Wilkerson would have it.[26] It's basic classism—economic status, family lineage, job status, and level of education—that holds down the Youngers and all poor people like them. "For she did not believe," Bob Nemiroff later wrote, "the enemy was *whiteness* [his italics], or a blanket, amorphous, all-inclusive 'white America,' but, rather, a specific economic, political and social system, American capitalism, one of the central features of which was the use of 'whiteness' and the trap of racism as a central device to divide the people and thus perpetuate itself and the exploitation and oppression—in vastly different degrees, to be sure—of the great majority, black and white (and of all races and ethnicities), both here and abroad."[27]

The Youngers have dreams—they must, so they can carry on. Walter plans to use his father's insurance money to make a down payment on a liquor store, which will make him a member of the black establishment. That's the nature of success in this country, according to Hansberry. "His dream is not a *Negro* dream, but an *American* one. . . . Acquisition is the logical end to a man who is encompassed in a culture which exalts acquisition."[28]

Beneatha, the sister, has a dream that is humanitarian: she plans to go to medical school and practice somewhere in the world where she's needed.

Her choice is meant to symbolize Hansberry's hope for what "mankind will ultimately worship in place of the old and useless Gods—science."[29] Lorraine gives Beneatha two boyfriends, like the daughter in *Juno*, Mary Boyle, comparing two young black men with different values.

The first suitor is George Murchison. His surname sounds, maybe not coincidentally, like "merchant's son." Walter Lee sneers at George's preppy clothes and his level of education. "Why all you college boys wear them faggoty-looking white shoes?" Real men with big plans were bold and operated by instinct. But then, in the next breath, Walter gives away that he's envious. "How's your old man making out? I understand you all going to buy that big hotel on the Drive? Shrewd move. Your old man is all right, man." Perry Hansberry, in fact, was negotiating to buy a flophouse named the Pershing Hotel, at Sixty-Fourth and Cottage Grove, near Lakeshore Drive, when *A Raisin in the Sun* was written.

In spite of George's money, Beneatha isn't impressed with him. "The Murchisons are honest-to-God-real-foe-rich colored people, and the only people in the world who are more snobbish than rich white people are rich colored people."

Murchison actually serves no serious purpose in the play except as a straw man to make a point. Hansberry holds him up as an example of how capitalism and consumerism degrade black Americans and adulterate them. During her speech to the Negro writers conference, she excoriated "the villainous and often ridiculous money values that spill over from the dominant culture and often make us ludicrous in pursuit of that which has its own inherently ludicrous nature: acquisition for the sake of acquisition." Her attack was merciless. "The war against illusions must dispel the romance of the black bourgeoisie. Nor does this imply the creation of a modern kind of buffoon dressed up in a business suit, haplessly trying to imitate the white counterpart. On the contrary. These values have their root in an American perversion and no place else."[30]

Beneatha's second boyfriend is Asagai, a Nigerian, and Hansberry's favorite character: the play's "true intellectual," she said, a representative of an "articulate and deeply conscious colonial intelligentsia."[31] He repudiates the Tarzan-of-the-jungle stereotypes—"the myth of the 'cannibal' with a bone in his hair," as Alex Haley put it—the first time in American theater that an African national had been portrayed as a dignified person. Asagai claims to represent the sanity and progress that will evolve in a postcolonial Africa; although, he says, because he knows history, he is just as likely to "be butchered in my bed some night by the servants of empire" as by the revolutionary resistance of "my own black countrymen."[32] Beneatha is ecstatically pleased by his gift of African robes.

Beneatha personifies black Americans' "double consciousness," as Du Bois defined it in *The Souls of Black Folk*, which had impressed Hansberry when she read the copy in her parents' library. "Such a double life," Du Bois writes, "with double thoughts, double duties, and double social classes, must give rise to double words and double ideals, and tempt the mind to pretense or revolt, to hypocrisy or radicalism." Beneatha tells Asagai she is searching for her identity. She feels inside and outside mainstream culture. She's nostalgic for an Africa she doesn't really know, and yet she is as much of an American Dreamer, in terms of ambition and individualism, as her brother. For now, in response to Asagai's teasing about her confusion, she can only respond sharply, "I am not an assimilationist." Asagai makes overtures that she should come to Africa with him.

The responsibility of reeling in these dreams falls to Lena "Mama" Younger. She has to decide how to use the insurance check. Before her son can become a man of the world, or her daughter a doctor, an emotionally wrenching secret comes to light. Ruth confides in Lena that she's contemplating having an abortion because there isn't enough money. Hansberry condemns how, in the topsy-turvy world of capitalistic values, life is cheap and things are expensive. Somehow, Mama Younger must save her family from the human disintegration that comes from living in the ghetto.[33]

Much has been made in analyses of the play about how Lena Younger symbolizes the strong woman in black culture. Hansberry intended her to be "the black matriarch incarnate, the bulwark of the Negro family since slavery, the embodiment of the Negro will to transcendence. It is she who, in the mind of the black poet[,] scrubs the floors of a nation in order to create black diplomats and university professors. It is she, while seeming to cling to traditional restraints, who drives the young on into the fire hoses."[34]

But Hansberry also cautioned that strong mothers and wives are not unique to black culture. Hardship forces them to be strong. "The Irish reflect this, I think. There's a relationship between Mother Younger in this play and Juno which is very strong and obvious. . . . [A]mong oppressed peoples, the mother will assume a certain kind of role." And she dismissed the criticism that women like Lena emasculate black men. "I think it's a mistake to get [black female strength] confused with Freudian concepts of matriarchal dominance. . . . These women have become the backbone of our people in a very necessary way."[35] When Walter castigates black women for "not building their men up and making 'em feel like they somebody," his real argument is about feeling demeaned in the outside world, not with the women in his life who love him.

Lena takes action by depositing $3,500 on a home in a better neighborhood. She has a hankering for "a little old two-story somewhere, with a yard where Travis could play in the summertime." The house is located in Clybourne Park, a lower-middle-class white community. "Them houses they put up for colored in them areas way out all seem to cost twice as much as other houses. I did the best I could." Her choice is based on pragmatism, not out of a desire to advance the cause of integration, but because material conditions are squeezing the life out of her family. As black Southsider Buggy Martin exclaims in Frank London Brown's novel *Trumbull Park*, "I'm not trying to prove anything—I just want a better place to live!" Lena Younger, like the Roman goddess Juno, and her namesake in O'Casey's play, acts as protectress of the unborn grandchild, ensuring the continuation of the race. She's the goddess of domesticity and of the family hearth. Lena purchases a house in Clybourne Park not to defy the color barrier, but to save her family from physical and spiritual strangulation.

She gives $6,500 to Walter to deposit in the bank, hoping to bolster his ego by entrusting him with the family's future. A portion of it, $3,000, is for Beneatha's medical schooling; the rest, she instructs Walter, should go into a checking account. "And from now on any penny that come out of it or that go in it is for you to look after. For you to decide." She asks her son, in so many words, to step into his father's shoes and be the man of the family. Lena, being part of the older generation and southern-raised, falls back on administering a strong dose of traditional, patriarchal structure and material support to her suffering family.

Walter, seeing his chance, doesn't deposit the money in the bank. He hands over the entire $6,500 to his partners in the liquor store deal, Willy Harris and Bobo—an act of impulsive foolishness that bears out his late father's opinion of him. Such is the addictive effect of capitalism: making people want to acquire things at any cost. Without letting on what he's done, Walter Lee regales Travis with descriptions of how they will live once they are respectable. The transformation will be total. Even Walter's speech changes from black vernacular to standard English, discarding the spoken bond of solidarity among Negroes. It's interesting to imagine what would have been the reaction of Lorraine's family to this parody of the black bourgeoisie. Perhaps that's why the scene was cut from the original production:

> And I'll pull the car up on the driveway . . . just a plain black Chrysler, I think, with white walls—no—black tires. More elegant. Rich people don't have to be flashy . . . though I'll have to get something a little sportier for Ruth—maybe a Cadillac convertible to do her shopping in. . . . And I'll come up the steps to the house and the gardener will be clipping away at the hedges and he'll say, "Good evening, Mr. Younger." And I'll say, "Hello, Jefferson, how are you this evening?" And I'll go inside and Ruth will come downstairs and meet me at the door and we'll kiss each other and she'll take my arm and we'll go up to your room to see you sitting on the floor with the catalogues of all the great schools in America around you.

While the Youngers are happily packing up and preparing to move, there's a knock on the door. Enter Karl Lindner, who represents the white homeowners association in Clybourne Park. "It is one of these community organizations," he explains nervously, "set up to look after—oh, you know, things like block upkeep and special projects and we also have what we call our New Neighbors Orientation Committee." Lindner says the Youngers may not enjoy living in Clybourne Park, because "our Negro families are happier when they live in their *own* communities." For the good of everyone, he recommends, the Youngers should sell their new home to the association, at a profit. As Judge Feinberg pointedly told Carl Augustus Hansberry when he purchased the house on Rhodes Avenue in Woodlawn, then an all-white community, "I don't go where I'm not wanted."[36] Walter Lee, angered but not surprised, ushers Mr. Lindner out and tells him he will be in touch.

Lindner is right, even though he arrives like a villain in a melodrama to foreclose on the orphanage; privately, Hansberry called the meaning of his visit "sick." ("I've even been booed by whites outside the stage entrance when I leave at night," said the actor John Fiedler, who played Lindner, "you know, a friendly kidding." But blacks applauded him enthusiastically for playing his part so well.)[37] The residents of Clybourne Park are white, working-class homeowners with a realistic understanding of property values: blacks moving in will cause a steep decline in them—one speeded up, no doubt, by unscrupulous real estate speculators—so they are taking steps to protect their homes, the biggest investment of their lives. No one knows this scenario better than Hansberry. The Youngers are victims of structural unfairness in capitalism—private property. Hansberry wants to persuade the audience that it should be abolished. An unjust economic system can't be fixed through white guilt. "For the master's tools," wrote Audre Lorde, "will never dismantle the master's house. They may allow us to temporarily beat him at his own game, but they will never enable us to bring about genuine change."[38]

The Youngers scoff at Lindner's proposal, and then Bobo arrives. Black people in the audience laughed bitterly when they saw his hangdog expression. Another Negro dream has misfired, fizzled, gone up in smoke.[39] The other "partner" entrusted with the liquor store money, Willy Harris, Bobo confesses, has taken off with all of it. Every cent. When Lena finds out, she beats Walter Lee like a disobedient little boy. Her rage stems not only from his deception and her disappointment, but also, perhaps, from his failure to advance the family materially, the way Big Walter had. As Nelson Algren observed in *The Man with the Golden Arm*, also set in Chicago in the 1950s, "The great, secret and special American guilt of owning nothing, nothing at all, in the one land where ownership and virtue are one."[40] Walter Lee, humiliated, says he will sell to Lindner, and he gets down on his knees, pretending to beseech an imaginary white man for money in a grotesque display of self-abasement that shocks his family.

Lindner returns for the Youngers' decision about the house, confident that they will settle up. "Thirty pieces and not a coin less!" says Beneatha. If Walter Lee takes the offer, he will remain embittered, without access to the privileges of a materially better life—a good school for Travis, a wholesome home for his pregnant wife, the kind of future that will fulfill his mother's heart's desire.

But Hansberry has Walter Lee "draw upon the strength of an incredible people who, historically, have simply refused to give up."[41] He's not selling, he informs Lindner, "we have decided to move into our house because my father—my father—he earned it for us brick by brick. We don't want to make no trouble for nobody or fight no causes, and we will try to be good neighbors. And that's all we got to say about that." He chooses to push the destiny of his family higher. Lindner, flabbergasted and upset, leaves. Mama Younger says to Ruth about Walter's transformation, "He finally come into his manhood today, didn't he? Kind of like a rainbow after the rain . . ."

Walter's finding himself at last is patterned after the psychological trajectory in Du Bois's *The Souls of Black Folk* when double consciousness becomes self-realization: "to merge his double self into a better and truer self. In this merging, he wishes neither of the older selves to be lost. He does not wish to Africanize America . . . he does not wish to bleach his Negro blood in a flood of white Americanism. . . . He simply wishes to make it possible for a man to be both a Negro and an American . . . to be a co-worker in the kingdom of culture, to escape both death and isolation, and to husband and use his best powers."[42]

And this is where Hansberry parts with O'Casey. The Irish playwright chooses to end *Juno and the Paycock* with a raft of betrayed expectations: there won't be a legacy; daughter Mary Boyle's romantic dreams have been dashed; Johnny Boyle didn't escape retribution for his part in a political ambush; Captain Jack's pipe dream of never having to work again is no more; and Juno's wish to keep her family together has not been granted—an unflinching final scene in which it is clear that things will stay the way they are and that the rest was all self-delusion. This is where the dialectics of O'Casey's slum socialism led him.

Hansberry couldn't let her characters depart like that. Her solution was to throw out capitalism and replace it with a system that dignified people.

"I cannot promise you that Walter Lee Younger is a happy man at the end of Act III, but I do know that he knows he is not a failure."[43]

The audience at the Ethel Barrymore Theatre rendered the play an immediate standing ovation. They stamped, howled, and cheered. Jerry Tallmer, the drama critic for the *Village Voice*, who was surprised that the waitress from Potpourri could write, said he cried like a baby. For the whites on their feet and shouting "Author! Author!," the lessons about housing and private property probably went unnoticed. Their applause was for a family with many of the same hopes and frustrations as theirs. For blacks in the audience, what moved them was how Hansberry had rendered the pathology of racism and Walter Lee's moral rise in spite of it. Where they met, as an audience, was in agreeing that injustice is recognizable and requires good people to act.

As the cast of *A Raisin in the Sun* came out and stood at the edge of the stage bowing, Ruby Dee nudged Poitier and said, "Go get her." He jumped down, walked to the third row, and extended his hand to escort Lorraine around to the steps on the side that led to the stage. The two still weren't speaking, but they were beaming as they stood together, facing the roar of the auditorium.

"And this, I believe," wrote Bob Nemiroff, "is why, in that moment, the audience, however they may articulate it, feels elation, pride, the surge of triumph. Because, in Lorraine's terms, the Youngers have moved beyond what *is* to what is *possible*, and thereby affirmed *our own* possibilities. But it is worth emphasizing that this is not a triumph that says the battle is won or that all will be well from now on. . . . It says only that the family— and in particular Walter Lee—have found something in themselves that has given them the strength, if only for that moment in their lives, to stop blaming themselves and each other, and to confront, however imperfectly, the world that hems them in."[44]

Phil Rose had a limousine waiting to take Lorraine and Bob to Sardi's, on West Forty-Fourth, the traditional spot for first-nighters after a show. Lorraine felt panicky and wanted to go home. She was worried about the reviews. At midnight, the first twenty-five copies of the *New York Times* and the *New York Herald Tribune* would be rushed over to Sardi's with the review pages marked. Rose insisted that people would be disappointed if Lorraine didn't go. She relented, but on the way over, she couldn't calm down. As she entered the restaurant, everyone stood and applauded. She was escorted to the first-floor room that had been reserved for the guest of honor.

A jazz combo was playing, and Lorraine danced with Lloyd Richards. "I think the play was staged brilliantly. . . . I am warm and content in a way that I cannot express to most—knowing that where the play stop[ped] being mine and became yours—it became a larger and more powerful play."[45] Listening to the music was Renee Kaplan. Lorraine slipped over to her and, between sips of champagne, flirted outrageously with her. "I think our relationship started after—five minutes after—opening night," Kaplan said.[46]

When the newspapers arrived at midnight, Bob read Brooks Atkinson's review in the *New York Times*. "Lorraine Hansberry touches on some serious problems. No doubt her feelings are as strong as anyone's. But she has not tipped her play to prove one thing or other." Nemiroff wept from disappointment. It was too mild, and none of the themes or ideas were touched on about black family life, the stresses of poverty, the conflict of the generations—nothing. In the *New York Herald Tribune*, Walter Kerr praised the performances warmly and Lloyd Richards's direction for its "fluid, elusive, quick-tempered grace." But there was no indication that the play might inspire thought or controversy. Kerr would wait until the Sunday edition to think more deeply about what he'd seen. Lorraine Hansberry, he wrote, "reads the precise temperature of a race at that time in its history when it cannot retreat and cannot quite find the way to move forward. The mood is forty-nine parts anger and forty-nine parts control, with a very narrow escape hatch for the steam these abrasive contraries build up. Three generations stand poised, and crowded, on a detonating-cap."[47]

In the coming days, dozens of congratulatory letters arrived on Bleecker Street, one of them from Lorraine's uncle Leo Hansberry, at Howard University. He wished her father could have been in the audience. Another letter was postmarked Madison, Wisconsin: Ann Miler, the former housemother of Langdon Manor, never thought she'd see "one of my girls' names in lights on Broadway." Then there was one that began "Dear tousled, slim-hipped, elfin Miss Hansberry." The handwriting awoke memories in Lorraine that had been quiet for years. It was from Edythe Cohen, now married and living in a Chicago-area suburb. She had been at the opening night and had met Bob. "I liked your husband, Lorraine, very much." Hansberry replied that she was glad, because, she added mischievously, she liked Bob, too.[48]

On April 7, 1959, *A Raisin in the Sun* was awarded the New York Drama Critics' Circle Award for Best Play, over Archibald MacLeish's *J.B.*, Eugene O'Neill's *A Touch of the Poet*, and Tennessee Williams's *Sweet Bird of Youth*. It would run for 538 performances.[49]

Two weeks after that announcement, J. Edgar Hoover, at the Department of Justice, received a memo from the FBI's New York office. The agent in charge recommended that in light of the "considerable notoriety" that *A Raisin in the Sun* was receiving in the press, it was inadvisable to interview Hansberry because the "possibility exists that the Bureau could be put in an embarrassing position" if it were known that it had been investigating Hansberry and her play. The situation would be revisited in the fall.[50]

An interview was never scheduled.

21

Chitterlin' Heights

Twenty minutes to five. Without: white snow, black trees. The rapidly falling darkness. My soul leaps out of me. . . . [O]nly death or infirmity can stop me now. The writing urge is on.

—Lorraine Hansberry

"You've made history and quite creatively. It's all the more significant and brilliant because you're so young and a Negro woman, having to overcome a few more extra hurdles than the male of the species," wrote former New York City councilman Benjamin Davis in a letter to Hansberry, "so all of us should feel even more proud, and the men a little less smug in their 'supremacist' airs."[1]

Very quickly, *A Raisin in the Sun* turned Hansberry into a sought-after spokesperson for and authority on integration, housing, black families, social reform, and theater. She received requests to serve on panels, deliver keynote speeches, and attend teas, luncheons, and fundraising dinners, many from progressive causes, civil rights organizations, and civic groups. She was unaware that so much important work was being done.[2] Some days, she received up to thirty pieces of mail asking for a commitment.

Many black writers were reluctant to step into the nation's mainstream because it carried the risk of being co-opted and turned into a trophy speaker—a good catch in the net of racial capitalism that uses nonwhiteness as a commodity to sell tickets to an event or to provide a bit of social relevance to an affair. Yet talking about topics that mattered could be a major step in ending the racial segregation that existed in the republic of letters. Hansberry wanted to be part of the conversation swirling in the pages of such magazines as *Commonweal*, *The New Republic*, *The Nation*, and *The National Review*. It wasn't long before she was arguably the first black woman intellectual to become a national celebrity.

A great deal of speculation surrounded her private life, and her personal appearance contributed to the interest. A *New York Times* article described her as "voluble, energetic, pretty and small." Baldwin noticed there were "both black and white people who were unable to believe, apparently, that a really serious intention could be contained in so glamorous a frame."[3] Some seized on her origins and sophistication as reasons she shouldn't be taken seriously on racial issues: she wasn't black enough. Amiri Baraka accused her of speaking only for the middle class—the beginning of a fencing off of the Black Arts and Black Power movements, still on the horizon, as territory reserved for fist-raising black men. (Baldwin was disqualified from representing black males because he was out as a gay man.)[4]

Harold Cruse derided Hansberry's celebrity on the grounds that it showed the "utter impoverishment" of the black cultural left and how its mission had stalled. "Hansberry, talking to the television rostrum on art and culture *a la Negre* was like a solitary defender, armed with a dull sword, rushing out on a charger to meet a regiment."[5] The image of a woman brandishing a phallically "dull sword" and taking on a male regiment suggests that, this time, gender was the disqualifier.

These class- and gender-based criticisms were a replay of her childhood, in a sense. Her mother had insisted she wear a white fur coat to school, and the children on the playground had beaten her up. "The world is in fact divided in half as it is lived by me."[6] In her posthumous play *Les Blancs*, a character who's African born and married to a white woman announces that he's going to join the revolution to overthrow colonialism. "Which part of yourself will you drive into the sea?" a friend asks.

Regardless, Hansberry proved very adept in the public eye. Television interviewer Mike Wallace put this question to her: "Someone comes up to you and says: 'This is not really a Negro play; why, this could be about anybody! It's a play about people!' What is your reaction? What do you say?"

She replied, "Well, I hadn't noticed the contradiction because I'd always been under the impression that Negroes *are* people."[7]

Returning to Chicago in May 1959, she delivered a lunchtime speech at what was now Roosevelt University, comparing Willy Loman in *Death of a Salesman* to Walter Lee Younger. She spent the afternoon at her mother's apartment being interviewed by author and commentator Studs Terkel. That evening, she appeared live on local public television's *The Irv Kupcinet Show*, the first of a new genre in the medium: the late-night talk show. The other guest was Hollywood director Otto Preminger. Preminger was there to promote his film *Porgy and Bess*, starring Poitier. Lorraine had read the novel and didn't like it: "My feeling about stereotypes is something that's seldom said—that they constitute bad art." When Preminger pressed her to explain what she thought his motives were in making the film, she didn't take the bait. "We cannot afford the luxuries of mistakes of other people. So it isn't a matter of being hostile to you, but on the other hand, it's also a matter of never ceasing to try to get you to understand that your mistakes can be painful, even those which come from excellent intentions." When Preminger asked her what she thought of his film *Carmen Jones*, starring Hansberry's friend Harry Belafonte, she replied that it was "unfortunate." Preminger dismissed her as a "minority of one." Callers to the station objected to his remark twenty to one.[8] Black public intellectuals and artists who expressed complexity and enjoyed challenging talk about racial democracy were new in the media. "I'm sure I'll make some people angry by saying this," Lorraine said later, "but I believe that white people are dreadfully ignorant of Negro life in America."[9]

During the last five years and seven months of her life, from mid-1959 until January 1965, Lorraine divided her time between a new residence in the city and one in the country. She moved out of the apartment she shared with Bob on Bleecker Street and into a nineteenth-century carriage house in Greenwich Village.

One hundred twelve Waverly Place is a slender four-story row house between Washington Square West and Sixth Avenue, just a seven-minute walk from 337 Bleecker Street and around the corner from the gateway arch of Washington Square Park, where she and Bob had courted. A very desirable address on a quiet, narrow street. Bob had recommended it as an investment, although Lorraine thought the purchase price "sounds like a hell of a lot of money to me—I mean it just does."[10]

She moved in May 1959, two months after *A Raisin in the Sun* opened, when her share of the box office was about $35,000 a week in today's money. Her share of selling the film rights to Columbia Pictures was the equivalent of $1.5 million.[11]

Her new home had been built around 1827, in the Federal style, on a block of early nineteenth-century residences. She claimed the two-floor apartment at the top of the stairs and rented out the two units underneath. She was a Hansberry landlord now in her own right. The tenant in the second-floor apartment was Dorothy Secules, an employment manager for the Loftus Candy Company.[12] A native of Williamsport, Pennsylvania, Secules was fifteen years older than Lorraine, fair-haired, outgoing, and eager to talk politics.

Though it's not known if Lorraine was aware, 112 Waverly Place had an interesting past. Years before, a group of realist painters known as the Ashcan school for their somber scenes of city life had turned one of the apartments into a small theater. They called themselves the Waverly Players. Also, there had been a tenant known during the Gilded Age for his good works among the immigrant Italian poor. The Rev. Joseph Sanford Attwell, one of the first black ordained priests of the Protestant Episcopal Church, had moved from the South in 1875 to become rector of St. Philip's Church on Mulberry Street.[13]

The month of May was an auspicious time for Hansberry to be buying her first home. Her birthday was May 19; she was turning twenty-nine. Bob answered the phone calls that came to Bleecker Street asking for her. She wasn't available—no, she had "retreated" to her private residence to write. Were the Nemiroffs splitting up? "Where do such rumors come from?" Bob mused aloud to a reporter for the *New York Age*. "As far as I'm concerned, we're very much together and always have been."[14]

In the meantime, the Hansberry family lawyer filed the necessary papers to untangle Lorraine from Hansberry Enterprises, but he wasn't quick enough to avoid another embarrassment. In June, she was named a codefendant in a suit in Chicago Superior Court for failure to correct building violations "in slums of which she is a part owner." There were eight buildings involved, and the city had already seized one to satisfy the fines. Lorraine's mother called this "confiscated wealth."[15]

To retaliate, the family—Lorraine included—filed a motion to reinstate the one-million-dollar suit against the city from the year before. Their complaint was that Hansberry Enterprises was still being cited for building violations even while the business was making repairs. Ole Nosey, the *Chicago Defender* gossip columnist, provided an update on the Hansberrys' pursuit of justice. "Carl Hansberry of the famed Hansberry real estate family, hit the turn with a spanking new '59 air-conditioned Cadillac behind that $1 million suit against the city."[16]

Lorraine went on the offensive by giving an interview to a *New York Post* reporter. Seated on a couch, her feet tucked under her, she said it would have been easy to make clear that she had nothing to do with Hansberry Enterprises—"I'm not a slum landlord. I haven't derived a cent from the family since I came East nine years ago"—but she didn't want to give the impression that she was breaking with her brothers and sister, either. She said she knew nothing about the details of the city's lawsuit involving her family. Her name had been placed on a piece of paper "some years ago. I wasn't told about it. . . . Of all the things in the world I could have been hit with, this is the most painful."[17]

While the Hansberrys played rope-a-dope with Chicago's city hall, Perry closed the deal he'd been working on to buy the residential Pershing Hotel, on the South Side. With financial help from Lorraine, he got it at auction.[18] The seven-story Pershing had a two-thousand-seat ballroom where jazz luminaries had once played: Charlie Parker, Miles Davis, Lester Young, Dizzy Gillespie, Billie Holiday, Dinah Washington, and Sun Ra. The basement's Beige Room had been a cabaret. The Hansberrys, in honor of their parents, renamed the Pershing the Nan-Carl Hotel.

When a judge discovered that the Hansberrys were now in the hotel business, he found them in contempt for refusing to pay fines on their other properties. He ordered them arrested—but not Lorraine, for some reason.[19] Mamie and Perry fled to Los Angeles. Mrs. Hansberry went to stay with Lorraine until the storm blew over. After she was cleared to go to Los Angeles, Nannie began receiving $400 a month from Lorraine. (At one point, Lorraine sent $7,400; Mamie replied with a thank-you card that had a penny taped inside: "Here's your change.") Carl Jr. remained behind in Chicago, consolidating Hansberry Enterprises. He sold one of their buildings and paid $22,000 in fines—the largest such sum ever paid in Chicago until then.[20] Then he focused his attention on converting the Pershing's 164 rooms into kitchenettes.

After a year or so, the Nan-Carl turned a profit, "which goes to prove," Lorraine's mother wrote to her from Los Angeles, "that good management, pride of ownership and know how, pays off." Carl explained to Lorraine that some revenue came from vending machines, sports betting, and "other little games." He predicted that they would just about be able to make their bills. But eventually, he gave up; the utilities were costing too much. People's Gas and Light sued Hansberry Enterprises for nonpayment, and the family abandoned the building to creditors. "Why they would desert a building which they paid $380,000 for two years ago is beyond me," said the building manager. The tenants had no water, radiator heat, or telephone service that winter. In Los Angeles, Perry began putting together a deal to buy blocks of property in the then-middle-class, racially mixed suburban neighborhood of Compton. Mamie asked Lorraine for an itemized list of her assets to demonstrate the Hansberrys' credit worthiness, which she reluctantly supplied through her accountant, Seymour Baldash. "I do not, under any circumstances," she warned him, "wish to be associated with any of their purchases or enterprises."[21]

Louis Burnham, Hansberry's mentor and friend at *Freedom*, suffered a fatal heart attack on February 12, 1960, while delivering a speech on Negro history to an audience. He was forty-four. "The things he taught me were great things," Lorraine remembered, "that all racism is rotten, white or black; that everything is political; that people tend to be indescribably beautiful and uproariously funny."[22]

He had attended, with his wife Dorothy, the opening night of *A Raisin in the Sun* on Broadway. "I looked and you were beautiful," he wrote to her later. "I listened and your words were music. Perhaps we will not always agree on every point. But . . . the search, the quest is the thing. So you must know that you are both a culmination and a beginning; that all that has gone before, for all its blindness and aimlessness and senselessness, has been necessary; and that all that is to come, for all the anguish that yet portends, will be good."[23] The last time she saw him was just a few months before his death. He was sitting cross-legged on her living room floor in Waverly Place, eating walnuts and smiling as they discussed independence movements in Africa, the Cuban revolution, and a new publication, *Freedomways*, that would continue the work of Robeson's newspaper, combining race issues, the arts, and politics. Burnham would be the editor in chief, lifting some of the financial burden of trying to take care of his family when most of his commitments as an organizer were unpaid. He worried about that.[24] He was so busy that he tried to accommodate everything he wanted to do through an elastic time schedule that his friends called "Lou Daylight Saving Time," meaning he was often running late. He could only stay to talk to Hansberry for half an hour because he was needed somewhere; but he left, Lorraine noticed, "in a triumphant mood."[25]

Not long after the memorial service for her husband, Dorothy Burnham sent Lorraine a letter addressed to her that had been found in one of his suit pockets. He hadn't had the time to mail it. He wrote to say that he would stop by to see her again, perhaps in a week or so: "Maybe by then I won't be so tired. Although sometimes I don't know, because what I'm tired about often, I suspect, is building up somebody else's civilization. And that's not easy to get over in a week." He talked about ongoing school desegregation struggles in Arkansas under Gov. Orval Faubus. Faubus constantly challenged his critics to name which of his accomplishments they would end. Improvements to public education? Better pay for teachers? Hundreds of miles of paved roads? Improvements to the notoriously bad State Hospital for the mentally ill?

Burnham was troubled, he said, by "Faubusism," as the governor called it, and the capitalist system because of a paradox they posed for black Americans: "Can Negroes *succeed* in opposing a system which oppresses them if they share the very *success* obsession of that system?"[26]

Lorraine contributed two thousand dollars to the Louis E. Burnham Fund for Dorothy and their four children.

Hansberry and Dorothy Secules, her tenant on the second floor, fell in love. Lorraine made an annual self-inventory called "Myself in Notes." In the "Likes" column, she wrote, "The inside of a lovely woman's mouth" and doodled the name "Dorothy Secules" several times.

Dorothy was pleasant, chic, not complicated—a more mature version of the preppy girls Lorraine had dated in the Village. She claimed to be psychic. Lorraine rolled her eyes when Dorothy got on the subject of race, because she didn't know what she was talking about. They went to New Hope, Pennsylvania, for a weekend to take in dinner and a show at the Bucks County Playhouse. Lorraine had reserved a room at the Brookmore Motel, a mom-and-pop place on West Bridge Street. But the two women were informed at check-in that there were no rooms available. Lorraine engaged Clarence B. Jones, Martin Luther King Jr.'s attorney, and prepared to sue.[27] The suit was dropped, however, probably because the circumstances would have drawn attention to Hansberry's private life. There had been difficulties with getting her television script, *The Drinking Gourd*, produced because she had refused to sign a contract with a morality clause.[28] ("The writer agrees to conduct herself with due regard to public conventions and morals. Writer also agrees not to do or commit any act or things which degrade her or prejudice the writer's standing in the community in which she resides, or shock or offend the motion picture, theatrical, television[,] or entertainment industry in general.") Officially, NBC shelved her ninety-minute drama about slavery and southern plantation masters—the first in a series set to air during the American Civil War Centennial—because studio executives decided the subject was too depressing for television audiences.[29]

Regardless of the personal and professional challenges Lorraine faced, Bob remained a fixture in her life because she continued to rely on him. He was good at keeping her on task. "I won't be falsely modest about it," he said. "She wanted me to produce her work because I'm profoundly committed to the same values she was. Our values were what brought us together in the first place."[30] By her own admission, she had "goofed away" her first summer on Waverly Place, reassuring herself that "there's time."[31] Once a week, her theater friend Marie Rupert stopped by to hear new material and offer encouragement. She understood that Lorraine "had very little quiet time to digest the situation of celebrity and also to be creative." However, not everything was beyond her control. Playwriting requires discipline, but it was clear that, left to her own devices, "she was not paying attention,"

Rupert said, "like an adult professional." As fall turned to winter, she was still saying, "I can't get to it, I can't get to it."[32]

Bob came to the rescue. The problem was New York City. What Lorraine needed was a writer's retreat out in the country, where there would be fewer distractions. And he knew of a village that fit the bill: Croton-on-Hudson, in Westchester County, less than an hour away by train on the Metro-North, leaving from Grand Central. His parents had been friendly with a number of people there. It was quiet, off the beaten track, but not too far away, in case Lorraine needed to come into the city for rehearsals and so on. Her favorite poet, Edna St. Vincent Millay, had once lived there. It might be better for her health, too. Ever since *A Raisin in the Sun* opened on Broadway, she had been having problems with her stomach—sometimes, quite painful.

She took the train to Croton and began house hunting.

Croton was named by Dutch settlers after the indigenous American sachem Kenoten. Native Kitchawanc people are supposed to have greeted explorer Henry Hudson on the shores of what became Croton Point. In the 1930s, the village was popular among American Communists and socialists as well as artists and writers—a throwback to the old progressive values that Lorraine and Bob had been fighting for when they met in Washington Square.

There were plenty of older Cape Cod and Colonial-style homes available in Croton, but Lorraine was interested in a modern split-level ranch—a "large airy house (Not too large)," she noted happily in her journal, set on a wooded lot of several acres, accessible via a curving asphalt driveway that led up to a two-car garage.[33] Inside, the living room had a peaked cathedral ceiling with exposed wooden beams. At the back of the house, through the kitchen, was a very large window looking out on the trees and rolling lawn. Downstairs, there was a paneled, nearly soundproof study.

She bought it, and christened her new property Chitterlin' Heights, after chitterlings, a southern dish made from pig intestines. She hand-lettered a sign and nailed it to a tree, a humorous protest by a young black woman who had been rusticated to Westchester County, where commuters, as in the 1954 John Cheever short story, caught the 5:48 home to suburbs like Croton.

For weeks at a time, Hansberry "settled down and locked myself in the woods."[34] Waverly Place was for romance; Croton was for work. "I never could start anything other than, you know, the whole thing at one time and just—wham!—into it." What she couldn't control were episodes of depression and loneliness. "I sit at this desk for hours and hours, and sharpen pencils and smoke cigarettes and nothing happens. I begin to think more and more of doing something else with my life while I am still young. I mean, almost anything—driving an ambulance in Angola or running a ski lodge in upstate New York, instead of this endless struggle. I expect the theatre will kill me."[35]

Dorothy was unhappy about her lover spending months away. But there was nothing she could do about it, really. When Lorraine's friends like James Baldwin came out from New York to Chitterlin' Heights, they usually found Bob in residence. He had a bedroom to himself. Weekend cookouts with guests included games of doubles badminton, with Bob and Lorraine as a team. Spice, their dog from Bleecker Street, resided there, too, completing the former domestic scene.

"Bobby was very supportive in her work," Lorraine's theater director friend Miranda D'Ancona remembered. "I mean, he was the person. It was almost too much so. I could see that it was her need of his advice, support, nurture, and also criticism, as well as his need to hold on to that aspect of her, if he could have nothing else. She needed it, but he needed for her to need it."[36]

Bob didn't object to his wife dating men, either. He accepted that he was the sexually sidelined husband, just as he had been when she had dated women. "As for love affairs," Hansberry wrote Ann Morrissett, a Quaker friend whom she had met through the American Committee on Africa, "I did go out a few times recently with a seaman, the handsome, progressive sort of my youth-youth, only to find that the proletariat has become more proletarian than I remembered it. But I don't work at it anymore. I have lazily decided that love-life is probably like going to sleep: if one doesn't think about it too much, long for it too much, then it just settles down and takes over. True not always *when* you need it or from the source one might most desire—but that keeps the variety and I have decided that I do like *variety*. Which is one of the ideas that I used to giggle at in my former bolshevickian [sic] puritanism."[37]

There wasn't much to do at Chitterlin' Heights except roll another clean sheet of paper into her typewriter and get back to business. If she heard Bob open the front door, she liked to be found downstairs in her study working, and not having a drink or playing outside with the dog. She felt a responsibility to justify his constant, unyielding support.

She had so many writing ideas. For years she'd been thinking about a play or an opera about her hero Toussaint Louverture, the Haitian leader of the first black uprising against European colonialism. There was also the novel she had started in college, "All the Dark and Beautiful Warriors." Her file cabinets contained short stories, written and revised. And she wanted to get started on a play based on *The Marrow of Tradition*, a historical novel by Charles W. Chesnutt about the 1898 race riots in Wilmington, Delaware.

Bob encouraged her to focus on the kind of play that theatergoers and critics were expecting from her: a drama about social issues. Her métier was strong theater, he insisted, "to be really believable—and therefore persuasive to an audience."[38] So she concentrated on a two-act play that was the furthest along, *The Sign in Sidney Brustein's Window*, about a disenchanted Greenwich Village intellectual and his wife, Iris, an aspiring actress. Sidney was a bit windy, like Bob—as anyone who had received one of his multipage, stream-of-consciousness typed letters would have recognized.[39]

> Sidney: That which warped and distorted all of us is—(*Suddenly lifting his hands as if this were literally true*) all around; it is in this very air! *This* world—this swirling, seething madness—which you ask us to accept, to help maintain—has done this . . . maimed my friends . . . emptied these rooms and my very bed. And now it has taken my sister. *This* world! Therefore, to live, to breathe—I shall *have* to fight it!

But as she worked in Croton, Hansberry suffered the writer's bane of sitting alone in a room for hours, watching the seasons change out the window. She didn't seem to know anyone in town very well. Holidays continued to be hard for her, and on Easter 1962, she was depressed. "I am ashamed of being alone. Or is it my loneliness that I am ashamed of? I have closed the shutters so that no one can see. Me. Alone."[40] In Bronzeville, when she had lived at home on South Parkway, the stretch between Forty-Third and Fifty-First Streets had been the route of the biannual "promenade" every Easter and Christmas. Families and couples, dressed in their best finery, strolled along the sidewalk, greeting one another and admiring the homes of the wealthy.

By early summer 1962, she was making progress on *The Sign in Sidney Brustein's Window*, although now she had "first draftitis," meaning she dreaded going through it again from the beginning, revising scenes and finessing dialogue.[41] She worked at her desk "at all costs until five," and then she downed "two brave sized scotches," followed by talking her "fool head off" to Bob; or she yakked on the phone until she was too tired to stay awake any longer.[42] She laughed when she received a telegram from *Playboy* publisher Hugh Hefner inviting her to the Playboy Mansion in Chicago for a party with the beautiful people. Hefner knew nothing about her except that she was famous.

That winter, back on Waverly Place, she began feeling faint on the stairs up to her apartment. Sometimes, fumbling with her key in the door, she had to hurry inside before she vomited. She suspected that she was "a very sick girl." In April, she "almost conked out," and she saw her physician, Dr. Baldwin, the next day. He admitted her to University Hospital on First Avenue in Manhattan for tests. She was frightened of hospitals and would seldom visit even a close friend in one.[43]

Bob and Burt D'Lugoff—now "Dr. Burton C. D'Lugoff, internist"—made sure that Lorraine was being well taken care of. She wrote in her journal that she was "Enjoying the attention mightily."[44] As was customary at the time, Dr. Baldwin explained Lorraine's test results to Bob, the husband. Dr. D'Lugoff added his thoughts to Bob's: Lorraine was run-down, they told her; her stomach problems were from worrying too much; she needed to rest. She felt reassured. "They have discovered that I have ulcers and anemia and here I am," she wrote to a young playwright who had sent her a script for advice. "Nothing serious, but enough to keep me out of action for a bit."[45]

Bob thought the best thing for her was to finish *The Sign in Sidney Brustein's Window* and to start nothing else for the time being. Lorraine agreed. She could commit to speaking engagements and interviews, but only a reasonable number, given her health. It was a matter of being selective about how and when to participate.

In May 1963, she accepted an invitation from James Baldwin to meet with Attorney General Robert F. Kennedy to discuss racial justice. Lena Horne would be there, as would actor Rip Torn; Harry Belafonte; Jerome Smith, a Freedom Rider; and sociologist Kenneth B. Clark, among several others.

The three-hour meeting in Kennedy's family apartment on Central Park South was tense and disturbing. Kennedy tried to defend his brother's record on civil rights, which provoked scornful laughter at times. Hansberry thought Kennedy was avoiding looking her in the eye. "Look, if you can't understand what this young man [Smith] is saying, then we are without any hope at all because you and your brother are representatives of the best that a white America can offer; and if you are insensitive to this, then there's no alternative except our going in the streets . . . and chaos." She was so angry, she stalked out, the first to leave. Afterward, she walked down Fifth Avenue alone, her hands pressed hard against her middle, her face registering the pain in her stomach.[46]

She soldiered on anyway. In Croton, she chaired a fundraiser at Temple Israel for voter registration in the South.[47] Her shoulders were hurting now, too. She started taking Darvon, an opioid, washing the pills down with Scotch.

The work continued apace on *The Sign in Sidney Brustein's Window*. Bob made notes in the margin of the script. And when he thought a character or scene required it, he changed lines of dialogue. He didn't think he was overstepping by doing this. He and Burt were producing a musical called *Kicks and Co.*, and in the show's investor prospectus, he claimed that *A Raisin the Sun* was the product of "his critical judgment which initially isolated and helped shape this incompleted work as *the* play for her Broadway debut."[48] Often in correspondence, he used the plural pronoun *we* to mean him and Lorraine. As they worked, if Lorraine was feeling too tired to suggest anything, Bob made changes. His zigzag, heavy-pencil deletions crossed out and replaced entire scenes.

In late June, two weeks after the fundraiser at Temple Israel, Lorraine was admitted again to University Hospital, this time for an operation. She listened in the recovery room to Bob and Dr. D'Lugoff explaining what they said the surgery had revealed: that her disease was a not "necessarily progressive or fatal illness of the lower back" that, for some strange reason, affected only Scandinavians and Negroes. The pain in her shoulders was caused by calcium deposits. But there was no denying that the exploratory operation had been serious. Lorraine had been on the operating table quite a while. She told friends who visited her while she was resting at home, "I'll bet you didn't know I almost died while you were away."[49]

In early August, Dr. Baldwin sent her to the Lahey Clinic in Boston for another operation, this time performed by a noted surgeon. Her strength returned, and she made it back to Croton to deliver the keynote speech at a "Rally to Support the Southern Freedom Movement," again at Temple Israel. With the March on Washington for Jobs and Freedom only two weeks away, the news media was beginning a countdown to the event. Hansberry was listed as one of the "movie personalities" who would attend. If she had gone, she might have been seated in front of the Lincoln Memorial beside James Baldwin.

But instead, she watched the speeches while propped up in a hospital bed at Lahey, awaiting yet another surgery—her second in three weeks. While she recovered in the hospital—this time, it took a month—Bob stayed in Boston, at the nearby Copley Plaza Hotel. He visited her every day, bringing along the script of *The Sign in Sidney Brustein's Window*, in case she felt up to doing a little work.

In the autumn, back in Croton, the two wrote, revised, and restructured the play. But they couldn't work fast enough. Bob was aiming for a spring premiere, but the producer, Hal Prince, who had coproduced a half dozen Broadway shows, including *Damn Yankees*, *West Side Story*, and *Fiorello!*, knew they wouldn't be ready. In mid-December 1963, he ended his association with the show. Lorraine "was being too casual," he said, about getting the rewrites finished in time.[50] Bob was frustrated but undaunted. He moved the opening date to October 1964. Lorraine, as the weather grew colder, went back to Waverly Place.

On New Year's Day, after celebrating the previous night as much as her medicated and healing body would allow, she looked out her window and saw that a heavy snow was falling. It was quiet outside. She let herself languish in the half-light of the apartment, indulging herself with happy thoughts of the future. "Twenty minutes to five," she wrote in her journal. "Without: white snow, black trees. The rapidly falling darkness. My soul leaps out of me. . . . The work goes superbly! Yes: Sidney Brustein! His character for the first time—beckons feeling from us! I am pleased. I am anxious to get on to Toussaint soon—only death or infirmity can stop me now. The writing urge is on."[51]

As she sat at her desk, hand on chin, trying to push imaginary characters around on the page, she felt guilty at times. She wanted to be a participant in the civil rights movement and not a commentor or an observer. What physical risks was she willing to take? "Have the feeling I should throw myself back into the movement. Become a human being again. . . . Comfort. Apparently I have sold my soul for it. I think when I get my health back I shall go into the South to find out what kind of revolutionary I am."[52]

The run-up to the scheduled opening, on October 15, 1964, of *The Sign in Sidney Brustein's Window*, at the Longacre Theatre on Broadway, turned into a nightmare. Lorraine had hoped that *Les Blancs*, her most political play, set in colonial Africa, would be staged first because it was her most serious and her best work, she thought, but it wasn't ready.

A dispute between satirist Mort Sahl, cast as Sidney Brustein, who wasn't learning his lines, and Nemiroff and Burt D'Lugoff, the coproducers, had stopped rehearsals. Sahl walked out without explanation, and the director, Carmen Capalbo, quit, saying, "I can't do this. I cannot do this."[53] Bob hired a nonunion director, Peter Kass, a protégé of Clifford Odets. Then he contacted Lorraine's college friend from the Progressive Theater at Madison, Gerald Hiken, now a professional stage and television actor, to offer him the role of Sidney. But Hiken had just moved to California to start his own theater, and he turned the part down. Gabriel Dell was cast as Sidney, opposite Rita Moreno as his wife, Iris Brustein.

Hansberry checked into the Victoria Hotel, at Seventh Avenue and Fifty-First Street, to be close to the Longacre Theatre. Her legs felt numb, and she had a private nurse to help her manage. When the weather was fair, the nurse took her outside in a wheelchair to enjoy the sunlight. On a piece of paper, Hansberry drew an outline of her body and pressed the ballpoint around and around to make a dark, solid spot on the left side of her chest, with an arrow: "Lorraine's pain." "If anything should happen before 'tis done," she wrote in a notebook, "may I trust that all commas and periods will be placed and someone will complete my thoughts—this last should be the least difficult—since there are so many who think as I do."[54]

With only ten days remaining before the opening of *The Sign in Sidney Brustein's Window*, Rita Moreno, who had won an Academy Award for Best Supporting Actress in the film adaptation of *West Side Story*, coped with a "production that was in turmoil. Absolutely filled with turmoil." Gabriel Dell didn't have enough time to memorize Sidney's Hamlet-size speeches. He was writing his lines on the walls of the set to help him. Alice Ghostley, in the role of Moreno's sister, Mavis, seemed to be losing her grip. She thought there were hidden microphones everywhere.

Gratefully, Moreno accepted an invitation to lunch with Bob and Lorraine. Now at least she might be able to get some help with her character. "I said to [Lorraine], 'Can you please tell me about Iris?' Because I didn't understand why Iris would behave in certain ways." Lorraine listened. She was obviously very ill. "Because that's what people do," she replied. Moreno nodded and thought to herself, *I'm screwed.*[55]

Opening night, Bob sent Lorraine a three-page telegram that began, "Witness you ever-burning lights above: we nuts are up and at it again: fools who believe that death is a waste and love is sweet and people want to be better than they are. . . . It is a great play, Lorraine: a measured, remorseless, dimensional paeon to life such as no one—no one has the courage to write these days."[56] Lorraine watched from a wheelchair at the rear of the theater. Gabriel Dell, feeling insufficiently rehearsed, carried a script with him throughout the action. In act 2, scene 1, Moreno walked onto the living room set expecting to find milk bottles placed beside the sofa as props. Not seeing them, she continued into the bedroom offstage and shouted, "What are these milk bottles doing in here?"[57]

When the reviews came out, Bob and Dorothy Secules read them to Lorraine while she rested in bed at the Victoria Hotel. The notices were mixed; a few were positive, but most of the critics were baffled. One, thinking back on the play a few years later, characterized *The Sign in Sidney Brustein's Window* as "an unresolved chaos of liberalistic political and sexual ideas. . . . [A]t the opening there were scenes not yet rehearsed which therefore had to be dropped, with results as might be expected."[58]

Two days later, Lorraine called Bob from the hotel, panic-stricken. The numbness in her legs was now in her chest. She was taken to University Hospital, where she suffered convulsions, lost her sight, and went into a coma. Mamie flew out from Los Angeles. The press reported that the thirty-four-year-old playwright was critically ill but that the cause was unknown.

Nemiroff sent a letter to investors about the "tragic news" concerning his wife. At the end of its first week, *Sidney Brustein* was losing money. The "finest testimonial to her person and her talent," he said, "will be the continuation of her play before the public."[59] A full-page ad appeared in the *New York Times* endorsing the show, signed by actors and directors (Marlon Brando, Mel Brooks, Lillian Hellman, Mike Nichols, Ossie Davis and Ruby Dee, Paddy Chayefsky, and Arthur Penn). Sammy Davis Jr. urged his nightclub audiences to take in something special while they were in town and get tickets for *The Sign in Sidney Brustein's Window*. John O. Killens and his wife, Grace, using investor lists for addresses, stuffed thousands of envelopes. At the Longacre Theatre, after the cast finished taking a bow, Bob came out from behind the curtain and passed the hat for donations.

After four days in a coma, Lorraine stirred and opened her eyes. She could see, but her speech was impaired. She struggled to make herself understood. "Robert and I tried to keep her from being so frightened," Mamie said.[60] Hot baths relaxed her. From her bed on the eleventh floor of the hospital, she could see across the street to Renee Kaplan's window, from which Renee would wave to her between visits. Uncle Leo Hansberry arrived, bringing with him the winds of Africa. The University of Nigeria had established the Hansberry Institute of African Studies in his honor.

On December 22, *Sidney Brustein* was forced to vacate the Longacre Theatre and moved to Henry Miller's Theatre, another Broadway house. The actors agreed to take a cut in salary, and additional funds surfaced to keep the show going. At University Hospital, nurses decorated Lorraine's room for the holidays. On Christmas Eve, they sang to her and exchanged gifts with Mamie. Bob gave Lorraine a necklace of delicate gold and amber; he said she could wear it as soon as she got out of the hospital. "Do you really think so?" she whispered. "Oh God, if it could only be true—that I could wear it." She had applied for and been issued a new passport after moving into Waverly Place. Her dream was to take a three-month trip to England and France, but there had never been enough time.[61]

On the morning of January 12, 1965, she was smiling and talking a little. At 8:30 a.m., she grew faint and fell unconscious. Twenty minutes later, she died. That night, after 101 performances, *The Sign in Sidney Brustein's Window* closed.

Bob had known Lorraine was dying from pancreatic cancer, but he hadn't told her. "I had arranged it with the doctor that way. She knew it was an illness that could very likely be fatal but, in the same instance, she believed that there was a chance . . . a hope . . . she could survive. This enabled her to go on, with considerable reality but it's still not total hopelessness. She wrote right up to the end."[62] Together, they had also kept secret from the public that he had divorced her six months before her death, in Mexico, where only one spouse was needed to file suit. His grounds were "incompatibility." Asked by reporters why, then, he had continued to act as her husband right up until her death, he said the divorce "did not in any way affect the closeness of our friendship or the working relations between us," or "the size of my loss."[63]

Douglas Turner Ward, one of Lorraine's friends, felt ashamed that Bob had flogged the play into production night after night, with appeals to the audience for donations, to keep it alive because it was by Lorraine Hansberry. "We all knew she was terminally ill," he said, "and here Bob was going around promoting her as if she was still all right."[64]

Six hundred people attended the morning service held during a blizzard at Presbyterian Church of the Master, on Morningside Avenue in Harlem. As the service began, the doors at the back of the church opened, and a freezing gust accompanied the entrance of Malcolm X.[65] He had changed his name to "El Hajj Malik el Shabazz" following a pilgrimage to Mecca. Assassins were plotting to kill him, and in six weeks, they would.

The Rev. Eugene Callender read messages from James Baldwin, who was in France; and one from Martin Luther King Jr., who said of her, from *Romeo and Juliet*: "When she shall die, take her, and cut her in little stars, and she will make the face of heaven so fine, that the world will be in love with night." Paul Robeson, making one of his few public appearances, delivered the eulogy. James Forman, Lorraine's classmate at Englewood High School, now executive director of the Student Nonviolent Coordinating Committee, remembered how, when Lorraine was a teenager, she defended unpopular opinions. Nina Simone, accompanying herself on piano, performed with her trio. Renee Kaplan and Dorothy Secules were honorary pallbearers. The coffin was draped in white flowers.

Lorraine's family left the arrangements for internment to Bob. The site he chose was Bethel Cemetery, in Croton-on-Hudson, a Revolutionary War–era Methodist churchyard on the Old Albany and New York Post Road, overlooking the Hudson River—not in Los Angeles, where her family had relocated; nor beside her father, in Burr Oak Cemetery, south of Chicago. It's doubtful whether there are other black Americans in Bethel Cemetery. Until the very end, Lorraine's disposition in the world was in Nemiroff's hands.

Nemiroff was named the executor of her estate. In her will, she gave her mother the privilege of choosing to live in the Croton house. Mrs. Hansberry remained in Los Angeles instead, where she died two years later. The house stayed in the Nemiroff family for many years, as did the Bleecker Street residence. Dorothy Secules received an annual sum.

All of Hansberry's intellectual property went to Bob—writings both published and unpublished; all letters, memoranda, and drafts; and all essays, articles, and fiction, "without limitation." Her shares in the joint theatrical production company Vivian Productions Inc. (her middle name) were to be divided between Bob and Burt D'Lugoff. By the terms of the will, Bob was instructed to make periodic contributions to civil rights organizations of his choice. Mrs. Hansberry approved the will, and no family members contested it. *Jet* magazine summarized all this under the headline "Divorced White Husband Gets Most of Hansberry's Rich Estate."

Readers phoned the magazine, wanting to know what had happened.[66] The February issue carried a summary of Hansberry's final wishes and an interview with Nemiroff. He pledged that he would perpetuate the legacy of Lorraine Hansberry, playwright, public intellectual, and civil rights activist. "A good deal of my energy from this point on is going to be devoted to trying to make sure that the world knows and experiences as much of the remaining body of her work as possible." He promised "many things produced from works she had not published."[67]

He began by collecting and curating his former wife's papers, inventorying items such as the notebook in the drawer beside her hospital bed. In Croton, he removed the few *New Yorker* cartoons she had taped to the wall in the downstairs study and filed them separately. He inventoried the books and articles left on her desk. He emptied her file cabinets of drafts for plays, short stories, essays, and whatever else seemed valuable.

Epilogue

Bob Nemiroff spent the year after Hansberry's death organizing her materials. He hired Charlotte Zaltzberg, a Croton neighbor, as his assistant. She became, as Bob had been for Lorraine, his collaborator and creative adviser. In 1967, Nemiroff married his third wife, literary scholar Jewell Handy Gresham, who became coexecutor of the Hansberry estate.[1]

During the next two decades, Nemiroff and Zaltzberg contacted Lorraine's friends, classmates, and family members asking for originals or copies of correspondence and photographs—as Nemiroff explained, "[I]t is impossible for the outsider to evaluate what may or may not be important."[2] He kept "tracings," as he called them, a record of reaching out to people who knew his former wife.

On the second anniversary of her death, January 1967, Nemiroff coordinated readings by sixty theater professionals of excerpts from Lorraine's diaries, correspondence, and plays for a two-hour radio broadcast, "Lorraine Hansberry in Her Own Words." The following year, a play titled *To Be Young, Gifted and Black* ran at the Cherry Lane Theatre in Greenwich Village, using many of the same materials. The script became the source for the "informal autobiography" *To Be Young, Gifted and Black: Lorraine Hansberry in Her Own Words*, edited by Nemiroff and published after the play closed.

By the end of the 1960s, *A Raisin in the Sun* was in danger of becoming a cultural mile marker left behind. But Nemiroff would not let Lorraine be lost. From her papers, he retrieved a draft of *Les Blancs*, the first major play by a black American to treat colonialism in Africa. He went at it with a red pencil: "Act 1, sc. 3 cut and edit, combine with original . . . Act 2, sc. 2, rework completely. . . . Act 2, sc. 4, vastly condense."[3] He wrote his own dialogue, he said, "to bridge gaps, deepen relationships or tighten the drama along the lines we had explored together."[4]

When *Les Blancs* premiered at Broadway's Longacre Theatre in 1970, reviewers dismissed it as "a preachy play, a sermon play," and "a cliché." It closed after forty performances. Two years later, Nemiroff published *Les Blancs: The Last Collected Plays of Lorraine Hansberry*, which included *The Drinking Gourd*, Hansberry's never-produced play for television about slavery, and *What Use Are Flowers?* about the world after a nuclear war.

In 1974, the musical *Raisin* ran for nineteen months on Broadway, the longest show of the season—with music by Judd Woldin, lyrics by Robert Brittan, and book by Robert Nemiroff and Charlotte Zaltzberg. It was nominated for nine Tony awards and won the award for Best Musical.

Jamaican American poet June Jordan challenged Nemiroff to explain the extent to which he was coauthor of *The Sign in Sidney Brustein's Window*, written when Hansberry was ill, and of the posthumous *Les Blancs*. He replied, "I am *not*—as you seem to be saying, perhaps without meaning to—*Lorraine*. I cannot speak for her, as much as I do admire her 'craft' generally—which is not to say invariably—and share her politics, I cannot claim responsibility for the plays you ascribe (or interpret me as ascribing) to 'her partial authorship.' These are, with the exception of my relatively minor contribution to *Les Blancs*, entirely *hers*."[5]

Nemiroff died in 1991. He devoted a good part of the last twenty-five years of his life to editing and publishing Hansberry's work. Whether he exceeded his mandate as her literary executor will be left to theater historians and scholars to determine.

What's certain in retrospect is that *A Raisin in the Sun* marked a new direction in American theater. Since the 1930s, black folk culture had been portrayed on the stage as a national, oppositional culture, a theater of leftist protest against oppression. Hansberry inspired a different type of honesty and intelligence in dramatizing the black experience. Like Alice Childress, she believed an emphasis on the real-life situations, conditions, and circumstances of black Americans should form the core value for black theater. The Youngers are convincing because their authenticity is unforced and unself-conscious. They use black vernacular because it is natural; they speak intimately to one another. The plot is driven by their character, instead of being bent to represent a political agenda. The play's popularity banished stereotypes, and the black playwrights, actors, and directors whom it influenced became part of the coming revolution in black consciousness.

A Raisin in the Sun also became something to push off from. The Black Arts Movement, the loci of which were Douglas Turner Ward's Negro Ensemble Company, in downtown New York, and the New Lafayette Theatre, in Harlem, introduced new aesthetics in black theater. Unlike Hansberry, these playwrights use symbolism, mythology, critique, and iconology that deliberately keeps white audiences at a distance. Instead of a protagonist, the black community itself becomes a character, the point being that the artist should not be alienated from his people. Street Sounds, a play by Ed Bullins for the New Lafayette Theatre, presents a succession of monologues by forty different characters on a Harlem street, who speak of liberation and self-determination. Ntozake Shange's For Colored Girls Who Have Considered Suicide / When the Rainbow Is Enuf is a feminist, antiracist "choreopoem" combining dance, music, and a series of twenty poetic monologues voiced by seven young black women. August Wilson later found a middle ground to create dramas about blackness in the realistic vein of Hansberry.

Today, the National Theater lists A Raisin in the Sun as one of the one hundred most significant works of the twentieth century. At almost any time of the year, a professional theater company is presenting the dreams of the Younger family. Sixteen million students read the play as part of the required curriculum at twenty thousand high schools in forty-three states using the federal Common Core Standards. Audiences around the world, on every continent, have seen A Raisin in the Sun acted in thirty languages.

Notes

Chapter 1: Infant of the Spring

1. James Baldwin, "Sweet Lorraine," *Esquire*, November 1, 1969, p. 139.
2. Samuel G. Freedman, "Yale Marking 25th Anniversary of 'Raisin in the Sun,'" *New York Times*, November 1, 1983, p. C-13.
3. Lorraine Hansberry [hereafter "LH"], "On Summer," *Playbill*, June 27, 1960 [hereafter "LH, 'On Summer,' in *Playbill*].
4. P. Preston Reynolds, "Professional and Hospital Discrimination and the US Court of Appeals Fourth Circuit 1956–1967," *American Journal of Public Health* 94, no. 5 (2004): 710–20.
5. Cook County Clerk, *Cook County Clerk Genealogy Records*, Cook County Clerk's Office, Chicago: Cook County Clerk, file number 6021383.
6. Rosetta James, *A Raisin in the Sun Notes* (Lincoln, NE: CliffsNotes, 1992), 2.
7. F. A. McGinnis, "Education and the Negro: An Address Delivered before the Sen Mer Rekh Honor Society," Wilberforce University, *The Boule Journal* (May 1938). The Sigma Pi Phi Fraternity was founded in Philadelphia, Pennsylvania, in 1904 and often referred to as the "Grand Boule," meaning "council of noblemen."
8. LH remarks, "The Black Revolution and the White Backlash," forum at Town Hall, sponsored by the Association of Artists for Freedom, New York City, June 15, 1964.
9. Robert Nemiroff, "From These Roots: Lorraine Hansberry and the South," *Southern Exposure* (September/October 1984): 33.
10. Amite County, MS, Marriage Book, no. 15, p. 476.
11. Leah Wright Rigueur, *The Loneliness of the Black Republican: Pragmatic Politics and the Pursuit of Power* (Princeton, NJ: Princeton University Press, 2014), 9.
12. Dolan Hubbard, ed., *The Collected Works of Langston Hughes*, vol. 4: *The Novels: Not without Laughter and Tambourines to Glory* (Columbia: University of Missouri Press, 2001), 194–95.
13. LH, "We Are of the Same Sidewalks," foreword to gallery brochure, Charles White exhibit, ACA Gallery (1961), reprinted in "Lorraine Hansberry: Art of Thunder, Vision of Light," *Freedomways* 20 (Winter 1980): 198.
14. Why certain blocks and streets in the city gradually turned into spaces that were Catholic and not Jewish, Italian and not Mexican, generally resulted from certain gravities acting on newcomers' choices about where to live. Employment was important. Neighborhoods abutting industrial zones were prevailingly made up of Irish, Italian, Polish, Lithuanian, and Yugoslav immigrants. Germans and Scandinavians found work in the warehouses, shops, and breweries of the Near North Side. Communities thickened because of other elements in the soup,

too: languages spoken, churches serving certain denominations, the location of settlement houses, and so on, which created, on sociologists' colored maps, a mosaic of little worlds. Consequently, there's a loss of social capital when people who are different move into ethnic neighborhoods. As the number of congregants at the parish church declines (or the number of kosher delis available, for that matter), residents will feel uneasy about diversity—just as gentrification riles residents of black neighborhoods. See Jonathan Haidt, *The Righteous Mind: Why Good People Are Divided by Politics and Religion* (New York: Random House, 2012), 360–61.

15. The plantation analogy isn't far-fetched. From the 1930s to the 1950s, the Bronx Slave Market in New York City was where black women waited to be hired by white women to clean house for the day. Sometimes, they were sent home with no pay because the mistress claimed to be dissatisfied. See Ella Baker and Marvel Cooke, "The Bronx Slave Market," *The Crisis* 42, November 1935, p. 330.

16. "Make New Sounds: Studs Terkel Interviews Lorraine Hansberry," radio interview, WFMT Radio, Chicago, May 12, 1959, transcript reprinted in *American Theater* (November 1984): 6 [hereafter "Make New Sounds"].

17. Wallace D. Best, *Passionately Human, No Less Divine: Religion and Culture in Black Chicago, 1915–1952* (Princeton, NJ: Princeton University Press, 2007), 37; Craig R. Prentiss, *Staging Faith: Religion and African American Theater from the Harlem Renaissance to World War II* (New York: New York University Press, 2013), 15; "Overstepping the Bounds," *Chicago Defender*, August 4, 1917, p. 12; Ben Baker, "A Few Do and Don'ts," *Chicago Defender*, July 13, 1918, p. 16. The theme of collective uplift touched even the youngest members of the community. The children of Bronzeville were better school attenders in elementary and high school and had higher rates of graduation than those living in Back of the Yards, a predominantly Polish and Lithuanian community on the southwest border of Bronzeville. Paul Street, "The 'Best Union Members': Class, Race, Culture, and Black Worker Militancy in Chicago's Stockyards during the 1930s," *Journal of American Ethnic History* 20, no. 1 (Fall 2000): 34.

18. Hansberry wrote "African" in the space for "race" on his draft registration card in 1917, perhaps out of deference to his father, the classical historian. But as he rose in the world, he left this identification behind.

19. "R.W. Hunter & Co., Bankers and Brokers," *Chicago Defender*, November 2, 1918, p. 11.

20. Display advertisement, *Chicago Defender*, July 20, 1918, p. 10.

21. Anne Cheney, *Lorraine Hansberry* (Boston: Twayne, 1984), 2n4.

22. Cheney, *Lorraine Hansberry*, relies on Mamie Hansberry Mitchell, who said in an interview that her grandfather the Reverend Perry became a bishop of the African Methodist Episcopal Church. Nothing corroborates this in histories of the AME Church available online at the Princeton Theological Seminary.

23. Society section, *The Nashville Globe*, April 12, 1918, p. 5. Even in Lorraine's lifetime, "acting black" was met with the jibe "You ain't ready for integration."

24. 1920 U.S. Census, Chicago, Ward 3, Cook County, Illinois, Roll T625_313, 9A. "All the Dark and Beautiful Warriors," *Village Voice*, August 16, 1983, p. 16.

25. Karen Grigsby Bates and Jason Fuller, "Red Summer in Chicago: 100 Years after the Race Riots," NPR/WBEZ radio, July 17, 2019.

26. Chicago Commission on Race Relations, *The Negro in Chicago: A Study of Race Relations and a Race Riot* (Chicago: University of Chicago Press, 1922), 666. The violence wasn't confined to the South Side. "A mob of white civilians, soldiers, and sailors, who had been chasing Negroes through the 'Loop' district for the previous two or three hours, beating and robbing them, and destroying property where Negroes were not found, entered one of Thompson's restaurants where [Paul] Hardwick was breakfasting. Another Negro, one King, was also in the restaurant. The mob set upon them, throwing food and dishes. Hardwick dodged into the street and King hid behind a dish counter, where he was wounded with a knife. Failing to catch Hardwick as he fled down Adams Street, one of the rioters stepped to the curb and fired

a revolver at him, bringing him down. Several of the crowd robbed the corpse" (Bates and Fuller, "Red Summer in Chicago," 666). See also James T. Farrell's often-anthologized short story "The Fastest Runner on Sixty-First Street," *Commentary*, June 1950.

27. Gwendolyn L. Shelton, "David Augustine Elihue Johnston," *The Encyclopedia of Arkansas*, online. The physician, Dr. L. H. Johnston, Lorraine's uncle, was married to her mother's sister Zelia A. Perry. The Elaine Massacre was by far the deadliest racial confrontation in Arkansas history and possibly the bloodiest racial conflict in the history of the United States. It began as a protest by black sharecroppers demanding better payments for their cotton crops.

28. LH to Kenneth Merryman, April 27, 1962, box 57, file 7, LH Papers, Schomburg Center for Research in Black Culture (SCH). Also, in LH, *To Be Young, Gifted and Black: Lorraine Hansberry in Her Own Words*, adapted by Robert Nemiroff, with an introduction by James Baldwin (New York: Vintage Books, 1995), 213–14.

29. Christopher Robert Reed, *The Rise of Chicago's Black Metropolis, 1920–1929* (Urbana: University of Illinois Press, 2011), 91–92.

30. "Creditors' Wand Changes Banker into Bankrupt," *Chicago Tribune*, December 20, 1919, p. 10. White-owned newspapers routinely mocked the ambitions and misfortunes of blacks.

31. "Neighborhood Pride," *Chicago Defender*, September 29, 1923.

32. "The Opening of the Binga State Bank," *Broad Ax*, December 22, 1922, p. 12; Will Cooley, "Moving on Out: Black Pioneering in Chicago, 1915–1950," *Journal of Urban History* 36, no. 4 (July 2010): 166n139; Lynne Feldman and John N. Ingham, eds., *African-American Business Leaders: A Biographical Dictionary* (Westport, CT: Greenwood Press, 1994), 78.

33. Mamie Hansberry Mitchell, Lorraine's elder sister, quoted in Cheney, *Lorraine Hansberry*, 2.

34. Ida Mae Cress: "Our family lived in a nice, large apartment, but we were forced to move out of it so they could cut it up and make smaller kitchenettes out of it, and that also made it harder for people like us to find a regular-sized apartment because the landlords could make so much more money by renting out all those smaller units. And one of the people who made good money on that type of housing was a man by the name of Carl Hansberry" (Timuel D. Black Jr., *Bridges of Memory: Chicago's First Wave of Black Migration* [Evanston, IL: Northwestern University Press, 2003], 80, 281).

Chapter 2: "The King of the Kitchenettes"

1. Mamie quoted in Pat McKissack and Frederick McKissack, *Young, Black, and Determined: A Biography of Lorraine Hansberry* (New York: Holiday House, 1998), 6.

2. St. Clair Drake and Horace R. Cayton, *Black Metropolis: A Study of Negro Life in a Northern City* (New York: Harcourt, Brace and Company, 1945), 576.

3. Wendy Plotkin, "Kitchenettes," in Encyclopedia of Chicago, Chicago Historical Society, 2004, http://www.encyclopedia.chicagohistory.org/pages/692.html; Drake and Cayton, *Black Metropolis*, 576–77.

4. Cheney, *Lorraine Hansberry*, 2.

5. Cooley, "Moving on Out," 488n17.

6. Cooley, "Moving on Out," 488n18.

7. Drake and Cayton, *Black Metropolis*, 659–60; Black, *Bridges of Memory*, 80.

8. Horace Cayton, "Negro Housing in Chicago," *Social Action* 6, no. 4 (April 1940).

9. *Bulletin of the Chicago Housing Authority*, March 1941, p. 3.

10. Richard Wright, *12 Million Black Voices* (New York: Viking Press, 1941), 105–6, 113, 116, 123, 124. See note 4: Wright's address is on the cover of the materials he prepared for the Illinois Writers' Project. In *Native Son*, his protagonist, Bigger Thomas, lives at 3721 Indiana Avenue.

11. Edith Abbot and Sophonisba P. Breckinridge, *The Tenements of Chicago, 1908–1935* (Chicago: University of Chicago Press, 1936), 126, 136–37.

12. Thomas Sancton quoted in Cheryl Greenberg, *Or Does It Explode? Black Harlem in the Great Depression* (New York: Oxford University Press, 1991), 185; David McBride, *From TB*

to AIDS: Epidemics among Urban Blacks Since 1900 (Albany: State University of New York Press, 1991), 36–37; Cooley, "Moving on Out," 490n30.

13. Fitchett's dissertation, "The Free Negro in Charleston, South Carolina," was almost finished in 1935. Interfering with his research was the policy of Charleston Library Society, which allowed only whites to use its collection. See Robert Harris Jr., "Committee on Negro Studies, 1941–1950," *Journal of Black Studies* 12, no. 3 (March 1982): 315.

14. Like the best black humanists of his day, Leo Hansberry had been adding to his education by taking a semester here and there at a northern university. As yet, there were no degree programs in African or black American studies. Cobbling together coursework that would satisfy college examiners for a graduate degree took a long time. Lawrence P. Jackson, *The Indignant Generation: A Narrative History of African American Writers and Critics, 1934–1960* (Princeton, NJ: Princeton University Press, 2011), 148.

15. "Alpha Group Hears Talk on Ethiopia," *Chicago Defender*, September 1, 1935, p. 23; "Good Shepherd to Hear Prof's Ethiopia Talk," *Chicago Defender*, September 7, 1935, p. 12.

16. Cheney, *Lorraine Hansberry*, 19.

17. Harold R. Isaacs, "Five Writers and Their African Ancestors, Part II," *Phylon* 21, no. 4 (1960): 333.

18. Isaacs, "Five Writers and Their African Ancestors, Part II," 333.

19. LH, *To Be Young, Gifted and Black*, 64.

20. Worth Kamili Hayes, *Schools of Our Own: Chicago's Golden Age of Black Private Education* (Evanston, IL: Northwestern University Press, 2019), 21.

21. Judith E. Smith, *Visions of Belonging: Family Stories, Popular Culture, and Postwar Democracy, 1940–1960* (New York: Columbia University Press, 2004), 286; "Millions Spent in Betterments for West Side," *Chicago Tribune*, August 29, 1937, p. 37. The overcrowding and double shifts impaired instruction: "I was given during the grade school years one-half of the amount of education prescribed for each child by the Board of Education of my city. This was so because the children of the Chicago ghetto were jammed into a segregated school system. To this day, I do not add, subtract, or multiply with ease. Our teachers, devoted and indifferent alike, had to sacrifice something to make that system work at all, and in my case it was arithmetic which got put aside most often" (LH, "The Scars of the Ghetto," *Monthly Review*, February 1965).

22. Lillian Ross, "How Lorraine Hansberry Wrote 'A Raisin in the Sun,'" *The New Yorker*, May 9, 1959.

23. LH, *To Be Young, Gifted and Black*, 64.

24. LH, *To Be Young, Gifted and Black*, 39.

25. LH, *To Be Young, Gifted and Black*, 68.

26. As further evidence that she was different from the rest of her classmates, she suspected, in retrospect, that she was the only child in her class who didn't come from a family receiving some form of federal assistance during the Great Depression of the 1930s. But it's hard not to hear a note of pride in this; her Republican parents certainly would have been proud. See LH, *To Be Young, Gifted and Black*, 36. Re: "maggot," see Robert Nemiroff interview of Mamie Hansberry Mitchell, box 71, file 3, n.d., p. 14, LH Papers, SCH [hereafter "Nemiroff interview of Mamie Hansberry Mitchell"]. Mamie recalled Lorraine being accused of plagiarism by a teacher who insinuated that a black child couldn't have written anything that coherent.

27. LH, *To Be Young, Gifted and Black*, 65–66.

28. LH, *To Be Young, Gifted and Black*, 48–49; Margaret B. Wilkerson, "Excavating Our History: The Importance of Biographies of Women of Color," *Black American Literature Forum* 24, no. 1 (Spring 1990): 77–78; Letter from LH to Madrue Wright (the dance teacher), August 2, 1959, box 2, file 10, LH Papers, SCH. Lorraine said her mother cherished "The Little Mama Doll" dress and kept it for years. See letter from Madrue Wright to Nemiroff, circa 1984, box 70, files 4-5, LH Papers, SCH.

29. Cheney, *Lorraine Hansberry*, 4.

30. LH, "All the Dark and Beautiful Warriors," *Village Voice*, August 16, 1983, p. 13.

31. LH, *To Be Young, Gifted and Black*, 48–49.

32. LH, *To Be Young, Gifted and Black*, 20.

33. LH, *To Be Young, Gifted and Black*, 19.

34. "Our studies confirmed the general impression that the rent paid by Negroes was appreciably higher than that paid by people of any other group. Cases were found of the actual doubling of rents when a building was given over to Negro tenants. . . . [T]he immigrant, for a smaller amount of money, may live in a better house than a Negro" (Abbot and Breckinridge, *The Tenements of Chicago, 1908–1935*, 124–25).

35. "African Americans, like other groups, have always tried to translate upward class mobility into geographic mobility" (Mary Pattillo-McCoy, *Black Picket Fences: Privilege and Peril among the Black Middle Class* [Chicago: University of Chicago Press, 1999], 23). "The Negro invaders of the subdivisions during the Depression seem to have been a culturally and economically advantaged group. Of the six whose names are given as among the first to move in, two had the title of 'Dr.,' one was an attorney" (Frederick Burgess Lindstrom, "The Negro Invasion of the Washington Park Subdivision" [master's thesis, University of Chicago, 1941], 37).

36. James Nelson Simms, *Simms' Blue Book and National Negro Business and Professional Directory* (Chicago: James N. Simms, 1923); Cooley, "Moving on Out," 487.

37. Harold I. Kahen, "Validity of Anti-Negro Restrictive Covenants: A Reconsideration of the Problem," *The University of Chicago Law Review* 12, no. 2 (February 1945): 206n39.

38. "Realtor Tells His Role in Covenant Case," *Chicago Defender*, November 23, 1940, p. 9.

39. Arnold R. Hirsch, "Restrictive Covenants," Encyclopedia of Chicago, http://www.encyclopedia .chicagohistory.org/pages/1067.html; "Iron Ring in Housing," *The Crisis* 47, no. 2, July 1940, p. 205.

40. Covenants created business for lawyers, bankers, and real estate agents, and a little pocket money for someone like Mr. Sheedy, for instance, who was paid for getting signatures. He received a call one morning from a property association member, Mr. Nathan. "I got a kike here who will sign. Come on over." Sheedy went to an address where Nathan was waiting with an older couple named Katz who spoke broken English. Faced with the reality that the area was poor and already ethnically mixed, the association was focused on preventing Negroes from moving in. While Nathan and Sheedy stood by, the Katzes conversed in Yiddish. Finally, they agreed to sign. It meant Sheedy would get 50 to 75 percent of their first year's dues as new members of the association. In return, the association promised to fight for the Katz family as homeowners—in court, if necessary. Each covenant was notarized and filed with the Recorder of Deeds. If any Negroes moved into the area, they were reported, a suit was filed against their occupancy, and an injunction obtained. See University of Virginia, Papers of the NAACP, Part 12: "The Campaign against Residential Segregation, 1914–1955," Series C: The Midwest.

41. Kahen, "Validity of Anti-Negro Restrictive Covenants," 198–213; Hirsch, "Restrictive Covenants"; Wendy Plotkin, "Deeds of Mistrust: Race, Housing, and Restrictive Covenants in Chicago, 1900–1953" (PhD diss., University of Illinois, 1999). False signatures representing churches and corporations were sometimes added to give a petition additional credibility, or to make it appear that a large majority in the neighborhood or community had signed.

42. "Realtor Tells His Role in Covenant Case," 9. Chicago Commission on Race Relations, *The Negro in Chicago*, 134; Michael Jones-Correa, "The Origins and Diffusion of Racial Restrictive Covenants," *Political Science Quarterly* 115, no. 4 (Winter 2000–2001): 562; Kenneth T. Jackson, *The Ku Klux Klan in the City, 1915–1930* (New York: Oxford University Press, 1967), 95.

43. Ron Grossman, "Chief of City's 1st Black-Owned Bank Emboldened Community," *Chicago Tribune*, December 2, 2018, p. 27.

44. Chicago Commission on Race Relations, *The Negro in Chicago*, 127–28.

45. Norris Vitchek, as told to Alfred Balk, "Confessions of a Block-Buster," *The Saturday Evening Post*, July 1962, pp. 15–19.

46. "The Hansberrys of Chicago: They Join Business Acumen with Social Vision," *The Crisis*, April 1941, p. 106.

47. Lindstrom, "The Negro Invasion," 24.

48. *Hansberry v. Lee*, 372 Ill. 369, 374, 24 N.E. 2d 37, 39–40 (1939).

49. Truman K. Gibson Jr. and Steve Huntley, *Knocking Down Barriers: My Fight for Black America* (Evanston, IL: Northwestern University Press, 2005), 44–48. Supreme Liberty Life was also eager to break into a housing market that would attract middle-class blacks who could pay their mortgages, according to Robert C. Puth—a case of prudent business going hand in hand with social good. The default rate by borrowers and life insurance holders after the crash of 1929 had driven the company into near bankruptcy in 1933. See Robert C. Puth, "Supreme Life: The History of a Negro Life Insurance Company," *The Business History Review* 43, no. 1 (Spring 1969): 13.

50. Gibson and Huntley, *Knocking Down Barriers*, 44–48. The Chicago community activist Bennett Johnson claims that "the two most important and active organizations in Chicago's black community in the early 1930s were the policy racket and the Communist Party, the former taking care of black entrepreneurs and the latter taking care of the people who were buying the numbers" (Mary Helen Washington, *The Other Blacklist: The African American Literary and Cultural Left of the 1950s*, ebook [New York: Columbia University Press, 2015]).

51. Gibson and Huntley, *Knocking Down Barriers*, 48.

Chapter 3: Stay Where You Belong

1. Anna M. Lee et al. vs. Paul [*sic*] A. Hansberry et al., Gen. no. 37C 6804, "Complaint to Enforce Restrictive Agreement Injunction and Other Relief," State of Illinois, Circuit Court of Cook County.

2. Box 60, file 15, LH Papers, SCH.

3. Transcript of Catherine Scheader's interview of Robert Nemiroff, n.d., for her book *They Found a Way: Lorraine Hansberry* (Chicago: Children's Press, 1978), box 67, file 1, Robert Nemiroff Biographical Information in LH Papers, SCH, 26 [hereafter "Scheader interview of Nemiroff"].

4. E. B. White, "Talk of the Town," interview with Lorraine Hansberry, *The New Yorker*, May 9, 1959, p. 35; C. Francis Stradford, Carl's attorney, graduated from Columbia Law School at the age of twenty and later cofounded the National Bar Association and the Cook County Bar Association as alternatives for black lawyers who, at that time, were excluded from membership in the American and Chicago Bar Associations. In 1963, his daughter, Jewel Stradford Lafontant-Mankarious, was the first black woman to argue a case before the U.S. Supreme Court. She was appointed vice chairman of the U.S. Advisory Commission on International, Educational and Cultural Affairs in 1969; representative to the General Assembly of the United Nations in 1972; and she became the first female deputy solicitor general in 1973.

5. Masco Young, a classmate of the older Hansberrys, remembers that they "drove to high school and college in Cadillacs, Buicks and Lincolns when most of us didn't even own bikes" (Masco Young, "Another Winner Added to Patti's Latest Album," *Philadelphia Daily News*, December 5, 1985, p. 84).

6. Dempsey J. Travis, *An Autobiography of Black Chicago* (Chicago: Urban Research Institute Press, 1981), 232.

7. McKissack and McKissack, *Young, Black, and Determined*, 6.

8. Nemiroff interview of Mamie Hansberry Mitchell, 17.

9. Marie J. Kuda, "Hansberry's A Raisin in the Sun: Chicago Tale Airs Nationally," *Windy City Times*, March 1, 2008.

10. Catherine Scheader's interview of Mamie Hansberry Mitchell, July 13, 1976, footnoted in *Lorraine Hansberry: Playwright and Voice of Justice*, 21; Hugh S. Gardner, "Residential 'War'

on in Chicago," *Pittsburgh Courier*, July 3, 1937, p. 7; LH, *Young, Gifted and Black*, 51; A. C. MacNeal, "Southsiders to Fight Residential Segregation," *Chicago Bee*, n.d.

11. Box 60, file 15, Lorraine Hansberry's notes for a short story, SCH.

12. LH's notes, SCH.

13. Cheney, *Lorraine Hansberry*, 3.

14. "Vandals Attack Realtor Who Bought House in White District," *Pittsburgh Courier*, June 17, 1937, p. 1.

15. Cooley, "Moving on Out," 494.

16. Lindstrom, "The Negro Invasion," 24; Allen R. Kamp, "The History Behind *Hansberry v. Lee*," *University of California, Davis Law Review* 20, no. 481 (1987): 486. With guidance from the University of Chicago, the Woodlawn Property Owners Association had successfully lobbied the Chicago Board of Education to change the attendance boundaries so as to remove practically all black children from Woodlawn schools. Many university faculty members resided in Woodlawn and Hyde Park. In the Englewood community, two miles west of Woodlawn, a member of the Chicago Real Estate Board informed members of the property association that while "Negroes had to live somewhere," they were "occupying three times as much territory as they needed" on the South Side. If they had to go anywhere, he suggested, they should go in the "right direction": to the stockyards. See Papers of the NAACP, Part 12: "The Campaign against Residential Segregation, 1914–1955," Series C: The Midwest, University of Virginia; Hayes, *Schools of Our Own*, 20n20.

17. The red-haired girl appears as a handwritten note under LH's memory of the brick story, box 1, file 5.

18. In 1941, with the support of the Chicago Board of Education and the Phi Delta Kappa Sorority, Madeline Stratton Morris began developing the "Supplementary Units for a Course in Social Studies." Morris's curriculum was the first adopted by a major school system in the United States to emphasize black contributions to American history. She eventually taught at A. O. Sexton Elementary, but too late for Hansberry.

19. Isaacs, "Five Writers and Their African Ancestors, Part II," 335. The Chicago artist Charles White, who attended Englewood High School a few years before Lorraine, found that his teachers "never mentioned a Negro in history." Like Lorraine, he began reading independently to discover himself. In Alain Locke's *The New Negro* (1925), for instance, White encountered "a new world of facts and ideas in diametric opposition to what was being taught in the classrooms and textbooks." He remembered being "so affected by the grotesque perversions of Negro culture, by the ridicule heaped upon everything Negro, that even . . . a touch of dialect, or the beautiful music of the spirituals, made us faintly ashamed" (Charles White, "Path of a Negro Artist," *Masses and Mainstream* [April 1955]: 35–36).

20. Isaacs, "Five Writers and Their African Ancestors, Part II," 334.

21. Isaacs, "Five Writers and Their African Ancestors, Part II," 334.

22. Mamie Mitchell Hansberry, quoted in Scheader, *They Found a Way*, 20.

23. "Feinberg Decision Shocks Chicago," *Pittsburgh Courier*, October 23, 1937, p. 2.

24. "Organize to Wipe Out Nation-Wide Restricted Areas," *Pittsburgh Courier*, July 31, 1937, p. 3. The NAACP was also strongly behind the passage of the Wagner-Steagall Act of 1937, also called the Public Housing Act, which for many years was the nation's prime affordable housing effort. Walter White and the leadership didn't rely only on eliminating covenants to improve living conditions.

25. Nemiroff interview of Mamie Mitchell Hansberry.

26. Gibson and Huntley, *Knocking Down Barriers*, 44.

27. There was a jeering mob when they left, according to Lucille Banta. But this writer also claims the Hansberrys had "all their possessions piled in a truck," which doesn't match Mamie's description of the way they left, or seem characteristic of the appearance-conscious Hansberrys. See Lucille Banta, "Lorraine Hansberry," *American Dialogue* 2 (1965): 25–27.

28. W. E. B. Du Bois, "Hopkinsville, Chicago and Idlewild," *The Crisis* 21–22, January 1, 1920, p. 158; Robert F. Williams (1925–1996), militant civil rights leader and author of *Negroes with Guns*, spent the last years of his life in the nearby town of Baldwin, in exile from his hometown of Monroe, North Carolina.

29. LH, "On Summer," in *Playbill*.

30. LH, "On Summer," in *Playbill*.

31. "The Hansborough-Hansbrough Family," website, administered by Michael Flanagan, http://flanaganfamily.net.

32. Frederick Douglass, *My Bondage and Freedom* (London: Partridge and Oakey, 1855), 1.

33. J. W. Hansborough, *History and Genealogy of the Hansborough-Hansbrough Family with Data on the Hanbury, Garrard, Lash, Devous, Davis, Wathen, and Bell Families* (privately printed, 1981).

34. Richard Holcombe Kilbourne Jr., *Debt, Investment, Slaves: Credit Relations in East Feliciana Parish, Louisiana, 1825–1885* (Tuscaloosa: University of Alabama Press, 1995). Kilbourne says the Taylors averaged about one hundred slaves per sale in Clinton in the 1850s, according to parish conveyance records (Kilbourne, "Re: Bills of Conveyance," email, March 3, 2019).

35. V. Elaine Thompson, *Clinton, Louisiana: Society, Politics, and Race Relations in a Nineteenth-Century Small Town*, ebook (Lafayette: University of Louisiana at Lafayette, 2014).

36. The figure "$1800" is repeated in handwritten notes about Hansberry, but there's no bill of conveyance in East Feliciana parish about him (Samuel H. Williamson and Louis Cain, "Measuring Slavery in 2016 Dollars," Measuring Worth, 2019, https://www.measuringworth.com/slavery.php).

37. Kilbourne explains the practice of taking mortgages on human beings as property. The Civil War ruined planters who had speculated on slaves as assets. They wrote angry letters to the federal government accusing Congress of depriving them of their property without compensation.

38. The papers of Alton Kelly, private collection. I am indebted to Claudette Smith-Brown of Baton Rouge, Louisiana, for sharing with me materials gathered by the late Mr. Kelly. See also Susan Sinott, *Lorraine Hansberry: Award-Winning Playwright and Civil Rights Activist* (Newburyport, MA: Conari Press, 1991), 10.

39. Kilbourne, *Debt, Investment, Slaves*, 143.

40. Kwame Wes Alford, "Professor William Hansberry's Biographer to Moderate a Panel at the OAU/AU Celebration," Little Ethiopia.org.

41. Commissioner Woolfley was a naturalized Swiss immigrant. Unlike native-born Hansberry, he had been granted the guarantees and privileges of American citizenship quite easily. As a free white male of good character, when he arrived in the United States, he had declared before a court clerk, as required, his intention to become a citizen; and second, he had provided a modicum of personal information (birthplace, age, nation of allegiance, and country of emigration). After residing in the United States for five years, he was given the full protections of the Constitution as a citizen, including the right to vote. Information about F(rancis) A(ugustus) Woolfley is in the Civil War diary kept by George G. Thwing (January–November 1862), self-titled "A Memorandum of Butler's Expedition on the Mississippi River!! July 12th /62."

42. "Sunshine School," *Nashville Globe*, August 16, 1918, p. 7.

43. W. E. B. Du Bois, *The Autobiography of W. E. B. Du Bois: A Soliloquy on Viewing My Life from the Last Decade of Its First Century* (New York: International Publishers, 1968), 114.

44. Du Bois, *Autobiography*.

45. Du Bois, *Autobiography*.

46. Unpublished memoir quoted in Cheney, *Lorraine Hansberry*, 9.

47. "And Bird Blowin' Back: I Am!" in box 57, file 1, LH Papers, SCH. Chicago poet Gwendolyn Brooks describes a drive like this in her poem, "Beverly Hills, Chicago."

48. Box 2, file 1, LH Papers, SCH.

49. McKissack and McKissack, *Young, Black, and Determined*, 121.

50. Cheney interview of Mamie Hansberry Mitchell, 9.

51. Gibson and Huntley, *Knocking Down Barriers*, 48.

52. Douglas B. Chambers, ed., "Richard Wright, Citizen of the World: A Centenary Celebration," *The Southern Quarterly* 46, no. 2 (Winter 2009): 9–39. Wright contributed descriptions of the Bronzeville neighborhood in 1936 to the Federal Writers' Project. In *American Hunger*, he ridiculed Negro Communists in Washington Park because, he said, they spoke with an English accent, like their political counterparts at Speakers' Corner in London's Hyde Park.

53. Randi Storch, *Red Chicago: American Communism at Its Grassroots, 1928–35* (Urbana: University of Illinois Press, 2008), 99–100, 114.

54. LH, *To Be Young, Gifted and Black*, 21.

55. Gibson and Huntley, *Knocking Down Barriers*, 45.

56. Editorial in the *Pulse*, reprinted in "Jim Crow in Chicago," *Chicago Defender*, November 11, 1939, p. 15.

57. "Open Letter of Carl A. Hansberry: Setting Forth Program and Purposes of His Candidacy for Congress," Deborah Holton Papers, Woodson Regional Library, Vivian G. Harsh Research Collection of Afro-American History and Literature, CPL.

58. "Hopes of GOP for Seats in Congress Rise," *Chicago Tribune*, March 24, 1940, 106. He "was hurt," said Mamie Hansberry Mitchell, "but we never realized how much until it was too late" (McKissack and McKissack, *Young, Black, and Determined*, 27).

59. "Iron Ring in Housing," 205, 210.

60. Gibson and Huntley, *Knocking Down Barriers*, 50.

61. "The Hansberry Case," *Chicago Defender*, November 30, 1940, 14. The proponents of racism and institutionalized discrimination doubled down after the Hansberry decision. The Chicago Title and Trust Company, the city's major land deed repository, owned by George F. Harding, a slumlord and benefactor of the Art Institute of Chicago, refused to stop issuing titles with restrictive covenants included. The University of Chicago continued to retain the white-shoe law firm representing Harding to preserve around its campus a white residential buffer. Realtors maneuvered blacks away from middle-class neighborhoods that had better housing, to keep those property values stable.

62. LH, *To Be Young, Gifted and Black*, 7; McKissack and McKissack, *Young, Black, and Determined*, 31.

63. "The Hansberrys of Chicago," 106.

64. Cooley, "Moving on Out," 494n69.

65. Thomas Schelling, "Micromotives and Macrobehavior," chapter 4 in *Sorting and Mixing: Race and Sex* (New York: W. W. Norton, 1978), 137–62. Regarding affiliation, a 2014 study found that neighborhoods in Chicago that are "more black"—greater than 40 percent—tend not to gentrify. See Jackelyn Hwang and Robert J. Sampson, "Divergent Pathways of Gentrification: Racial Inequality and the Social Order of Renewal in Chicago Neighborhoods," *American Sociological Review* 79, no. 4 (2014): 726–51. "This is really a sobering finding," Hwang, the paper's lead author, said. "Even in neighborhoods that are showing change, even when we control for things like crime, perception of disorder, and proximity to amenities, race still matters." On the other side of the coin, the year the study above was published, filmmaker Spike Lee gave a talk to an audience of art students at Brooklyn's Pratt Institute, during which he inveighed against "white New Yorkers" who were changing the culture of Fort Greene in Brooklyn, where he was raised.

66. The FHA relied on a property grading system devised by the appraisal industry, which believed that a mixing of the races would lead to a decline in property values. Often, the FHA would insure home loans for black applicants only if they built or bought in black neighborhoods, where there was no "blight" yet. Unable to purchase homes in better areas destined to appreciate in value, or to obtain loans for property upgrades, black Americans watched their wealth—a home is a person's single biggest investment—be destroyed. Because wealth

is passed on from parents to children, black homeowners of the mid-twentieth century had much less than whites to hand down, even after the tremendous postwar boom times of the 1950s, a setback in financial progress still evident today. See Beryl Satter, *Family Properties: How the Struggle over Race and Real Estate Transformed Chicago and Urban America* (New York: Picador, 2010), 41–42.

67. "Housing Survey Reports on Seven Areas," *Chicago Tribune*, January 19, 1941. The survey was conducted by the Chicago Planning Commission.

68. The Hansberrys owned $250,000 worth of real estate. Hansberry Enterprises received a gross annual total of $100,000 ("The Hansberrys of Chicago"). For historical parallels to Woodlawn and the Hansberrys, see N. D. B. Connolly, *A World More Concrete: Real Estate and the Remaking of Jim Crow South Florida* (Chicago: University of Chicago Press, 2014).

69. Gibson and Huntley, *Knocking Down Barriers*, 51. "Rents in black areas ranged from fifteen percent to fifty percent higher than that paid by whites for similar accommodations, the Illinois Inter-racial Commission wrote in 1944. The difference was especially great, they added, in areas just beginning the process of racial succession" (Ta-Nehisi Coates, "The Ghetto, Public Policy, and the Jewish Exception," *The Atlantic*, February 28, 2013).

Chapter 4: American Princess

1. "Miss Freeman in Bow to Nashville Society," *Chicago Defender*, February 10, 1945, p. 15.

2. Cornel West has a very interesting analysis of American blacks and British cosmopolitanism as a phenomenon of "triple consciousness" in his first book, *Prophesy Deliverance! An Afro-American Revolutionary Christianity* (Philadelphia: Westminster Press, 1982).

3. "Miss Freeman in Bow to Nashville Society," 15.

4. "Miss Freeman in Bow to Nashville Society," 15.

5. Zelda J. Ormes, "Social Whirl," *Chicago Defender*, April 14, 1945, p. 14.

6. LH, "Origins of Character," Address to the American Academy of Psychotherapists on October 5, 1963, reprinted as "Playwriting: Creative Constructiveness," in Jules Barron and Renee Nell, eds., *Annals of Psychotherapy*, Monograph No. 8: *The Creative Use of the Unconscious by the Artist and the Psychotherapist* 5, no. 1 (1964): 14 [hereafter LH, "Origins of Character"]; "Love letters," in box 1, file 1, LH Papers, SCH.

7. LH to Edythe Anne Cohen, November 14, 1948, box 2, file 11, LH Papers, SCH.

8. "200 Students Leave Classes," *Decatur Daily Review*, September 27, 1945, p. 1.

9. LH, "All the Dark and Beautiful Warriors," 13–14. There was no fighting. The Englewood assistant superintendent told the striking students to take up their complaints with their parents and aldermen. The strike ended after a few days, when the students were threatened with suspension. As Hansberry writes later in a portion of the story never quoted, the black teenagers "had arrived as *allies*. Except nothing was happening. They might as well all go home. . . . They were disappointed with the strike."

10. See Margo Jefferson, *Negroland: A Memoir* (New York: Alfred A. Knopf, 2016), 163–64. Hansberry's upbringing was very similar to Jefferson's. Jefferson's father was head of pediatrics at Provident Hospital, where Hansberry was born.

11. Because of the parents' prominence in civic and political life, a fair number of Chicago's lesser-known mechanics in the urban panorama came through the Hansberry home as well: political favor seekers, party workers, ministers, deacons, and charity organizers.

12. Robert Nemiroff, "A Critical Background," in Lorraine Hansberry, *Les Blancs: The Collected Last Plays* (New York: Vintage Books, 1994), 27. Leo Hansberry befriended many African students, including Nnamdi Azikiwe, the first president of postcolonial Nigeria.

13. Sharon Fitzgerald, "Charles White in Person," *Freedomways* 20, no. 3 (Third Quarter 1980): 159.

14. Gwendolyn Cherry et al., eds., *Portraits in Color: The Lives of Colorful Negro Women* (New York: Pageant Press, 1962), 150. A legend persists that Lorraine "spent many evenings at the knee" of a "Marxist mentor" named Raymond Hansbrough, a steelworker and Communist

organizer known to the FBI. Hansbrough supposedly developed Lorraine's "perceptions of painful class differences into an appreciation of working-class racial resistance." A longtime Bronzeville resident recalled seeing Lorraine when she was eleven years old talking to Hansbrough, "whose progressive ideas," one historian claimed, "had helped to change her life!" (Lerone Bennett Jr. and Margaret G. Burroughs, in "A Lorraine Hansberry Rap," *Freedomways* 19, no. 4 [Fourth Quarter 1979]: 228); Smith, *Visions of Belonging*, 290; Margaret Wilkerson, "A Life in Theater and Higher Education," interview conducted by Nadine Wilmot, 2003–2004, Regional Oral History Office, Bancroft Library, University of California, Berkeley. It's inconceivable that the Hansberrys would expose her to the teachings of a Communist. Hansbrough's criticisms of the American system and capitalism contradicted everything Carl and Nannie Hansberry stood for. In fairness to Wilkerson, she temporized, "Hansbrough did not school her in the doctrinaire views of the Communist party but rather nurtured in her democratic ideas of freedom and social justice for all people and, especially, African Americans" (Margaret Wilkerson, "Political Radicalism and Artistic Innovation in the Works of Lorraine Hansberry," in *African American Performance and Theater History: A Critical Reader*, ed. Harry J. Elam Jr. and David Krasner [New York: Oxford University Press, 2001], 47).

15. Albert Shaw, "The Carolina Playmakers," in *American Review of Reviews* 60 (July–December 1919): 303.

16. Prentiss, *Staging Faith*, 38–41.

17. "Lorraine Hansberry Goes into B'Way Orbit with Socko 'Raisin in the Sun,'" *Pittsburgh Courier*, February 14, 1959, 23; "Make New Sounds."

18. "Lorraine Hansberry Goes into B'Way Orbit with Socko 'Raisin in the Sun,'" 45.

19. Nemiroff interview of Mamie Hansberry Mitchell, 15.

20. Nemiroff interview of Mamie Hansberry Mitchell, 15.

21. Jackson, *The Indignant Generation*, 98–99.

22. "NNPA Meet at Shiloh Baptist Here Sunday," *Indianapolis Recorder*, June 23, 1943, p. 2.

23. "Prize Winners (1st Division) in Essay Contest," *Pittsburgh Courier*, February 20, 1943, p. 6.

24. William H. Green, Daniel Gaines, Carl A. Hansberry, and Howard D. Geter (plaintiffs) . . . a dozen individuals, two supply companies, and the National Rig Company (defendants)— complaint to dissolve partnership and other equitable relief, April 15, 1941, National Archives at Chicago; "Liquid Gold Brings Grief to Men Who Found Illinois Wells," *Indianapolis Recorder*, November 22, 1941, pp. 1, 3.

25. McKissack and McKissack, *Young, Black, and Determined*, 30; Nemiroff interview of Mamie Hansberry Mitchell, 19.

26. Nemiroff interview of Mamie Hansberry Mitchell, 4.

27. LH quoted in Smith, *Visions of Belonging*, 288.

28. Nemiroff interview of Mamie Hansberry Mitchell, 5.

29. All three telegrams are in box 1, file 3, LH Papers, SCH.

30. On the day Burr Oak Cemetery was dedicated in 1927, local residents, with the assistance of police, drove away the first burial party. They returned with a deputy sheriff, delegated by the Republican state attorney's office, and succeeded in consecrating the cemetery. The body of Emmett Till is interred in Burr Oak.

31. LH, *To Be Young, Gifted and Black*, 48; LH, "Letter to the Editor," *New York Times*, April 23, 1964; Lloyd W. Brown, "Lorraine Hansberry as Ironist: A Reappraisal of 'A Raisin in the Sun,'" *Journal of Black Studies* 4 no. 3 (March 1974): 243–44; White, "Talk of the Town," 34.

Chapter 5: Entering into a Romance

1. LH, "All the Dark and Beautiful Warriors" (unpublished draft), 88, Deborah Holton Papers, unprocessed, CPL [hereafter "LH, 'All the Dark and Beautiful Warriors' (unpublished draft)"].

2. E. David Cronon and John W. Jenkins, *University of Wisconsin, Renewal to Revolution, 1945–1971*, vol. 4: *Renewal to Revolution* (Madison: University of Wisconsin Press, 1999), 18.

3. Leo Hansberry's teammate in defeating Fisk University, winning three rounds to zero, was Walter White, the future executive secretary of the NAACP. James Forman, later a spokesperson for the Student Nonviolent Coordinating Committee and the Black Panthers, was in Hansberry's homeroom, where students discussed current events every Friday, such as capital punishment, the United Nations, and an antilynching bill in Congress. Sometimes, he and Hansberry were on the same side of the question. Forman wrote, however, "Englewood High School—like all schools for ghetto children—did not have a curriculum suited to the needs of its students." Despite the racial connotation of "ghetto," two-thirds of the students in the late 1940s were ethnic Americans from middle- and lower-middle-class families. See James Forman, *The Making of Black Revolutionaries* (Seattle: University of Washington Press, 1997), 47.

4. "Chicago Heiress," *Our World*, April 1952.

5. LH, "On Summer," in Gerald Levin, ed., *Short Essays* (New York: Harcourt Brace Jovanovich, 1977), 52–55 [hereafter "LH, 'On Summer,' in Levin, ed."]; Mamie Hansberry quoted in McKissack and McKissack, *Young, Black, and Determined*, 31.

6. LH, "On Summer," in Levin, ed., 52–55; Mamie Hansberry, quoted in McKissack and McKissack, *Young, Black, and Determined*, 31.

7. Scheader interview of Nemiroff.

8. LH, "Mailbag: O'Casey-Hansberry" (letters to the editor), *New York Times*, June 28, 1959.

9. LH, "All the Dark and Beautiful Warriors" (unpublished draft), 90.

10. Cronon and Jenkins, *The University of Wisconsin: A History: 1945–1971*, vol. 4: *Renewal to Revolution*, 390. Giving enrolling students a list of approved housing was routine, as others have recounted about their experiences at Wisconsin during the postwar years, and not an indication, by itself, that Hansberry wasn't permitted to move into the dormitories, as some have alleged. Chinese student Cynthia Waiying Wu Wilcox arrived from California in September 1950: "The housing department secretary gave us a list of available houses near campus. Dormitories on campus were all filled at this late date" (*The Love of Lotus* [Redwood City, CA: Tyde House Books, 2007], 111–12). Wu Wilcox also moved into Langdon Manor.

11. The student who led the *Cardinal* protest was H. Jack Geiger, who later became president of Physicians for Human Rights (Geiger interview, Southern Oral History Program, Civil Rights History Project, National Museum of African American History and Culture and the Library of Congress, Smithsonian Institution, Washington, DC, March 16, 2013); "Greeks Can Lose Recognition: Board—Bias Clauses in Constitutions Could Be Basis for Action," *Daily Cardinal*, November 28, 1951.

12. Nemiroff interview of Mamie Hansberry Mitchell, 10.

13. JoAnn Beier, letter to Nemiroff, November 16, 1969, box 69, file 2, LH Papers, SCH [hereafter "Beier to Nemiroff"]; Dorothy Sinclair, *You Can Take the Girl Out of Chicago . . . Tales of My Wayward Youth* (Bloomington, IN: iUniverse, 2013), 45.

14. Nemiroff interview of Mamie Hansberry Mitchell, 11.

15. Beier to Nemiroff.

16. Stuart D. Levitan, *Madison: 1856–1931* (Madison: University of Wisconsin Press, 2006), 238.

17. African American dancer Mary De Haven Hinkson, Hansberry's instructor for a dance class, and later a principal dancer with the Martha Graham Dance Company, defrayed the cost of her lodging by washing dishes and sweeping at the Groves Women's Cooperative.

18. Roma Borst, letter to Nemiroff, February 10, 1968, box 69, files 6–7, LH Papers, SCH [hereafter "Borst to Nemiroff"]; Beier to Nemiroff.

19. LH, "All the Dark and Beautiful Warriors" (unpublished draft), 90.

20. Alan M. Wald, "Theodore Ward (September 15, 1902–May 8, 1983)," in Steven C. Tracy, ed., *Writers of the Black Chicago Renaissance* (Chicago: University of Illinois Press, 2011), 322.

21. Cheney, *Lorraine Hansberry*, 1; William J. Weatherby, *James Baldwin: Artist on Fire* (New York: Random House Value, 1991), 149.

22. Beier to Nemiroff.

23. Borst to Nemiroff.

24. Borst to Nemiroff; Wu Wilcox, *The Love of the Lotus*, 117; LH, "All the Dark and Beautiful Warriors" (unpublished), 92 and 84.

25. LH, "All the Dark and Beautiful Warriors" (unpublished), 18; LH, "On Summer," in Levin, ed., 52–55.

26. Box 1, file 5, LH Papers, SCH.

27. LH, "This Complex of Womanhood," *Ebony*, August 1960, 40 [hereafter "LH, 'This Complex of Womanhood' (1960)"].

28. LH, "All the Dark and Beautiful Warriors" (unpublished), 85; LH to Alice (no surname), March 15, 1963, box 2, file 11, LH Papers, SCH.

29. W. E. B. Du Bois, *Black Folk Then and Now: An Essay in the History and Sociology of the Negro Race* (New York: Oxford University Press, 2014), 1. Du Bois popularized ideas about ancient African civilization that William Leo Hansberry devoted his life to studying, though almost in obscurity. Du Bois explains in *The World and Africa* (1946): "I have read Eduard Meyer's *Geschichte des Altertums* [*History of Antiquity*] (1910–1913); but of greatest help to me has been Leo Hansberry. Mr. Hansberry, a professor at Howard University, is the one modern scholar who has tried to study the Negro in Egypt and Ethiopia." Why, then, was Hansberry not better known? "I regret that he has not published more of his work," Du Bois continues. "The overwhelming weight of conventional scientific opinion on Africa has overawed him, but his work in manuscript is outstanding." In other words, Hansberry didn't publish very much in his lifetime. However, historians of Africa who came after him appreciate that "conceptualizing, writing and teaching what Leo Hansberry calls pre-European History of Africa and Africana Studies at a time of open denial and advancement of [the] notion of African inferiority will always remain as his great legacy" (Ayele Bekerie, "Leo Hansberry, Founder of Ethiopian Research Council," *Tadias Magazine*, February 23, 2009).

30. George Lakoff, *Women, Fire and Dangerous Things: What Categories Reveal about the Mind* (Chicago: University of Chicago Press, 1987), 161.

31. LH, "All the Dark and Beautiful Warriors" (unpublished), 94–95.

32. Ross, "How Lorraine Hansberry Wrote 'A Raisin in the Sun.'"

33. Robert G. Lowery, "The Socialist Legacy of Sean O'Casey," *The Crane Bag* 7, no. 1 (1983): 128–34.

34. James Joyce, "The Race," in *Dubliners* (1914; reprint New York: Penguin Classics, 2014), 30.

35. Bernard Shaw, "Mr. Shaw's Works of Fiction: Reviewed by Himself," in *Selected Non-Dramatic Writings of Bernard Shaw*, ed. Dan H. Laurence (Cambridge, MA: Riverside Press, 1965), 309–14.

36. LH, *Young, Gifted and Black*, 65.

37. LH, *Young, Gifted and Black*, 65.

38. LH, "Origins of Character," 14.

39. Author interview with Douglas Turner Ward, June 21, 2018. Why, then, were the ethnic Irish in America and American Negroes at each other's throats when they seemed to have much in common? The question troubled W. E. B. Du Bois. The reasons for it, he believed, stemmed from historical materialism. "It happened unfortunately that the first Irish immigration to the United States took place just as the free Negroes of the North were making their most impressive forward movement. Irishmen and black men came, therefore, in bitter industrial competition in such cities as Boston, New York, and Philadelphia. Riots and street fights ensued." Regardless, despite the hostility of Irish Americans toward Negroes, "This fact does not for a moment invalidate the justice of the Irish cause," he said, "and I shall at all times defend the right of Ireland to absolute independence." Du Bois, "Ireland" in *The Crisis*, and Du Bois to the Rev. D. J. Bustin, March 30, 1921, Special Collections and University Archives, the University of Massachusetts, Amherst.

40. "The New Negro," in *The New Negro*, ed. Alain Locke (New York: A. & C. Boni, 1925), 7.

41. Henry Louis Gates Jr., *The Henry Louis Gates, Jr. Reader* (New York: BasicCivitas Books, 2012), 525. Smith, *Visions of Belonging*, 313.

42. "At the Union," *Wisconsin State Journal*, April 6, 1948.

43. Lorraine's use of dashes to capture natural speech is similar to that of Jane Austen, who was brilliant at creating conversation; Lorraine's epistolary style is an early indicator of her skill at dialogue. See LH to Edythe Anne Cohen, "A Day in June," 1948, box 1, file 5, LH Papers, SCH.

44. After college, Roma, ever interested in new experiences, produced a radio show for local listeners in her hometown. Once a week, farmers going about their chores were treated to a lively one-hour broadcast of *Musica Latina*. Later, she received a PhD in Spanish.

45. Borst to Nemiroff.

46. Beier to Nemiroff.

47. Borst to Nemiroff. In elementary school, Roma was enthralled by Richard Halliburton's travel books. Halliburton, the only surviving child of a farm and timber broker in Memphis, Tennessee, disappeared in 1939 attempting to sail a Chinese junk from Hong Kong to San Francisco. Roma wrote a letter of condolence to his father, Wesley Halliburton, offering to be his granddaughter because Richard had died without children. He proposed that she be "their little friend" instead and asked her to "occasionally send out to us a happy thought from faraway Wisconsin," beginning a correspondence that would continue another twenty-five years, until his death at ninety-five. See Wesley Halliburton to Roma Borst, December 18, 1941, private collection.

48. LH to Edythe Anne Cohen, July 31, 1948, and August 9, 1948, box 1, file 5, LH Papers, SCH.

Chapter 6: The Young Progressives

1. Why she wrote "parents" when her father had been gone for two years is a mystery. Perhaps she hadn't subconsciously accepted his death yet. See LH to Edythe Anne Cohen, letter dated "Harvest Time" (1948), box 1, file 5, LH Papers, SCH [hereafter "LH to Cohen 'Harvest Time'"].

2. LH, "A Challenge to Artists," speech delivered at Rally to Abolish the House Un-American Activities Committee, Manhattan Center, New York City, October 27, 1962.

3. The former Communist National Committee member Bella Dodd asserts in her 1954 memoir, *School of Darkness*, that the Progressive Party had Wallace as its voice and "inspirational leader," but that it was actually controlled by top U.S. Communists. Thomas W. Devine, *Henry Wallace's 1948 Presidential Campaign and the Future of Postwar Liberalism* (Chapel Hill: University of North Carolina Press, 2013); Karl M. Schmidt, *Henry A. Wallace, Quixotic Crusade 1948* (Syracuse, NY: Syracuse University Press, 1960), iii.

4. LH, "A Challenge to Artists."

5. LH, "All the Dark and Beautiful Warriors" (unpublished draft), 85.

6. LH, unpublished essay on Ibsen, 9, box 89, file 10, LH Papers, SCH.

7. LH, *Young, Gifted and Black*, 4.

8. Author interview with Kate Weiskopf Resek, March 9, 2020 [hereafter "Author interview with Resek"].

9. Author interview with Resek.

10. "Introducing YPA," Student Organizations file, September 30, 1949, University of Wisconsin–Madison Archives.

11. "Communist Methods of Infiltration: Hearings before the Committee on Un-American Activities, House of Representatives," 83rd Cong., 1st Sess. (1953), 2091.

12. LH to Cohen, "Harvest Time."

13. Rhoda Winter to LH, July 16, 1950, box 1, file 5, LH Papers, SCH.

14. Sara S. Schmidt, "'Americanized' Zionism: The Forgotten Role of Horace M. Kallen," *American Jewish Archives* (April 1976), 60; author interview with Lisa Mersky, Deborah Mersky, and Ruth Pool, May 1, 2020. Mersky went on to become a respected university law librarian.

15. LH, "All the Dark and Beautiful Warriors" (unpublished draft), 86.

16. LH to Cohen, "Harvest Time."

17. Unpublished essay for *The Urbanite* (circa 1961), box 89, file 10, LH Papers, SCH; "Frank Lloyd Wright Denounces University Buildings as 'Heresy,'" *Daily Cardinal*, October 15, 1948.
18. LH to Edythe Cohen, November 14, 1948, box 1, file 5, LH Papers, SCH.
19. Author interview with Gerald Hiken, February 18, 2020.
20. Author interview with Hiken.
21. Paul L. Trump, Dean of Men, University of Wisconsin, to Erich A. Walter, Dean of Students, University of Michigan, February 19, 1949, Holton Papers, unprocessed, CPL.
22. LH to Edythe Anne Cohen, November 12, 1948, box 1, file 5, LH Papers, SCH.
23. LH, "All the Dark and Beautiful Warriors" (unpublished draft), 16.

Chapter 7: Mexico

1. For a summary of the art workshop in Ajijic, see "Mexican Trip Open to KSU Artists," *Kent Stater* 13, no. 113 (May 26, 1948).
2. Steven R. Carter, "Commitment amid Complexity: Lorraine Hansberry's Life in Action," *Melus* 7 (Fall 1980): 41; Banta, "Lorraine Hansberry," 25–27.
3. LH to Edythe Anne Cohen, May 2, 1949, box 1, file 5, LH Papers, SCH.
4. Irma Jonas to LH, September 20, 1949, box 1, file 5, LH Papers, SCH.
5. Tobias Schneebaum, *Secret Places: My Life in New York and New Guinea* (Madison: University of Wisconsin Press, 2000), 7. Henry Miller scholars haven't found evidence of this.
6. Tony Burton, "Mexican Artist Ernesto Butterlin (1917–1964), aka Linares," LakeChapalaArtists.com, August 14, 2015; Zoe Kernick, "Ajijic," *Mexican Life*, April 1951.
7. Christina A. Sue, *Land of the Cosmic Race: Race Mixture, Racism, and Blackness in Mexico* (New York: Oxford University Press, 2013), 117.
8. Nemiroff interview of Mamie Hansberry Mitchell, 4.
9. Hazel Rowley, *Richard Wright: The Life and Times* (New York: Henry Holt, 2001), 197; Arnold Rampersad, *The Life of Langston Hughes*, vol. 1: *I, Too, Sing America: 1902–1941* (New York: Oxford University Press 1986), 40; Daniel Zizumbo-Colunga, "Study Reveals Racial Inequality in Mexico, Disproving Its 'Race-Blind' Rhetoric," *The Conversation*, December 13, 2017.
10. Sybille Bedford, *A Visit to Don Otavio: A Traveller's Tale from Mexico* (New York: Counterpoint, 2003), 193.
11. Lizzetta LeFalle-Collins and Shifra M. Goldman, "The Mexican Connection: The New Negro Border Crossings," in *In the Spirit of Resistance: African American Modernists and the Mexican Muralist School* (New York: American Federation of Arts, 1996), 37, 41–43, 46–47.
12. LH, *To Be Young, Gifted and Black*, 90.
13. "Make New Sounds."
14. Beier to Nemiroff.
15. Beier to Nemiroff.
16. Burton, "Alexander Nicolas Muzenic (1919–1976), Student of Josef Albers," January 8, 2015, LakeChapalaArtists.com. Tobias Schneebaum was an abstract expressionist who was more interested in anthropology than in pursuing a career as an artist. One day, he would walk into the Peruvian rain forest and live for seven months with the Arakmbut cannibals.
17. LH to Elaine (no surname), Thursday, n.d., 2, box 2, file 15, LH Papers, SCH. As a social realist, Hansberry disliked nonobjective painting for the same reason she disliked existentialism: embracing uncertainty struck her as decadent. Yet, if she had looked deeper, she would have found that unpredictability, according to these parallel strains of philosophy and art, was a call to action. "As an artist stood facing a blank canvas, a block of stone, or a pile of metal, wondering how (although seldom whether) he or she should begin, the Existentialists said there was only one answer to that question—they must act. They must travel to the deepest part of themselves, 'where fear and trembling start,' in the service of art." Mary Gabriel, *Ninth Street Women: Lee Krasner, Elaine De Kooning, Grace Hartigan, Joan Mitchell, and Helen Frankenthaler: Five Painters and the Movement That Changed Modern Art* (New York: Little, Brown and Company, 2017), 170.

18. LH to Hoyt Fuller, July 12, 1962, box 2, file 15, LH Papers, SCH.

19. LH, *To Be Young, Gifted and Black*, 253–54; *What Use Are Flowers?* in *The Collected Last Plays*, 223–60; letter to Mme. Chen Jui-Lan, *To Be Young, Gifted and Black*, 223.

20. Robbie Lieberman, *The Strangest Dream: Communism, Anticommunism, and the U.S. Peace Movement, 1945–1963* (Syracuse, NY: Syracuse University Press, 2000), 43.

21. "The Soviet Union's Nuclear Test Programme," Comprehensive Nuclear-Test-Ban Treaty Organization, www.ctbto.org.

22. Scheader interview of Nemiroff; Bob Teague, *Letters to a Black Boy* (New York: Lancer Books, 1969), 45.

23. Beier to Nemiroff.

24. Scheader interview of Nemiroff and repeated in other sources.

25. LH, *To Be Young, Gifted and Black*, 71; Carter G. Woodson, *The Mis-Education of the American Negro* (Washington, DC: Associated Publishers, 1933).

26. LH, "All the Dark and Beautiful Warriors" (unpublished), 89.

27. LH, "Written: Chicago Illinois—June 1949, 19 years old," box 1, file 5, LH Papers, SCH.

28. Young Communist League of America, Resolution adopted by the United Communist Party, January 1921, document 679, "Communist Methods of Infiltration," M-1085, reel 940, Department of Justice/FBI files, National Archives and Records Administration, 2091.

29. Labor Youth League, "NACCP March to Washington," January 17, 1950, announcement of March in Washington to support civil rights laws (e.g., antilynching bill); Brooklyn College, "Political Flyers and Papers," the Archives and Special Collections.

30. Federal Bureau of Investigation, Lorraine Vivian Hansberry Nemiroff file, May 10, 1950, Special Agent in Charge, FBI, Milwaukee, 100–3–7–1477, pp. 59 and 60 [hereafter "LH FBI file"].

31. LH FBI file; L. R. Forney to J. Edgar Hoover, September 30, 1943, 100-HQ-235405-1; Smith, *Visions of Belonging*, 285.

32. Athan Theoharis, *Chasing Spies: How the FBI Failed in Counterintelligence but Promoted the Politics of McCarthyism in the Cold War Years* (Chicago: Ivan R. Dee, 2002).

33. Sarah Jaffe, "The Unexpected Afterlife of American Communism," *New York Times*, June 6, 2017.

34. "The Election Petition of the Communist Party and the List of Names and Addresses Filed with the Secretary of State in the State of Illinois: Official Report Prepared by and for the Confidential Use of the Special Committee on Un-American Activities," Committee on Un-American Activities, 1940 (Chicago: Committee on Un-American Activities), Illinois State Library.

35. LH FBI file, 59 and 60.

Chapter 8: "Flag from a Kitchenette Window"

1. Vivian Gornick, "What Endures of the Romance of American Communism," *New York Review of Books*, April 3, 2020; Vivian Gornick, *The Romance of American Communism* (New York: Basic Books, 1977), 7.

2. Wright, quoted in Gornick, *The Romance of American Communism*, 9; Wright excerpt in Richard H. Crossman, ed., *The God That Failed* (New York: Columbia University Press, 2001), 118.

3. Wright, *12 Million Black Voices*, 108; Plotkin, "Kitchenettes."

4. Arnold R. Hirsch, *Making the Second Ghetto: Race and Housing in Chicago 1940–1960* (Chicago: University of Chicago Press, 1998), 36, 101.

5. "Court Orders Warrants," *Chicago Daily Tribune*, March 5, 1950, p. 201.

6. "In Memoriam: Judge John V. McCormick," *Loyola University Chicago Law Journal* 3, no.1 (Winter 1972); "Judge Opines Owners of Flats Is No Santa Claus: Fine: $50," *Chicago Daily Tribune*, September 23, 1951, p. 217.

7. Scheader interview of Nemiroff.

8. Sidney Fields, "Housewife's Play Is a Hit" (interview), *New York Daily Mirror*, March 16, 1959, p. 21; Borst to Nemiroff. Roma tried helping Lorraine with her Spanish at Wisconsin.

9. Lynn Y. Weiner, "The Leading Edge of Social Justice," *Roosevelt Review*, June 17, 2020.

10. "She did a little work with a small theater group in Chicago and took some courses at Roosevelt College," in "Negro Playwright's Drama Wins Honor," Associated Press, *Daily Independent Journal*, April 9, 1959, p. 31; LH's FBI file reports, "Has Worked with the Wisconsin Players, the Southside Community Skyloft Players, and the Progressive Theater Group at Madison [Wisconsin]," FBI, New York, 100–107297-51.

11. Anne Meis Knupfer, *The Chicago Renaissance and Women's Activism* (Urbana: University of Illinois Press, 2006), 46–47.

12. Winter to LH.

13. Julian Markels, *From Buchenwald to Havana* (Sacramento, CA: Evening Street Press, 2012), 41. Markels was Elbein's classmate.

14. Investigation of the University of Chicago and Roosevelt College 1949, Seditious Activities Investigation Commission, State of Illinois (Springfield, Illinois), 1949, p. 54.

15. Committee on Un-American Activities, "Report on the Communist 'Peace' Offensive: A Campaign to Disarm and Defeat the United States," April 1, 1951, U.S. House of Representatives, Washington, DC, 80.

16. Paul Robeson Jr., "Paul Robeson: Black Warrior," *Freedomways* 11, no. 2 (1971): 27.

17. Washington, *The Other Blacklist*, 17.

18. Emily Jones [LH], "Flag from a Kitchenette Window," *Masses and Mainstream* 3, no. 9 (September 1950): 38. It isn't clear why Hansberry included Algiers with Salerno. Black American soldiers weren't part of the North African campaign; the Ninety-Second Division, the Buffalo Soldiers, received twelve thousand decorations for combat service in Italy.

19. Author interview with Resek.

20. LH, "Willy Loman, Walter Younger, and He Who Must Live," *Village Voice* 4, no. 42 (August 12, 1959).

21. Author interview with Resek.

22. In the 1960s, the Albert became home to musicians. Many of them used the Albert's basement for rehearsals and impromptu jam sessions. The sound quality was good down there; but, writes Lillian Roxon, author of *The Rock Encyclopedia*, you had to play "among the pools of water and the cockroaches."

23. "From Hotel Albert, New York, August 1950," box 87, file 9, LH Papers, SCH.

24. LH to Edythe Cohen, July 1951, box 2, file 11, LH Papers, SCH; "Project 'N'" (October 1950), box 87, file 9, LH Papers, SCH.

25. Course catalogue, 1950, New School for Social Research, New York.

26. Shauneille Perry, "Miss Hansberry Makes History," *Chicago Defender*, February 14, 1959, p. 1. The fiction workshop was taught by Irma Brandeis, a professor of literature at Bard College and an authority on Dante; the Western Civilization course by Horace M. Kallen, who conceived, with Alain Locke, the concept of multiculturalism. Hansberry's untitled short story for Brandeis (September 1950) is in her papers at the Schomburg Center.

27. Alain Locke, "Harlem," *The Survey Graphic* 6, no. 6 (March 1925): 629.

28. Lofton Mitchell, "The Small Town," *Freedomways* (Fall 1964): 469.

29. Carla J. DuBose-Simons, "Movin' on Up: African Americans in the South Bronx in the 1940s," *New York History* 95, no. 4 (2014): 543–57.

30. "Gordon Parks and 'Harlem Gang Leader,'" The Gordon Parks Foundation, www.gordonparksfoundation.org.

31. LH, undated fragment, box 87, file 10, LH Papers, SCH; LH to Edythe Cohen, July 1951, box 2, file 11, LH Papers, SCH.

32. "Make New Sounds."

33. Simone de Beauvoir, *America Day by Day* (Berkeley: University of California Press, 1999), 35.

34. *The Autobiography of Malcolm X: As Told to Alex Haley* (1965; repr. New York: Ballantine, 1992), 79.

35. LH, undated fragment, box 5, file 14, LH Papers, SCH.

Chapter 9: *Freedom*

1. Francine to LH, November 6, 1951, box 2, file 14, LH Papers, SCH.

2. LH, fragments, box 5, file 14, LH Papers, SCH. While in Harlem in 2018, I saw a man standing on the subway platform wearing a T-shirt that read, "Make Harlem Black Again."

3. Carole Boyce Davies, *Left of Karl Marx: The Political Life of Black Communist Claudia Jones* (Durham, NC: Duke University Press, 2007), 2. "Howard Johnson, an African-American Party leader who left abruptly in 1956, recalls that Hansberry was a committed member who met several times a week with Claudia Jones." See Dubravka Juraga and M. Keith Booker, eds., *Socialist Cultures East and West: A Post–Cold War Reassessment* (Westport, CT: Praeger, 2002), 167n6; Margaret B. Wilkerson, "Lorraine Hansberry: The Making of a Woman of the Theatre," speech delivered to the College of Fellows of the American Theatre, April 23, 1995, John F. Kennedy Center for the Performing Arts, Washington, DC, p. 3.

4. "Dear Comrade Foster: The Following Is the Autobiographical (Personal, Political, Medical) History That I Promised . . . Comradely, Claudia Jones" (December 6, 1955), *American Communist History* 4, no. 1 (2005): 85–93.

5. Kate Weigand, *Red Feminism: American Communism and the Making of Women's Liberation* (Baltimore: Johns Hopkins University Press, 2001), 89–90.

6. Claudia Jones, "An End to the Neglect of Women," reprinted from *Political Affairs*, June 1949, p. 3.

7. Jackson, *The Indignant Generation*, 119–20.

8. Earl Browder, "After V-E Day—What Next?" *Political Affairs*, June 1945, pp. 485–86.

9. LH, fragment, box 88, file 11, LH Papers, SCH.

10. "For Irma Brandeis's class at the New School for Social Research" (September 1950), box 88, file 10, LH Papers, SCH.

11. LH, "Some Rather Indecisive Thoughts on M. Gide and His 'Corydon,'" box 56, file 18, LH Papers, SCH.

12. Carter, "Commitment amid Complexity," 41.

13. LH, "Freedom's First Struggling 3 Years—A Proud Record," *People's World*, February 4, 1954.

14. Howard Eugene Johnson and Wendy Johnson, *A Dancer in the Revolution: Stretch Johnson, Harlem Communist at the Cotton Club* (New York: Fordham University Press, 2014), 66–67.

15. LH, remarks read at a memorial service for Louis E. Burnham, February 15, 1960, box 2, file 13, LH Papers, SCH.

16. LH remarks at Burnham memorial.

17. LH, *To Be Young, Gifted and Black*, 78.

18. Alice Childress, "Tribute," in *Paul Robeson: The Great Forerunner*, ed. by the editors of *Freedomways* (New York: Dodd, Mead and Company, 1978), 272–73.

19. LH, *To Be Young, Gifted and Black*, 79; Wilkerson, "Lorraine Hansberry: The Making of a Woman of the Theatre," 3; Paul Robeson, *The Negro People and the Soviet Union* (New York: New Century Publishers, 1950), 12.

20. Bayard Rustin to Ethel Perry, July 29, 1947, box 45, General and family correspondence, 1944–1965, Bayard Rustin Papers, Library of Congress, Washington, DC. From "The Strange Case of Paul Robeson": "We refuse to be stampeded by the hysterical protests broadcast by the Civil Rights Congress and the Council on African Affairs over the refusal of authorities in Peoria, Illinois and Albany, New York to allow Robeson to sing in public-owned auditoriums. Mr. Robeson asked for just such a reaction by going about the country interrupting his program to lecture on political subjects which most of his auditors did not pay to hear and in

which the vast majority of them did not have the slightest interest" (*Pittsburgh Courier*, May 3, 1947, p. 6). See Lauren McConnell, "Understanding Paul Robeson's Soviet Experience," *Theatre History Studies* 30 (2010): 138–53.

21. Paul Robeson, "To You Beloved Comrade," *New World Review* 21, no. 4 (April 1953). During his 1949 Moscow tour, Robeson asked to see his friend the Yiddish poet Itzik Feffer. Feffer was being held in the infamous Lubyanka prison, but Soviet officials made him presentable and brought him to Robeson's hotel room. Feffer whispered to Robeson that the room was bugged. By hand signs and written notes, he told him that anti-Semitism was on the increase and indicated that he would be killed soon. When Robeson didn't understand, Feffer drew his finger across his throat. A few years later, Feffer was shot. Robeson said nothing publicly about the episode in his hotel room. Ronald Radosh, "The Price of Self-Delusion," *The American Interest*, August 27, 2019.

22. *Paul Robeson Speaks: Writings, Speeches, Interviews, 1918–1974* (Secaucus, NJ: Carol Publishing Group, 1978), 261.

23. Rebeccah E. Welch, "Black Art and Activism in Postwar New York, 1950–1965" (PhD diss., New York University, 2002), 20n38.

24. Welch, "Black Art and Activism," 190–91n76; Brian Dolinar, *The Black Cultural Front: Black Writers and Artists of the Depression Generation* (Jackson: University Press of Mississippi, 2012), 214. Burnham was not a regular church attender, but his affirming attitude and optimism had a spiritual side to it. "He would sing at home," said his daughter Margaret Burnham. "I remember, on Sundays, he would sing both spirituals as well as blues, and he was very, very engaged with music" (author interview with Margaret Burnham, July 8, 2020).

25. LH to Edythe Cohen, n.d. (circa 1951), box 2, file 14, LH Papers, SCH [hereafter "LH to Cohen, n.d."].

26. Welch, "Black Art and Activism," 66; Sarah E. Wright, "The Negro Woman in American Literature," *Freedomways* 6, no. 1 (1966): 8.

27. LH to Cohen, n.d.

28. Box 62, file 4, LH Papers, SCH.

29. Thomas Patrick Doherty, *Hollywood's Censor: Joseph I. Breen and the Production Code Administration* (New York: Columbia University Press, 2007), 240.

30. Box 58, files 3, 12–14, LH Papers, SCH.

31. Nemiroff, "Typed from [LH's] Notebook, New York," box 88, file 15, LH Papers, SCH.

Chapter 10: "A Young Harriet Tubman"

1. Author interview with Douglas Turner Ward, June 21, 2018.

2. Ossie Davis, *With Ossie and Ruby: In This Life Together* (New York: HarperCollins/It Books, 2000), 102.

3. John Oliver Killens, "Lorraine Hansberry: On Time!" *Freedomways* 19 (1979): 273–74.

4. LH, *"A Raisin in the Sun": The Unfilmed Original Screenplay* (New York: Plume, 1992), 132–34.

5. Author interview with Ward, June 21, 2018.

6. LH, *To Be Young, Gifted and Black*, 80.

7. LH, *To Be Young, Gifted and Black*, 80; LH to Edythe Cohen, July 15, 1951, box 1, file 5, and box 2, file 14, LH Papers, SCH; author interview with Ward, December 12, 2019.

8. Jessica Mitford, *A Fine Old Conflict* (New York: Vintage Books, 1978), 160–94.

9. LH, "The Statue of Nathan Hale," box 56, file 19, and "Communism—Labor Youth Defense," 1950–54, n.d., box 66, file 2, LH Papers, SCH.

10. LH, Douglas Turner Ward trial notes, "Communism—Labor Youth Defense," 1950–54, n.d., box 66, file 2, LH Papers, SCH.

11. Sarah Hart Brown, *Standing against Dragons: Three Southern Lawyers in an Era of Fear* (Baton Rouge: Louisiana State University Press, 1998), 106. Ward's sentence was reduced to two years' mandatory residence in Louisiana. His conviction was overturned by the U.S.

Supreme Court (Roosevelt [Douglas Turner] Ward, "This Happened in Penn Station," *Freedom* 1, no. 10 [October 1951]: 7); LH, "News Item," box 66, file 2, LH Papers, SCH.

12. Douglas Turner Ward said Jackson and Hansberry didn't live together, and comparisons of addresses and dates indicate they didn't, either.

13. McKissack and McKissack, *Young, Black, and Determined*, 63.

14. Author interview with Ward, June 22, 2018.

15. LH, "Women Demand Justice Done," *Freedom* 1, no. 10 (October 1951): 6.

16. LH, "The Negro Writer and His Roots: Toward a New Romanticism," *The Black Scholar* 12, no. 2 (1981): 8.

17. LH, "Life Challenges Negro Youth," *Freedom*, March 1955, p. 7.

18. LH, "Books," *Freedom*, April 1953, p. 7.

19. LH to Cohen, July 15, 1951.

20. LH, "Negroes Cast in Same Old Roles in TV Shows," *Freedom*, June 1951, p. 7. Watching the *Amos 'n' Andy* Christmas episodes was an annual event in black and white homes. See Henry Louis Gates Jr., "An 'Amos 'n' Andy' Christmas," *New York Times*, December 23, 1994.

21. Killens, "Lorraine Hansberry: On Time!," 273–74.

22. Loyle Hairston, "Lorraine Hansberry: Portrait of an Angry Young Writer," *The Crisis*, April 1979, p. 123.

23. Harold W. Cruse, "Replay on a Black Crisis," *Negro Digest*, November 1968, pp. 21, 23.

24. Washington, *The Other Blacklist*. The threat to the bottom line from the rightward shift is illustrated by the *National Guardian*, a radical leftist independent weekly newspaper established in 1948 in New York City. Among its editorial priorities were reporting on the civil rights movement in America, integrating the educational system, expanding voting rights, and ending discrimination in housing and employment. Paid circulation was seventy-five thousand in 1950; when the paper came out against the Korean War, it lost a third of its subscribers almost immediately.

25. Julian Mayfield, "Autobiography" (unpublished), box 15, file 9, Julian Mayfield Papers, SCH [hereafter "Mayfield 'Autobiography' (unpublished)"].

26. Killens, "Wanted: Some Black Long Distance Runners," *Black Scholar* 5, no. 3 (1973): 2–7.

27. "College Football; NYU Honors Protesters It Punished in '41," *New York Times*, May 4, 2001, sec. A, 1.

28. Angela Calomiris, "Red Masquerade: Tells How Commies Pay Way with US Gold," *Daily News*, February 21, 1951, 42; Danton Walker, "Broadway," *Daily News*, December 10, 1949, p. 25.

29. Author interview with Resek, March 9, 2020. The folk music movement came out of places like Camp Woodland, where children learned square dancing, folk songs from different cultures, and homespun crafts (Bill Horne, *The Improbable Community: Camp Woodland and the American Democratic Ideal* [self-published: Bill Horne, 2016]).

30. Welch, "Black Art and Activism," 110n24; Mark Naison, *Communists in Harlem during the Depression* (Urbana: University of Illinois Press, 1983), 281.

31. Author interview with Jane Bond, December 17, 2019. Bond, a cousin of Julian Bond, was an undergraduate at Sarah Lawrence when she and Hansberry became friends and began to correspond. Ms. Bond used the word *chasm* to describe the difference Lorraine said she felt between herself and young people in Harlem.

32. Dafora's contributions to the dance world influenced many future artists, especially African American artists such as Pearl Primus, Esther Rolle, and Katherine Dunham.

33. LH, "Poem," *Freedom*, November 1950, 7.

34. LH to Robert Nemiroff, "Dear Boobie," summer 1954, box 66, file 5, LH Papers, SCH.

35. *Trouble in Mind* was optioned for Broadway. But as an indictment of racism in American commercial theater, the play, as written, was considered too edgy and ironic for audiences who were there to take in the delights of the very institution being criticized. Childress refused to change the script. See Lofton Mitchell, *Black Drama: The Story of the American Negro in Theater* (New York: Hawthorn Books, 1967), 169.

36. Alice Childress to Robert Sherwood, March 3, 1956, box 3, file 1, Alice Childress Papers, SCH. Sherwood's letter must have lain under her pile of correspondence for quite a while. By the time she responded, Sherwood had been dead for almost four months.

37. Adrienne Macki Braconi, "African American Women Dramatists, 1930–1960," in *The Cambridge Companion to African American Theatre*, ed. Harvey Young (Cambridge, UK: Cambridge University Press, 2012), 124–25. Childress herself had worked as a domestic between acting jobs.

38. Samuel A. Hay, *African American Theatre: An Historical and Critical Analysis* (Cambridge, UK: Cambridge University Press, 1994), 26–27.

39. Childress to Trudier Harris, January 7, 1980, box 3, files 4–6, Alice Childress Papers, SCH.

40. Washington, *The Other Blacklist*.

41. Mary Helen Washington, "Lorraine Hansberry and 'Freedom': A Founding Text of Black Left Feminism," in *Left of the Color Line: Race, Radicalism, and Twentieth-Century Literature of the United States*, ed. Bill V. Mullen and James Smethurst (Chapel Hill: University of North Carolina Press, 2003), 194; "Make New Sounds."

Chapter 11: The Passport

1. Quoted in Gerald Sorin, *Howard Fast: Life and Literature in the Left Lane* (Bloomington: Indiana University Press, 2012), 231.

2. Robert C. Ruark, "War Beaters," *Pittsburgh Press*, January 10, 1951, p. 23; Martin B. Duberman, *Paul Robeson* (New York: Alfred A. Knopf, 1988), 394.

3. Walter White, "The Strange Case of Paul Robeson," *Ebony*, February 1951.

4. Davis, *With Ossie and Ruby*, 205–6.

5. Penny Von Eschen, *Race against Empire: Black Americans and Anticolonialism 1937–1957* (Ithaca, NY: Cornell University Press, 1997), 1, 124.

6. LH, "Simone de Beauvoir and 'The Second Sex': An American Commentary," in *Words of Fire: An Anthology of African-American Feminist Thought*, ed. Beverly Guy-Sheftall (New York: The New Press, 1995), 134.

7. LH FBI file, 100–393031, November 27, 1953; LH to Edythe Cohen, July 1951, box 1, file 5, and box 2, file 14, LH Papers, SCH.

8. LH to Cohen, July 1951.

9. LH, "Journey Notes," box 66, file 3, LH Papers, SCH.

10. LH, "Simone de Beauvoir and 'The Second Sex,'" 134–35.

11. LH, "'Illegal' Conference Shows Peace Is Key to Freedom," *Freedom*, April 1952.

12. LH, "'Illegal' Conference." The findings of the Women's International Democratic Federation are contained in "We Accuse! Report of International Women's Commission to Investigate the Atrocities Committed by American and Syngman Rhee Troops in Korea." A retrospective look at the work of the fact-finding mission and the price that some of the women paid is described in Taewoo Kim, "Frustrated Peace: Investigatory Activities by the Commission of the Women's International Democratic Federation (WIDF) in North Korea during the Korean War," *Sungkyun Journal of East Asian Studies* 20, no. 1 (2020): 83–112.

13. LH, "'Illegal' Conference."

14. "Vivian" to Roosevelt Jackson, Radiograma, n.d.; Roosevelt Jackson to LH, Western Union, March 29, 1952.

15. LH, "Journey Notes," box 66, file 3, LH Papers, SCH.

16. LH, "What Makes You So Suspicious?" box 88, file 15, LH Papers, SCH.

17. Author interview with Douglas Turner Ward, June 21, 2018.

18. LH, "Dear Rosie," "Thurs. nite," circa spring 1952, box 2, file 14, LH Papers, SCH.

19. LH, "Suspicious?" box 88, file 15, LH Papers, SCH.

20. LH, "The Negro Writer and His Roots," 2–12.

21. LH, Letter to *The Ladder* 1, no. 4 (January 1957): 39.

22. George B. Murphy Jr., "Robeson Birthday Tour Will Benefit Freedom Fund," *Freedom*, March 1952, p. 2.
23. Marvin E. Gettleman, "'No Varsity Teams': New York's Jefferson School of Social Science, 1943–1956," *Science and Society* 66, no. 3 (Fall 2002): 343.
24. Letter to Robert Nemiroff by one of Hansberry's former students, January 15, 1968, box 69, files 6–7, LH Papers, SCH.
25. Gerald Sorin, *Howard Fast: Life and Literature in the Left Lane* (Bloomington: Indiana University Press, 2012), 141.
26. There were no female FBI agents until 1972. United States of America v. Carl A. Hansberry, Perry Hansberry, M. L. Hansberry, and C.A. Enterprises, U.S. District Court, Northern District of Illinois, Eastern Division at Chicago, Civil Action Case 52C339.
27. LH, "A Negro Woman Speaks for Peace," *Daily Worker*, June 22, 1952.
28. LH FBI file, 100–26009.
29. LH FBI file, 100–393031 and 100–27468.
30. United States Code, 2006 Edition, Supplement 5, Title 18—Crimes and Criminal Procedure, June 25, 1948, ch. 645, 62 Stat. 771; June 27, 1952, ch. 477, title IV, §402(a), 66 Stat. 275; Pub. L. 94–550, §5,
31. LH FBI file, 100–27468: "obtained the subject's passport from her mother."
32. McKissack and McKissack, *Young, Black, and Determined*, 63.

Chapter 12: "I Do Love You"

1. Cheney, *Lorraine Hansberry*, 21–22.
2. Jones, "Dear Comrade Foster," 85–93.
3. Author interview with Esther Cooper Jackson, April 10, 2020.
4. Cheney, *Lorraine Hansberry*, 21–22.
5. William A. Raidy, "Eight Years Later 'Raisin' Reaches the Musical Stage," *Philadelphia Inquirer*, September 16, 1973, p. 84.
6. Federal Bureau of Investigation, Robert Barron Nemiroff file, FBI, 100–95240, January 4, 1954, National Archives at College Park, Maryland.
7. Nemiroff FBI file, 100–106019, July 1953.
8. A venue other than Prague had to be found for the 1948 festival because the Soviet Union overthrew the Czech government and ruled the country from Moscow. Noncommunist leaders went sent to prison or into exile.
9. Nemiroff FBI file, 100–106019, July 1953; American Youth for Democracy, "With a Lot of Gripes and Hopes," *Spotlight* 1, no. 1 (March 15, 1948).
10. Carl Hansberry's fundraising in Ole Nosey, "Everybody Goes When the Wagon Comes" (gossip column), *Chicago Defender*, September 18, 1943, p. 12; McKissack and McKissack, *Young, Black, and Determined*, 30.
11. Civil Action Case 44C720, *Perry Hansberry v. Franklin D. Roosevelt, Commander in Chief of the U.S. Army and Navy et al.*, Records of the District Courts of the United States (Record Group 21), National Archives, Chicago.
12. Evelyn Goldwasser, a Langdon Manor housemate who was active in Hillel at Wisconsin, returned to New York and remained a lifelong friend.
13. LH, "Genet, Mailer and the New Paternalism," *Village Voice*, June 1, 1961, 11, 14, 15. Baldwin remarked, "Until Norman sees us with no more romanticism than he views Jewish storekeepers, he'll never understand or be on to what's happening, *really* happening beneath the surface of this country" (W. J. Weatherby, *James Baldwin: Artist on Fire* [New York: Dell, 1989], 221) [hereafter "Weatherby, *James Baldwin* (1989)"].
14. "Young Negro Writer's Work Gains Popularity," UPI, *Lubbock Avalanche-Journal*, June 14, 1969.
15. The notorious case of Leo Frank, a Jewish factory manager in Georgia, lynched for his alleged

killing of a young Christian woman in 1915, spurred Jewish Americans to join the NAACP from a belief that anti-Semitism and racism were the same enemy.

16. James Baldwin, "From the American Scene: The Harlem Ghetto: Winter 1948," *Commentary*, February 1948.

17. Ruth R. Wisse, "Irving Kristol, Jewish Realist," *National Affairs* 44 (Summer 2020).

18. *Claudia Jones: Beyond Containment: Autobiographical Reflections, Essays, and Poems*, ed. Carole Boyce Davies (Oxford: Ayebia Clarke Publishing Limited, 2011), passim.

19. "Mention of [the people] attests to [one's] proper leftist sympathies," writes John Carey in *The Intellectual and the Masses*: "Their function is, in effect, to vouch for the intellectual who observes them" ([Chicago: Chicago Review Press, 2002], 38).

20. Dan Wakefield, *New York in the '50s* (New York: St. Martin's Griffin, 1999), 158.

21. Nemiroff to LH, September 1952, pp. 7, 9, 11, box 2, file 15, LH Papers, SCH.

22. "For white progressive women and men, and especially for Communists, the question of social relations with Negro men and women is above all a question of strictly adhering to social equality" (Claudia Jones, "An End to Neglect," 13).

23. Cheney, *Lorraine Hansberry*, 20.

24. George B. Murphy Jr. to LH, October 2, 1952, box 2, file 14, LH Papers, SCH.

25. Cheney, *Lorraine Hansberry*, 21–22.

26. Cheney, *Lorraine Hansberry*, 21–22.

27. Nannie Hansberry to LH, Western Union, November 10, 1952, box 2, file 1, LH Papers, SCH.

28. Cheney, *Lorraine Hansberry*, 21–22.

29. Cheney, *Lorraine Hansberry*, 21–22; Nemiroff to LH, Western Union, December 30, 1952, box 2, file 14, LH Papers, SCH.

30. Isaacs, "Five Writers and Their African Ancestors Part II," 336.

31. Ethel Payne, "Washington Society Opens Doors for Inaugural Guests," *Chicago Defender*, January 31, 1953, p. 13.

32. W. E. B. Du Bois, "Seminar of Africa," April 20, 1953, box 1, file 5, LH Papers, SCH.

33. LH, "Du Bois Talk," box 2, file 15, LH Papers, SCH. By coincidence, while she was taking the class, her uncle Leo Hansberry was on a Fulbright-sponsored sabbatical trip to Egypt, the Sudan, and Ethiopia to research ancient black Africa. However, as Kwame Alford points out in his unpublished biography of her uncle, "Upon his return to Howard University in 1954, Hansberry learned from a former student—and quite by accident—that the university had just received a Ford Foundation grant to develop its own African Studies Program. The news was bittersweet. While overjoyed to see his dream come to fruition, Hansberry was also stunned, hurt, and disappointed. After his own grant application was denied just prior to the news, no one in the administration bothered to inform him of this major accomplishment. Not only had the Howard administration made a conscious decision to keep Hansberry in the dark about the award, they also determined that although his paradigm formed the nucleus for the African Studies Program at the university, they left him out of the planning and implementation of a curriculum that had been at the heart of this scholar's/activist's life for over 30 years." Instead, Howard adopted the Melville Herskovits–led African Studies Association model favored by white universities, the federal government, private foundations, and philanthropic associations, according to Kwame Wes Alford, *In Defense of a People: William Leo Hansberry and the Struggle for African World Liberation, 1894–1965* (unpublished, n.d.).

34. David Levering Lewis, *W. E. B. Du Bois: A Biography, 1868–1963* (New York: Henry Holt, 2009), 682.

35. LH speech at memorial for DuBois in Carnegie Hall, February 23, 1964, in *Black Titan: W.E.B. Dubois*, ed. John H. Clarke et al. (Boston: Beacon Press, 1970), 17.

36. LH, "Hansberry Notes in Her Books," box 61, file 9, LH Papers, SCH.

37. "Art D'Lugoff, Oral History Memoir," December 1993, William E. Weiner Oral History Library of the American Jewish Committee at the New York Public Library.

38. LH, "Reflections during a Season of Murder: A Memorial in Three Parts," box 58, file 21, LH Papers, SCH.

39. LH, "Reflections during a Season of Murder."

40. LH, "Reflections during a Season of Murder."

41. LH to Charles Browning, November 4, 1953, box 2, file 15, LH Papers, SCH. Although Hansberry said Carey was her pastor, she may have meant that as "spiritual adviser." She didn't attend Quinn Chapel AME on South Wabash Avenue, where Carey was the pastor. Carey had delivered a stirring speech at the Republican Convention in Chicago the previous July, often quoted and sometimes not attributed to him: "We, Negro Americans, sing with all loyal Americans: My country 'tis of thee, Sweet land of liberty, Of thee I sing. Land where my fathers died, Land of the Pilgrims' pride, From every mountainside, Let freedom ring! That's exactly what we mean—from every mountainside, let freedom ring. Not only from the Green Mountains and White Mountains of Vermont and New Hampshire; not only from the Catskills of New York; but from the Ozarks in Arkansas, from the Stone Mountain in Georgia, from the Blue Ridge Mountains of Virginia. Let it ring not only for the minorities of the United States, but for the disinherited of all the earth! May the Republican Party, under God, from every mountainside, *Let freedom ring!*" "Address of Archibald J. Carey Jr. at the Republican National Convention, 1952," Quinn Chapel A.M.E. Church, box 2, file 26, CPL.

42. Cheney, *Lorraine Hansberry*, 21–22.

43. LH, "Reflections during a Season of Murder."

Chapter 13: Camp Unity

1. "Camp Unity, 1917–1998," Robert Steck Papers, Tamiment Library and Robert F. Wagner Labor Archives, New York University.

2. "My gentle husband": caption under a photo of Nemiroff in her scrapbook; "Lorraine Hansberry; Village Intellect Revealed," *New York Times*, October 11, 1964, X1; Scheader interview of Nemiroff, 17.

3. "Addenda: Notes on 'The Quarter,'" n.d., box 61, file 18, and box 62, file 1, LH Papers, SCH.

4. David Kennedy, "An Interview with Kenneth Koch," August 5, 1993, http://writing.upenn.edu/~afilreis/88/koch.html; John Strausbaugh, *The Village: 400 Years of Beats and Bohemians, Radicals and Rogues—A History of Greenwich Village* (New York: Ecco, 2013), 296; "Neighbor to Neighbor: Notes to a Greenwich Village Meeting on 'the Open Community,'" September 22, 1959, p. 2, box 56, file 15, LH Papers, SCH.

5. David W. Dunlap, "A Marriage Born Where Tables for 2 Women Were Common," *New York Times*, March 26, 2013.

6. Gunnar Myrdal, *An American Dilemma: The Negro Problem and Modern Democracy* (1944; repr. New York: Routledge, 1995), 1:62.

7. Welch, "Black Art and Activism," 112.

8. Author interview with Hettie Jones, October 18, 2019.

9. Baldwin, "From the American Scene."

10. James Smethurst, "Don't Say Goodbye to the Porkpie Hat: Langston Hughes, the Left, and the Black Arts Movement," *Callaloo* 25, no. 4 (2002): 1–14.

11. Box 66, file 4, LH Papers, SCH.

12. Amiri Baraka, *Autobiography of LeRoi Jones* (Chicago: Lawrence Hill Books, 1997), 192–99.

13. William S. Anderson, CPA, to Seymour L. Baldash, CPA, July 29, 1957, box 2, file 17, LH Papers, SCH. Hansberry received a distributive share of the partnership during 1954–56, in the amount of about $1,300 per year (or $12,500 in today's money).

14. Ann Serrane to LH, July 7, 1953, box 66, file 4, LH Papers, SCH.

15. "Dozen New York Summer Camps Have Red Tinge," Associated Press, *Lansing State Journal*, July 5, 1954.

16. Elise McCurties, "Red Roots, Radical Fruit: Children of the Old Left in the Civil Rights Movement and the New Left" (PhD diss., Michigan State University, 2001). "To his young leftist

audience [Pete] Seeger sang lullabies of world peace, the brotherhood and sisterhood of all races, and the innate goodness in all mankind. Idealistic campers, suffering from their own troubled childhood experiences, desperately wanted to believe these concepts." Camp Unity and others like it were the incubators of social justice–minded children who became leaders in the 1960s of Students for a Democratic Society, the Free Speech Movement, voter registration drives in the South, and the Weathermen.

17. "Camp Policy," box 1, file 21, Robert Steck Papers, Tamiment Library and Robert F. Wagner Labor Archive, New York University.
18. "Camp Policy."
19. "Darling," n.d., box 66, file 5, LH Papers, SCH.
20. Federal Bureau of Investigation, Louis Pasternak (manager of Camp Unity while Hansberry was there) file, FBI, New York, 100–79725; LH to Nemiroff, July 1953, box 66, file 5, LH Papers, SCH.
21. Pettis Perry, "The Struggle against White Chauvinism," *Political Affairs*, June 1949, p. 10.
22. "An Evaluation of the Organizational Level of the Fight against White Chauvinism," n.d., box 66, file 5, LH Papers, SCH; "Camp Unity: Accounts," box 1, folder 20, Robert Steck Papers.
23. George Tabori, "Baby, You Could Be Jesus in Drag," *Village Voice* 12, no. 17, February 9, 1967; Letter to Charlotte Zaltzberg (Nemiroff's associate), August 9, 1968, box 69, files 6–7, LH Papers, SCH.
24. Wil Haygood, "45 Years Ago, a 'Raisin' to Cheer," *Washington Post*, March 28, 2004; LH to Nemiroff, Summer 1954, box 66, file 5, LH Papers, SCH.
25. LH to Edythe Cohen, circa 1951, box 1, file 5, and box 2, file 14, LH Papers, SCH.
26. LH, *The Final Glory: A Contemporary Drama in Three Acts*, box 50, files 8–9, LH Papers, SCH.
27. "Doug Ward: The Early Years," *Ward Quarterly*, September 16, 2010, https://douglasturner ward.wordpress.com.
28. "Doug Ward: The Early Years."
29. LH to Nemiroff, summer 1954.
30. LH to Nemiroff, "Dear Boobie," box 66, file 5, LH Papers, SCH.
31. LH to Nemiroff, summer 1954.
32. "Camp Unity," box 66, file 5, LH Papers, SCH.
33. "Camp Policy."
34. LH to Nemiroff, summer 1954; Nemiroff to LH, Thursday, 1954, box 66, file 5, LH Papers, SCH.

Chapter 14: "One Becomes a Woman"

1. Catherine Scheader interview of Robert Nemiroff, August 1, 1976, p. 5, box 67, file 2, LH Papers, SCH.
2. Burt D'Lugoff became a partner in his brother Art's famous restaurant and club, the Village Gate.
3. Paul Laurence Dunbar, "A Negro Love Song" in *The Book of American Negro Poetry*, ed. James Weldon Johnson (New York: Harcourt, Brace and Company, 1922).
4. LH, "'Raisin' Author Tells Meaning of Her Play," *New York Age*, December 20, 1958, p. 27.
5. LH, "We Are of the Same Sidewalks."
6. The comic strip was *Winnie Winkle*, introduced around the time of World War I.
7. LH, "Images and Essences: Dialogue with an Uncolored Egg-Head," *Urbanite*, May 1961.
8. Leon Wofsy, "Lorraine Hansberry: The Writer, Her Times and Our Times," a symposium at University of California at Berkeley, February 19, 1998. Though not openly a Communist publication, *New Challenge* was accused of being pro-Communist in an issue of *Counterattack: The Newsletter of Facts to Combat Communism* 9/10 (1955): 19. The cover of the first issue of *New Challenge*, in August 1954, featured Raymonde Dien, a young Communist Frenchwoman imprisoned for ten months for protesting the French colonial war in Indochina.

9. Nemiroff, writing as "Bob Rolfe," "Is Wedlock a Padlock?" *New Challenge*, December 1954, pp. 27–29.

10. Antero Pietila and Stacy Spaulding, "The Afro-American's World War II Correspondents: Feuilletonism as Social Action," *Literary Journalism Studies* 5, no. 2 (Fall 2013): 49.

11. LH to Nemiroff, September 1954, Chicago, box 2, file 1, LH Papers, SCH.

12. LH to Nemiroff, September 1954.

13. United States of America v. Carl A. Hansberry, Perry Hansberry, and C.A. [Hansberry] Enterprises, Civil Action Case 53C840, Eastern Division at Chicago, Northern District of Illinois, U.S. District Court (1953).

14. "Society Women Drape in Mink for 'Dripping in Mink' Extravaganza," *Chicago Defender*, October 9, 1954, p. 13.

15. LH to Nemiroff, September 1954.

16. Julian Mayfield, "Eddies and Streams," in "Autobiography" (unpublished).

17. "Negro Job Watch Is Set on Radio-TV," *New York Times*, January 19, 1955, p. 16.

18. Claude Brown, *Manchild in the Promised Land* (1965; repr. New York: Simon and Schuster, 2012), xii.

19. Mayfield, "Eddies and Streams."

20. Arnold De Mille, "Once Over Lightly," *New York Age Defender*, September 18, 1954, p. 8. Robeson's passport was restored in 1958, but the damage to his professional career was done. He performed for a few more years before retiring in the 1960s, although the FBI continued to investigate him until his death in 1976 at age seventy-seven.

21. The FBI maintained files on black artists from many walks of life: Ruby Dee, Ossie Davis, Sidney Poitier, Harry Belafonte, Hazel Scott (jazz and classical pianist, singer, and actor), Canada Lee (actor), Lena Horne, Elizabeth Catlett (graphic artist and sculptor), Charles White (artist), and Alice Childress. Most of them, and other artists on the left—Orson Welles, Lillian Hellman, Leonard Bernstein—had appeared in *Red Channels: The Report of Communist Influence in Radio and Television* (1950), assembled by three former FBI agents.

22. Bosley Crowther, "Negroes in Film," *New York Times*, October 31, 1954, X1.

23. LH, unpublished letter to Bosley Crowther, November 3, 1954, box 63, file 8, LH Papers, SCH.

24. Perhaps this advice from da Vinci on creating monsters came in handy for something she was working on: *Simon's House: A Fantastic Drama in Seven Scenes*, New York City, 1955, box 51, file 10, LH Papers, SCH.

25. "Finding 'Raisin' Backers (for Film) Took Time," interview, *Cleveland Press*, October 26, 1960.

26. LH, "Simone de Beauvoir and 'The Second Sex,'" 133, 129; LH, "Some Rather Indecisive Thoughts."

27. Simone de Beauvoir, *Memoirs of a Dutiful Daughter* (1958; repr. HarperCollins 2005), 104.

28. Beauvoir, *The Mandarins* (1956; repr. New York: W. W. Norton, 1999), 315. Algren may have fallen for her, in part, because he was transgressing boundaries. "With us [Americans]," he told her, "beautiful and ugly, grotesque and tragic, and also good and evil—each has its place. Americans don't like to think that these extremes can mingle" (Beauvoir, *America Day by Day*, 98).

29. Beauvoir, *The Second Sex* (New York: Vintage Books, 1980), 683.

30. McKissack and McKissack, *Young, Black, and Determined*, 121. When Bob later said Mamie had a mind that had never "fulfilled its potential" and, instead, she relied on being "the perfect hostess, perfect conversationalist," he likely heard this assessment of his sister-in-law from Lorraine first. See Scheader interview of Nemiroff, 9; LH, "Simone de Beauvoir and 'The Second Sex,'" 129.

31. LH, "Simone de Beauvoir and 'The Second Sex,'" 139, 141.

32. LH, "Autobiographical Notes 1957–1963," fragment, October 19, 1956, box 1, files 1–2 , LH Papers, SCH.

33. LH, "Simone de Beauvoir and 'The Second Sex,'" 140; LH, "Notes on Women's Liberation" (unpublished), November 11, 1955, box 56, file 6, LH Papers, SCH.

34. LH, "Autobiographical Notes 1957–1963."

35. Wright was influenced by existentialists Genet, Sartre, Beauvoir, and the others after he moved to Paris in 1947, the year he met Beauvoir. LH, *A Raisin in the Sun*, and *The Sign in Sidney Brustein's Window* (New York: Vintage Books, 1995), 283. The quotation is from *The Sign*.

36. Cheryl Higashida, "To Be(come) Young, Gay, and Black: Lorraine Hansberry's Existentialist Routes to Anticolonialism," *American Quarterly* 60, no. 4 (December 2008), 901. It needs to be mentioned that Hansberry's understanding of existentialism was sketchy and based mainly on reading Camus. Had she read Beauvoir's *The Ethics of Ambiguity* (1947), she would have seen that it ends by declaring, first, the necessity of assuming one's freedom; and second, by asserting that it is only through action that freedom makes itself possible.

37. LH, "Simone de Beauvoir and 'The Second Sex,'" 133; LH, "Some Rather Indecisive Thoughts."

38. LH, "Personal Feelings," box 62, file 4, LH Papers, SCH.

39. LH, under pen name Emily Jones, "Chanson du Konallis," *The Ladder* 2, no. 12 (September 1958): 8–10, 20–26.

40. Robert Nemiroff, foreword to LH, *To Be Young, Gifted and Black*, xxiii [hereafter "Nemiroff foreword"].

41. How Beauvoir rejects the exclusionary practices of identity politics brings to mind Adrienne Rich's image of a "lesbian continuum" and freedom to move in either direction. Margaret A. Simon, "Lesbian Connections: Simone de Beauvoir and Feminism," *Signs* 18, no. 1 (1992): 140; Beauvoir, *The Second Sex*, 436.

42. Manuscript for Nemiroff's foreword to *Young, Gifted and Black*, vi, box 44, file 3, LH Papers, SCH.

43. LH, "Author's Notes on Characterization, Structure and Content," 2, box 50, files 4 and 11–13, LH Papers, SCH. Sex was "in" as a subject and taken as an indication of the nation's health and character during the Cold War. The Kinsey Reports, two scholarly books about the range of people's sexual identities and behaviors, became bestsellers. This, combined with the boom in interest in psychoanalysis, turned morality and modern culture into fashionable but serious topics of discussion. Harvard sociologist and expert on the family, Carl Zimmerman, commented, "If you cannot control the values of the womb, you cannot control the values of the bomb."

44. LH, "Author's Notes," 2, box 50, file 4, LH Papers, SCH.

45. *Flowers for the General*, box 50, file 11, LH Papers, SCH. Cheryl Higashida offers the most thorough discussion of these two early plays: *Black International Feminism: Women Writers of the Black Left, 1945–1995* (Urbana: University of Illinois Press, 2011).

46. LH, "Author's Notes," box 50, file 4, LH Papers, SCH.

47. Buzz Johnson, *"I Think of My Mother": Notes on the Life and Times of Claudia Jones* (London: Karia Press, 1985), 121.

48. Federal Bureau of Investigation, Claudia Jones file (FBICJF), FBI Memo, New York, 100–18676; "Claudia Jones Loses," *New York Times*, November 10, 1955, p. 39; "Red Agrees to Leave the Country," *New York Times*, November 18, 1955, p. 10; "Fire Records," *New York Times*, November 15, 1955, p. 66; Carole Boyce Davies, *Left of Karl Marx: The Political Life of Black Communist Claudia Jones* (Durham, NC: Duke University Press, 2008), 2.

49. Davies, *Left of Karl Marx*, 118.

50. Halois Robinson to LH, July 7, 1960. "To make a long story short, she is in need of about two hundred dollars to tide her over this latest hurdle."

51. Jones, "An End to the Neglect of Women," 3.

52. LH, "This Complex of Womanhood," *Ebony* 18, no. 11 (September 1963): 88.

53. Cheney, *Lorraine Hansberry*, 22. *Slave Songs* is still in print in a handsome edition from the University of Georgia Press.

54. LH, "Chicago—Christmas 1955 . . . the late hours," box 2, file 1, LH Papers, SCH.

Chapter 15: "I Ain't Sick"

1. Scheader interview of Nemiroff.
2. R. C. Baker, "The *Voice*'s First Ever Restaurant Review," *Village Voice*, October 26, 1955.
3. LH, "Arnold," a short story, circa February 1956, p. 3, box 60, file 2, LH Papers, SCH.
4. LH, uncompleted draft, 4, box 60, file 2, LH Papers, SCH.
5. Cheney, *Lorraine Hansberry*, 22.
6. Cheney, *Lorraine Hansberry*, 22.
7. Jerry Tallmer, "Father of the Revolution," *AMNY Magazine* 76, no. 8 (July 12–18, 2006).
8. In Karen Malpede, *Women in Theatre: Compassion and Hope* (New York: Drama Book Publishers, 1983), 171.
9. Tallmer, "Father of the Revolution."
10. Robin Patric Clair and Lauren Berkshire Hearit, "The Meaning of Work and the Absence of Workers in 'Les Mandarins': Irony at Work through the 'Essential Accessory,'" *Tamara Journal of Critical Organisation Inquiry* (Warsaw) 15, no. 1–2 (March/June 2017): 203–15.
11. LH to Nemiroff, "Sunday," July 1, 1956, box 2, file 1, LH Papers, SCH.
12. "Khrushchev's Secret Speech: 'On the Cult of Personality and Its Consequences,' Delivered at the Twentieth Party Congress of the Communist Party of the Soviet Union," February 25, 1956, History and Public Policy Program Digital Archive, from the *Congressional Record*: Proceedings and Debates of the 84th Cong., 2nd Sess. (May 22, 1956–June 11, 1956), C11, Part 7 (June 4, 1956), pp. 9389–403. Robert Conquest in *The Great Terror* (1968) gives a carefully accumulated total for the Stalin years (at least twenty million killed); Iosif G. Dyadkin, a Soviet geophysicist, did a demographic analysis of excess Soviet deaths, 1926–54, in *Unnatural Deaths in the USSR* (1983) and concludes that Soviet repression killed 23,100,000 to 32,000,000 Soviet citizens during this twenty-nine-year period.
13. LH to Nemiroff, "Sunday."
14. LH to Nemiroff, "Sunday." Nemiroff later attempted to distance Hansberry from Soviet-style communism: "Whatever her reservations about the Soviet system, she did not then, because of its revolutionary origins and rhetoric and its actual support for many third world revolutions, recognize its parallel threat to democratization and socialism."
15. Julian Mayfield, notes for a proposed autobiography, box 1, file 2 (Biographical Sketches), Julian Mayfield Papers, SCH.
16. Loften Mitchell, "The Negro Writer and His Materials," in *The American Negro Writer and His Roots: Selected Papers from the First Conference of Negro Writers* (New York: American Society of African Culture, 1960), 57.
17. Mayfield, "Eddies and Streams."
18. LH, "What's New about the 'New Negro'?" unpublished Letter to the Editor, *New York Times Sunday Magazine*, March 4, 1956, box 63, file 25, LH papers, SCH.
19. LH, fragment, box 62, file 4, LH Papers, SCH.
20. Scheader interview of Nemiroff.
21. Michael Adams, "Lorraine Hansberry," in *Dictionary of Literary Biography: Afro-American Writers after 1955: Dramatists and Prose Writers* (Farmington Hills, MI: Gale Publishing, 1985); LH, "The Negro Writer and His Roots"; Philip Rose, *You Can't Do That on Broadway! "A Raisin in the Sun" and Other Theatrical Improbabilities* (New York: Proscenium Publishers, 2001), 56.
22. "'Whites Dreadfully Ignorant of Negro Life,'" interview by Don Ross, *New York Herald Tribune*, March 13, 1960, p. 3; LH, "Village Intellect Revealed," *New York Times*, October 11, 1964, in Cherry et al., eds., *Portraits in Color*, 150.
23. Cheney, *Lorraine Hansberry*, 24.
24. LH to Nemiroff, June 29, 1956, box 1, files 1–2, LH Papers, SCH.
25. Metropolitan Housing and Planning Council, Accession 74–20, box 13, file 143, Daley Library, Chicago; "The Father of Modern American Theater," Lloyd Richards interview, Academy of Achievement, February 15, 1991, https://achievement.org/achiever/lloyd-richards/ [hereafter "The Father of Modern American Theater"].

26. LH to Nemiroff, "Sunday."

27. LH to Nemiroff, "Sunday."

28. LH to Nemiroff, June 29, 1956.

29. LH to Nemiroff, "Sunday."

30. LH to Nemiroff, June 29, 1956; LH to Nemiroff, "Sunday."

31. LH to Nemiroff, "Sunday."

32. LH to Nemiroff, "Sunday."

33. Robbie Lieberman, *My Song Is My Weapon: People's Songs, American Communism, and the Politics of Culture, 1930–1950* (Champaign: University of Illinois Press, 1989), 143. The first concert organized by People's Artists was a Peekskill, New York, performance in 1949 of Paul Robeson and others. Local vigilantes broke it up. A second concert resulted in the Peekskill Riot; one hundred fifty people were hospitalized.

34. "Ex-Communist Says Party Used Summer Camps, Social Events in Recruiting Youths," Associated Press, February 7, 1952. The informant was Harvey Matusow, the most notorious of the paid snitches for the Communist witch hunters of the 1950s. He testified before HUAC against hundreds of Americans, the Girl Scouts, the American Legion, and the *New York Times*. Most of it was lies, he confessed later. He would spend forty-four months in prison for perjury.

35. "Neighborhood Source: Chinese Hand Laundry, 339 Bleecker Street," LH FBI file, New York, 100–107297–231. The FBI, according to its records, had photographs of Hansberry that agents showed to informants when they sought information about her.

36. LH FBI files, New York, 100–107297 and 100–107297–04, July 1956.

37. Shane Vogel, *Stolen Time: Black Fad Performance and the Calypso Craze* (Chicago: University of Chicago Press, 2018), 40.

38. Michael S. Eldridge, "Bop Girl Goes Calypso: Containing Race and Youth Culture in Cold War America," *Anthurium: A Caribbean Studies Journal* 3, no. 2 (2005).

39. LH, fragment, October 19, 1956, box 1, file 1, LH Papers, SCH.

40. Fragments, box 62, file 4, LH Papers, SCH.

41. Ted Poston, "We Have So Much to Say" (interview with Hansberry), *New York Post*, March 22, 1959, p. M2.

Chapter 16: "Cindy, Oh Cindy"

1. Garvey quoted in John Henrik Clarke, *Marcus Garvey and the Vision of Africa* (New York: Vintage Books, 1974), 346.

2. Cheney, *Lorraine Hansberry*, 22.

3. LH to Nemiroff, June 29, 1956.

4. Killens, "Lorraine Hansberry: On Time!," 337.

5. LH, "Provincetown, Monday evening, 1 am," box 2, file 15, LH Papers, SCH.

6. LH, unpublished essay on Ibsen, 9.

7. In 1966, Robert Starobin joined the history faculty at the University of Wisconsin–Madison and became involved with reforming the history department and with student protest groups. He pioneered the first black studies course at Wisconsin in 1968, and he published articles and spoke on his research interests in black history and the Black Power movement. But he felt unaccepted by the Black Panthers and by black academics because he was white. His marriage broke up, and his wife moved back to California in 1968. At the end of 1969, he resigned from the University of Wisconsin–Madison and accepted a teaching position at the State University of New York at Binghamton. He committed suicide in 1971. From the guide to the Joseph R. Starobin and Robert S. Starobin Papers, 1945–1976, Department of Special Collections and University Archive, Stanford University Libraries.

8. Joseph R. Starobin to Nemiroff, January 11, 1968, box 69, files 6–7, LH Papers, SCH.

9. LH, "Provincetown, Monday evening, 1 am."

10. A discussion of why theater workers weren't subjected to McCarthyism can be found in

James Edward Smethurst, *The New Red Negro: The Literary Left and African American Poetry, 1930–1946* (New York: Oxford University Press, 1999), 252.

11. "And yet this didn't disrupt her celebrity and influence." Imani Perry, *Looking for Lorraine: The Radiant and Radical Life of Lorraine Hansberry*, ebook (New York: Beacon Press, 2018).

12. "During the 1950s and until her untimely death in 1965, Hansberry remained committed to an anticolonial/anti-imperialist political project that challenged the supremacy of American capitalism and advocated for some variant of socialist development at the height of McCarthy-ism and beyond" (Fanon Che Wilkins, "Beyond Bandung: The Critical Nationalism of Lorraine Hansberry, 1950–1965," *Radical History Review* 95 [Spring 2006]: 192).

13. Phillip Deery, *Red Apple: Communism and McCarthyism in Cold War New York* (New York: Empire State Editions, 2016), 109n226.

14. Joel Dinerstein, *The Origins of Cool in Postwar America*, ebook (Chicago: University of Chicago Press, 2017).

15. LH, "Provincetown, Monday evening, 1 am."

16. LH, "Provincetown, Monday evening, 1 am."

17. Lowery, "The Socialist Legacy of Sean O'Casey," 130.

18. LH, "We Are of the Same Sidewalks," 198.

19. Keith Clark, *Black Manhood in James Baldwin, Ernest J. Gaines, and August Wilson* (Urbana: University of Illinois Press, 2004), 116–17.

20. A voice-over narration cut from Hansberry's screenplay for *A Raisin in the Sun*. Michael Tritt, "A View from the Stockyards: Lorraine Hansberry's Allusion to 'The Jungle' in the Unfilmed Screenplay of 'A Raisin in the Sun,'" *ANQ: A Quarterly Journal of Short Articles, Notes and Reviews* 21, no. 1 (Winter 2008): 54.

21. Rough draft/thoughts about contemporary drama, 1, box 89, file 10, LH Papers, SCH; Notes from *The Apples of Autumn* reading, box 62, file 4, LH Papers, SCH.

22. Rough draft/thoughts about contemporary drama, 1; Notes from *The Apples of Autumn* reading.

23. Studs Terkel, "An Interview with Lorraine Hansberry," *Chicago Perspective* (WFMT Chicago Fine Arts Guide) 10, no. 4 (April 1961): 10.

24. Albert Murray, *The Omni-Americans: Some Alternatives to the Folklore of White Supremacy* (1970; repr. New York: Penguin/Library of America, 2020), 58. In the play *On Whitman Avenue*, a white liberal coed sublets a second-floor flat in her parents' house to a Negro veteran and his family while her parents are away on vacation. This causes a furor in her suburban community, causing a rift in her family and devastating the black family, whose only offense was needing a home. The play had difficulty getting financing because most white producers considered it too controversial. Margo Jones, an overlooked figure in American theater history, was the Broadway director, and later the codirector of Williams's *The Glass Menagerie*.

25. Patricia Marks, "Lorraine Hansberry Interview," WNYC Radio, New York, March 30, 1961; Terkel, "An Interview with Lorraine Hansberry"; Interview by Walter Lister Jr., "Audiences Spread Word on 'Raisin,'" *New York Herald Tribune*, March 1, 1959, pp. 1 and 4.

26. Israel Shenker, "Moody Man of Letters: Portrait of Samuel Beckett, Author of the Puzzling Waiting for Godot," *New York Times*, May 6, 1956. Later, Hansberry parodied Beckett in a short story, "The Arrival of Todog," which ends with three travelers dancing and singing an existential tautology: "We are here because we are here because we are here."

27. LH, unpublished essay, 14, box 89, file 10, LH Papers, SCH.

28. LH, "The Negro Writer and His Roots," 7.

29. Miller, *Death of a Salesman*, Requiem.

30. LH to Fuller.

31. Poston, "We Have So Much to Say."

32. Philip Rose, *You Can't Do That on Broadway!: "A Raisin the Sun" and Other Improbabilities* (2001; repr. New York: Limelight Editions, 2004), 56–64 [hereafter "Rose, You Can't Do That" (2004)"].

33. Rose, *You Can't Do That* (2004), 56–64; author interview with Sidney Eden, January 20, 2020.
34. Rose, *You Can't Do That* (2004), 56–64; author interview with Sidney Eden, January 20, 2020.

Chapter 17: The Invisible Lesbian
1. LH to Nemiroff, "Sunday."
2. "Me in Notes," box 1, file 1, LH Papers, SCH; Kevin Mumford, "Opening the Restricted Box: Lorraine Hansberry's Lesbian Writing," OutHistory.org, https://outhistory.org/exhibits/show /lorraine-hansberry/lesbian-writing.
3. The U.S. Senate launched an investigation into allegations of homosexuals "and other perverts" in federal government jobs in 1950. According to the Senate report, gays "lack the emotional stability of normal persons"; "sex perversion weakens the individual"; and "espionage agents could blackmail them." Many were quietly dismissed from the military, government employment, teaching positions, and university posts. (Sherry Wolf, "The Roots of Gay Oppression," *International Socialist Review* 37 [September–October 2004]).
4. Audre Lorde, *Zami: A New Spelling of My Name* (Trumansburg, New York: Crossing Press, 1982), 221.
5. Ann Aldrich, *We Walk Alone* (1955; repr. New York: The Feminist Press, 2006), 133. Novelist Patricia Highsmith, whom Hansberry later met, was like many who viewed homosexuality as a psychological defect; but she wasn't interested in being adjusted. When her analyst suggested she join a therapy group of "married women who are latent homosexuals," Highsmith wrote in her diary, "Perhaps I shall amuse myself by seducing a couple of them" (Margaret Talbot, "The Passions Behind Patricia Highsmith's 'The Price of Salt,'" *The New Yorker*, November 30, 2015).
6. LH, requests sent to *One* and *The Ladder*, January 16, 1957; April 18, 1957; January 9, 1958; and February 2, 1959, *One* National Gay and Lesbian Archives, University of Southern California Libraries.
7. Linsey Scriven, "Reaching across Land and Ocean: Daughters of Bilitis, Minorities Research Group, and Resistance Formation in the International Lesbian Network" (master's diss., University of Nevada, Las Vegas, 2017).
8. Elise Harris, "The Double Life of Lorraine Hansberry," *Out*, September 1999, p. 99.
9. Harris, "The Double Life of Lorraine Hansberry," 176.
10. Lorde, *Zami*.
11. Lorde writes, "However imperfectly, we tried to build a community of sorts where we could, at the very least, survive within a world we correctly perceived to be hostile to us; we talked endlessly about how best to create that mutual support which twenty years later was being discussed in the women's movement as a brand new concept. Lesbians were probably the only black and white women in New York City in the fifties who were making any real attempt to communicate with each other; we learned lessons from each other, the values of which were not lessened by what we did not learn" (*Zami*, 179).
12. Lorraine Hansberry, letter to *The Ladder* 1, no. 8 (May 1957): 26–28.
13. LH, "Simone de Beauvoir and 'The Second Sex'"; LH, "This Complex of Womanhood" (1960), 40; LH, "The Negro Writer and His Roots"; LH, *To Be Young, Gifted and Black* (New American Library edition), 98, 226; Letter "On Arthur Miller, Marilyn Monroe, and 'Guilt,'" n.d.; on Lena Younger (Mama) and "Matriarchy," see "Make New Sounds"; LH, "Origins of Character"; *A Raisin in the Sun* (New American Library edition), 82–83; and *The Sign in Brustein's Window* (New American Library edition), 233–34, 300–305.
14. LH, "Notes on Women's Liberation." Hansberry anticipates bell hooks: "From the onset of my involvement with the women's movement I was disturbed by the white women's liberationist's insistence that race and sex were two different issues. My life experience had shown me that the two issues were inseparable, that at the moment of my birth, two factors determined my destiny, my having been born black and my having been born female. . . . I voiced my conviction that the struggle to end racism and the struggle to end sexism were naturally

intertwined, that to make them separate was to deny a basic truth of our existence, that race and sex are immutable facets of human identity" (bell hooks, *Ain't I a Woman: Black Women and Feminism* [New York: Routledge, 2014], 12–13).

15. LH, "Simone de Beauvoir and 'The Second Sex,'" 128–42. Hansberry's "fantasy slave" image fits with Beauvoir, who applies Hegel's master-slave dialectic to explain how woman is twice oppressed: first, because she's a slave, and second, because she works to embody her master's self-fulfilling vision of her *as a slave*.

16. LH, "Simone de Beauvoir and 'The Second Sex,'" 128–42; LH, "Notes on Women's Liberation."

17. "In Defense of Equality of Men," written in 1961 and published in Sandra M. Gilbert and Susan Gubar, eds., *The Nation: Anthology of Literature by Women* (New York: W. W. Norton, 1985), 2056–68.

18. Letter signed "L.N." [Lorraine Nemiroff], *The Ladder* 1, no. 11 (August 1957).

19. Using the pen name "Emily Jones," Hansberry later contributed three lesbian-themed short stories to *One*: "The Budget," "The Anticipation of Eve," and "Renascence"; and one, "Chanson du Konallis," to *The Ladder*.

20. Beauvoir quoted in Higashida, *Black International Feminism*, 66.

Chapter 18: "Go the Way Your Blood Beats"

1. "Negro Playwright's Drama Wins Honor," Associated Press, April 5, 1959.

2. Langston Hughes to Lorraine Hansberry, April 5, 1958, box 63, file 15, LH Papers, SCH.

3. LH to Nemiroff, March 10, 1958, box 2, file 15, LH Papers, SCH.

4. LH's journal, Easter 1958, box 2, file 15, LH Papers, SCH.

5. "'Raisin in the Sun' Author Invented Own Formula," United Press International, *Democrat and Chronicle* (Rochester, NY), March 29, 1959; Cecil Smith, "'Raisin in the Sun' Was an Accident," *Los Angeles Times*, October 4, 1959, p. 108; Carter, "Commitment amid Complexity," 41.

6. "Make New Sounds."

7. Lloyd Richards directed six of Wilson's ten plays on Broadway: *Ma Rainey's Black Bottom* (1985); *Fences* (1988), for which Lloyd received the Tony Award; *Joe Turner's Come and Gone* (1988); *The Piano Lesson* (1990); *Two Trains Running* (1992); and *Seven Guitars* (1996).

8. Jeffrey Marsten, "Playwriting: Authorship and Collaboration," in *A New History of Early English Drama*, ed. John D. Cox and David Scott Kastan (New York: Columbia University Press, 1997), 358. Case in point: Hecate's speech in *Macbeth* is so lugubrious and unlike Shakespeare that it might have been written by an actor in the troupe who was unhappy with not being onstage often enough.

9. Colleen Karen Brown argues that collaboration draws on feminine strengths. "Playwriting and Authority: Collaborative Art and Feminine Production" (master's diss., Oregon State University, 1992).

10. Sandra G. Shannon, "From Lorraine Hansberry to August Wilson: An Interview with Lloyd Richards," *Callaloo* 14, no. 1 (1991): 124.

11. Interview with Lloyd Richards, conducted by Woodie King Jr., videotaped on November 16, 2004, for the Theatre on Film and Tape Archive, New York Public Library for the Performing Arts at Lincoln Center, New York [hereafter "Woodie King Jr. interview of Lloyd Richards"]. I have edited Richards's oral transcript to eliminate places where he digresses, while he's thinking, before returning to Hansberry.

12. "Therefore Choose Life: Paul Mann, 1913–1985," interviews with actors and directors about Mann, box 1, file A, Paul Mann Collection, Howard Gotlieb Archival Research Center, Boston University. Three of Mann's students—Mazursky, Poitier, and Vic Morrow—were together in the film that made them breakout stars: *The Blackboard Jungle* (1955); author interview with Douglas Turner Ward, December 18, 2019.

13. "The Father of Modern American Theater."

14. Woodie King Jr. interview of Lloyd Richards.

15. Poston, "We Have So Much to Say."
16. Author interview with Douglas Turner Ward, December 18, 2019.
17. Woodie King Jr. interview of Lloyd Richards.
18. Woodie King Jr. interview of Lloyd Richards; Haygood, "45 Years Ago, a 'Raisin' to Cheer."
19. Woodie King Jr. interview of Lloyd Richards.
20. ". . . alas, the original, which was lost . . ." Robert Nemiroff, "On Mama and Matriarch," 25, unprocessed, Deborah Holton Papers, Chicago Public Library; "Make New Sounds." There's also a note to Hansberry in her papers from someone expressing sadness over the lost manuscript, and it seems to have been written when Hansberry moved from Bleecker Street to Waverly Place. Did she leave the manuscript with Bob?
21. James Baldwin interviewed by Richard Goldstein, *Village Voice*, June 26, 1984.
22. James Baldwin, *Giovanni's Room* (1956; repr. New York: Penguin Books, 2010), 84.
23. Baldwin, *Giovanni's Room*, 3.
24. Weatherby, *James Baldwin* (1989), 144; David Leeming, *James Baldwin: A Biography* (1994; repr. New York: Arcade, 2015), 151; James Baldwin, *The Cross of Redemption: Uncollected Writings*, ed. Randall Kenan (New York: Pantheon Books, 2010), 135.
25. Cruse, "Replay on a Black Crisis," 21, 23–24.
26. Roger Maxwell, "The Last Days of Lorraine Hansberry," *Detroit News*, March 15, 1966.
27. Baldwin, "Sweet Lorraine."
28. Marc Lombardo, "James Baldwin's Philosophical Critique of Sexuality," *Journal of Speculative Philosophy* 23, no. 1 (2009): 41; Meredith Joan Wiggins, "Setting His House in Order: The Crisis of Paternity in James Baldwin's *Giovanni's Room*" (master's diss., University of Alabama, 2012); Nicholas Buccola, *The Fire Is upon Us: James Baldwin, William F. Buckley Jr., and the Debate over Race in America* (Princeton, NJ: Princeton University Press, 2019), 29.
29. Albert Murray, *The Omni-Americans: Some Alternatives to the Folklore of White Supremacy* (1970; repr. New York: Library of America, 2020), 38; Herb Boyd, *Baldwin's Harlem: A Biography of James Baldwin* (New York: Atria Books, 2008), 38; Leeming, *James Baldwin: A Biography*, 159. Baldwin, for the white readers of *Esquire* magazine, described the first private housing project in Harlem, Riverton, as a "slum," where enraged residents "had scarcely moved in, naturally, before they began smashing windows, defacing walls, urinating in the elevators, and fornicating in the playgrounds." It was, in fact, the pride of the area, populated by middle-class residents, some of whom had been on a waiting list for years. Reporting on a reunion of seven hundred members of the Riverton Old Timers Association in 1985, the *New York Times* described the buildings "as Harlem's first middle-income housing development and for many years the most attractive concentration of such housing open to blacks in New York City. . . . Riverton took on a special chemistry, becoming a haven of strivers far larger than the nearby block of brownstones known as Strivers' Row" (Carlyle Douglas, "Ex-Tenants Fondly Recall a Haven in Harlem," *New York Times*, March 15, 1985).
30. LH, *The Movement: Documentary of a Struggle for Equality* (New York: Simon and Schuster, 1964), 48.
31. Norman Mailer, "The White Negro: Superficial Reflections on the Hipster," *Dissent* (Fall 1957).
32. LH, "The Negro Writer and His Roots," 2–12; Untitled Lecture, Brandeis University, April 27, 1961, box 56, file 3, LH Papers, SCH.
33. LH, "The Negro Writer and His Roots," 2–12. "But you can't be a member of the beat generation, the fashionable word at the moment in marketing, unless you starve a little. Yet who wants to be beat? Not Negroes" (Langston Hughes, "Writers: Black and White," paper presented at the First Conference of Negro Writers, March 1959, American Society of African Culture, New York, 1960, p. 45).
34. Mailer, "The White Negro."
35. Perry Meisel, "From Bebop to Hip Hop: American Music after 1950," in *A Concise Companion*

to *Postwar American Literature and Culture*, ed. Josephine Hendin (Hoboken, NJ: Blackwell Publishing, 2004), 95.

36. Cheney, *Lorraine Hansberry*, 29n52; James Baldwin et al., "The Negro in American Culture," *CrossCurrents* 11, no. 3 (1961): 205–24.

37. Baldwin, "Sweet Lorraine."

38. Julian Mayfield, box 9, file 1: Publishers and Agents, Julian Mayfield Papers, SCH.

39. James Baldwin interviewed by Richard Goldstein, *Village Voice*, June 26, 1984; Douglas Field, *All Those Strangers: The Art and Lives of James Baldwin* (New York: Oxford University Press, 2015), 78.

40. Civil rights leaders asked Baldwin and Bayard Rustin to stay in the wings of the movement. "The crucial charge against Baldwin had little to do with his politics, or his literary craftsmanship, or even for that matter his precise position on the race questions. The argument was that Baldwin's homosexuality, his unconfident masculinity, is the hidden root of all his writing and completely disqualifies him as a representative spokesman" (Morris Dickstein, *Gates of Eden: American Culture in the Sixties* [New York: Basic Books, 1977], 168); John D'Emilio, "Homophobia and the Trajectory of Postwar American Radicalism: The Career of Bayard Rustin," in *Modern American Queer History*, ed. Allida M. Black (Philadelphia, PA: Temple University Press, 2001); LH, *To Be Young, Gifted and Black*, 201.

41. James Baldwin, "The Artist's Struggle for Integrity" in Kenan, ed., *The Cross of Redemption*; LH to the editor of *Commentary* (March 5, 1963), in response to Norman Podhoretz's article "My Negro Problem and Yours," in *Commentary* (February 1963).

42. Studs Terkel, James Baldwin interview, in Fred L. Standley and Louis H. Pratt, eds., *Conversations with James Baldwin* (Jackson: University Press of Mississippi, 1963), 3–23; Isaacs, "Five Writers and Their African Ancestors Part II," 326.

43. Michael Anderson, "A Landmark Lesson in Being Black," *New York Times*, March 7, 1999, sec. 2, p. 7.

44. Bruce McConachie, *American Theater in the Culture of the Cold War: Producing and Contesting Containment, 1947–1962* (Iowa City: University of Iowa Press, 2003), 1.

45. Rose, *You Can't Do That* (2004), 72.

46. Muriel I. Symington to W. E. B. Du Bois, June 2, 1958, https://credo.library.umass.edu/view/full/mums312-b148-i384, Special Collections and University Archives, University Libraries, University of Massachusetts, Amherst.

47. Howard Morley Sachar, *A History of Jews in America* (New York: Vintage Books, 1993), 666.

48. Anna Arnold Hedgeman, "Why You Should See 'Raisin,'" *New York Age*, July 18, 1959, p. 9.

49. Author interview with Douglas Turner Ward, December 18, 2019.

50. LH to Miss Watson, May 1 and 14, 1963, box 8, file 1, LH Papers, SCH.

51. Mitchell, *Black Drama*, 170.

52. Smith, *Visions of Belonging*, 310n120.

53. Hay, *African American Theatre*, 89–90. Ossie Davis also wrote and directed a one-act about Rosa Parks, *Montgomery Footsteps* (1956), for Service Employees International Union Local 1199 Healthcare Workers in New York.

Chapter 19: "Something Urgently on Its Way"

1. Kevin J. Mumford, *Not Straight, Not White: Black Gay Men from the March on Washington to the AIDS Crisis* (Chapel Hill: The University of North Carolina Press, 2016), 19.

2. Harris, "The Double Life of Lorraine Hansberry," 96–101.

3. Harris, "The Double Life of Lorraine Hansberry," 96–101.

4. Harris, "The Double Life of Lorraine Hansberry," 96–101.

5. Audre Lorde, *I Am Your Sister: Collected and Unpublished Writings of Audre Lorde* (New York: Oxford University Press, 2011), 148.

6. Margaret A Simons, "Lesbian Connections: Simone de Beauvoir and Feminism," *Signs* 18, no. 1 (1992): 149.

7. Eve Kotchever (better known by her pseudonym, Eve Adams) opened her tearoom at 129 MacDougal Street. She was a Polish-Jewish lesbian immigrant. Convicted by New York's Vice Squad for keeping a disorderly house and publishing her book, *Lesbian Love Stories*, she was deported to Europe in the late 1920s. In Paris, she ran a bookstore and café until, during German occupation, she was sent to Auschwitz and murdered in 1943.

8. Harris, "The Double Life of Lorraine Hansberry," 96–101.

9. Lorde, *Zami*, 180 and 220.

10. Lillian Faderman, *Odd Girls and Twilight Lovers* (New York: Columbia University Press, 1991), 160.

11. Schelling, "Micromotives and Macrobehavior," 150.

12. Lorde, *Zami*, 222.

13. Audre Lorde, "The Master's Tools Will Never Dismantle the Master's House" (1984), in *Sister Outsider: Essays and Speeches* (New York: Crossing Press, 2007), 111.

14. Nicholas Buccola, *The Fire Is upon Us*, 24.

15. LH, "Some Rather Indecisive Thoughts."

16. Perry, *Looking for Lorraine*.

17. Mary Oliver, *Our World* (New York: Beacon Press, 2009).

18. Maxine Wood to LH, May 17, 1959, box 8, file 1, LH Papers, SCH.

19. LH, "On Summer," in *Playbill*.

20. Charles McHarry, "On the Town," *Daily News*, July 30, 1958, C14.

21. Lorde, *Zami*, 217.

22. Harris, "The Double Life of Lorraine Hansberry," 96–101.

23. Simons, "Lesbian Connections," 140, 160.

24. LH to Nemiroff, August 18, 1958, box 2, file 1, LH Papers, SCH.

25. William S. Anderson, CPA, to Seymour L. Baldash, CPA, July 29, 1957; Baldash to Anderson, July 31, 1957; Anderson to Baldash, July 29, 1957, box 2, file 17, LH Papers, SCH; LH to Nemiroff, August 18, 1958, box 2, file 1, LH Papers, SCH; Metropolitan Housing and Planning Council Accession 74–20, box 13, file 143, Daley Library, Chicago, IL. Violations (by year: 1955, 8; 1956, 13; 1957, 22; 1958, 58; 1959, 11; 1960, 3) ranged from rats and roaches to rotten floors to substandard partitions to fire hazards. At least one case was the result of tenant injury.

26. Cheney, *Lorraine Hansberry*, 12.

27. "$22,122 in Building Fines Paid by Hansberry Family," *Chicago Sun-Times*, August 24, 1960.

28. "Daley Insists on Trial of Building Suits," *Chicago Tribune*, May 9, 1958.

29. "Six Hansberrys Sue City for $1 Million," *Chicago Defender*, June 27, 1959, p. 1; "Landlord Suing City for Million," *Chicago American*, July 12, 1958.

30. LH, *To Be Young, Gifted and Black*, 18.

31. LH, *To Be Young, Gifted and Black*, 63.

32. McKissack and McKissack, *Young, Black, and Determined*, 29.

33. LH, *To Be Young, Gifted and Black*, 120.

34. Weatherby, *James Baldwin* (1989), 150.

35. "The Father of Modern American Theater."

36. Haygood, "45 Years Ago, a 'Raisin' to Cheer."

37. Haygood, "45 Years Ago, a 'Raisin' to Cheer."

38. LH FBI file, 100–107297, September 5, 1958.

39. Dale Wright to LH, September 19, 1958, box 63, file 7, LH Papers, SCH.

40. Mitchell, *Black Drama*, 138.

41. Thurgood Marshall to LH, October 7, 1958, box 7, file 7, LH Papers, SCH. The dinner was at the home of Joseph Buttinger and his wife. Buttinger was an Austrian refugee from Nazism who developed programs for the International Rescue Committee. He also subsidized the socialist magazine *Dissent*.

42. "Limited Partnership Agreement of the Raisin in the Sun Company, 1958," box 86, file 3, Waldo Salt Papers, Performing Arts Special Collections, UCLA Library.

43. Email from Howard Swibel, May 20, 2019; Alexander Polikoff, *Waiting for Gautreaux: A Story of Segregation, Housing, and the Black Ghetto* (Evanston, IL: Northwestern University Press, 2006), 43; Adam Cohen and Elizabeth Taylor, *American Pharaoh: Mayor Richard J. Daley, His Battle for Chicago and the Nation* (New York: Back Bay Books/Hachette, 2001), 401; Ruth Moore to Harold Strauss, April 30, 1959, box 257, file 7, Alfred A. Knopf Papers, Harold Ransom Center. Among the other backers were Anne Bancroft, Robert Nemiroff, Doris Belack, Harry Belafonte, Burt D'Lugoff, Juanita Poitier, producer Harold Prince, Philip Rose, and screenwriter Waldo Salt. The 2014 revival of *Raisin* with Denzel Washington was coproduced by Charles R. Swibel's grandson Brian, his father, Howard, said.

44. Anderson, "A Landmark Lesson in Being Black," sec. 2, p. 7.

45. Perry, *Looking for Lorraine*; Marie J. Kuda, "A Woman in the Sun: Lorraine Hansberry," in *Out and Proud in Chicago: An Overview of the City's Gay Community*, ed. Tracy Baim (Evanston, IL: Agate Surrey, 2009), 61.

46. Harris, "The Double Life of Lorraine Hansberry," 96–101.

47. Harold Clurman, *On Directing* (New York: Simon and Schuster, 1997), 25.

48. Everett C. Dixon, "Lloyd Richards in Rehearsal" (PhD diss., York University, 2013).

49. Dixon, "Lloyd Richards in Rehearsal"; Tallmer, "Father of Revolution."

50. "Accident Creates Hit, 'Raisin in the Sun,'" *Los Angeles Times*, October 4, 1959.

51. Act 2, scene 2, *A Raisin in the Sun*, 25th anniversary ed. (New York: Samuel French, 1984), pp. 139–40; Nemiroff, "On Mama and Matriarch," 25.

52. Sidney Poitier, *This Life* (New York: Alfred A. Knopf, 1980), 235.

53. *A Raisin in the Sun*, box 5, files 116–17, Philip Rose Papers, Beinecke Rare Book and Manuscript Library, Yale University, New Haven, CT. Later, MacNeil began signing her letters and telegrams "the star of *A Raisin in the Sun*." Hansberry approached Alice Childress about playing Mama Younger, but Childress was petite and cast in romantic leads. "I want your play to succeed," she said.

54. Poitier, *This Life*, 236.

55. Porgy and Bess Debate, *The Theatre*, box 63, file 28, LH Papers, SCH.

56. Quoted in Wilkerson, "Political Radicalism and Artistic Innovation in the Works of Lorraine Hansberry," 43.

57. LH, *To Be Young, Gifted and Black*, 109; Nannie Hansberry to LH, Western Union, January 21, 1959, box 7, files 4–5, LH Papers, SCH.

58. Margaret B. Wilkerson. "'A Raisin in the Sun': Anniversary of an American Classic," *Theatre Journal* 38, no. 4 (1986): 442.

59. Scheader interview of Nemiroff, 30.

60. Smith, *Visions of Belonging*, 315.

61. From a speech delivered by Wofsy at a symposium commemorating Loraine Hansberry and *A Raisin in the Sun* at the University of California at Berkeley, February 19, 1998. Writing in her scrapbook of reviews, Hansberry agreed with Daniel Gottlieb's review in the *Hartford Times*: the playwright "manages to weave the threads of the Negro-white conflict, materialism vs. spiritualism, and the individual vs. his conscience into the play" (January 24, 1959).

62. Lorraine Hansberry, "Willie Loman, Walter Younger, and He Who Must Live," *Village Voice*, August 12, 1959, pp. 7–8.

63. LH, "Willy Loman, Walter Younger, and He Who Must Live," 7–8; "Appraising a Prize," *Christian Science Monitor*, reprinted in *Journal Gazette* (Mattoon, IL) (April 21, 1959), 4.

64. Scheader interview of Nemiroff, 38.

65. This was written in Hennich's hand on the FBI memo about the play. LH FBI file, 100–393031–28.

66. Khrushchev asked the question during an interview given to a correspondent of *Le Figaro*, March 19, 1958.

67. The details about Hennrich are taken from his FBI personnel file, "Hennrich, Carl E.," at

the Internet Archive, https://archive.org/details/foia_Hennrich_Carl_E.-2; LH FBI file, 100–107297, September 5, 1958.

68. LH FBI file, Office Memorandum, 100–44090, February 5, 1959; see William J. Maxwell's interpretation of the FBI review/report in *F.B. Eyes: How J. Edgar Hoover's Ghostreaders Framed African American Literature* (2015; repr. Princeton, NJ: Princeton University Press, 2016). Word of the play spread through the black community via entertainment journalists Billy Rowe, nicknamed "the black Walter Winchell," and Conchita Nakatani, who contacted local clubs, resulting in blocks of tickets being purchased (Jack Saunders, "I Love a Parade," *Philadelphia Tribune*, January 24, 1959).

69. Scheader, *Lorraine Hansberry*, 67–68.

70. Cheney, *Lorraine Hansberry*, 25.

71. "The Father of Modern American Theater"; Bennett and Burroughs, "A Lorraine Hansberry Rap," 226.

72. Claudia Cassidy, "Warm Heart, Backbone, Funnybone in Blackstone Play and Cast," *Chicago Tribune*, February 11, 1959, p. 27.

73. George Leighton to Seymour L. Baldash, August 7, 1962, box 2, file 17, LH Papers, SCH.

74. "The Father of Modern American Theater."

75. Arnold Rampersad, *The Life of Langston Hughes*, vol. 2: *1947–1967, I Dream a World*, 2nd ed. (New York: Oxford University Press, 2002), 294.

Chapter 20: Dismantling the Master's House

1. "Whites Dreadfully Ignorant of Negro Life," 3.

2. *The American Negro Writer and His Roots*, 1–3, 8, 41, 58.

3. "A Playwright, A Promise," Faye Hammel interview with LH, *Cue*, February 28, 1959, pp. 20, 43.

4. LH, "The Negro Writer and His Roots," 2–12.

5. Washington, *The Other Blacklist*. How the CIA worked with foundations—and they weren't reluctant to receive the support—is explained in Frances Stonor Saunders's excellent *The Cultural Cold War: The CIA and the World of Arts and Letters* (New York: The New Press, 2013), 297–301.

6. Phil Rose to LH, Western Union, March 11, 1959, box 7, files 4–5, LH Papers, SCH; LH to Phil Rose, March 11, 1959, Production Files, 1957–2007, box 17, Oversize, Series 2, Philip Rose Papers, Beinecke Rare Book and Manuscript Library, Yale University, New Haven, CT.

7. Hughes to Arna Bontemps, March 17, 1959, in Charles Harold Nichols, ed., *Arna Bontemps–Langston Hughes Letters, 1925–1967* (New York: Athena, 1990).

8. Poston, "We Have So Much to Say"; Scheader interview of Nemiroff, 32.

9. During rehearsals for *The Sign in Sidney Brustein's Window*, Nemiroff was always "just *there*," Moreno said, "getting hamburgers or something" (Author interview with Rita Moreno, December 10, 2019).

10. Author interview with Douglas Turner Ward, December 18, 2018. Lonne Elder was in the cast as an understudy as well.

11. Harris, "The Double Life of Lorraine Hansberry," 96–101.

12. LH to Mamie Hansberry, January 19, 1959, box 7, file 7, LH Papers, SCH.

13. Ernest Hemingway, "The Art of Fiction No. 21," *Paris Review* 18 (Spring 1958).

14. Nan Robertson, "Dramatist Against Odds," *New York Times*, March 8, 1959, p. X3; Harold Cruse, *The Crisis of the Negro Intellectual* (1967; repr. New York Review of Books, 2005), 222, 267, 282–83.

15. Robin Bernstein, "Inventing a Fishbowl: White Supremacy and the Critical Reception of Lorraine Hansberry's 'A Raisin in the Sun,'" *Modern Drama* 42, no. 1 (1999): 23.

16. LH to Nan Robertson, March 27, 1959, box 7, file 7, LH Papers, SCH.

17. Poston, "We Have So Much to Say"; Cecil Smith, "'Raisin in the Sun' Was an Accident," *Los Angeles Times* (October 4, 1959), 108.

18. LH to Lloyd Richards, "Friday" (March 1959), box 42, files 424–25, Lloyd Richards Papers, Beinecke Rare Book and Manuscript Library, Yale University, New Haven, CT.

19. LH, quoted in Stephen R. Carter, *Hansberry's Drama: Commitment and Complexity* (Urbana: University of Illinois Press, 1990), 65.

20. Rough draft/thoughts about contemporary drama, p. 1; Notes from *The Apples of Autumn* reading.

21. Freedman, "Yale Marking 25th Anniversary of 'Raisin in the Sun'"; Woodie King Jr., "Lloyd Richards: Teacher, Director, Friend," *New World Review* 1, no. 1 (2007).

22. McConachie, *American Theater in the Culture of the Cold War*, 181–83.

23. LH, "Mailbag," sec. 2, part 1, X3; Samuel A. Boyea to Seán O'Casey, July 6, 1959, MS 38, 110, Seán O'Casey Papers, Manuscripts Department, National Library of Ireland.

24. Lowery, "The Socialist Legacy of Sean O'Casey," 133–34; LH, *To Be Young, Gifted and Black*, 209.

25. Oliver C. Cox, *Caste, Class, and Race* (1948), quoted in McConachie, *American Theater in the Culture of the Cold War*, 180.

26. Isabel Wilkerson, *Caste: The Origin of Our Discontent* (New York: Random House, 2020), 41.

27. Nemiroff, "On LH's View of Assimilation, Integration, Separatism, Black Liberation & the Way Ahead," unprocessed, Holton Papers, CPL.

28. LH to Peter Buitenhuis, February 3, 1959, box 63, file 5, LH Papers, SCH.

29. LH to Buitenhuis, February 3, 1959.

30. LH, "The Negro Writer and His Roots," 2–12.

31. "Make New Sounds."

32. Asagai seems to take his philosophy from French West Indian intellectual Franz Fanon, whom Hansberry may have read. Fanon advocated black consciousness, a revolt against racist colonialism, putting Marxism into practice, and transforming society in the developing world through revolution.

33. In an analysis of *Juno and the Paycock*, one scholar discusses Juno's role as it relates to the play's theme, which can be applied to Lena's function as a pragmatist in *Raisin*, too. "The governing idea of the play, I have been suggesting, is the ironic (if not wholly tragic) juxtaposition of human realities in conflict with the grandiose illusions of Irish Romanticism and the meaningless abstractions of politics and war. . . . It is against such abstractions that Juno has constantly to struggle in her attempt to hold a disintegrating world together" (Errol Durbach, "Peacocks and Mothers: Theme and Dramatic Metaphor in O'Casey's Juno and the Paycock," *Modern Drama* 15, no. 1 [Spring 1972], 15–25).

34. LH, "Origins of Character," 14.

35. "Make New Sounds." Nemiroff attributed this criticism to the "prevailing notions of the establishment—i.e., white, sexist—sociology (the Moynihan 'thesis') which confuses leadership with 'dominance' to denigrate the black male and divide the liberation struggle" (Nemiroff to Susan McHenry, November 27, 1978, unprocessed, Holton Papers, CPL. Black feminist scholar bell hooks makes the same point: "The dominant role white women played in the 19th century domestic household has not led scholars to theorize about ineffectual white masculinity; quite the opposite has occurred. . . . Like their slave-owning ancestors, racist scholars acted as if black women fulfilling their role as mothers and economic providers were performing a unique action that needed a new definition even though it was not uncommon for many poor and widowed white women to perform this dual role. Yet they labeled black women as matriarchs—a title that in no way accurately described the social status of black women in America. No matriarchy has ever existed in the United States" (hooks, *Ain't I a Woman: Black Women and Feminism*, 72).

36. "Feinberg Decision Shocks Chicago," 2.

37. LH to Pauline Oehler, March 8, 1959, box 63, file 5, LH Papers, SCH; Joseph Wershba, "John Fielder: The White Man in 'A Raisin in the Sun,'" *New York Post*, May 20, 1959.

38. McConachie, *American Theater in the Culture of the Cold War*, 188; Lorde, "The Master's Tools Will Never Dismantle the Master's House," 111.

39. Robert Nemiroff to Chris Bigsby, July 2, 1982, unprocessed, Holton Papers, CPL.

40. Nelson Algren, *The Man with the Golden Arm* (New York: Seven Stories Press, 2011), 19. Original edition, Doubleday, 1950.

41. LH, "Willie Loman, Walter Lee Younger, and He Must Live," 7–8.

42. W. E. B. Du Bois, "Of Our Spiritual Strivings," in *The Souls of Black Folk* (1903). "You may wish also to add 'potentiated double consciousness' to your analysis. It is from what Paget Henry first called 'potentiated second sight' and then Jane Anna Gordon transformed into 'potentiated double consciousness.' The idea is that a form of growth occurs when African Americans realize that it is the governing force of the United States' commitment to making the country a white wealthy nation that makes black people into problems. Understanding that they are not in-and-of-themselves the problem, they can become active in addressing the society's contradictions and articulate a different future" (email, Lewis R. Gordon, PhD, February 7, 2019).

43. LH, "Willie Loman, Walter Lee Younger, and He Must Live," 8.

44. Nemiroff to Bigsby.

45. LH to Lloyd Richards, March 13, 1959, box 42, files 424–25, Lloyd Richards Papers, Beinecke Rare Book and Manuscript Library, Yale University, New Haven, CT.

46. Harris, "The Double Life of Lorraine Hansberry," 96–101.

47. Walter Kerr, "No Clear Path and No Retreat," *New York Herald Tribune*, Lively Arts, March 22, 1959, pp. 1–2.

48. Leo Hansberry to LH, March 26, 1959, box 7, file 6; Ann Miler to LH, n.d., box 7, file 6; Edythe Cohen to LH, March 12, 1959, box 7, file 6; LH to Edythe Cohen, March 25, 1959, box 8, file 1, LH Papers, SCH.

49. *A Raisin in the Sun* didn't ensure the success of two other Broadway plays that were similar in spirit. A year later, Lloyd Richards directed *The Long Dream*, based on a novel by Richard Wright, at the Ambassador Theatre. It closed after five performances. And *The Cool World*, based a novel by Warren Miller, said by Baldwin to be the best ever written about Harlem, closed at the Eugene O'Neill Theater after only two performances.

50. LH FBI file, 100–393031–37, April 21, 1959.

Chapter 21: Chitterlin' Heights

1. Benjamin Davis to LH, May 4, 1959, file: "Lorraine Hansberry, Correspondence Personal Left," LH Papers, SCH.

2. Ross, "How Lorraine Hansberry Wrote 'A Raisin in the Sun.'" Hansberry was asked to participate on President's Kennedy Commission on the Status of Women because, the invitation said, she was a "leader in the mass media field" (Esther Peterson to LH, February 15, 1963, file: "Lorraine Hansberry Correspondence Organizations Government," LH Papers, SCH).

3. James Baldwin, "Preface" to LH, *To Be Young, Gifted and Black*, xix.

4. See bell hooks, *Ain't I a Woman*, 4–6; and Olga Barrios, *The Black Theatre Movement in the United States and in South Africa* (València: Publicacions Universitat de València, 2009), 31; Cruse, *The Crisis of the Negro Intellectual*, 102.

5. Cruse, *The Crisis of the Negro Intellectual*, 102.

6. LH, *To Be Young, Gifted and Black*, 39.

7. "Television Portrait Gallery of Interesting People: Lorraine Hansberry," interview with Mike Wallace, May 8, 1959, on *Lorraine Hansberry Speaks Out: Art and the Black Revolution*, Caedmon cassette, CDL 51352.

8. "At Random," Irv Kupcinet's (of the *Chicago Sun-Times*) weekly television program (May 16, 1959); Jack Pitman, in *Variety*, May 27, 1959; Ian Gregory Strachan and Mia Mask, eds., *Poitier Revisited: Reconsidering a Black Icon in the Obama Age* (New York: Bloomsbury Academic, 2014), 109.

9. "'Whites Dreadfully Ignorant of Negro Life,'" 3.

10. LH to Nemiroff, May 13, 1959, box 2, file 15, LH Papers, SCH. The purchase price was $80,000—ten times that in today's money.

11. "'Raisin' Proves Bonanza for Lorraine Hansberry," *The Afro-American*, July 18, 1959. All amounts are given in 2018 dollars.

12. Author interview of Amy Secules, March 3, 2017.

13. Roberta Kyle, "Brownstone Biographies," Patricia D. Klingenstein Library, New York Historical Society. The Ashcan School: Robert Henri (1865–1929), William James Glackens (1870–1938), George Luks (1866–1933), John Sloan (1871–1951), and Everett Shinn (1876–1953), whose apartment it was that was used as a bohemian theater.

14. "Lorraine Hansberry's Husband Denies Split," *New York Age*, June 20, 1959.

15. "Slum Play Author Sued as Slumlord," *New York World Telegram*, June 13, 1959, p. 2; Nannie Hansberry to LH, January 5, 1961, box 2, file 1, LH Papers, SCH.

16. Ole Nosey, "Everybody Goes When the Wagon Comes," 18; "Slum Landlord Eludes City in Jail: Hansberry Freed Before Process Server Arrives," *Chicago Daily News*, June 22, 1960. Journalists scoffed at how Carl had been in jail for a night after being arrested by a deputy court bailiff, but before a process server from municipal court got to him, he had already walked out a free man again, owing $19,000 in fines.

17. Helen Dudar, "Counterpoint to 'A Raisin in the Sun,'" *New York Post*, July 1, 1959.

18. Carl Hansberry Jr. to LH, April 20, 1961, box 2, file 2, LH Papers, SCH.

19. "Hansberry Family of Chicago Forced to Flee City to Escape Arrest on Contempt of Court Charges; They Refused to Pay Fines on Housing Violations; about $20,000.00," *Jet*, July 7, 1960.

20. "$22,122 Is Paid in Hansberry Building Fines," *Chicago Tribune*, August 24, 1960, p. 14.

21. "Slum Play Author Sued as Slumlord," 2; Nannie Hansberry to LH, January 5, 1961, box 2, file 1, LH Papers, SCH; Carl Hansberry Jr. to LH, April 20, 1961, box 2, file 2, LH Papers, SCH; "Is Pershing Hotel Jinxed?" *Chicago Defender*, February 23, 1963; LH to Seymour Baldash, "Sunday"; S.L. Baldash to Mamie Tubbs, February 10, 1962, box 2, file 17, LH Papers, SCH.

22. Box 2, file 17, LH Papers, SCH.

23. Louis Burnham to LH, March 11, 1959, box 2, file 13, LH papers, SCH.

24. Author interview with Margaret Burnham, July 4, 2020.

25. Box 2, file 17, LH Papers, SCH.

26. Louis Burnham to LH, March 11, 1959, box 2, file 13, LH Papers, SCH.

27. The Brookmore was sold in the 1970s and became a popular resort for LGBTQ guests under the name "The Raven."

28. Memorandum RE Draft Agreement Between Henry Rogers Benjamin and Lorraine Hansberry, July 20, 1961, "Paragraph 16: Morals clause . . . must be eliminated," box 11, folder 36, Arthur Kinoy Papers, Wisconsin Historical Society, Madison, WI.

29. *Lorraine Hansberry: The Collected Last Plays* (New York: New American Library, 1983), 143–50; Maire Torre, "Dore Schary Tells Why TV Shies from Civil War," *New York Herald Tribune*, August 30, 1960, B1; Edward W. Farrison, "Lorraine Hansberry's Last Dramas," *College Language Association Journal* 16, no. 2 (December 1972): 188–97. A soldier in *The Drinking Gourd* explains that slavery is capitalism at its most basic level—it's the same system that employs small white children in northern mills. It's about labor, merchandise, and profit, he says. Hansberry anticipates the work of scholars such as Edward E. Baptist in *The Half Has Never Been Told: Slavery and the Making of American Capitalism*. Nemiroff heavily revised *The Drinking Gourd* and tried for twenty years to get it produced and aired.

30. Jan Herman, "The Sweet Dreams of Black Playwright Lorraine Hansberry," *Chicago Sun-Times*, October 16, 1983, p. 10.

31. Cecil Smith, "Time Ran Out, but the Message Is There," *Los Angeles Times* (April 25, 1965).

32. Harris, "The Double Life of Lorraine Hansberry."

33. LH, journal entry, October 1962, box 1, files 1–2, LH Papers, SCH.

34. LH to Alice [no surname], March 15, 1963, box 2, file 18, LH Papers, SCH.

35. LH, *To Be Young, Gifted and Black*, 125.

36. Harris, "The Double Life of Lorraine Hansberry."

37. Letter to Ann Morrissett Davidon, May 1962, box DG 144, file 7, Ann Morrissett Davidon and William C. Davidon Papers, Swarthmore College Peace Collection, Swarthmore College, Swarthmore, PA.

38. Robert Nemiroff to June Jordan, October 27, 1979, box 40, file 8, June Jordan Papers, Schlesinger Library, Radcliffe Institute, Harvard University, Cambridge, MA.

39. *The Sign in Sidney Brustein's Window* (New York: Samuel French, 1993), 120.

40. LH, *To Be Young, Gifted and Black*, 146.

41. "News of the Rialto: Hansberry's Plays," LH interview with Milton Esterow, *New York Times*, July 1, 1962.

42. LH to Ann Morrissett Davidon, May 1962, Ann Morrissett Davidon and William C. Davidon Papers, Swarthmore College Peace Collection, Swarthmore College, Swarthmore, PA.

43. LH, *To Be Young, Gifted and Black*, 218; Robert Nemiroff, introduction, xix; McKissack and McKissack, *Young, Black, and Determined*, 110.

44. LH, *To Be Young, Gifted and Black*, 218.

45. LH to Miss Watson, May 1 and 14, 1963; LH, *To Be Young, Gifted and Black*, 218.

46. Arthur Meier Schlesinger, *Robert Kennedy and His Times* (1978; repr. Boston: Houghton Mifflin, 2002), 332; Leeming, *James Baldwin*, 225.

47. The car that Michael Schwerner, James Chaney, and Andrew Goodman were riding in when they were murdered outside Philadelphia, Mississippi, was purchased with the money raised at the temple.

48. Investor prospectus from box 11, file 45, Arthur Kinoy Papers, Wisconsin Historical Society, Madison, WI.

49. Maxwell, "The Last Days of Lorraine Hansberry."

50. Dorothy Kilgallen, "The Voice of Broadway" (syndicated column), December 31, 1963.

51. LH, *To Be Young, Gifted and Black*, 225.

52. LH, *To Be Young, Gifted and Black*, 249–50.

53. Author interview with Rita Moreno.

54. LH, *To Be Young, Gifted and Black*, 261.

55. Author interview with Rita Moreno.

56. Nemiroff to LH, Western Union, October 15, 1964, box 27, file 1, LH Papers, SCH.

57. Author interview with Rita Moreno.

58. Maxwell, "The Last Days of Lorraine Hansberry."

59. D'Lugoff and Nemiroff to "Dear Partners," October 21, 1964, box 26, file 11, LH Papers, SCH.

60. McKissack and McKissack, *Young, Black, and Determined*, 133.

61. Harris, "The Double Life of Lorraine Hansberry"; LH FBI file, 100–393031–38, July 6, 1959.

62. Raidy, "Eight Years Later 'Raisin' Reaches the Musical Stage."

63. Harris, "The Double Life of Lorraine Hansberry"; Lee Silver, "Reveal Hansberry was Divorced," *Daily News*, February 5, 1965.

64. Author interview with Douglas Turner Ward, June 21, 2018.

65. At a party hosted by Ossie Davis and Ruby Dee in 1963, Lorraine made a point of telling Malcolm X that she objected to his remarks condemning interracial marriages. He apologized and explained that he had believed interracial marriages were wrong, but he had since changed his mind. "Eyes on the Prize One Interviews," interview with Ossie Davis by Madison Davis Lucy Jr., July 6, 1989, Washington University Digital Gateway Texts, Washington University Film and Media Archive, Henry Hampton Collection.

66. Author interview with Douglas Turner Ward, June 21, 2018.

67. "Divorced White Husband Gets Most of Hansberry's Rich Estate," *Jet*, February 18, 1965.

Epilogue

1. Jewell Handy Gresham-Nemiroff was a professor of language and literature who taught at Tuskegee Institute, New York University, Hofstra University, Nassau Community College, and Vassar College.
2. Nemiroff to Madrue Wright, December 18, 1967, box 69, file 3, LH Papers, SCH.
3. *Les Blancs*, boxes 32–33, LH Papers, SCH.
4. LH, *Les Blancs: The Collected Last Plays*, ed. and with an introduction by Robert Nemiroff (New York: Vintage Books, 1973), 45.
5. Nemiroff to June Jordan, October 27, 1979, box 40, file 8, June Jordan Papers, Schlesinger Library on the History of Women in America, Radcliffe Institute for Advanced Study, Cambridge, MA.

Selected Bibliography

Abbot, Edith, and Sophonisba P. Breckinridge. *The Tenements of Chicago, 1908–1935*. Chicago: University of Chicago Press, 1936.

Abdell, Joy. L. "African/American: Lorraine Hansberry's 'Les Blancs' and the American Civil Rights Movement." *African American Review* 35 (2001).

Baldwin, James. "Sweet Lorraine." In *The Price of the Ticket: Collected Nonfiction, 1948–1985*. New York: St. Martin's/Marek, 1985.

Barrios, Olga. *The Black Theatre Movement in the United States and in South Africa*. Valencia: Universitat de València, Spain, 2008.

Bernstein, Robin. "Inventing a Fishbowl: White Supremacy and the Critical Reception of Lorraine Hansberry's 'A Raisin in the Sun.'" *Modern Drama* 42, no. 1 (1999).

Bower, Martha G. *Color Struck Under the Gaze: Ethnicity and the Pathology of Being in the Plays of Johnson, Hurston, Childress, Hansberry, and Kennedy*. Westport, CT: Praeger, 2003.

Brown, Lloyd W. "Lorraine Hansberry as Ironist: A Reappraisal of 'A Raisin in the Sun.'" *Journal of Black Studies* 4, no. 3 (1974).

Carter, Steven R. "Commitment amid Complexity: Lorraine Hansberry's Life in Action." *Melus* 7 (Fall 1980).

Chambers, Douglas B., ed. "Richard Wright, Citizen of the World: A Centenary Celebration." *The Southern Quarterly* 46, no. 2 (Winter 2009).

Cheney, Anne. *Lorraine Hansberry*. Boston: Twayne, 1984.

Chicago Commission on Race Relations. *The Negro in Chicago—A Study of Race Relations and a Race Riot*. Chicago: University of Chicago Press, 1922.

Cooley, Will. *Moving Up, Moving Out: The Rise of the Black Middle Class in Chicago*. DeKalb: Northern Illinois University, 2018.

Cruse, Harold. *The Crisis of the Negro Intellectual: A Historical Analysis of the Failure of Black Leadership*. 1967; repr. New York Review Books, 2005.

Dolinar, Brian. *The Black Cultural Front: Black Writers and Artists of the Depression Generation*. Oxford: University Press of Mississippi, 2012.

Drake, St. Clair, and Horace R. Cayton. *Black Metropolis: A Study of Negro Life in a Northern City*. 1945; repr. Chicago: University of Chicago Press, 2015.

Effiong, Phillip Uko. "History, Myth, and Revolt in Lorraine Hansberry's 'Les Blancs.'" *African American Review* 3, no. 2 (1998).

Gettleman, Marvin E. "'No Varsity Teams': New York's Jefferson School of Social Science, 1943–1956." *Science and Society* 66, no. 3 (Fall 2002).

Gibson, Truman K., Jr., with Steve Huntley. *Knocking Down Barriers: My Fight for Black America.* Evanston, IL: Northwestern University Press, 2005.

Gilyard, Keith. *John Oliver Killens: A Life of Black Literary Activism.* Athens: University of Georgia Press, 2010.

Gornick, Vivian. "What Endures of the Romance of American Communism." *New York Review of Books,* April 3, 2020.

Gresham-Nemiroff, Jewell Handy. "Foreword to the Vintage Edition." In *A Raisin in the Sun* and *The Sign in Sidney Brustein's Window,* edited by Robert Nemiroff. New York: Vintage Books, 1995.

Hairston, Loyle. "Lorraine Hansberry—Portrait of an Angry Young Writer." *The Crisis* 86, no. 4 (April 1979).

Hansberry, Lorraine. "The Black Revolution and the White Backlash." In *Black Protest: History, Documents and Analysis: 1619 to the Present,* edited by Joanne Grant. New York: Fawcett, 1968. Originally delivered as part of a forum sponsored by the Association of Artists for Freedom. Town Hall, New York, June 15, 1964.

———. "A Challenge to Artists." Speech delivered at Rally to Abolish the House Un-American Activities Committee. Manhattan Center, New York City, October 27, 1962.

———. "In Defense of the Equality of Men." In *The Norton Anthology of Literature by Women,* edited by Sandra M. Gilbert and Susan Gubar. New York: W. W. Norton, 1985.

———. "Make New Sounds: Studs Terkel Interviews Lorraine Hansberry." Transcript of radio show. WFMT Radio, Chicago, May 12, 1959. Reprinted in *American Theater* (November 1984), 6.

———. *The Movement: Documentary of a Struggle for Equality.* New York: Simon and Schuster, 1964.

———. "The Negro Writer and His Roots: Toward a New Romanticism." *The Black Scholar* 12, no. 2 (1981).

———. "On Strindberg and Sexism." In *Women in Theatre,* edited by Karen Malpede. New York: Limelight Editions, 1985. Originally published as a letter to the *Village Voice* in February 1956.

———. "Origins of Character." Address to the American Academy of Psychotherapists, October 5, 1963. Reprinted as "Playwriting: Creative Constructiveness." In Jules Barron and Renee Nell, eds., *Annals of Psychotherapy* (Monograph No. 8: *The Creative Use of the Unconscious by the Artist and the Psychotherapist*) 5, no. 1 (1964).

———. "Simone de Beauvoir and 'The Second Sex': An American Commentary." In *Words of Fire: An Anthology of African American Feminist Thought,* edited by Beverly Guy-Sheftall. New York: New Press, 1995.

———. *To Be Young, Gifted and Black: Lorraine Hansberry in Her Own Words.* Adapted by Robert Nemiroff. Hoboken, NJ: Prentice-Hall, 1969.

———. *To Be Young, Gifted and Black: Lorraine Hansberry in Her Own Words.* Adapted by Robert Nemiroff. New York: Vintage Books, 1995.

———. "Willy Loman, Walter Younger, and He Who Must Live." *Village Voice,* August 12, 1959.

"The Hansberrys of Chicago: They Join Business Acumen with Social Vision." *The Crisis,* April 1941.

Harris, Trudier. "This Disease Called Strength: Some Observations on the Compensating Construction of Black Female Character." *Literature and Medicine* 14, no. 1 (1995).

Higashida, Cheryl. "To Be (Come) Young, Gay and Black: Lorraine Hansberry's Existentialist Routes to Anticolonialism." *American Quarterly* 60, no. 4 (2008).

Hirsch, Arnold R. *Making the Second Ghetto: Race and Housing in Chicago 1940–1960.* Chicago: University of Chicago Press, 1998.

Hodin, Mark. "Lorraine Hanberry's Absurdity: 'The Sign in Sidney Brustein's Window.'" *Contemporary Literature* 50, no. 4 (Winter 2009).

Hughes, Langston. *The Big Sea: An Autobiography.* 1940; repr. New York: Hill and Wang, 1993.

Ingle, Zachary. "'White Fear' and the Studio System: A Re-evaluation of Hansberry's Original Screenplay of 'A Raisin in the Sun.'" *Literature/Film Quarterly* 37, no. 3 (July 2009).

"Iron Ring in Housing." *The Crisis* 47, no. 7 (July 1940).

Isaacs, Harold R. "Five Writers and Their African Ancestors Part II." *Phylon* 21, no. 4 (1960).

Jackson, Lawrence P. *The Indignant Generation: A Narrative History of African American Writers and Critics, 1934–1960.* Princeton, NJ: Princeton University Press, 2011.

Jaffe, Sarah. "The Unexpected Afterlife of American Communism." *New York Times*, June 6, 2017.

Jeffries, Devair. "Black Feminine Identity: An Examination of Historical and Contemporary Dramatic Texts Through a Critical Race Theory Framework." Master's thesis, University of South Carolina, 2013.

Jones, David C. *Apart and a Part: Dissonance, Double Consciousness, and the Politics of Black Identity in African American Literature, 1946–1964.* PhD diss., University of Manchester, 2015.

Kahen, Harold I. "Validity of Anti-Negro Restrictive Covenants: A Reconsideration of the Problem." *The University of Chicago Law Review* 12, no. 2 (February 1945).

Kamp, Allen R. "The History Behind *Hansberry v. Lee.*" *University of California at Davis Law Review* 481 (1987): 20.

Keppel, Ben. *The Work of Democracy: Ralph Bunche, Kenneth B. Clark, Lorraine Hansberry, and the Politics of Race.* Cambridge, MA: Harvard University Press, 1995.

Leighton, Jared E. *Freedom Indivisible: Gays and Lesbians in the African American Civil Rights Movement.* PhD diss., University of Nebraska–Lincoln, 2013.

Levitan, Stuart D. *Madison: 1856–1931.* Madison: University of Wisconsin Press, 2006.

Lieberman, Robbie. *The Strangest Dream: Communism, Anticommunism, and the U.S. Peace Movement, 1945–1963.* Syracuse, NY: Syracuse University Press, 2000.

Lieberman, Robbie, and Clarence Langs, eds. "Another Side of the Story: African American Intellectuals Speak Out for Peace and Freedom during the Early Cold War Years." In *Anticommunism and the African American Freedom Movement: Another Side of the Story.* New York: Palgrave Macmillan, 2009.

Lindstrom, Frederick Burgess. "The Negro Invasion of the Washington Park Subdivision." Master's thesis, University of Chicago, 1941.

Lipari, Lisbeth. "Hansberry's Hidden Transcript." *The Journal of Popular Culture* 46, no. 1 (2013).

———. "The Rhetoric of Intersectionality: Lorraine Hansberry's 1957 Letters to *The Ladder*," 220–48. In *Queering Public Address: Sexualities in American Historical Discourse*, edited by Charles E. Morris III. Columbia: University of South Carolina Press, 2007.

Locke, Alain. "Harlem," *The Survey Graphic* 6, no. 6 (1925).

Maxwell, William J. *F. B. Eyes: How J. Edgar Hoover's Ghostreaders Framed African American Literature.* Princeton, NJ: Princeton University Press, 2015.

———. *New Negro, Old Left: African-American Writing and Communism between the Wars.* New York: Columbia University Press, 1999.

McConnell, Lauren. "Understanding Paul Robeson's Soviet Experience." *Theatre History Studies* 30 (2010).

McDuffie, Erik S. "Black and Red: Black Liberation, the Cold War, and the Horne Thesis." *The Journal of African American History* 96, no. 2 (Spring 2011).

———. "'A New Day Has Dawned for the UNIA': Garveyism, the Diasporic Midwest, and West Africa, 1920–80." *Journal of West African History* 2, no. 1 (Spring 2016).

Mitchell, Lofton. *Black Drama: The Story of the American Negro in Theater.* New York: Hawthorn Books, 1967.

Mullen, Bill, and James Edward Smethurst, eds. *Left of the Color Line: Race, Radicalism, and Twentieth-Century Literature of the United States.* Chapel Hill: University of North Carolina Press, 2003.

Nemiroff, Robert, ed. "A Critical Background." Preface to *'Les Blancs': The Collected Last Plays.* New York: Vintage Books, 1994.

——. "From These Roots: Lorraine Hansberry and the South." *Southern Exposure* (September/October 1984).

——. "A Note about This Revised Edition." *"The Sign in Sidney Brustein's Window": A Drama in Two Acts, Revised Stage Edition by Lorraine Hansberry.* Acting Edition. New York: Samuel French, Inc., 1993.

——. "The 101 Final Performances." Introduction. *The Sign in Sidney Brustein's Window.* With a Foreword by John Braine. New York: Random House, 1965.

——. "Production Notes." In *"Les Blancs": A Drama in Two Acts by Lorraine Hansberry.* Final text adapted by Robert Nemiroff; script associate, Charlotte Zaltzberg. Acting Edition. New York: Samuel French, Inc., 1972.

Parks, Sheri. "In My Mother's House: Black Feminist Aesthetics, Television, and 'A Raisin in the Sun.'" In *Theatre and Feminist Aesthetics*, edited by Karen Laughlin and Catherine Schuler. Madison, NJ: Fairleigh Dickinson University Press, 1995.

Plotkin, Wendy. "Deeds of Mistrust: Race, Housing, and Restrictive Covenants in Chicago, 1900–1953." PhD diss., University of Illinois, Chicago, 1999.

——. "Kitchenettes." Encyclopedia of Chicago, Chicago Historical Society, 2004, http://www.encyclopedia.chicagohistory.org/pages/1067.html.

Prentiss, Craig R. *Staging Faith, Religion and African American Theater from the Harlem Renaissance to World War II.* New York: New York University Press, 2013.

Prince, Valerie Sweeney. *Burnin' Down the House: Home in African American Literature.* New York: Columbia University Press, 2004.

Rampersad, Arnold. *The Life of Langston Hughes.* Vol. 1: *1902–1941: I, Too, Sing America.* New York: Oxford University Press, 1986.

Reed, Christopher Robert. *The Rise of Chicago's Black Metropolis, 1920–1929.* Urbana: University of Illinois Press, 2011.

Rigueur, Leah Wright. *The Loneliness of the Black Republican: Pragmatic Politics and the Pursuit of Power.* Princeton, NJ: Princeton University Press, 2014.

Saber, Yomna. "Lorraine Hansberry: Defining the Line Between Integration and Assimilation." *Women's Studies* 39, no. 5 (July 2010).

Schmidt, Karl M. *Henry A. Wallace: Quixotic Crusade 1948.* Syracuse, NY: Syracuse University Press, 1960.

Shannon, Sandra G. "From Lorraine Hansberry to August Wilson: An Interview with Lloyd Richards." *Callaloo* 14, no. 1 (Winter 1991).

Simons, Margaret A. "Lesbian Connections: Simone de Beauvoir and Feminism." *Signs* 18, no. 1 (1992).

Smethurst, James Edward. *The Black Arts Movement: Literary Nationalism in the 1960s and 1970s.* Chapel Hill: University of North Carolina Press, 2005.

——. *The New Red Negro: The Literary Left and African American Poetry, 1930–1946.* New York: Oxford University Press, 1999.

Smith, Judith E. *Visions of Belonging: Family Stories, Popular Culture, and Postwar Democracy, 1940–1960.* New York: Columbia University Press, 2004.

Smith, Preston H. *Democracy and the Black Metropolis: Housing Policy in Postwar Chicago.* Minneapolis: University of Minnesota Press, 2012.

Teele, James E. *E. Franklin Frazier and the Black Bourgeoisie.* Columbia: University of Missouri Press, 2002.

Theoharis, Athan. *Chasing Spies: How the FBI Failed in Counterintelligence but Promoted the Politics of McCarthyism in the Cold War Years.* Chicago: Ivan R. Dee, 2002.

Tracy, Steven C., ed. *Writers of the Black Chicago Renaissance.* Urbana: University of Illinois Press, 2011.

Travis, Dempsey J. *An Autobiography of Black Chicago.* Chicago: Urban Research Institute Press, 1981.

Tritt, Michael. "A View from the Stockyards: Lorraine Hansberry's Allusion to 'The Jungle' in the

Unfilmed Screenplay of 'A Raisin in the Sun.'" *ANQ: A Quarterly Journal of Short Articles, Notes and Reviews* 21, no. 1 (2008).

Vassell, Olive, and Todd Steven Burroughs. "No Common Ground Left: 'Freedomways,' Black Communists vs. Black Nationalism/Pan-Africanism." *Journal of Pan African Studies* 9, no. 1 (March 2016).

Vose, Clement E. "NAACP Strategy in the Covenant Cases." *Case Western Law Review* 6, no. 2 (1959).

Wald, Alan M. *American Night: The Literary Left in the Era of the Cold War*. Chapel Hill: University of North Carolina Press, 2012.

——. *Exiles from a Future Time: The Forging of the Mid-Twentieth Century Literary Left*. Chapel Hill: University of North Carolina Press, 2012.

Washington, Mary Helen. "Lorraine Hansberry and 'Freedom': A Founding Text of Black Left Feminism." In *Left of the Color Line: Race, Radicalism, and Twentieth-Century Literature of the United States*, edited by Bill V. Mullen and James Smethurst. Chapel Hill: University of North Carolina Press, 2003.

——. *The Other Blacklist: The African American Literary and Cultural Left of the 1950s*. New York: Columbia University Press, 2015.

Weigand, Kate. *Red Feminism: American Communism and the Making of Women's Liberation*. Baltimore: Johns Hopkins University Press, 2001.

Welch, Rebeccah E. "Black Art and Activism in Postwar New York, 1950–1965." PhD diss., New York University, 2002.

——. "Spokesman of the Oppressed? Lorraine Hansberry at Work: The Challenge of Radical Politics in the Postwar Era." *Souls* 9 (2007).

Wilkerson, Margaret B. "The Dark Vision of Lorraine Hansberry: Excerpts from a Literary Biography." *The Massachusetts Review* 28, no. 4 (1987).

——. "Excavating Our History: The Importance of Biographies of Women of Color." *Black American Literature Forum* 24, no. 1 (Spring 1990).

——. "Lorraine Hansberry: The Making of a Woman of the Theatre." Delivered to the College of Fellows of the American Theatre, John F. Kennedy Center for the Performing Arts, Washington, DC, April 23, 1995.

——. "Political Radicalism and Artistic Innovation in the Works of Lorraine Hansberry." In *African American Performance and Theater History: A Critical Reader*, edited by Harry J. Elam Jr. and David Krasner. New York: Oxford University Press, 2001.

——. "The Sighted Eyes and Feeling Heart of Lorraine Hansberry." *Black American Literature Forum* 17, no. 1 (1983).

Wilkins, Fanon Che. "Beyond Bandung: The Critical Nationalism of Lorraine Hansberry, 1950–1965." *Radical History Review* 95 (Spring 2006).

Winger, Stewart. "Unwelcome Neighbors." *Chicago History Magazine* 21, nos. 1 and 2 (Spring/Summer 1992).

Acknowledgments

I am indebted to the following institutions and their reference specialists for their assistance and for making critical materials available for the writing of this book. Their generosity is deeply appreciated:

J. D. Boyd Library, Alcorn State University; Bucks County Historical Society, Doylestown, Pennsylvania; Chicago History Museum; Hall Branch and the Vivian G. Harsh Research Collection, Chicago Public Library; Oral History Archives, Columbia University; Dedalus Foundation; Stuart A. Rose Manuscript, Archives, and Rare Book Library, Emory University; Criminal Justice Information Services Division, Federal Bureau of Investigation; John Hope and Aurelia E. Franklin Library, Fisk University; Arthur and Elizabeth Schlesinger Library on the History of Women in America and the Radcliffe Institute for Advanced Study, Harvard University; Moorland-Spingarn Research Center, Howard University; Manuscript Division, Library of Congress; Monroe Library Special Collections and Archives, Loyola University New Orleans; Manuscripts Department, National Library of Ireland; New York Historical Society; Theatre on Film and Tape Archive and the Billy Rose Theater Division, New York Public Library for the Performing Arts; Tamiment Library and Robert F. Wagner Labor Archives, Elmer Holmes Bobst Library, New York University; Seeley G. Mudd Manuscript Library, Princeton University; Rhodes College; Roosevelt University; Manuscripts, Archives and Rare Books Division, Schomburg Center for Research in Black Culture;

Special Collections, Smith College; Swarthmore College Peace Collection, Swarthmore College; Team Englewood Community Academy, Chicago; U.S. National Archives and Records at Chicago; U.S. National Archives, College Park, Maryland; Charles E. Young Research Library, Special Collections, University of California at Los Angeles; Special Collection Research Center, University of Chicago; Special Collections, University of Delaware Library; Special Collections and University Archives, Richard J. Daley Library, University of Illinois at Chicago; Rare Book and Manuscript Library, University of Illinois at Urbana-Champaign; ONE National Gay and Lesbian Archives, University of Southern California; Harry Ransom Center, University of Texas at Austin; Manuscript Reading Room, University of Virginia; Steenbock Memorial Library, University Archives, University of Wisconsin; Wisconsin Historical Society; Beinecke Rare Book and Manuscript Library, Yale University.

One of the pleasures of writing a literary biography of a midcentury American author is meeting the subject's friends, colleagues, and family and those who played an important part in shaping the era. The following people were especially helpful to me and my research:

Joi Gresham, director and trustee, Lorraine Hansberry Literary Trust; Arnold Rampersad, for his thoughts and guidance; Claudette Smith-Brown, David Dreyer, and Kwame Wes Alford, for sharing unique materials about the Hansberry family; genealogist and family researcher Deb Stone; Richard Kilbourne, for delving into and explaining the slave economy in Louisiana; and the following members of the Hansberry family for sharing their memories: Gail Adelle Hansberry, Myrtle Kay Hansberry, Carl Hansberry (nephew), and Taye Hansberry.

These persons provided details and insights, through interviews or correspondence: the late David McReynolds, the late Douglas Turner Ward, Amy Secules, Frank McCabe, Margaret B. Wilkerson, Robert Nedelkoff, Dawn Durante, Dolan Hubbard, Andrew Berman, Jamila Wignot, Stephen G. Hall, Deborah Holton, Alan Rinzler, Peter Der Manuelian, Howard J. Swibel, Timothy Sutphin, the late Leon Wofsy, Dan Wakefield, Tony Burton, Risa L. Goluboff, Kate Weiskopf Resek, Amy Weiskopf, David A. Leeming, Peter B. Hoff, Gerry Max, J. Michael Lennon, Lisa Mersky, Deborah Mersky, Ruth Pool, Margaret Burnham, Harriet Scarupa, Hettie Jones, Mark B. Cohen,

Esther Cooper Jackson, Jane Bond, Rita Moreno, Erika Kelsaw, and the late Gerald Hiken.

Will Cooley and Lillian Faderman, respected scholars in their fields, read excerpted chapters, and I thank them for their advice and suggestions. Charly Simpson, dramatist and sensitivity reader, reviewed the manuscript, and her clarifying remarks were indispensable. Longtime friend and colleague Dennis Lynch read it carefully for sense and sensibility, giving the benefit of his many years teaching composition.

Linda Justice has expertly transcribed hundreds of hours of interviews for this and other books and has become a friend—an unforeseen benefit of working with her.

For ten years, Dr. Daniel Cudin has been my guide, my Virgil, through the labyrinth of gods and monsters one encounters in life.

And for twenty years, my agent, Jeff Kleinman of Folio Literary Management, has advised me on every important decision related to publishing and has been my advocate—and for that, I am tremendously grateful. My editor, Serena Jones, provided me with the kind of professionalism, tact, and solid judgment I've come to rely on from Henry Holt and Company.

Illustration Credits

Salubria: Library of Congress

William Hansberry: Hansberry family

Carl and Nannie Hansberry: New York Public Library

Kitchenette: Russell Lee, Library of Congress

Lorraine Hansberry at Englewood High School: Englewood High School yearbook, 1947

Paul Robeson: Bettman/Getty Images

Bob Nemiroff at NYU: New York University yearbook, 1951

Lorraine in Montevideo: Courtesy of *People's World*

Douglas Turner Ward: Bert Andrews, Negro Ensemble Company

On Whitman Avenue: Bauer-Toland

Charles R. Swibel: Courtesy of Howard J. Swibel

Bob and Lorraine in apartment: Ben Martin/Getty Images

Lorraine and Lloyd Richards at Sardi's: Gordon Parks/Getty Images

Nelson Algren: Walter Albertin, Library of Congress

Bob Nemiroff, Carole King, and Paul Simon: Michael Ochs/Getty Images

Lorraine at Brandeis: Courtesy of the Robert D. Farber University Archives & Special Collections Department, Brandeis University

Dorothy Secules: Courtesy of Amy Secules

Richard Nixon and Mamie Hansberry: Charles Williams, Tom and Ethel Bradley Center, California State University, Northridge

Croton-on-Hudson: Courtesy of Caroline Curvan

Index

About the Author

Charles J. Shields is the author of the bestselling biography *Mockingbird: A Portrait of Harper Lee*, the Kurt Vonnegut biography *And So It Goes*, and the biography of John Edward Williams, *The Man Who Wrote the Perfect Novel*. Shields has spoken to hundreds of audiences in the United States and abroad, and his work has been reviewed in newspapers and magazines worldwide.